lonely planet

# Normandy

## Jeanne Oliver

**LONELY PLANET PUBLICATIONS**
Melbourne • Oakland • London • Paris

English Channel
(La Manche)

Alderney (UK)

rk (UK)

Cap de la Hague

Beaumont-Hague

St-Pierre-Eglise

Barfleur

**Cherbourg**

Quettehou

Dielette

St Vaast-la-Hougue

Les Pieux

N13

D902

**Valognes**

D904

Bricquebec

D2

Ste-Mère-Eglise

Utah Beach

Grandcamp-Maisy

Pointe du Hoc

**D-DAY BEACHES**
Scene of the 1944 Allied landings
and the ferocious Battle of Normandy

Carteret

St Sauveur-le-Vicomte

D900

N13

Carentan

N13

Omaha Beach

Arromanches-les-Bains

Plateau du Calvados

Juno Beach

Luc-sur-Mer

Portbail

Cotentin Peninsula

Courseulles-sur-Mer

Sword Beach

D650

La Haye-du-Puits

**Bayeux**

Douvres-la-Délivrande

Quistreham

JERSEY
(UK)

Lessay

Périers

**BAYEUX**
The epic Bayeux Tapestry
and a majestic cathedral

N13

Tilly-Seulles

**Caen**

St-Helier

D900

D972

Balleroy

A84

**St-Lô**

CALVADOS

D2

Caumont

D562

ÎLES
CHAUSEY

Agon-Coutainville

**Countances**

MANCHE

A84

N158

D7

D999

Tessy

**CAEN**
Fine museums, historic
abbeys and an enormous
11th-century chateau

Lengronne

Percy

N174

D511

Bréhal

Gavray

N175

**Granville**

Villedieu-les-Poêles

Vire

D512

D973

D524

D977

**MONT ST-MICHEL**
High tide at Normandy's
most dramatic abbey

St-Pois

Sourdeval

**Flers**

D924

Putanges-Pont-Ecrepin

**St-Malo**

Cancale

Mont-St-Michel

Avranches

Brécey

Pointel

Mortain

D962

D18

La Ferté-Macé

Dol-de-Bretagne

N176

A84

St-Hilaire-du-Harcouët

**Domfront**

D908

Pontorson

St-James

N176

N176

Bagnoles de l'Orne

CÔTES
D'ARMOR

D155

Louvigné-de-Désert

Couptrâin

Antrain

D177

**ORNE**
The attractive spa town
of Bagnoles de l'Orne and
atmospheric Alençon

A84

**Fougères**

D23

N12

ILLE - ET - VILAINE

D798

N12

MAYENNE

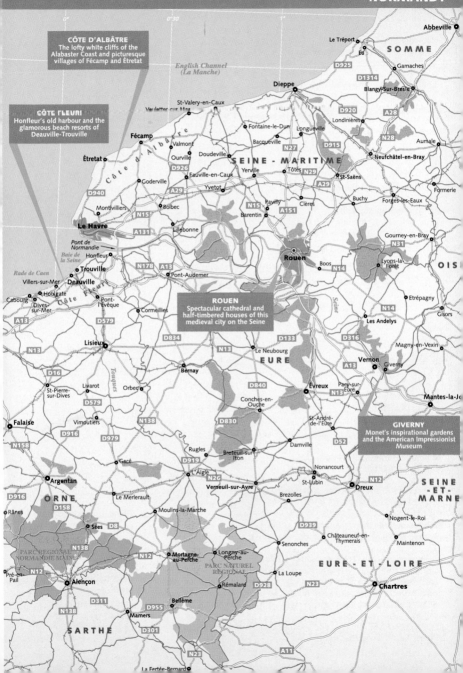

Abbeville

Le Tréport

Ed

**SOMME**

Gamaches

D925

D1314

Blangy-Sur-Bresle

**CÔTE D'ALBÂTRE**
The lofty white cliffs of the
Alabaster Coast and picturesque
villages of Fécamp and Étretat

Dieppe

St-Valery-en-Caux

Veulettes-sur-Mer

D920

A28

Londinières

N28

**CÔTE FLEURI**
Honfleur's old harbour and the
glamorous beach resorts of
Deauville-Trouville

Fontaine-le-Dun

Longueville

Aumale

Fécamp

Valmont

Ourville

Doudeville

Bacqueville

N27

D915

Neufchâtel-en-Bray

Étretat

Fauville-en-Caux

Yerville

Tôtes

St-Saëns

Formerie

Goderville

D926

A29

Yvetot

N29

Buchy

Forges-les-Eaux

Montivilliers

N15

Bolbec

N15

Ravilly

Clères

A151

Gournay-en-Bray

**SEINE - MARITIME**

Barentin

Le Havre

A131

Lillebonne

Rouen

Boos

N14

Lyons-la-
Forêt

N31

OIS

Pont de
Normandie

Baie de
la Seine

Honfleur

Rade de Caen

Trouville

N178

A13

Pont-Audemer

Seine

Etrépagny

N14

Gisors

Villers-sur-Mer

Deauville

**ROUEN**
Spectacular cathedral and
half-timbered houses of this
medieval city on the Seine

Les Andelys

Cabourg

Houlgate

Pont-
l'Évêque

Cormeilles

Vernon

Giverny

Magny-en-Vexin

Dives-
sur-Mer

A13

D579

D834

D133

D316

Mantes-la-Jo

Lisieux

D13

**EURE**

Le Neubourg

A13

D16

Bernay

Pacy-sur-
Eure

St-Pierre-
sur-Dives

Livarot

Orbec

D840

Évreux

N13

D579

Conches-en-
Ouche

St-André-
de-l'Eure

**GIVERNY**
Monet's inspirational gardens
and the American Impressionist
Museum

Falaise

Vimoutiers

N138

D830

Damville

D52

D916

D979

Rugles

Breteuil-sur-
Iton

Nonancourt

**SEINE
-ET-
MARNE**

Gacé

D919

St-Lubin

N12

Argentan

L'Aigle

N26

Brezolles

Dreux

**ORNE**

Verneuil-sur-Avre

D916

Le Merlerault

Nogent-le-Roi

D158

Moulins-la-Marche

D939

Châteauneuf-en-
Thymerais

Maintenon

Rânes

Sées

D8

Senonches

**EURE - ET - LOIRE**

Pré-en-
Pail

**PARC RÉGIONAL
NORMANDIE MAINE**

N138

N12

Mortagne-
au-Perche

Longny-au-
Perche

**PARC NATUREL
RÉGIONAL**

La Loupe

N12

Alençon

Rémalard

D928

N23

Chartres

D311

Bellême

D955

Mamers

N138

La Fertée-Bernard

D301

**SARTHE**

N23

A11

Normandy
1st edition – June 2001

Published by
Lonely Planet Publications Pty Ltd  ABN 36 005 607 983
90 Maribyrnong St, Footscray, Victoria 3011, Australia

Lonely Planet Offices
Australia Locked Bag 1, Footscray, Victoria 3011
USA 150 Linden St, Oakland, CA 94607
UK 10a Spring Place, London NW5 3BH
France 1 rue du Dahomey, 75011 Paris

Photographs
Most of the images in this guide are available for licensing from
Lonely Planet Images.
email: lpi@lonelyplanet.com.au

Front cover photograph
Fishing boats in Honfleur's old harbour
(Robert Everts, Tony Stone Images)

ISBN 1 86450 098 0

GR and PR are trademarks of the FFRP (Fédération Française de la
Randonnée Pédestre).

Printed by SNP SPrint (M) Sdn Bhd
Printed in Malaysia

Although the authors
and Lonely Planet try
to make the informa-
tion as accurate as
possible, we accept
no responsibility for
any loss, injury or
inconvenience sus-
tained by anyone
using this book.

# Contents – Text

1

# 2 Contents – Text

## MAP LEGEND                                                                                          back page

## METRIC CONVERSION                                                                          inside back cover

# Contents – Maps

# MAP INDEX

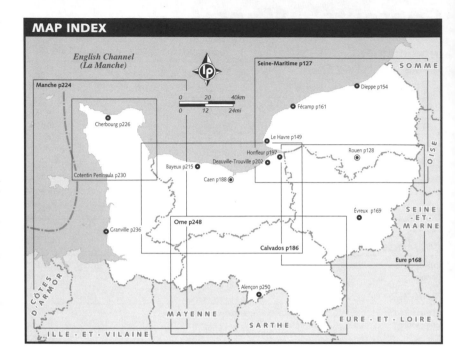

English Channel
(La Manche)

Seine-Maritime p127

SOMME

Manche p224

Dieppe p154

0   20   40km
0   12   24mi

Fécamp p161

Cherbourg p226

Le Havre p149

Honfleur p197

Rouen p128

OISE

Cotentin Peninsula p230

Bayeux p215

Deauville-Trouville p202

Caen p188

Évreux p169

SEINE
- ET -
MARNE

Granville p236

Orne p248

Calvados p186

Eure p168

D. CÔTES D'ARMOR

Alençon p250

MAYENNE

SARTHE

EURE - ET - LOIRE

ILLE - ET - VILAINE

# The Author

## Jeanne Oliver

Born in New Jersey, Jeanne spent her childhood mulling over the *New York Times* travel section and plotting her future voyages. After a BA in English at the State University of New York at Stony Brook and a stint at the *Village Voice* newspaper, Jeanne got a law degree. After working as a prosecutor in the Manhattan District Attorney's office, Jeanne started her own legal practice. It was interrupted by ever-more-frequent trips to far-flung destinations and eventually she set off on a round-the-world trip that landed her in Paris. A job in the tourist industry leading tours through Normandy led to freelance writing assignments for magazines and guidebooks. She joined Lonely Planet in 1996 and has written 1st editions of Lonely Planet's *Croatia*, *Crete* and *Crete Condensed* as well as updating chapters on Crete, Croatia and Slovenia in *Greece*, *Mediterranean Europe*, *Central Europe* and *Eastern Europe*. She currently lives in the south of France.

## FROM THE AUTHOR

First of all I'd like to thank the Normandy regional tourist office for their efficiency and knowledge. Throughout Normandy, the staff of local tourist offices were incredibly patient and went out of their way to find and provide useful information.

I had a wonderful time in Normandy, largely due to the kindness and generosity of Augustin and Colette Prod'homme in Caen, and M and Mme Nguyen Tu Bon in Rouen, who ensured that I was comfortably housed. Both Jean-Philippe Touzet and Françoise Chevalier both have a tremendous knowledge of Normandy and I am indebted to them. Thanks also to Harvey Rosen for his enthusiasm and advice on the D-Day landings as well as for being a great friend.

I appreciate the patience and support of the Lonely Planet London office, especially Paul Bloomfield and Sara Yorke. Finally, thanks must go to fellow author Jeremy Gray whose text in *France* formed a valuable basis for parts of this book.

# This Book

## This Book

This book was researched and written by Jeanne Oliver, based on the relevant text from Lonely Planet's *France* guide.

## From the Publisher

This 1st edition of *Normandy* was edited and proofed in Lonely Planet's London office by Michala Green. Sam Trafford and Sally Schafer assisted with editing and the book was proofed by Sally and Michala. Jimi Ellis was responsible for mapping, design and layout, with help from David Wenk, James Timmins and Jolyon Philcox. Paul Edmunds drew the climate charts, Andrew Weatherill designed the cover with help from Adam McCrow, and Jim Miller drew the back-cover map. Lonely Planet Images provided photographs and illustrations were drawn by Jane Smith. Thanks to Tim Fitzgerald for his last-minute checks, to Quentin Frayne and Emma Koch for producing the language chapter, and to Jeanne for her extremely thorough work.

Special thanks to the City of Bayeux for permission to reproduce sections of the Bayeux Tapestry, and to the Australian War Memorial for images of the D-Day landings.

# Foreword

## ABOUT LONELY PLANET GUIDEBOOKS

The story begins with a classic travel adventure: Tony and Maureen Wheeler's 1972 journey across Europe and Asia to Australia. Useful information about the overland trail did not exist at that time, so Tony and Maureen published the first Lonely Planet guidebook to meet a growing need.

From a kitchen table, then from a tiny office in Melbourne (Australia), Lonely Planet has become the largest independent travel publisher in the world, an international company with offices in Melbourne, Oakland (USA), London (UK) and Paris (France).

Today Lonely Planet guidebooks cover the globe. There is an ever-growing list of books and there's information in a variety of forms and media. Some things haven't changed. The main aim is still to help make it possible for adventurous travellers to get out there – to explore and better understand the world.

At Lonely Planet we believe travellers can make a positive contribution to the countries they visit – if they respect their host communities and spend their money wisely. Since 1986 a percentage of the income from each book has been donated to aid projects and human rights campaigns.

**Updates** Lonely Planet thoroughly updates each guidebook as often as possible. This usually means there are around two years between editions, although for more unusual or more stable destinations the gap can be longer. Check the imprint page (following the colour map at the beginning of the book) for publication dates.

Between editions up-to-date information is available in two free newsletters – the paper *Planet Talk* and email *Comet* (to subscribe, contact any Lonely Planet office) – and on our Web site at www.lonelyplanet.com. The *Upgrades* section of the Web site covers a number of important and volatile destinations and is regularly updated by Lonely Planet authors. *Scoop* covers news and current affairs relevant to travellers. And, lastly, the *Thorn Tree* bulletin board and *Postcards* section of the site carry unverified, but fascinating, reports from travellers.

**Correspondence** The process of creating new editions begins with the letters, postcards and emails received from travellers. This correspondence often includes suggestions, criticisms and comments about the current editions. Interesting excerpts are immediately passed on via newsletters and the Web site, and everything goes to our authors to be verified when they're researching on the road. We're keen to get more feedback from organisations or individuals who represent communities visited by travellers.

Lonely Planet gathers information for everyone who's curious about the planet – and especially for those who explore it first-hand. Through guidebooks, phrasebooks, activity guides, maps, literature, newsletters, image library, TV series and Web site we act as an information exchange for a worldwide community of travellers.

**Research** Authors aim to gather sufficient practical information to enable travellers to make informed choices and to make the mechanics of a journey run smoothly. They also research historical and cultural background to help enrich the travel experience and allow travellers to understand and respond appropriately to cultural and environmental issues.

Authors don't stay in every hotel because that would mean spending a couple of months in each medium-sized city and, no, they don't eat at every restaurant because that would mean stretching belts beyond capacity. They do visit hotels and restaurants to check standards and prices, but feedback based on readers' direct experiences can be very helpful.

Many of our authors work undercover, others aren't so secretive. None of them accept freebies in exchange for positive write-ups. And none of our guidebooks contain any advertising.

**Production** Authors submit their raw manuscripts and maps to offices in Australia, USA, UK or France. Editors and cartographers – all experienced travellers themselves – then begin the process of assembling the pieces. When the book finally hits the shops, some things are already out of date, we start getting feedback from readers and the process begins again ...

## WARNING & REQUEST

Things change – prices go up, schedules change, good places go bad and bad places go bankrupt – nothing stays the same. So, if you find things better or worse, recently opened or long since closed, please tell us and help make the next edition even more accurate and useful. We genuinely value all the feedback we receive. A well-travelled team reads and acknowledges every letter, postcard and email and ensures that every morsel of information finds its way to the appropriate authors, editors and cartographers for verification.

Everyone who writes to us will find their name in the next edition of the appropriate guidebook. They will also receive the latest issue of *Planet Talk*, our quarterly printed newsletter, or *Comet*, our monthly email newsletter. Subscriptions to both newsletters are free. The very best contributions will be rewarded with a free guidebook.

Excerpts from your correspondence may appear in new editions of Lonely Planet guidebooks, the Lonely Planet Web site, *Planet Talk* or *Comet*, so please let us know if you *don't* want your letter published or your name acknowledged.

Send all correspondence to the Lonely Planet office closest to you:

**Australia:** Locked Bag 1, Footscray, Victoria 3011
**USA:** 150 Linden St, Oakland, CA 94607
**UK:** 10A Spring Place, London NW5 3BH
**France:** 1 rue du Dahomey, 75011 Paris

Or email us at: talk2us@lonelyplanet.com.au

**For news, views and updates see our Web site: www.lonelyplanet.com**

## HOW TO USE A LONELY PLANET GUIDEBOOK

The best way to use a Lonely Planet guidebook is any way you choose. At Lonely Planet we believe the most memorable travel experiences are often those that are unexpected, and the finest discoveries are those you make yourself. Guidebooks are not intended to be used as if they provide a detailed set of infallible instructions!

**Contents** All Lonely Planet guidebooks follow roughly the same format. The Facts about the Destination chapters or sections give background information ranging from history to weather. Facts for the Visitor gives practical information on issues like visas and health. Getting There & Away gives a brief starting point for researching travel to and from the destination. Getting Around gives an overview of the transport options when you arrive.

The peculiar demands of each destination determine how subsequent chapters are broken up, but some things remain constant. We always start with background, then proceed to sights, places to stay, places to eat, entertainment, getting there and away, and getting around information – in that order.

**Heading Hierarchy** Lonely Planet headings are used in a strict hierarchical structure that can be visualised as a set of Russian dolls. Each heading (and its following text) is encompassed by any preceding heading that is higher on the hierarchical ladder.

**Entry Points** We do not assume guidebooks will be read from beginning to end, but that people will dip into them. The traditional entry points are the list of contents and the index. In addition, however, some books have a complete list of maps and an index map illustrating map coverage.

There may also be a colour map that shows highlights. These highlights are dealt with in greater detail in the Facts for the Visitor chapter, along with planning questions and suggested itineraries. Each chapter covering a geographical region usually begins with a locator map and another list of highlights. Once you find something of interest in a list of highlights, turn to the index.

**Maps** Maps play a crucial role in Lonely Planet guidebooks and include a huge amount of information. A legend is printed on the back page. We seek to have complete consistency between maps and text, and to have every important place in the text captured on a map. Map key numbers usually start in the top left corner.

Although inclusion in a guidebook usually implies a recommendation we cannot list every good place. Exclusion does not necessarily imply criticism. In fact there are a number of reasons why we might exclude a place – sometimes it is simply inappropriate to encourage an influx of travellers.

# Introduction

Normandy is a gentle land with a tumultuous history.

Its long coast made a tempting target for the Viking invasions and then became the launching pad for another great invasion, the Norman Conquest of England in 1066. The magnificent Bayeux Tapestry depicts William the Conqueror's epic struggle with Harold, which linked the destiny of the two lands for many centuries. Colossal fortresses arose as the English and French battled for Normandy's natural treasures. Chateaux at Caen, Falaise, Gisors and Les Andelys swung between English and French control as Normandy lay poised between the two cultures.

Even amidst the turmoil, a remarkable cultural life flourished in Normandy. Learned and architecturally sophisticated Benedictine monks scattered Romanesque abbeys throughout Normandy – at St-Wandrille, Jumièges, Le Bec-Hellouin, Fécamp, Mont St-Michel – that attracted the region's best minds. The next age brought towering Gothic cathedrals to Coutances, Sées, Évreux and Rouen. Normandy's museums are rich with the works of artists who lived and worked in Normandy: Monet in Giverny, Boudin in Honfleur, Braque in Varengeville, Dufy in Deauville.

Rural Normandy is pastures and apple orchards, forests and farms, grazing cows and gambolling horses. A turn away from the main road might bring a village of stone houses peeping out from a mass of ivy or a few rows of half-timbered houses festooned with flowers leaning over a splashing river. Rare is the town in Normandy without a river running through it, usually with banks manicured into a small park or promenade. In Upper Normandy the River Seine carves its way through a verdant valley, just grazing Rouen's medieval centre. Lower Normandy's waterways wind through a bucolic patchwork of grain fields and rolling slopes webbed by hedgerows.

The slow rhythms of agricultural life rule the interior but the pace quickens on the

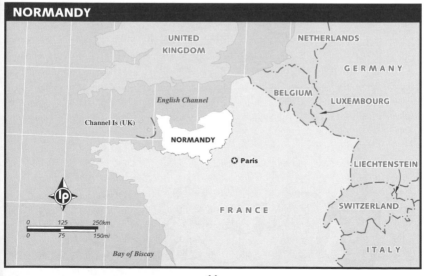

NORMANDY

coast. Boats, tankers and ferries lumber into Le Havre and Cherbourg while fishing boats putter into the ports of Barfleur, Granville, Honfleur, Fécamp and Dieppe, depositing their briny loads on the dock. In Deauville and Trouville sleek and haughty Parisians loiter on the promenade, murmuring into their mobile phones. Along the Alabaster Coast, oh-so-cute villages and frayed resorts cower under a white wall of cliffs, waiting for the summer onslaught of visitors. Around the Cotentin peninsula, surging tides push against lonely beaches and marshes before rushing off to Mont St-Michel.

It is along the middle coast that the darker contours of Normandy emerge. From Pointe du Hoc past Omaha beach to Arromanches, reminders of history's greatest amphibious landing abound. The cost of the Battle of Normandy is apparent in the military cemeteries, war museums and monuments that fan out from the D-Day beaches following the Allied march to victory. Modern cities, rebuilt towns, new bridges and roads, all constructed upon the ashes of postwar Normandy, testify to the enormity of the civilian sacrifice.

Normans approach the art of living with the same attention to detail that Monet brought to his garden at Giverny. One of the main pleasures of visiting the region is to slip into the Norman way of life. Assemble a picnic at a weekly market; sample an artfully composed salad from the local delicatessen; spread a creamy Camembert over a freshly baked baguette; relax over a four-course lunch and a bottle of cider. And on Sunday, hop on a bike or put on your walking shoes and head to the countryside with the locals to enjoy the lush delights of this beautiful region.

# Facts about Normandy

## HISTORY
### Prehistory

France has been inhabited since at least the Middle Palaeolithic period (about 90,000 to 40,000 BC) when Neanderthal people – thought to be early representatives of *Homo sapiens* – hunted animals, made crude tools and lived in caves. During a dramatic change of climate about 35,000 years ago, the Neanderthal people disappeared. They were followed by Cro-Magnon people. Much taller than their predecessors (over 170cm), these people had nimble hands; larger brains; long, narrow skulls and short, wide faces. They were skilful hunters, and with their improved tools and hunting techniques were able to kill reindeer, bison, horses and mammoths.

In the Mesolithic period, which began about 13,000 years ago, hunting and fishing became very efficient and wild grains were harvested. Remnants of Stone Age settlements have been found primarily in Upper Normandy and around Caen. The Neolithic period (about 7500 to 4000 years ago), also known as the New Stone Age, saw the advent of polished stone tools. Warmer weather caused great changes in flora and fauna, ushering in the practice of farming and stock rearing. Communities were therefore more settled and villages were built. The use of pottery became common, as did woven fabric.

By the time of the Bronze Age (2500 BC) it appears that the ancient Normans had begun to trade with the British Isles. Swords, hatchets, spears and helmets found around Caen and Falaise were made from forged copper, a metal imported from England. After the introduction of more durable bronze, forts were built and a military elite developed. Over the next millennium, iron was introduced in various parts of Europe, but it was a scarce, precious metal and used only for ornaments and small knives. It did not come into common use until the arrival of the Celts.

## The Gauls & the Romans

The Celtic Gauls moved into what is now France between 1500 and 500 BC, joining the native Ligurians and Iberians. The new settlers formed tribes throughout the region. Although their later Roman conquerors regarded them as little more than primitive boozers and brawlers other evidence indicates that the early Gauls were already raising cows, pigs and horses, as well as mining enough iron to manufacture weapons and coin money.

The Romans swept through in 56 BC, defeating the Gallic chief Viridorix in the swamps around Carentan and finishing their conquest of Gaul with the defeat of Vercingétorix in 52 BC. In their new Gallic territory, the Romans set up a road grid and administrative capitals at Rotomagus (Rouen), Augustodurum (Bayeux), Noviomagus (Lisieux) and Juliabona (Lillebonne). They bestowed upon the province all the trappings of their civilisation – amphitheatres, temples, theatres and aqueducts – and lived in splendid dwellings ornamented with marble, mosaics and frescoes. The richest archaeological discoveries in Normandy were unearthed at Lillebonne where the outlines of a Roman amphitheatre are still visible.

In the 3rd century, the Gallo-Roman territory came under attack by Saxons and Frankish pirates, harbingers of the more serious invasions to come two centuries later. Strongholds such as Rouen and Bayeux were reinforced. Meanwhile Christianity was taking root. Rouen, Bayeux, Avranches, Évreux, Sées, Lisieux and Coutances developed into archbishoprics and many ecclesiastical buildings were constructed.

## The Merovingians & the Carolingians

Germanic tribes invaded Gaul early in the 5th century and, as the Roman Empire crumbled, a new leader appeared on the scene: Clovis, king of the Franks. Clovis created the first stirrings of national identity by uniting the disparate tribes and completely defeating the confederation of Germanic tribes, known as the Alamanni, by 506. His baptism in 496 bound the French kings to Christianity, a bind that lasted for 13 centuries. Clovis launched the Merovingian dynasty and his name, Gallicised as 'Louis', was given to 18 French kings.

Under the Merovingian kings that ruled after Clovis' death in 511, Normandy began to assume recognisable contours. Counties such as Cotentin and Pays de Caux emerged and great abbeys arose at St-Wandrille, Fécamp, Jumièges and Mont St-Michel. The great administrative centres of antiquity – Rouen, Avranches, Évreux – became great clerical centres. The proliferation of religious construction attracted more sculptors, painters and artisans to work on the new buildings.

The Merovingians were succeeded by the Carolingians, descendants of Emperor Charlemagne, in the 8th century. It was a peaceful time for France and Normandy. The agrarian economy was based an large landholdings and was sufficiently prosperous to pay for significant extensions to several large abbeys.

## The Norman Fury

Prosperity ended when the Vikings arrived. Their task facilitated by weak and divided Carolingian kings, the 'Norse-men' (hence the word 'Norman') ripped through Rouen, Évreux, Bayeux, Lisieux and Sées in the 9th century causing immense destruction. They hailed from Scandinavia, mostly Denmark, and sailed unusually rapid ships called drakkars. With eyes on the prizes in Normandy's rich abbeys and cathedrals, the Vikings sailed up the Seine, attacking cities along the way, and then dragged their boats overland with horses to set sail on other rivers, unleashing more havoc. In 841, the Vikings attacked Rouen mercilessly before burning and pillaging the abbeys of Jumièges and St-Wandrille. *'A furore Normannorum libera nos, domine'* (God, spare us from the Norman fury), prayed the

monks, but to no avail. The inhabitants were unprepared for such an onslaught and either fled or paid tribute to the Viking leaders in an attempt to buy their way out of trouble.

When bribes and ransom failed to dam the flood of Viking invaders, King Charles (the Simple) tried to negotiate. In 911 at St-Clair-sur-Epte, he ceded Rouen and the territory between the rivers Bresle, Epte, Avre and Risle (roughly half of modern-day Normandy) to the Viking leader Rollo.

Rollo was a man of large appetites (supposedly so gigantic that no horse could carry him) who continued to devour Normandy. By 924 he had forced his way into Bayeux, Sées and most of Lower Normandy. After his death in 933, his son, Guillaume Long-Epée completed his work by seizing Cotentin and the lower Manche, thus setting the boundaries for most of modern Normandy.

## The Norman Dukes

Guillaume was followed by Richard I (942–96) and Richard II (996–1027) who assumed the title duke of Normandy. Although the Danish origins of Normandy are apparent in many geographical names – *bec* (stream), *hoc* (point) – the Danish were quickly assimilated into local culture. The language disappeared within a generation.

The first Norman leaders presided over a hierarchical society in which peasants, although nominally free, were cruelly repressed. Periodic revolts were met with fierce countermeasures. At the same time, the economy was flourishing with the growth of metalworking and the spread of agriculture and cattle breeding. Protected by thick walls, the cities of Rouen, Caen, Falaise, Alençon, Dieppe and Argentan grew more populous.

The early Norman rulers encouraged religious life. The great abbeys destroyed by Viking invasions – St-Wandrille, Jumièges, Mont St-Michel and Fécamp – were rebuilt and extended. At Mont St-Michel, the learned Benedictine monks created an influential intellectual centre, and in the abbeys of Bec-Hellouin and Fécamp the abbots Lanfranc and Guillaume de Volpiano reformed and expanded the prestige of their orders.

Normandy was flourishing economically and culturally but ridden with internal warfare when Guillaume le Batard (William the Bastard, later known as 'the Conqueror') assumed the throne in 1035. As the illegitimate son of Robert I, duke of Normandy, and Arlette, a tanner's daughter, William's origins were hardly auspicious. His father had quelled a revolt by his barons and repelled a threat by Brittany before leaving for the Holy Land where he died in 1035. As his designated successor, William ascended to the throne at the age of seven. After a long regency, the adult duke managed to unite his fractious barons and establish a strong central authority. He then began to think about expanding Norman influence and seized the crown of England after the Battle of Hastings in 1066 (see the boxed text 'William Conquers England').

William's death in 1087 ushered in a new climate of insecurity in the region. Although William had bequeathed Normandy to his oldest son, England to the next eldest and left his youngest, Henri Beauclerc with only a sum of money, ambitious Henri soon took over. He strong-armed his oldest brother out of the picture when the brother left for the Holy Land and the next eldest died. Upon assuming power in 1100 Henri, like his father, unified his warring subjects enough to allow continued prosperity. He lavished money on churches and monasteries, erected new fortified castles and blocked the advance of another ambitious neighbour, the French king, Louis VI (the Fat).

## The Plantagenets

William the Conqueror's line came to an end in a tragic shipwreck. In 1120, the *Blanche Nef* sank off the coast of Normandy with Henri's son and sole heir, William, aboard. A power struggle ensued between partisans of Henri's daughter Mathilde (married to Geoffroy Plantagenet) and Etienne de Blois, grandson of William the Conqueror. Mathilde and Geoffroy

controlled Normandy and the Loire region and Etienne controlled England. In 1153 the death of Etienne's only son forced him to cede his claim in favour of Geoffroy and Mathilde's son, Henri Plantagenet. Henri became King Henry II of England and duke of Normandy, Maine, Anjou and Touraine. With his marriage to the powerful Eleanor of Aquitaine, his empire stretched from the Scottish to the Spanish border.

Normandy was in a plum position in the middle of the Plantagenet kingdom. All the Norman ports prospered from the increased trade, but none more so than Rouen. A rich mercantile class developed from the trade in wine, salt and textiles, while a spreading bureaucracy managed real estate, finance and tax collection. A municipal structure implemented in Rouen became the model for other Norman cities, ensuring an administrative system responsive to royal authority.

Henri II was succeeded by Richard the Lion-Heart in 1189, an able administrator, better known in his southern territories than in Normandy. His main rival on the continent was the French king, Philippe-Auguste, who became nearly obsessed with attaching Normandy to the French crown. The two kings parted on Crusade together in 1190 but Philippe-Auguste fell ill, or claimed to fall ill, and hurried home in 1191. Richard was captured in 1192 and held for ransom. The price fell hard on Norman taxpayers, each noble, cleric and merchant obliged to surrender one-quarter of their earnings. Meanwhile, his younger brother John Lackland struck a bargain with Philippe-Auguste surrendering all of Upper Normandy except for Rouen in exchange for the French king's recognition of his claim to the English throne.

When Richard was freed and landed in Barfleur in 1194, he launched a war to recover the territory. His fortress on the Seine, Chateau Gaillard, was meant to protect Rouen from French encroachment and worked well, but Richard was killed in 1199. The kingdom passed to John Lackland who lost Normandy to Philippe-Auguste in 1204.

## William Conquers England

Edward the Confessor, king of England and William's cousin, promised William that upon his death, the throne would pass to the young Norman ruler. And when the most powerful Saxon lord in England, Harold Godwinson of Wessex, was shipwrecked on the Norman coast, he was obliged to swear to William that the English crown would pass to Normandy.

In January 1066 Edward died without an heir. The great nobles of England (and very likely the majority of the Saxon people) supported Harold's claim to the throne, and he was crowned on 5 January. He immediately faced several pretenders to his throne, William being the most obvious. But while William was preparing to send an invasion fleet across the Channel, a rival army consisting of an alliance between Harold's estranged brother Tostig and Harold Hardrada of Norway landed in the north of England. Harold marched north and en-

JANE SMITH

**William the Conqueror – the first Norman king of England**

gaged them in battle at Stamford Bridge, near York, on 25 September. He was victorious, and both Harold Hardrada and Tostig were killed.

Meanwhile, William had crossed the Channel unopposed with an army of about 6000 men, including a large cavalry force. They landed at Pevensey before marching to Hastings. Making remarkably quick time southwards from York, Harold faced William with about 7000 men from a strong defensive position on 13 October. William put his army into an offensive position, and the battle began the next day.

Although William's archers scored many hits among the densely-packed and ill-trained Saxon peasants, the latter's ferocious defence terminated a charge by the Norman cavalry and drove them back in disarray. For a while, William faced the real possibility of losing the battle. However, summoning all the knowledge and tactical ability he had gained in numerous campaigns against his rivals in Normandy, he used the cavalry's rout to draw the Saxon infantry out from their defensive positions, whereupon the Norman infantry turned and caused heavy casualties on the undisciplined Saxon troops. The battle started to turn against Harold – his two other brothers were slain, and he himself was killed late in the afternoon. The embattled Saxons fought on until sunset and then fled, leaving the Normans effectively in charge of England. William immediately marched to London, ruthlessly quelled the opposition and was crowned king of England on Christmas Day.

William thus became king of two realms and entrenched England's feudal system of government under the control of Norman nobles. Ongoing unrest among the Saxon peasantry soured his opinion of the country, however, and he spent most of the rest of his life after 1072 in Normandy, only going to England when compelled to do so. He left most of the governance of the country to the bishops.

In Normandy, William continued to expand his influence by military campaigns or by strategic marriages; in 1077, he took control of the Maine region, but then fought Philip I of France over several towns on their mutual border. In 1087 he was injured during an attack on Mantes. He died at Rouen a few weeks later and was buried at Caen.

## Medieval Normandy

As a new part of France, the French kings left Normandy's administrative structure in place but installed their own people in the higher posts. In 1315, King Louis X signed the Normandy Charter which guaranteed the uniqueness of Normandy and set up a sovereign court of justice in Rouen. The local legal system and body of Norman common law remained undisturbed but the price of this local autonomy was increased taxes. Although comprising only an eighth of French territory, wealthy Normandy was paying a quarter of the total tax revenues well into the Middle Ages.

The high tax burden caused little trouble because the Norman economy was operating in high gear throughout the 13th century. Trade links with England kept the big port cities bustling, while smaller ports netted money with their fishing fleets, and interior cites such as Rouen, St-Lô and Évreux were turning out textiles, leather, woodworks and precious metals.

Churches and monasteries also benefited from the rising tide of wealth. As major landholders, their coffers swelled with revenue. Monks grew fat and rich and their churches reached ever-loftier heights with the new wave of Gothic architecture rolling in from Paris. The cathedrals of Caen, Bayeux, Coutances, Lisieux and Rouen mark the pinnacle of Norman Gothic architecture.

## The Hundred Years' War

By the middle of the 14th century the struggle between the Capetians (the descendants of the 10th-century king, Hugh Capet) and England's King Edward III (a member of the Plantagenet family) over the powerful French throne degenerated into the Hundred Years' War, which was fought on and off from 1337 to 1453. The death of Charles IV, in 1328, marked the end of the Capetian line in France and launched a new power struggle for the French throne. Philippe VI of Valois became king and in 1337 seized Aquitaine from the English. The following year Edward III of England invaded France. His first campaign amounted to little but in

1346 he landed at St-Vaast-la-Hougue and marched upon St-Lô, Caen and Lisieux. He eventually inflicted a major defeat upon the French at Crécy and went on to win Calais, but the drain on English resources was so severe that the war lapsed into a tentative truce.

The English were not the only ones who coveted Normandy. The Count of Évreux, known as Charles the Bad with good reason, had a boiling hatred for Philippe VI's successor, the incompetent (and mysteriously named) King Jean the Good, who had confiscated some of Charles' southern lands. Charles struck back by assassinating one of Jean's most trusted confidants and Jean declared Charles' Normandy properties confiscated. Charles appealed to the English for help and drew support from portions of Norman landowners. Rival gangs tore through the Norman countryside pillaging and looting as the peasant population cowered in the woods or in fortified castles and churches. As if political confusion didn't wreak enough misery, the bubonic plague (or Black Death) arrived in Normandy in 1348 and left a wave of death unlike any the world had seen.

The combination of warfare and disease reduced much of Normandy to abject poverty and yet the king still squeezed the landowners with new taxes to pay for the country's defence against the English. His unpopularity only increased when he arrested Charles the Bad at a banquet in Rouen and executed the popular Norman Count of Harcourt for treason. The effect of these unwise moves was to drive Normandy's nobility into the arms of the English, imploring Edward III for help against the French king.

Edward launched a new invasion later in the year that resulted in the king's capture in the Battle of Poitiers. The defeat of the flower of French nobility at Poitiers had a devastating effect on morale. Edward demanded a huge sum for King Jean's release which remained unpaid, and the king died in captivity in 1364.

The next king, Charles V (the Wise), ran into immediate trouble with Charles the

Bad, now released from prison and rumbling about his claims to either the French throne or the duchy of Normandy. Charles V found a gifted warrior in the Breton Bertrand Du Guesclin and placed the defence of Normandy in his hands. Du Guesclin's troops massed in Cocherel on the right bank of the Eure and cleverly lured the forces of Charles the Bad down from the hill to a devastating defeat, thus ending Charles the Bad as a threat.

Some stability returned to Normandy, marred only by an uprising over taxes in Rouen in 1383. Rouen and Dieppe resumed commercial activities but it was a short respite. The Armagnacs and the Burgundians went to war in 1407 after the assassination of Louis d'Orleans, brother of Charles VI. The English sided with the Burgundians and raided the Côte d'Albâtre, destroying Fécamp in 1410. The crushing French defeat at Agincourt in 1415 marked the beginning of a relentless English advance. Henry V landed on the Norman coast near Deauville-Trouville in 1417 capturing Honfleur, Caen, Bayeux and finally Rouen after a six-month siege. Only Mont St-Michel resisted the English onslaught, remaining loyal to the uncrowned French dauphin, Charles.

In the hands of their old masters, Normandy fared comparatively well. Henry VI founded a university at Caen, and law courts functioned in Rouen. Commerce also flourished in Rouen as suppliers rushed to fill the needs of the occupying army. Just as some Normans collaborated with the English, others fled to neighbouring regions or organised periodic revolts. In 1422 John Plantagenet, duke of Bedford, was installed as regent of France for England's King Henry VI, then an infant. Henry was crowned as king of France at Notre Dame less a decade later, and the English might have remained in power if a 17-year-old peasant girl hadn't intervened.

In 1429, the teenage Jeanne d'Arc (Joan of Arc) persuaded the French dauphin Charles that she had a divine mission from God to expel the English from France and bring about Charles' coronation. She rallied the French troops to defeat the English near Orléans, and Charles was crowned at Reims as Charles VII. However, Joan of Arc failed in her attempt to take Paris, and in 1430 she was captured by the Burgundians and sold to the English. Convicted of witchcraft and heresy by a tribunal of French ecclesiastics, she burned at the stake two years later in Rouen. Charles VII returned to Paris in 1437, but it wasn't until 1453 that the English were entirely driven from French territory (with the exception of Calais).

## Postwar Prosperity

The postwar period was a time of rebuilding in Normandy. Louis XI (The Spider King, so called because of his ruthless cunning) granted Normandy a substantial degree of autonomy both financially and politically. International trade reawoke, bringing prosperity to Rouen, Dieppe, Fécamp, Honfleur and Cherbourg who exported metal, salt, textiles, spices and fish. Explorers set forth from Normandy's shores. The Canary Islands, Senegal and Newfoundland were 15th-century acquisitions and, in 1523, Verrazano left from Dieppe to found Manhattan. In 1550, Le Havre native Guillaume Le Testu sailed the coast of Brazil and in 1555 a new Le Testu expedition left from Le Havre to colonise the bay of Rio de Janeiro. Ivory, spices and slaves flowed into Normandy's ports from French colonies on the west coast of Africa, allowing commercial shippers to amass fortunes. Jean Ango from Dieppe was one of the most notable. With all the money flowing into the region, opulent chateaux sprouted throughout the countryside.

## The Reformation

International trade made the Normans broadminded and the region fertile terrain for the spread of Protestantism. Normandy became a battleground for warring bands of religious fanatics in the latter half of the 16th century. The Catholic nobility attempted to preserve a power base, the English helped the Protestants and, as usual, the common people bore the brunt of the massacres and spasms of violence. In 1562, the

Huguenots, with the support of the English, attacked and pillaged churches and monasteries. Charles IX, with the connivance of his mother and regent Catherine de Médicis, retaliated by attacking Rouen and pillaging the city for eight days. The St Bartholomew's Day massacre of 1572 left 500 Huguenots dead in Rouen and spawned sporadic killing in Caen and Dieppe. Peace only returned after Henri IV issued the Edict of Nantes in 1598, granting freedom of worship.

The expansion of royal authority under his successor, Louis XIII, and his gifted advisor, Cardinal Richelieu, boded poorly for Normandy's autonomy. Rouen's independent-minded Parliament was reduced to a simple law court. As a final blow, the young king assaulted the chateau of Caen in 1620 for its fidelity to Marie de Médicis and forced the city into submission.

## Louis XIV & the Ancien Régime

Yet still the money kept rolling in. Louis XIV's Finance Minister, Jean-Baptiste Colbert, set up a number of profitable industries in Normandy. Ceramics in Rouen, textiles in Elbeuf and Alençon lace were some of his brainchildren that produced high returns for the region throughout the 17th century. The coastline also remained a launching pad for global expeditions. Colbert set up the West Indies Company in 1664 and put its headquarters in Le Havre. Robert Cavelier de La Salle was born in Rouen and went on to discover Ohio, the Mississippi and then claimed Louisiana for his king. Rich merchants commissioned the most fashionable Parisian architects and designers to create extravagant mansions. Mansard and Le Notre, fresh from their triumph at Versailles, rode out to lend their skills to Normandy's chateaux.

The revocation of the Edict of Nantes in 1685, which had allowed religious freedom, was a disaster for Normandy however. Protestantism had gained a strong foothold and numerous churches were destroyed in Caen, St-Lô and Argentan. Many citizens simply walked out rather than face persecution. Rouen alone lost 20,000 inhabitants, mostly skilled artisans who took their money and know-how to England, France and Germany. The region slid back into poverty.

## The French Revolution

By the 18th century, France had entered a financial and social crisis. Louis XIV had spent heavily on his castle at Versailles and his successor, Louis XV pursued a ruinously expensive Seven Years' War with Austria against England and Prussia. The royal treasury was saddled with heavy debt and high interest payments that the antiquated and unfair taxation system could not finance. Bread shortages added to the woes of the peasantry, who were also shouldering a high tax burden. At the same time, a new generations of philosophers – Voltaire, Rousseau and Montaigne – were talking about inalienable rights that belonged to the people.

In 1789 Louis XVI called a meeting of the États Généraux (Estates General) as a means of warding off popular discontent. Made up of representatives of the nobility and clergy (the First and Second Estates), the convention ran into trouble with the increasingly powerful Third Estate, which represented the other 90% of the population. They wanted the convention to adopt a system of proportional voting in order to avoid being repeatedly outvoted by the nobility and clergy. Failing to secure this system, they banded together with a few members of the first two estates, proclaimed themselves the National Assembly and demanded a constitution.

If Louis XVI had acted more decisively, he might have been able to retain power under a constitutional monarchy, but instead he took a hard line against the new National Assembly. His recognition of the rights of the Third Estate came too late; suspicion of the monarchy had reached boiling point. Anticipating a royal attack, crowds assaulted the Bastille on 14 July thereby securing an important symbolic victory against the crown.

The Normans enthusiastically supported the Revolution of 1789 and demolished the old chateau-prison of Rouen soon after the fall of the Bastille. The new government's administrative reorganisation of France in 1790 divided Normandy into the same five departments that exist today. Although the revolutionary government's hostility to the clergy was unpopular in abbey-strewn Normandy, the region stayed loyal to Paris until the purge of the moderate Girondin party and the ascendancy of the radical Jacobins in 1793. Caen became the centre of the Fédéralist party, opposed to the bloody Reign of Terror emanating from Paris. The Terror claimed few victims in Normandy but many churches and abbeys were pillaged, especially in Rouen and Caen. In July 1793 Charlotte Corday – a young woman disgusted by the excesses of the Revolution – left Caen for Paris where she found Jacobin leader Marat in his bath. She stabbed him to death and was then executed herself.

The years from 1793 to 1800 were a time of great political confusion in Normandy. The government's forced recruitment of young men provoked anti-recruitment riots in Calvados. The Fédéralist movement failed to attract adherents in large numbers but certain parts of Normandy – near Brittany, the Orne and Calvados departments and the southern Manche – supported the Chouannerie, royalist sympathisers. The economy also suffered as the recruitment drive robbed the region of workers and a blockade affected trade with England, Africa and the Antilles.

## The Golden 19th Century

Normandy thrived under all the 19th-century regimes from Napoleon to the Third Republic. Once the debris of the Revolution had been cleared, the region set about doing what it had always done best – make money. The revolutions of 1830 and 1848 and the 1870 war hardly touched Normandy. Politics took place in Paris, close in distance but far from the economic concerns that preoccupied Normans.

The century opened with Napoleon's decision in 1811 to create a vast naval port at Cherbourg, the city he called *'la véritable France'* (the real France). At the time, the English blockade of France was stifling Normandy's economy which depended on cross-Channel trade. The Cherbourg project was completed in 1831 under Napoleon III and coincided with the opening of the Paris–Cherbourg railroad line, allowing transatlantic passengers to disembark at Cherbourg and hop on a train to Paris.

The establishment of the first sea-bathing station in Dieppe in 1806 opened Norman shores to an entirely different activity – tourism. Queen Hortense of Holland, Napoleon's sister-in-law, was the first celebrity to try the curative effects of water in Dieppe, followed by the illustrious Duchesse of Berry in 1824. Other persons of prestige soon followed. Trouville was the next town to benefit from the sea-bathing fashion. The writer Alexandre Dumas publicised it well and soon writers, artists and nobility made it a must for the fashionable set. The opening of the Paris–Rouen railroad line in 1846 also helped coastal tourism by cutting travel time down to only four hours.

The 19th century saw a rich artistic output in Normandy. The spectacular coastline and picturesque ports became favourite subjects for artists beginning with the English landscapist, Joseph Turner, who painted Dieppe in 1825, and continuing through the luminous seascapes and impressionistic gardens of Claude Monet at the end of the century. Writers drew their inspiration from town life in Normandy. Balzac wrote about 19th-century Alençon and Flaubert's *Madame Bovary* was set in a provincial French village modelled after Normandy's Ry.

It was also in the 19th century that Normandy's countryside underwent a transformation into the large areas of pastureland that are typical of the region today. Dairy products became big business as all of France turned to Normandy for its cream, butter and famous Camembert and livarot cheeses. A spreading network of roads and railways helped distribute Norman products and maritime connections kept England as a major customer.

The contrasts between Lower and Upper Normandy became evident as the Lower region turned away from its small industries – wool, linen, lace – and became more rural, as Upper-Normandy cities such as Rouen developed a stronger manufacturing base. The steel business expanded in Caen as rural areas gradually became depopulated.

## World Wars

The First World War took place far from Normandy's borders but Norman soldiers were renowned for their bravery. 'I'm calm. The Normans are here,' the great Marshall Foch remarked about Norman participation in the battles of Charleroi, the Marne, Verdun and Chemin des Dames. From 1914 the village of Ste-Adresse, next to Le Havre, became the seat of the Belgian government. The economic effects of the war were disastrous for Normandy, as for the rest of France. The trend towards depopulation, begun in the 19th century, continued and Normandy's politics became increasingly conservative, emphasising the protection of local interests.

The Second World War was another story, as all the world knows. The Germans entered Normandy at Forges-les-Eaux on 7 June 1940 and Rouen on 9 June 1940, causing immense destruction before pursuing their advance to the Channel Islands where they stayed until 1945. A wave of bombardments accompanied their advance, driving the civilian population from their homes. For four years Normandy suffered all the indignities and cruelties of occupation: deportations, forced labour, arrests and executions.

The Allied debacle at Dieppe further demoralised the population. In 1942 Allied commanders persuaded themselves that it was time to launch a cross-Channel invasion. Winston Churchill was dubious about the feasibility of the plan but his commanders convinced him that a Second Front was necessary both to cement American involvement in the war effort and relieve German pressure on the Red Army.

The raid was astoundingly ill-conceived. An Anglo-Canadian force was to land at a strongly fortified port in the hopes that surprise would somehow carry the day. On the morning of 19 August battalions of Canadian infantry and tanks attempted to land east of the harbour but were met by heavy German fire even before they could get to shore. Pushing ahead, they blew a gap in the sea wall and a few managed to get to the cliffs beyond, but most were machine-gunned down.

The second wave met the same fate. A landing party in the centre of the harbour fared no better, with few of their tanks reaching the promenade and access to the town blocked by defensive concrete. Trapped on the beach, the tank crews were steadily eliminated by German fire.

At the end of the morning, only 2110 of the 4963 Canadians survived unscathed, leaving a casualty rate of 65%. Despite a 12 to 1 numerical superiority, the Germans had managed to destroy nearly all of the tanks and 106 British Royal Air Force aircraft. Clearly the Allies needed to rethink entirely their invasion strategy.

As a result of the disaster at Dieppe, Allied planners decided to abandon any idea of directly assaulting a fortified port. German planners decided that they needed further fortifications and began reinforcing the Atlantic wall, a 3200km defensive system along the Belgian and French coast. The Germans hired Fritz Todt to build the first gun batteries and then celebrated Nazi architect Albert Speer to complete the job. The string of pillboxes, blockhouses and gun emplacements were compared to links in a chain and were strongest around the narrowest part of the Channel, in the Pas de Calais, far northern France.

When German Field Marshal Rommel was placed in charge of the Atlantic defence in 1944 he further strengthened the fortifications by planting antitank obstacles on the beach and underwater obstructions offshore. He also laid nearly six million mines, mostly in Normandy. The Atlantic wall gave Allied troops less trouble on D-Day than the Germans anticipated largely because the invasion avoided the heavily fortified Pas de Calais and Channel ports in favour of the Cotentin beaches. Remnants of the Atlantic wall are still visible in Pointe du Hoc and Granville.

The largest amphibious operation in human history kicked off on 6 June 1944 in rough weather and heavy seas. For nearly three months bombs had rained down on Normandy and northern France, cutting rail lines, bridges and arms depots. Resistance fighters on the ground supplemented the air campaign primarily by sabotaging rail lines, preventing German reinforcements from reaching the coast. They were deployed inland since the Germans had effectively quarantined the Normandy coast to a depth of at least 50km inland, making sure that only proven loyalists were allowed near the coastal zone. Allied commanders and resistance fighters communicated via coded messages broadcast on the BBC. Despite the difficulties, by D-Day plus one resistance fighters had cut the main lines in Normandy, preventing a critical Panzer division from reaching the front.

The events of D-Day are covered in more detail in the special section, pages 25 to 32.

During the ensuing Battle of Normandy, Bayeux was the first city to be liberated. The British forces that had landed on Gold Beach reached Bayeux by the evening of 6 June and met no resistance. The city became a safe haven for civilians fleeing the chaos of the rest of Normandy and the British soon set up hospitals and a medical centre. On 14 June General De Gaulle arrived in Bayeux, making his first speech in free France. He was welcomed as a hero, helping to put to rest Allied suspicions that he might have little support among the French. He then turned Bayeux into the seat of his provisional government, setting up an administration and issuing currency.

Bayeux was one of the few Norman cities to emerge unscathed from the invasion. When the smoke cleared, it turned out that

## Military Cemeteries

### German Cemeteries

The largest German cemetery is at **La Cambe** which holds 21,400 tombs buried beneath a well-kept lawn. In the centre of the cemetery stands a six-metre high burial mound topped by an iron cross flanked by two statues. Around the mound are gravestones embedded in the ground carrying the names of those German soldiers that could be identified. Others are marked simply with 'Ein Deutscher Soldat'. Le Cambe is 20km north-west of Bayeux on the N13.

The ossuary at **Huisnes-sur-Mer**, 4km south-east of Mont St-Michel on the D275, is a striking memorial. The two-storey circular building has 34 chambers that contain nearly 12,000 human remains stored in concrete tiers.

Other German cemeteries in Normandy are St-Desir de Lisieux near Lisieux with 3735 graves, Marigny between St-Lô and Coutances with 11,169 graves and Orglandes south of Valognes with 10,152 graves. Hundreds of other German dead were buried in the Commonwealth cemeteries, including the one in Bayeux.

### British Cemeteries

By tradition, soldiers from the Commonwealth killed in the war were buried near where they fell. As a result, the Commonwealth military cemeteries follow the line of advance of British and Canadian troops. They are always open. The largest British cemetery in Normandy is the horseshoe-shaped burial ground at **Bayeux**, which contains 4868 tombs. As in all Commonwealth cemeteries, each gravestone is marked with personal and military information about the soldier as well as an inscription chosen by his family, making the visit almost unbearably personal. A monumental gate across the road is inscribed with the names of 1837 soldiers missing in action.

The British cemetery at **Ranville** (12km north-east of Caen), near the Pegasus bridge, contains over 2000 graves of soldiers of the British 6th Airborne Division as well as 80 Canadian and 100 German graves.

some 200,000 buildings had been destroyed. Calvados was particularly hard-hit, and St-Lô became known as the 'capital of ruins' with roughly 90% of its buildings destroyed by D-Day plus one. Falaise, Le Havre and the villages of the Suisse Normande were 85% destroyed; Caen lost 9000 of its 15,000 buildings; Coutances, Rouen, Évreux and Argentan lost 40 to 50% of their buildings.

## Modern Normandy

Postwar rebuilding was swift and, with a flood of Allied funds, largely completed by 1951. Speed was essential since housing stock needed to be replenished, but each city approached the task of reconstruction with a different aesthetic. The idea was to conserve reminders of the past, while adapting to the demands of modernity. Rouen erected bland, functional buildings along its devastated riverbanks but replicated the medieval style of half-timber buildings in the old town. Caen constructed modern buildings out of its traditional white stone and placed its famed university outside the city centre in the style of American campuses.

Le Havre is the most aggressively modern with a grid of wide streets interrupted by some strange architectural experiments. Smaller towns and villages tended to keep to the original layout of streets winding around riverbanks and allowed the new, low buildings to suggest rather than replicate the older structures.

Honouring the dead was another postwar priority. Soldiers who had been buried where they fell during the Battle of Normandy were disinterred, sorted and reburied in proper cemeteries. For details see the boxed text 'Military Cemeteries'.

## Military Cemeteries

Other British cemeteries in Normandy are at Banneville-Sannerville, between Caen and Troarn, with 2175 graves; Brouay, between Caen and Bayeux, with 377 graves; Cambes-en-Plaine, between Caen and Courseulles, with 224 graves; Chouain (Jérusalem), between Bayeux and Tilly-sur-Seulles with 40 graves; Douvres-la-Delivrande, between Caen and Luc-sur-Mer, with 927 graves; Fontenay-le-Pesnel, between Caen and Caumont-l'Eventé, with 520 graves; Hermanville-sur-Mer, on the coast, with 986 graves; Hottot-les-Bagues, between Caen and Caumont-l'Eventé, with 965 graves; Ryes-Bazenville, between Bayeux and Arromanches, with 987 graves; St-Manvieu, between Caen and Caumont-l'Eventé, with 2186 graves; Secqueville-en-Bessin between Caen and Bayeux, with 117 graves; Tilly-sur-Seulles between Caen and Balleroy with 1224 graves; and St-Charles de Percy, near Bény-Bocage, with 792 graves.

### Canadian Cemeteries

About 3km south of Dieppe in **Hautot-sur-Mer** is a cemetery with graves of nearly 700 Canadian and over 200 British soldiers who died in the 1942 raid on Dieppe.

Other Canadian cemeteries are Beny-sur-Mer, near Courseulles, with 2048 graves and Cintheaux, between Caen and Falaise, with 2959 graves.

### American Cemeteries

The largest American cemetery is at **St-Laurent-sur-Mer**, dramatically located over Omaha beach near Colleville-sur-Mer. The austere rows of white crosses and Stars of David marking the graves of 9386 American soldiers were used to powerful dramatic effect in Steven Spielberg's 1999 film *Saving Private Ryan*.

There's a smaller American cemetery in the same style at St-James, 16km south of Avranches, which contains the graves of 4410 soldiers killed during the fighting in Brittany and in the Loire Valley.

The positive side of a destroyed economy and infrastructure is the opportunity to start from scratch. A network of new roads and rail lines connected Normandy's cities with Paris, which opened Normandy's coast and countryside to Parisians looking for either seaside vacations or second residences. At the same time, France began moving towards a policy of building economic centres throughout the country rather than leaving Paris as the seat of all economic opportunity, which benefited Normandy enormously.

The region has attracted much industry as well as relying on its traditional agricultural base. Normandy's natural beauty has led many Parisians to buy second homes in the countryside. Tourists love the coastline in the summer and many come to pay homage to the fallen heroes of WWII.

## GEOGRAPHY

Normandy covers an area of 29,847 sq km including a 550km coastline that stretches from Le Tréport in the north-east to Mont St-Michel in the south-west. North of the Seine estuary at Honfleur the coastline is composed of the high chalky cliffs that gave the coastline its name, the Côte d'Albâtre. South of the estuary the Côte Fleuri (Flowered Coast) offers long stretches of sand interspersed by low cliffs, sand dunes and salt marshes that continue to the Côte de Nacre (Mother-of-Pearl Coast) west of Caen. The coastline of the Cotentin peninsula is marked by rocky inlets with occasional stretches of sandy beach.

The interior is gentle, rarely surpassing 200m in height. Inland from the Côte d'Albâtre, the Pays de Caux is a vast chalky plateau bordered on the south by the fertile Seine Valley and sliced by the rivers Bresle and Béthune. The wheat, rape and sugar beet fields of the Pays de Caux stretch east to the Vexin Normand between the rivers Epte and Andelle.

South of the Seine, the River Iton cuts through the wheatfields of the St-André plain which is flanked on the west by the wooded plateau of the Pays d'Ouche and on the south by the hilly Perche. In the east, Normandy's other major river, the Eure,

flows into the Seine. In the western portion of the Pays d'Ouche, the rivers Risle and Charentonne wind through flat meadows. Further west, the rivers Touques and Dives and their many tributaries water the Pays d'Auge, a plateau that marks the beginning of bocage country. These parcels of land divided by hedgerows run south-west to the Armorican massif, which forms the backbone of Brittany and Normandy. On the edge of the Armorican massif, there's a narrow strip of land, the Bessin, marked by clay soil. Dairy cows and horses graze peacefully in the rolling pastures. The northern part of the Armorican massif is the Cotentin peninsula whose rugged tip, Cap de la Hague, marks the furthest edge of Normandy. The crests of the Armorican massif extend east to the highest points in Normandy – Mount des Avaloirs and Signal de la Forêt d'Écouves at 417m. The central axis that runs from Caen to Falaise is a vast, treeless plain now given over to cattle rearing. Continuing south to Alençon are chalk regions in which cereal production is giving way to more cattle rearing.

## CLIMATE

The climate of Normandy is strongly influenced by the ocean. Summers are comfortable, and winters rarely become cold along the coast but are colder in the interior, especially around the heights of the Perche region. The littoral only gets 20 freezing days per year compared with 60 days in the interior. Normandy is a rainy region, and Upper Normandy is somewhat rainier than Lower Normandy. It can rain up to 88 days a year in Upper Normandy and 81 days a year in Lower Normandy. The lowest rainfall is in July and August and the highest is from November to January. The quantity varies between 700mm and 1000mm per year, with more rain on the hills and on the coast. December 1999 bore an unusual and highly destructive tempest throughout France that mowed down trees in a number of Normandy forests and damaged some monuments.

*[continued on page 33]*

D-Day Landings

# D-DAY LANDINGS

Barfleur

Cherbourg

*Peninsula*

*Cotentin*

English Channel
(La Manche)

Valognes

82nd
Airborne

Ste-Mère-
Église

Carteret

101st
Airborne

Pointe
du Hoc

La Haye-du-Puits

Carentan

Vierville

St-Laurent

Colleville

**US FORCES**

American
4th Infantry

American
1st Infantry

*Utah*

*Omaha*

Port-en-Bessin

Arromanches

**BRITISH, CANADIAN,
COMMONWEALTH, FREE
FRENCH & POLISH FORCES**

British
Forces

Canadian
Battalions

British
3rd Infantry

*Gold*

*Juno*

*Sword*

Courseulles

Lessay

Périers

St-Lô

*Vire*

Bayeux

Creully

Douvres

Ouistreham

Pegasus
Bridge

Ranville

6th Airborne

Caen

Coutances

Balleroy

Caumont

Tilly-Seulles

Villers-Bocage

*Drôme*

*Seulles*

*Orne*

Granville

Villedieu-les-Poêles

Vire

Falaise

Cancale

Avranches

St-Hilaire-du-
Harcouët

| | = US Paratroopers | | = US Movements |
|---|---|---|---|
| | = British Paratroopers | | = British Movements |

0   10   20km
0   6   12mi

Peaceful Omaha Beach as it stands today belies the tumultuous scenes here of 6 June 1944.

# The Battle of Normandy

The need for an invasion of continental Europe became apparent to Allied commanders as early as 1942. Early plans for a full-scale invasion called for a US–British contingent to land between Le Havre and Boulogne but the operation, code-named Roundup, was shelved. German submarine warfare was raging in the North Atlantic, preventing the transport of American troops to Britain and forcing shipyards to build escort vessels instead of landing craft. Allied efforts were instead directed towards North Africa and the Mediterranean.

American victories in the Pacific and the German defeat in Russia and North Africa turned the tide in 1943. Planning of an invasion of northern France, code-named Operation Overlord, began in earnest in January 1943 along with an invasion of Sicily, intended to divert German forces away from France. In December 1943 General Dwight D Eisenhower was appointed Supreme Commander of the Allied Expeditionary Force, soon followed by the appointment of British General Bernard Montgomery to head British and Canadian forces.

The target date for the invasion was May 1944 and the Allies settled on the beaches of the Cotentin peninsula as a landing site. The most obvious landing point was the Pas de Calais, which lies closest to Britain, but it was extremely well-defended. Other parts of the coast were either backed by high cliffs or too far from Britain.

Allied intelligence went to extraordinary lengths to encourage the German belief that the landing would be north of Normandy. The disinformation effort, code-named Operation Fortitude, involved the creation of phoney airfields and military bases replete with dummy tanks, landing craft and aeroplanes across from the Pas de Calais. To confuse the Germans even further, the Allies sent a Montgomery lookalike to impersonate him in the Mediterranean shortly before the D-Day landings.

**Title page:** The American Military Cemetery at Colleville-sur-Mer. (photograph by Martin Moos)

**Right:** Allied soldiers poured onto Normandy's beaches in the early hours of 6 June 1944 before advancing inland.

AUSTRALIAN WAR MEMORIAL NEGATIVE NUMBER P02018.223

Although the original invasion plan called for a force of three divisions followed by 12 more, Montgomery sought and received authorisation to expand the landing area and add more divisions, postponing the landing date until the beginning of June. The final plan entailed an assault by three paratroop divisions and five seaborne divisions, along with an armada of 13,000 aeroplanes and 6000 vessels. The initial invasion force was 45,000, and 15 divisions were to follow once successful

JANE SMITH

beachheads had been established. The landing area was to stretch over 80km of the coast from Caen to Ste-Mère-Église. The five sectors involved were code-named Sword, Juno, Gold, Omaha and Utah beaches.

To overcome likely logistical problems stemming from the lack of a harbour, the Allies devised the remarkable 'Mulberry Harbours'. These were enormous floating harbours that were towed from England, and set up off the Norman coast. They were indispensable, allowing large amounts of supplies to be taken quickly off ships and onto the roads leading to the front. A big storm from 19 to 22 June, however, destroyed the harbour stationed at Omaha Beach and damaged the Arromanches installation.

For three months prior to the invasion, bombs rained down on northern France cutting transportation and communication links. As the date drew closer, men in the assault divisions moved into their encampments, held virtually prisoner now that the target for the attack was finally revealed to them. A mood of pessimism prevailed among the Allied commanders as the possibility of a colossal failure loomed.

The invasion was carefully timed to take advantage of a full moon for the three airborne divisions and low tides for the landings. Conditions would be optimal only from 5 to 7 June. The invasion was set for 5 June, but the weather turned nasty on 4 June after the invasion force had already embarked, putting Eisenhower in an excruciating position. A delay could fatally imperil the vital secrecy of the operation and force the Allies to resupply the invading army in a period of even worse weather. Meteorologists predicted a window of opportunity on 6 June and Eisenhower gave the go-ahead.

# D-Day – 6 June 1944

Shortly after midnight on the night of 5–6 June, three Allied airborne divisions filled the skies over Normandy with gliders and parachutes. The American 82nd and 101st Airborne secured the base of the

**Top:** Supreme Allied Commander General 'Ike' Eisenhower – mastermind of the D-Day invasion.

Cotentin peninsula after suffering heavy casualties. The British 6th Airborne achieved its objectives of seizing bridges over the River Orne and Caen canal, including Pegasus bridge, which prevented enemy reinforcements.

By 3 am a few German commanders realised that something like an invasion might be taking place, but the most senior German Commander in Normandy was absent. Informed that an invasion was unlikely because of poor weather, Field Marshal Rommel was in Germany for his wife's birthday.

A preliminary bombing began at 3 am, followed by artillery fire from the offshore fleet. Even then the scale of the invasion was not apparent to Normandy's German defenders. The high command persisted in the belief that the naval bombardment was a diversionary tactic for an attack elsewhere. Around 6.30 am men began pouring out of their landing crafts.

## Sword, Juno & Gold Beaches

These beaches, stretching for about 30km from Ouistreham to Arromanches, were attacked by the British 2nd Army, which included sizeable detachments of Canadians and smaller groups of Commonwealth, Free French and Polish forces.

At Sword Beach (Colleville beach), the British 3rd Infantry Division disembarked at 7.25 am. The area was only lightly defended and the British were met by only moderate fire. The resistance was quickly overcome and the beach secured after about two hours. The infantry pushed inland from Ouistreham to link up with paratroops around Ranville, but soon suffered heavy casualties as their supporting armour fell behind, trapped in a huge traffic jam on the narrow coastal roads. Nevertheless, they were within 5km of Caen by 4 pm, but a heavy German armoured counterattack by the crack 21st Panzer division

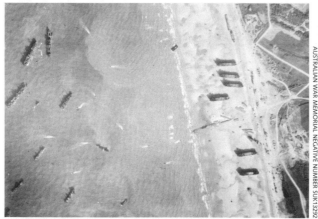

**Right:** Ships off the Normandy coast provided artillery fire as well as delivering troops and supplies.

forced them to dig in. Thus, in spite of the Allies' successes, Caen, one of the prime D-Day objectives, was not taken on the first day as planned. The British suffered 630 casualties.

At Juno Beach (Courseulles, Bernières and St-Aubin beaches), nine Canadian battalions attacked one German battalion but, despite the numerical advantage, underwater obstacles and steady artillery fire took a heavy toll. The offshore bombardment had done little damage to the German blockhouses. Even though their tanks had managed to land, the Canadians had to systematically clear the Germans trench by trench before moving inland. Two hours later a quarter of the force was still tied down in the landing area, but by noon they were south and east of Creully. Late in the afternoon, the German armoured divisions that had halted the British from Sword were deflected towards the coast and held Douvres, thus threatening to drive a wedge between the Sword and Juno forces. However, the threat of encirclement caused them to withdraw the next day. At the end of the day, the Canadians had 1000 casualties, including 335 dead.

At Gold Beach, which included the town of Arromanches, the attack by the British forces was at first chaotic; unexpectedly high waters obscured the German underwater obstacles, leading to the loss of numerous armoured vehicles. Fortunately the offshore bombardment had silenced most of the German big guns. By 9 am Allied armoured divisions were on the beach and several brigades pushed inland. By afternoon, they had joined up with the Juno forces and were only 3km from Bayeux – the first town in France to be freed. The British had suffered 400 casualties in securing the beachhead.

On all three beaches, odd-looking 'Funnies' – specially designed armoured amphibious vehicles designed to clear minefields, breach walls and wire entanglements, and provide support and protection for infantry – proved their worth. Their construction and successful deployment was due to the ingenuity and foresight of British Major-General Hobart.

# Omaha & Utah Beaches

The struggle on Omaha Beach (Vierville, St-Laurent and Colleville beaches) was by far the bloodiest of the day. Omaha Beach stretched 10km from Port-en-Bessin to the mouth of the River Vire and was backed by 30m-high cliffs. The beach was heavily defended by three battalions of heavily armed, highly trained Germans supported by an extensive trench system, mines and underwater obstacles. The Allied commanders failed to realise that the veteran German 352nd Infantry Division had only recently been moved into position here for training exercises.

The 1st US Infantry Division, known as the 'Big Red One', launched the attack on Omaha Beach and ran into immediate difficulty. The seas were choppy; winds and strong currents buffeted the landing crafts from one end of the beach to the other. Men disembarked under heavy German fire; the naval bombardment had done little damage to

German positions at the top of the cliffs. Those who weren't picked off by German gunners as they stepped off the boats, drowned under the weight of their heavy packs. Of the 29 Sherman tanks expected to support the troops, only two made it to shore. The situation was so critical that General Omar Bradley, in charge of the sector, considered calling off the landing.

Under relentless German enfilade fire, the men tried to collect themselves in small exhausted groups to seek some shelter under the sea wall or behind the beach obstacles. Man by man and metre by metre, the GIs managed to gain a precarious toehold on the beach and scaled the cliffs. Eventually a naval destroyer opened fire, forcing the Germans to fall back a short distance, and the men were finally able to get off the deadly beach. Nevertheless, 1000 soldiers were killed at Omaha on D-Day, out of a total of 2500 American casualties.

Matters were no better north-west at Pointe du Hoc where Colonel Earl Rudder's Texas Ranger Battalion was struggling up 30m cliffs. His mission was to seize German howitzers, whose fire could imperil the landing at Omaha Beach. His men had been trained on the Isle of Wight and came equipped with ropes and ladders, but nothing went as planned. A navigational error caused the men to come under direct German fire and casualties were heavy. The Germans had moved the howitzers but the Rangers engaged in two days of bloody fighting before they were finally relieved.

At Utah Beach the 4th US Infantry Division faced little resistance. By noon, the beach had been cleared with the loss of only 12 men. Pockets of troops held large tracts of territory to the west of the landing site, and the town of Ste-Mère-Église was captured.

**Top:** For three months prior to the invasion, bombers flew over France, cutting valuable transport and communication links.

## The Interior

By the end of D-Day, it was clear that the essential conditions for a successful invasion had been met. Surprise was total; the Allies had achieved complete mastery of the air and the Germans were unable to reinforce their units.

The bad news was that none of the military objectives had been met, and the Allies had lost 10,000 men, two warships, 127 aeroplanes and 300 landing craft.

Four days later, the Allies held a coastal strip about 100km long and 10km deep, but the Germans were firmly entrenched around Caen. General Montgomery's plan was to win a war of attrition with the Germans in the British sector, leaving the US army farther west to consolidate and push northwards up the Cotentin peninsula. A rapid advance was central to his plan but German resistance proved unexpectedly stiff and the situation threatened to degenerate into a stalemate. Villers-Bocage was the hub of a crucial road network for the region, but the British armoured thrust there on 13 June was defeated, as was an infantry offensive west of Caen from 25 to 29 June.

AUSTRALIAN WAR MEMORIAL NEGATIVE NUMBER P02018.306

**Left:** British troops file through the ruins of Caen after heavy bombing – 80% of the city was destroyed.

The German commitment in the British–Canadian sector allowed the Americans to enter the base of the Cotentin peninsula and move towards the important port of Cherbourg. The port was a major prize; after a series of fierce battles it fell to the Allies on 29 June. However, its valuable facilities were blown up by the retreating Germans, so it remained out of service until the autumn.

The grim Battle of the Hedgerows was fought mainly by the Americans up and down the Cotentin peninsula. The land of the *bocage*, divided into countless fields bordered by walled roads and hedgerows, made ideal territory for defending and the Germans made brilliant use of it. Since the nature of the terrain was not indicated on available maps, Allied commanders failed to foresee the difficulties of fighting in bocage country; the cost in men and morale was high.

On 18 July, American troops captured the vital communications centre of St-Lô after a bombing campaign that so destroyed the city it became known as the 'capital of ruins'. Taking advantage of their position as well as the fall of Cherbourg, which released three divisions, General Omar Bradley decided that the time was right for a major offensive, code-named Operation Cobra, to break out of the murderous bocage country. In late July, he began a thunderous bombing campaign of the German positions along the St-Lô–Périers road, which ran parallel to the advance route to Avranches. By 28 July, three infantry divisions followed by four armoured divisions finally succeeded in punching a hole in the German lines.

Bradley was quick to exploit the advantage, turning to fiery General George S Patton. Patton was ordered to take his army out of Normandy and into Brittany. After taking the 4th Armoured Division 40km in 36 hours, Patton captured Avranches on 31 July, the exit door from Normandy, leaving the way clear to Brittany.

The Germans decided to counterattack on 7 August. Hitler put

AUSTRALIAN WAR MEMORIAL NEGATIVE NUMBER 128328

**Right:** The cathedral of Coutances stands miraculously unscathed among the rubble of the rest of the city.

together a force of Panzer divisions, which then moved towards Mortain, intending to cut off the American forces south of Avranches and in Brittany. Allied interception of German radio communications allowed them to mount a sturdy air and land defence that inflicted heavy losses on the Germans and stopped the advance cold. The new position of German troops presented Allied commanders with an unexpected opportunity to inflict a potentially fatal blow

AUSTRALIAN WAR MEMORIAL NEGATIVE NUMBER SUK12844

to the German army. After finally liberating Caen on 19 July, the Canadians moved towards Falaise. Meanwhile, Patton's army was ordered to swing east and then north from Le Mans with the intention of meeting the Canadians at Falaise and trapping the German army in what became known as the Falaise pocket. In one of the more controversial decisions of the war, General Bradley ordered Patton to remain at Argentan, apparently fearing a 'friendly battle' between American and Canadian forces.

German commanders sensed the trap and began moving their divisions east just as Polish and American forces raced to close the Falaise–Argentan gap. The Germans fought with the fury of the damned and some quarter of a million men managed to escape to the Seine before the gap was closed on 19 August. Ultimately, their struggle was hopeless. The Germans lost some 10,000 men in the Falaise pocket, with another 50,000 taken prisoner. Allied forces pressed on to the Seine and beyond. The Battle of Normandy was over. On 15 August, the Allies also landed in southern France and, after a brief insurrection, Paris was liberated on 25 August by Allied forces.

Throughout the region, towns and cities have been rebuilt, road and rail links re-established and war debris removed, but countless reminders of Normandy's thousand-year heritage perished in the ferocious air campaign and are lost forever. However, the casualty figures for the Battle of Normandy are a more eloquent testimony to the price of this epic struggle. The Germans lost 200,000 men and as many were taken prisoner. Some 53,000 Allied soldiers were killed, more than 150,000 were wounded and nearly 20,000 were listed as missing in action. Some 15,000 to 35,000 Norman civilians also lost their lives.

**Top:** The Allies achieved complete mastery of the air, ensuring the success of the D-Day invasion.

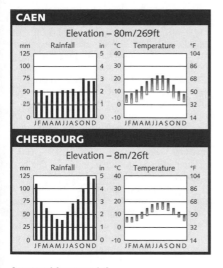

*[continued from page 24]*
Repairs of the monuments have largely been completed but replacing the patches of fallen trees will take decades.

## ECOLOGY & ENVIRONMENT
### Ecology
If Normandy was colour-coded to reflect ecological problems, the tip of the Cotentin peninsula would be bright red. The nuclear power plant at Flamanville produces about 15 billion kWh of electricity a year, equivalent to the consumption of Lower Normandy and Brittany combined. There is some radioactive discharge but it pales in comparison to that discharged by the nuclear waste treatment plant at nearby COGEMA. With 230 million litres of waste pumped into the Channel each year, Greenpeace has labelled COGEMA 'the single largest source of radioactive contamination in the EU'. The health effects of the contamination are a matter of hot debate. A study conducted by the *Association pour le Contrôle de la Radioactivité de l'Ouest*, an independent laboratory, found a statistically significant increase in deaths from leukaemia among residents living within a 10km radius of the plant, especially those who consumed large quantities of seafood or who frequently played at the beach as children. Published in the *British Medical Journal*, the study unleashed a storm of criticism based upon its methodology. The risk of eating seafood was further confirmed by a 1997 Greenpeace study finding that crabs from the COGEMA area had levels of radioactivity greatly exceeding EU regulations. In 1998 Greenpeace discovered that low tides left a radioactive discharge pipe exposed at the public beach, Plage des Moulinets. Radiation at the pipe's surface measured some 2000 times higher than normal background radiation. There's some hope on the horizon however. A recent European conference on the maritime environment in north-eastern Europe banned the dumping of nuclear waste into the sea. Although not legally binding on France, it's hoped that public pressure will force the government to exercise some control over COGEMA's practices.

What is not likely to change is France's reliance on nuclear power for its energy needs. Since the late 1980s, the state-owned electricity company, Electricité de France (EDF), has produced about three-quarters of the country's electricity using nuclear power. In addition to the power plant at Flamanville, Normandy has a smaller plant at Paluel on the Côte d'Albâtre.

Recent shipping accidents off Normandy's shores have also resulted in serious environmental damage. At the end of October 2000, the chemical tanker *Ievoli Sun*, carrying 6000 tons of toxic chemicals, sunk in the Channel north-west of Cap de la Hague. It was not the first accidental spill. In 1980 a container of pesticides sunk in the Channel and in the mid 1990s another cargo of toxins landed on the ocean floor. While the environmental effects of the latest spill are being evaluated, a lawsuit brought by the Manche department is trying to force the EU to introduce safer standards for ships passing through the Channel.

### Environment
The areas of Normandy under the most environmental pressure are the littoral, the Seine Valley and the Seine estuary, which are important bird habitats. The Seine bay between Le Havre and Honfleur receives

industrial and domestic pollution from the Paris region and the industrial zones of Le Havre and Rouen. The fertile alluvial deposits of the River Orne near Caen and the urbanised littoral of western Calvados are also environmentally degraded. The natural flushing action of the sea keeps the northwestern Manche far less polluted but the use of pesticides, as well as cattle breeding, in the intensively farmed Caen-Falaise plain has left unacceptably high levels of nitrates and pesticides in the ground water. Agrobusiness contributes up to 60% of the organic pollution in the region. The Calvados coast between Courseulles and Honfleur is also subject to occasional outbreaks of toxic algae, which impacts unfavourably on the region's fish and shellfish business.

Sea water in Upper Normandy is generally cleaner than that in Lower Normandy. The primary threat to the Upper Normandy coastline is erosion, which has eaten away at the chalky cliffs of the Côte d'Albâtre. The interior forests have been intensively logged for centuries, partly in order to create Normandy's distinctive half-timbered houses. Between just 1970 and 1980, some 25,0000 acres of forest was lost. Replanting is underway but the situation has only been stabilised, not reversed.

## FLORA & FAUNA
### Flora
Most Norman flora is concentrated in the forests and wetlands. Upper Normandy is more thickly wooded, with 20% of the surface covered by forests, mostly beech and oak with some yew trees. Non-deciduous trees such as Douglas pines and firs have been introduced only since the 19th century but tend to spread rapidly and impoverish the soil.

The Seine estuary is rich in reeds and saltloving plants while the Vernier marsh in the Parc Régional de Brotonne is replete with peat bogs. The peat bog of Heurteauville, near Jumièges is graced with a variety of rare plants such as giant ferns.

### Fauna
Some 270 species of mammals, reptiles, amphibians and birds are found in Normandy, not including millions of kinds of insects and fish. Nevertheless, there once were more. The wolf has disappeared since the end of the 19th century; wildcats, otters, civet, martens and ermine are also gone as well as peregrine falcons, sea eagles and royal kites. Wildlife is thin in Normandy's forests but you may spot warblers, crested tits, wrens, woodpeckers, jays and buzzards. Mammal life includes squirrels, fox, deer and wild boar.

The wetlands are rich in wildlife. The bay of Mont St-Michel hosts a large population of native ducks feeding on the watery grasses and is an international thoroughfare for migrating birds such as grey geese and black scoters. Seals arrive each year to nurse their young and large dolphins travel in schools seeking cuttlefish.

On the south-east of the Cotentin peninsula, the *Baie des Veys* is one of the best spots in Normandy for bird life. Covering some 32,000 acres, this vast swamp at the confluence of salt and fresh water harbours a nesting population of sheldrakes and ducks, while thousands of rails arrive in winter. Shrikes, sandpipers and grey curlews also make an appearance. The bay is under the protection of the World Wide Fund for Nature.

The cliffs of Étretat are host to arctic auks that come to the temperate coastal climes for three months each year to reproduce. They lurk in the cracks of the cliffs and lay one sole egg. Unfortunately, these trusting birds make an easy target for hunters who decimate the population each spring.

The *Marais Vernier* is a vast 5060-hectare marsh in the Seine Valley that has exceptional birdlife. Grey herons and white swans were recently reintroduced and you'll also find black-tailed godwits, white spoon-bills and avocets.

White Camargue horses and Scottish cows have also been introduced into the marsh; they are not indigenous species. For more on the horse and cow-breeding tradition in Normandy, see the boxed text 'Horses in Normandy' and, in the Manche chapter, 'Normandy Cows'.

## Horses in Normandy

Thoroughbreds, trotters and workhorses are honoured parts of the Normandy landscape. The Orne, Calvados and Manche departments raise some 70% of French thoroughbreds and trotters, bred in the national stables of St-Lô and Le Pin as well as scattered private stud farms. Horses that don't make the cut for a racing career are pressed into service for weekend riders and horse lovers at hundreds of local stables.

Normandy's tradition of breeding racehorses dates back to the early 18th century. The elite thoroughbreds are descended from Arabian stallions and English mares, carefully chosen for speed and endurance. With an average career of only three years, the elegant horses are evaluated early. Deauville hosts a yearling sale each August while brood mares and foals go to market in November.

Norman trotters have a somewhat longer career, working first at the race track and then as hire horses. Descended from Norman mares and English stallions, the trotter is also a pure breed, with a carefully charted heritage.

Cobs are sturdy horses with short legs and a comfortable riding gait, good for a long day in the saddle touring the farm. Although not strong enough for heavy loads, they are often used for pulling small carriages of tourists on sightseeing jaunts.

Normandy's most famous horse breed is the Percheron. These grey or black horses are immensely powerful and were once indispensable on the farm. Although the breed may extend back to the Middle Ages, all of today's Percherons are descended from one (busy) 19th-century stallion, Jean Le Blanc. Their docility and strength made them the workhorse of choice a century ago, but modern farming has less need of their powerful fore and hindquarters. Sadly, the Percherons have failed to find a role in the Norman economy, except on the dinner table. Since there's no work for them, they can't run fast and aren't lovely to look at, Percherons are coming to an inglorious end at the butcher shop.

## Endangered Species

The primary habitats for flora and fauna are the forests, the littoral, the bocage and the river estuaries. Industrial pollution has posed the most serious threat to watery habitats resulting in a loss of bird life, while the loss of forestland has destroyed the habitat of land creatures. Some protection for threatened habitats has followed the establishment of *Zones Naturelles d'Intérêt Écologique, Faunistique et Floristique* (ZNIEFF), an ecological protection program.

France counts some 1.7 million hunters, many of whom head to the forests and woodlands with their dogs as soon as the five-month season begins at the end of September. To safeguard the passage of migratory birds, long a target of hunters, a Brussels directive was introduced in 1979 to protect wild birds, their eggs, nests and habitats; it applies to all Member States of the EU. The French government signed the directive but didn't make its provisions part of French law, so birds that can safely fly over other countries may still be shot as they cross France. As a result, environmentalists have in the past rented entire mountain passes on birds' flight paths in order to keep hunters away.

## Regional Parks

Normandy has four *parcs naturels régionaux* (regional parks) established both to improve (or at least maintain) local ecosystems and to encourage economic development, the maintenance of local crafts and tourism. They are large, locally managed spaces that include small towns and villages and often have special visitors programs, ecomuseums and cultural tours. For further information on the regional parks contact the Fédération des Parcs Naturels Régionaux de France (☎ 01 44 90 86 20, fax 01 45 22 70 78, ✉ info@ parcs-naturels-regionaux.tm.fr), 4 rue de Stockholm, 75008 Paris, or see the Web site at www.parcs-naturels-regionaux.tm.fr.

The Parc Naturel Régional de Normandie Maine is the southernmost park and includes part of the Orne department and the Maine department in the Loire Valley. The countryside is a luscious combination of wooded cliffs, forests, bocage and open countryside. Of all the park's forests, the loveliest is the Forêt d'Écouves, within easy reach of Alençon.

The Parc Naturel Régional des Marais du Cotentin et du Bessin covers the bird sanctuary Baie des Veys as well as 74,000 acres of wetlands, home to species of migrating birds. The marshes also harbour small mammals and many insects.

The Parc Naturel Régional du Perche lies at the far southern tip of Lower Normandy and contains a number of oak and beech forests, most notably the Forêt de Bellême, with many kilometres of shady trails. This regional park is particularly rich in plant life with some 1200 different species, 140 of which are protected.

In Upper Normandy, the Parc Naturel Régional de Brotonne includes the vast Forêt de Brotonne, with its towering beech and oak trees, as well as the Marais Vernier wetlands. Over-logging has reduced the number of oak trees that once predominated in the forest, but replanting should eventually increase the population. The park spans the northern and southern banks of the Seine, linked by the soaring Pont de Brotonne near Caudebec-en-Caux which makes a good base for exploring the park.

## GOVERNMENT & POLITICS

France has long been a highly centralised state. Before the Revolution, the country consisted of about two dozen major regions and a variety of smaller ones. Their names (and those of their long-extinct predecessors) are still widely used, but for administrative purposes the country has, since 1790, been divided into units of about 6100 sq km called *départements* (departments).

There are five departments within Normandy: Seine-Maritime and Eure in Upper Normandy, and Calvados, the Manche and the Orne in Lower Normandy. The departments are commonly known by their two-digit code, which appears as the first two digits of all postcodes in the department and as the last two numbers on number plates of cars registered there.

Within the departments there are a number of areas *(pays)* that serve no administrative purpose but reflect various geographical and geological features. The Pays d'Auge, le Perche, Pays de Bray, Pays de Risle-Charentonne, Pays d'Ouche, Suisse Normande, Cotentin, Côte d'Albâtre, Côte Fleuri and Pays de Caux are some of the regions-within-regions mentioned in this book.

The national government is represented in each department by a *préfet* (prefect). A department's main town, where the government and the prefect are based, is known as a *préfecture* (prefecture). It is also the seat of an elected *conseil général* (general council). You can tell if a town is a prefecture because the last three digits of the postcode are zeros.

A department is subdivided into a number of *arrondissements* (for a national total of 324), each of whose main town is known as a *sous-préfecture* (subprefecture). The arrondissements are further divided into *cantons* and these are further split into *communes*, the basic administrative unit of local government. Each commune is presided over by a *maire* (mayor) based in a *hôtel de ville* (town hall) or *mairie* (mayor's office). Almost one-third of the communes have populations of less than 200.

Because of their small size, the 96 departments of metropolitan France are ill-suited for carrying out modern regional coordination. Therefore, in 1972, the government divided France into 22 regions based roughly on the country's historical divisions. Each of these has an elected council and other organs, but its powers are limited and it plays no direct role in actual administration. The historical region of Normandy is divided into two administrative regions, Upper (Haute) and Lower (Basse) Normandy.

Although *conseils régionals* (regional councils) have little power in a centralised state, the local elections provide a good

## RÉGIONS & DÉPARTEMENTS

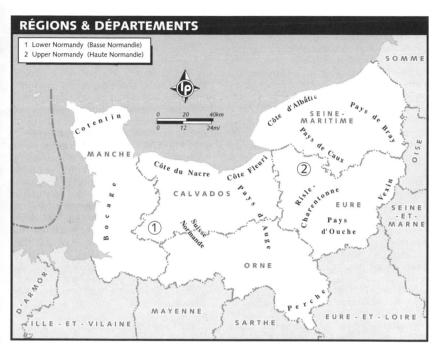

1  Lower Normandy  (Basse Normandie)
2  Upper Normandy  (Haute Normandie)

barometer of local political opinion. France is currently governed by president Jacques Chirac of the right-of-centre RPR and prime minister Lionel Jospin of the PS or Socialist Party. The split is reflected in Norman politics with Lower Normandy headed by the rightist UDF party and Upper Normandy in the hands of the Socialist Party.

The *bête-noire* of French politics is the extreme-right Front National (FN) which draws generally higher support in Upper Normandy than in the rest of France. The 1998 regional elections awarded nearly 20% of the vote in the Eure department to the FN (against a national average of 15%), 11.5% in the Manche, 10.3% in Calvados, 11.5% in the Orne and 14.8% in the Seine-Maritime. The election also sparked a bitter controversy when the RPR threw its support to an FN candidate in order to block a Communist vice-president of the regional counsel.

## ECONOMY

France's economy may not be the powerhouse of Europe, but French financial leaders have enough clout to help determine the course of European Monetary Union (EMU). Although Frankfurt, not Paris, was chosen as the headquarters of the new European Central Bank, the French won a victory in 1998 that surprised many European observers: the central bank's chief, a Dutchman, would have a much shorter reign than originally envisaged, and its second head would be a French official, Jean-Claude Trichet.

For the traveller the most important consequence of EMU will be the disappearance of many of Europe's banknotes and bills in 2002, when the euro becomes the standard EU currency (see the boxed text 'Adieu Franc, Bonjour Euro' in the Facts for the Visitor chapter).

To the surprise of many outsiders, the French *dirigiste* (interventionist) model of State ownership is still alive and well. More than 50% of GDP is spent by the government on a bureaucracy that employs one in every four French workers despite a series of heavyweight privatisations during the 1990s. The 'family silver' – including Air France, France Telecom and Aerospatiale – have been partly sold off, but enough other mammoth concerns such as car-maker Renault remain government-controlled.

Privatisation has helped France take advantage of a global economic boom: the French economy is turning over nicely (with growth predicted at around 3% in 2001) and unemployment was expected to fall to below 9%, the lowest level in over a decade. Growth could be slower than expected, however, if the US economy turns sharply downwards, sparking a global slowdown. Inflation is negligible (around 0.69%).

France is one of the world's most industrialised nations, with some 40% of the workforce employed in the industrial sector. About half of the economy's earnings come from industrial production. Large industries such as automobile manufacturing, machinery, electronics and pharmaceuticals have set up shop in Évreux, Lisieux, Caen and the Seine Valley, as they are well-linked to Paris. Falaise, Argentan, St-Lô and Granville have built industrial zones outside their centres to attract such industries.

France can also lay claim to being the largest agricultural producer and exporter in the EU. Its production of wheat, barley, maize (corn) and cheese is particularly significant. The country is to a great extent self-sufficient in food except for certain tropical products, like bananas and coffee. Normandy is second only to Brittany in cattle breeding for meat and dairy products and is France's primary producer of flax and carrots. The primary dairy production area lies in the bocage territory in west Normandy, which supplies the milk for the butter, cheese and cream found on supermarket shelves.

There are, however, clear differences between Upper and Lower Normandy. Upper Normandy is more industrialised and Lower Normandy relies more on its agricultural base. Industry employs one in three workers in Upper Normandy but only one in four in Lower Normandy.

Upper Normandy produces 20% of France's paper pulp, 30% of its cars and 50% of its plastics. The port of Le Havre is a major factor in the regional economy, representing some 8% of the total employment in Upper Normandy. In the Le Havre region, more than one job in five is linked to port activities. Rouen is also an important port in the region, contributing 6% of the total regional employment. Together, the ports handle wheat, corn, sugar, fertilisers, timber, wood pulp, chemical products and cars. Energy production is also a significant source of revenue with the refineries along the Seine in the Seine-Maritime department producing a third of France's refined fuel, and the nuclear power centre of Paluel on the Côte d'Albâtre producing 12% of its electricity. The construction sector has also been strong in the last few years as France's overall economic picture has improved, allowing wealthy Parisians to construct secondary residences in the region.

The Eure department is more agricultural than the Seine-Maritime, with plains that supply France with wheat and oil seed rape, but an industrial base is developing. Pharmaceuticals, printing and machinery are clustered around Évreux while the rest of the region has profited from its close transportation links to Paris to attract such diverse industries as automated packaging, space technology, chemicals and plastics.

Despite strong growth in 1998–9, Upper Normandy traditionally has had a stubbornly high unemployment rate. Although diminishing faster than the national average, at the end of 1999 Normandy still had an unemployment rate of 12.4%, 1.8% higher than the rest of France. Its traditional industrial base has seen improvements in productivity that don't necessarily translate into more jobs.

Lower Normandy has a more dynamic economy largely due to the strength of its small-business sector. Dairy, meat and cereal production employ one worker in five and horse-breeding has created 6000 jobs. The agricultural sector employs 15.6% of the region's workers, closely followed by the electrical and electronics industry centred in Caen and food processing centred in St-Lô. Plastics and pharmaceuticals complete the economic picture. Heavy industry is also represented. Caen is a steel centre and Cherbourg's shipyards are a major force in the local economy. Tourism is also a factor in the Lower Normandy economy employing 16,000/24,000 people in low/high season.

The economic figures are strong in Lower Normandy. In the last few years, its GDP has increased faster than any other region in France. The number of jobseekers decreased by a hearty 10,000 in 1999, leaving the total unemployment rate just under 10%.

The construction and automotive business was especially strong, again reflecting the overall health of the French economy.

The largest cloud on the economic horizon of Lower Normandy is the appearance of BSE or 'mad cow disease' in French beef cattle. Although meat is rigorously inspected and controlled, the fact that the disease has made its way into the food chain has caused the French consumers to shy away from beef, which could have a serious impact upon Normandy's beef industry.

## POPULATION & PEOPLE

Upper Normandy has a population of 1,780,000 and the Lower Normandy population is 1,420,000. There are large differences in population density between the regions. The Seine-Maritime is one of the most densely populated departments in France with 197 inhabitants per square kilometre as opposed to 89 inhabitants per square kilometre in the Eure. In the Seine-Maritime 86% of the inhabitants live in an urban environment, clustered around Rouen and Le Havre. In the Eure only 66% of the inhabitants live in an urban area, mostly around Évreux.

As a predominantly agricultural region, it's not surprising that Lower Normandy is more sparsely populated with an average density of only 77 inhabitants per square kilometre, dwindling to 50 in the interior Manche, central Orne and western Calvados. Although the population of both regions has increased in the last 10 years as a result

of higher birth and lower death rates, there have been changes in the distribution of the population. The decades-long depopulation of rural spaces has stopped, if not reversed. Upper Normandy has seen a higher increase in its rural population, especially in the areas close to Paris as more Parisians choose to live in the country and commute to work. The great urban centres of Rouen and Le Havre have seen an exodus, while in Lower Normandy the economic opportunities afforded by the Calvados region are proving attractive to young workers who are contributing to a population increase in the Caen region. The rural population of Lower Normandy has also increased since rural areas offer a quality of life unmatched in the cities.

The ethnic composition of the regions varies markedly. Upper Normandy has 48,000 immigrants, mostly of Algerian and Moroccan descent with some Portuguese. There are 20,000 immigrants in Lower Normandy, equally divided between Turks, Moroccans and Portuguese.

## EDUCATION

France's education system has long been highly centralised, a fact reflected in teachers' status as civil servants. Its high standards have produced great intellectuals and almost universal literacy, but equal opportunities are still not available to people of all classes.

Private schools, most of which are Catholic (though Protestant and Jewish schools also exist), educate about 17% of students – and also account for a quarter of all students planning to attend university. The State pays staff salaries and some of the operating costs at most private schools provided they follow certain curriculum guidelines. Tuition fees are thus very low.

## ARTS
### Literature

As the Vikings settled in Normandy in the 10th century, the region developed a particular dialect, Norman French, that incorporated elements from the Scandinavian language mixed with the language of northern France. Norman French is no longer spoken in the region but, in the 11th century, historical accounts were written in the language, which was a departure from the usual practice of writing in Latin. First to appear was Geoffrey Gaimar's *Estorie des Engles* (History of the English) in the early 12th century, followed by the Anglo-Norman chronicler Wace's *La Geste des Normands* (Heroic Achievements of the Normans) in the later part of the century.

The most celebrated early work attributed to a Norman poet was the 11th-century epic poem *Chanson de Roland* (Song of Roland). It was the earliest work of French literature and recounts the heroic death of Charlemagne's nephew Roland, ambushed on the way back from a campaign against the Muslims in Spain in 778.

Historical themes continued to predominate from the end of the 12th to the 13th century. The poet Fantosme chronicled the invasions of the Scots, Angier recounted the life of St Gregory, and Guillaume de Berneville wrote about the life of St Gilles. Anonymous poets wrote about Thomas à Becket, the English knight Bevis and Charlemagne. One of the last important works of Norman French was the 14th-century *Contes Moralisées* (Moral Tales) by Nicole Bozon.

By the 15th century poets turned their attention to matters of the heart. Alain Chartier of Bayeux began his career with a patriotic work recounting the French defeat at Agincourt and then launched the trend of romanticism by writing *La Belle Dame Sans Merci* (The Beautiful Woman Without Pity) which inspired the John Keats poem of the same title. Chartier's allegorical love poems became enormously popular.

The highlight of 16th-century Norman literature was François de Malherbe of Caen, whose work reflected a backlash against romanticism and lush language in its emphasis upon simplicity of expression. As court poet to Louis XIII and Henri IV, he wrote odes to King Louis and Marie des Médicis, Henri IV's wife, that brought a new rigour to the treatment of rhythm. He poetry was an early precursor of the French classical style that developed in the 17th century.

The 17th century is known as *le grand siècle* because it was the century of great French classical writers. Pierre Corneille of Rouen was a leading figure of the classical period and one of France's greatest playwrights. He began his career with comedy and tragicomedy and then turned out the celebrated *Le Cid* (El Cid) based upon the Spanish hero. Matters of conscience preoccupied his tragedies, especially the conflict between reason and romantic yearnings. He wrote three other fine tragedies – *Horace*, *Cinna* and *Polyeucte* set in ancient Rome – before inventing the comedy of manners in the 1643 *Le Menteur*.

French literature of the 18th century was dominated by philosophers who ushered in the Age of Enlightenment. The philosopher Fontenelle, also from Rouen, prefigured the rationality of the age with works attacking superstition and making scientific learning accessible to the general public.

The other great 19th-century theme was the back-to-nature movement espoused by Jean-Jacques Rousseau. The traveller and Le Havre native Bernardin de St-Pierre foreshadowed Rousseau's idealised love of nature in *Études de la Nature* (Nature Studies) in 1784 and *Paul et Virginie* in 1787. He later became a disciple of Rousseau in Paris.

The 19th century brought Gustave Flaubert, a Rouen native and author of *Madame Bovary*, a landmark in French literature. The shallow, corrupt Emma Bovary is portrayed with unflinching realism, marking a turn away from romantic, classical themes. Based upon a real-life story in Ry, near Rouen, the book sparked a government prosecution to have it banned for immorality which of course assured its popular success.

Guy de Maupassant was another influential Norman writer. Born in Fécamp, and a failed law student like his friend Flaubert, de Maupassant had a pessimistic view of human nature. His short-story collection *Contes de la Bécasse* (Tales of the Woodcock), written in Étretat, evoked the oppressive class hierarchy found in bourgeois Norman life, and his grim psychological study of two brothers *Pierre et Jean* was set in Le Havre.

Although many historical buildings perished during the Battle of Normandy, the rolling landscape is still liberally sprinkled with the traditional medieval half-timbered houses so typical of the region.

Creamy Camembert – *les pieds de Dieu!*

Shortbread souvenirs from Mont St-Michel

Apples are at the very heart of Norman cuisine.

Guess the secret recipe of this 16th-century drink.

Buy some 'sole' food in Rouen's covered market.

Enough garlic to take your breath away!

The Norman coastal village of Cabourg is the background for Proust's *A l'Ombre des Jeunes Filles en Fleur* (In the Shade of Young Girls in Flower) part of *À la Récherche du Temps Perdu* (Remembrance of Things Past). The writer spent time in the village as a child and returned each year until WWI. His largely autobiographical novel explores in evocative detail the true meaning of past experience recovered from the unconscious by 'involuntary memory'.

The 20th century opened with the philosopher-essayist Émile Chartier, known as Alain, born in Mortagne-au-Perche. His aphoristic essays, *Propos sur le Bonheur* (Words about Happiness) and *Sur l'Éducation* (On Education) expressed a humanistic philosophy opposed to war and political tyranny. Perhaps the best-known philosopher of the 20th-century was Jean-Paul Sartre whose existential philosophy was forcefully prefigured by his novel *Nausée*, written while he was teaching at Le Havre. His companion, philosopher and feminist Simone de Beauvoir, taught at the school in Rouen for four years.

## Architecture

**Gallo-Roman** The Romans constructed a large number of public works all over the country from the 1st century BC: aqueducts, fortifications, marketplaces, temples, amphitheatres, triumphal arches and bathhouses. They also established regular street grids at many settlements. Little remains of the Roman presence in Normandy except remnants of an amphitheatre at Lillebonne, foundations of Roman buildings in Lisieux and the Gallo-Roman wall at Évreux.

**Romanesque** After the 11th-century conquest of England, Normandy was rich in resources, and engaged in a flurry of new construction, rebuilding the Merovingian and Carolingian churches destroyed by the Viking invasions and erecting new churches and abbeys. The style endured throughout the 12th century and was called Romanesque because their architects adopted many architectural elements (eg, barrel vaulting) from Gallo-Roman buildings still standing at the time. Romanesque buildings typically have round arches, heavy walls whose few windows let in very little light, and a lack of ornamentation that borders on the austere. The effect is remarkably graceful, despite the architectural limitations of barrel vaulting which precluded the construction of large windows. Norman builders often constructed Oriental-style cupolas copied from the Carolingian churches or installed square lantern towers to create light. The naves usually had three storeys with wide, high bays; galleries broke the monotony of thick walls; and the facade was often flanked by tall towers in an H shape.

The Benedictine monks were the primary instigators of Normandy's 11th-century abbeys. They're in ruins now, but the abbeys of Jumièges and St-Wandrille still convey a sense of the majesty of the Norman Romanesque style. The abbey of Mont St-Michel, though expanded in later centuries, contains remains of the 11th-century structure. The abbeys in Caen – Abbaye aux Hommes and Abbaye aux Dames – are the best surviving examples of Romanesque architecture in Normandy.

**Gothic** The Romanesque style remained popular until the mid-12th century, when it was supplanted by the Gothic style, originating in the Ile de France. Gothic structures are characterised by ribbed vaults carved with great precision, pointed arches, slender verticals, chapels (often built by rich people or guilds) along the nave and chancel, refined decoration and large stained-glass windows. The use of flying buttresses to support the walls allowed windows to be larger, creating a light, spacious interior. The cathedral of Rouen was the first cathedral in Normandy to incorporate the Gothic style in the St-Romain tower but it was in the cathedral at Coutances, built between 1218 and 1275, that early Gothic style can be seen in its purest form. One of the other features of Gothic cathedrals are the huge, colourful rose windows as seen in Rouen cathedral.

In the 14th century, the Rayonnant (Radiant) Gothic style – named after the radiating tracery of the rose windows – developed, with interiors becoming even lighter thanks to broader windows and more translucent stained glass. One of the most beautiful Rayonnant buildings is the Église St-Ouen in Rouen, whose stained glass forms a sheer curtain of glazing.

By the 15th century, decorative extravagance led to Flamboyant Gothic, so named because its wavy stone carving was said to resemble flames. Beautifully lacy examples of Flamboyant architecture include Rouen cathedral's Tour de Beurre and the Église St-Maclou in Rouen.

**Renaissance** The Renaissance, which began in Italy in the early 15th century, set out to realise a 'rebirth' of classical Greek and Roman culture. It had its first impact on France at the tail end of the 15th century, when Charles VIII began a series of invasions of Italy. The king's chief minister, Georges d'Amboise, introduced the style to Normandy by importing Italian artists and artisans to build his chateau in Gaillon. In the beginning of the 16th century, the architect Rouland Le Roux applied elements of the new style to the Bureau des Finances (now the tourist office) in Rouen and the

## PARTS OF A CATHEDRAL

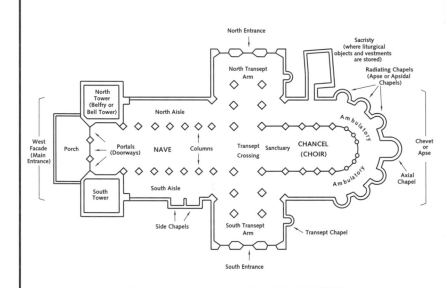

**NOTE:**
Very few churches incorporate all of the elements shown here, some of which are found only in Gothic cathedrals from certain periods. Romanesque churches have a much simpler layout.

Many Normandy cathedrals are oriented roughly east to west so that the chancel faces more or less east towards Jerusalem. As a result, the main entrance is usually at the base of the west facade and the transept arms extend north and south from the transept crossing as shown here.

tombs of the Amboise cardinals in Rouen's cathedral. In this early period, Renaissance decorative motifs (columns, tunnel vaults, round arches, domes and so on) were blended with the rich decoration of Flamboyant Gothic. In the Bureau des Finances, Renaissance pilasters and bas-reliefs combine well with Gothic canopies. Also in Rouen, the early Renaissance style is apparent in l'Aître St-Maclou, the Gros Horloge and the Parliament. The cathedral and St-Maclou church show Renaissance influences in several stained glass windows and sculptures. In Caen, the apse of the St-Pierre church is a wonderful example of the early Renaissance style.

Many private mansions in Normandy's cities were built in a Renaissance style and some smaller towns have 16th-century Renaissance churches. The exquisite carved porch of the Ry church is especially notable. The style became more mannered later on in the 16th century and fell out of favour in Normandy although there are scattered restored mansions from the period in Rouen, Honfleur, Bernay and Lyons-la-Forêt. Because French Renaissance architecture was very much the province of the aristocracy

## PARTS OF A CATHEDRAL

### USEFUL TERMS:

**Ambulatory**
The ambulatory, a continuation of the aisles of the nave around the chancel, forms a processional path that allows pilgrims relatively easy access to radiating chapels, saints' relics and altars around the chancel and behind the altar.

**Clerestory Windows**
The clerestory windows, a row of tall windows above the triforium (see below), are often difficult to see because they're so high above the floor.

**Cloister**
The cloister (cloître), a four-sided enclosure surrounded by covered, colonnaded arcades, is often attached to a monastery church or a cathedral. In monasteries, the cloister served as the focal point of the monks' educational and recreational activities.

**Crypt**
The crypt (crypte) is a chamber under the church floor, usually at the eastern end, in which saints, martyrs, early church figures and worthy personages are buried. In many Gothic churches, the crypt is often one of the few extant parts of earlier, pre-Gothic structures on the site. A visit to the crypt, usually reached via stairs on one or both sides of the chancel, may involve a small fee.

**Narthex**
The narthex is an enclosed entrance vestibule just inside the west entrance. It was once reserved for penitents and the unbaptised.

**Rood Screen**
A rood screen, also known as a jube (jubé), is an often elaborate structure separating the chancel from the nave. Because rood screens made it difficult for worshippers to see religious ceremonies taking place in the chancel, most were removed in the 17th and 18th centuries.

**Rose Window**
The circular stained-glass windows commonly found in Gothic cathedrals over the west entrance and at the northern and southern ends of the transept arms are known as rose or wheel windows. The stained-glass panels are usually separated from each other by elaborate stone bar tracery, which people inside the church see in silhouette.

**Treasury**
A treasury (trésor) is a secure room for storing and displaying precious liturgical objects. It may be open shorter hours than the church itself. Visiting often involves a small entry fee.

**Triforium**
The triforium is an arcaded or colonnaded gallery above the aisle, choir or transept. Most triforia are directly above the columns that separate the aisles from the nave or the ambulatory from the chancel. From the late 13th century, larger clerestory windows often replaced the triforium.

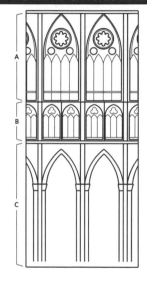

View of Nave Wall

A. Clerestory Windows

B. Triforium

C. Aisle (behind the columns)

and designed by imported artists, the middle classes – resentful French artisans among them – remained loyal to the indigenous Gothic style, and Gothic churches continued to be built throughout the 16th century.

**Baroque** During the Baroque period, which lasted from the end of the 16th century to the late 18th century, painting, sculpture and classical architecture were integrated to create structures and interiors of great subtlety, refinement and elegance.

In Normandy, the style was most often expressed in private mansions. François Mansart, the favourite architect of Louis XIII, brought the Baroque style to Normandy in the chateau of Balleroy. The chateau of Beaumesnil is another fine example.

**Neoclassicism** Neoclassical architecture, which emerged in about 1740 and remained popular in Paris until well into the 19th century, had its roots in the renewed interest in classical forms. It was a search for order, reason and serenity through the adoption of the forms and conventions of Graeco-Roman antiquity: columns, simple geometric forms and traditional ornamentation. The Château du Champ de Bataille embodies the ideals of classical architecture in a private mansion while the town hall of Caen, remodelled by Guillaume de la Tremblaye in the 18th century, demonstrates the sobriety of the style in civil architecture. The same architect rebuilt the monastic buildings of Le Bec-Hellouin in a classical style.

**Seaside Architecture** The Art Nouveau style so characteristic of turn-of-the-century Paris never made its way to Normandy but a unique resort architecture arose in the 19th century. All along the coast, from Deauville to Dieppe, exuberant buildings arose for the fashionable Parisians flocking to Normandy's shores. Using Normandy's traditional half-timbered houses for inspiration, designers created facades of dizzying geometrical shapes broken by bow windows and balconies. The arrangements of towers, chimneys, gables and steeply slanting roofs is deliberately and delightfully asymmetrical. Deauville-Trouville has numerous examples of the style, most notably the Villa Strassburger.

**Contemporary Architecture** When Normandy arose from the ashes of WWII, the need to create entire towns nearly from scratch forced town planners to take on some interesting architectural experiments. In Le Havre, Auguste Perret found that reinforced concrete perfectly expressed modern architecture's disdain for ornament and extraneous detail. His prefabricated buildings were intended to be more than cheap and easy to build – to also reflect a neoclassical ideal of purity. His Église St-Joseph, built with Raymond Audigier and Georges Brochard, is a stark, concrete structure. The architect Oscar Niemeyer, who designed Brasília (in Brasil), built a conical white cultural centre without doors or windows in Le Havre's town centre.

In Rouen, Louis Arretche's 1979 church, Église Ste-Jeanne d'Arc, in the form of an upturned boat, was initially unsettling but has worn well. The restoration of William the Conqueror's birth castle in Falaise has been less popular. Architect Bruno Decaris' decided to suggest the defensive function of the outer courtyard with a grey concrete wall rather than attempt to duplicate the materials or style of the original. The theory that the restoration of an ancient monument is an opportunity for expressionistic architectural statements proved unpersuasive to the local citizenry who responded with fury and lawsuits. Some have pointed out that if Decaris' theory had prevailed in postwar Normandy, most of the region would now be covered in grey concrete.

## Painting
**16th Century & Earlier** Sculpture and stained glass rather than paintings were the main adornments of the medieval Gothic cathedrals of Normandy, in part because the many windows left little wall space. In the 15th century, France might have served as a meeting ground for the rich traditions of Italy and Flanders, but the Hundred Years'

War got in the way. In the 16th century, the Wars of Religion further hampered the development of Norman painting. Most Renaissance painters copied Italian models with little passion or inspiration.

**17th Century** The Rouen painters Jean Jouvenet and Jean Restout achieved some note in Normandy with their religious paintings but it was Nicolas Poussin (1594–1665) who became the most influential painter of the age. Voltaire wrote that French painting began with Poussin, born near Les Andelys. At the beginning of the 17th century, the best place to study art was still Italy, which was where Poussin headed in 1624. He spent 17 years in Rome, came back to Paris for 18 months and then returned to Rome for the rest of his life. Influenced by Titian and Raphael at first, Poussin eventually developed a style based upon mathematically controlled composition, restrained colour and themes from antiquity. His classical style became the official 'Academic' style of French painting and the standard by which all succeeding painters were judged up to the 20th century. Several Poussin canvases are in display in the museum of Rouen.

**18th Century** By the 18th century, other landscape painters were becoming interested in Normandy. The Avignon painter Joseph Vernet was commissioned to execute a series of paintings of French ports that came to include *Le Ville et le Port de Dieppe*. More seaside paintings followed. Jules Noël painted Étretat and Hubert Robert painted the ports of Dieppe, Rouen and Le Havre. English landscapists, Eastlake, Cotman, Crome, Wilkie, Haydon, Edridge and Prout hurried to Normandy after the Revolution to turn out paintings, etchings and watercolours. The most influential of the late-18th-century English landscapists to fall in love with Normandy was Joseph Turner who made a point of coming to France each year. He produced several paintings of Normandy ports at Dieppe and Rouen that strongly influenced the later Impressionists. Monet's seminal *Impression,*

*Soleil Levant* strongly resembles a Turner watercolour of Rouen.

**19th Century** The 19th century was Normandy's golden age of painting. The century began with Rouen-native Théodore Géricault (1791–1824), who received classical training in Paris before falling under the spell of the Italian masters in Rome. His forceful, dramatic works realistically depicting human suffering launched the romantic movement in France. An entire room of Géricault paintings is part of Rouen's Beaux-Arts museum.

Gréville-born Jean-François Millet (1814–75) took a different approach. After studying art in Cherbourg and Paris, he joined the Barbizon school, a group of French painters living in the town of Barbizon on the Ile de France who devoted themselves to paintings of outdoors scenes. Millet painted peasants with extraordinary naturalism, rejecting the idealised historical scenes that the French Academy admired. The Barbizon school's emphasis on painting outdoors and its choice of everyday scenes foreshadowed Impressionism. Rouen's Musée des Beaux-Arts displays several Millet paintings.

When many painters left Normandy to work and study, Honfleur-born Eugène Boudin (1824–98) spent most of his life living and working on the Normandy coast. Enchanted with the opportunities afforded by working in the open air, Boudin took advantage of Normandy's new popularity to paint the elegantly dressed women frequenting the coastal resorts. Boudin's paintings are displayed in the museums of Le Havre, Honfleur, Trouville, Caen and Rouen, but he is mainly remembered as Claude Monet's first teacher.

The Dutch painter Johan Barthold Jongkind (1819–91) also influenced young Monet, educating his eye to observe varying intensities of light and subtleties of colour. Norman by choice if not by birth, Jongkind lived all along the coast where he painted Honfleur, Tréport and Le Havre. In the 1860s, Boudin, Jongkind and Monet were a frequent threesome around Honfleur, painting and socialising together.

## Monet in Normandy

Born in Paris in 1840, Claude Monet and his family moved to Le Havre five years later. After picking up rudimentary Impressionist techniques from Boudin and Jongkind, Monet decided to study in Paris, the centre of the universe as far as young painters were concerned. Monet entered the Academie Suisse in 1859 and met future Impressionists Renoir, Pissarro, Bazille and Sisley. After two years' military service in Algiers, he returned to Le Havre in 1862 and, in 1864, met the Le Havre shipowner, Gaudibert, who became Monet's first patron.

JANE SMITH

**Claude Monet – pioneer of the Impressionist movement**

In 1865 two of Monet's paintings of Honfleur were accepted by the Salon, a government sponsored exhibition in Paris that was the official arbiter of quality painting. Staying with his aunt in Ste-Adresse, Monet turned out the luminous *La Terrasse à Ste-Adresse* and worked on two paintings of the Le Havre port for the 1868 Salon show, only one of which was accepted. Monet stayed on the Normandy coast, painting at Fécamp, Étretat and Trouville, until the Franco-Prussian war broke out in 1870.

Fleeing to London with Pissarro, Monet met the dealer Paul Durand-Ruel, who began showing Monet's seascapes in London and ultimately became a great champion of the Impressionists. When Monet returned to France the following year he rented a house in Argenteuil, on the Seine, but returned to Le Havre to paint *Impression: Soleil Levant*. Exhibited outside the Salon in an independent show, Impression: Sunrise displayed the new technique of creating a fleeting impression by the swift application of bright, often unmixed colours. Critics were unkind. Accustomed to blended colours that created a polished effect they disparagingly dubbed the new style 'Impressionism'.

The rest of the 1870s were difficult for Monet. France was suffering financial hardship from the war, no one was buying art and Monet descended into poverty. To make matters worse, his wife Camille became ill and died in 1879. Monet set up house with his longtime mistress Alice Hoschedé

Of all the painters fascinated by the Norman landscape, Monet was the most influential and most rooted in the region. In his long life he spanned every phase of Impressionism, beginning with landscape painting in Le Havre and ending with the first steps towards abstraction in Giverny. Although he painted in London, the south of France and around Paris, the ever-changing skies of Normandy afforded him limitless opportunities to investigate light in all its daily and seasonal variations. He returned again and again, finally settling in Giverny where he spent the last 43 years of his life. Some of Monet's paintings are displayed in the museums of Honfleur, Le Havre, Rouen and Vernon.

Throughout the 19th century, painters made regular sojourns to the Normandy coast. Honfleur became the first painter's hub with a friendly inn outside town, La Ferme St-Siméon, welcoming Boudin, Bazille, Pissarro and Sisley among others. Étretat's cliffs and pebbly beach attracted Delacroix, Corot and Courbet in the 1860s and 1870s. Courbet found Trouville particu-

## Monet in Normandy

in Poissy but spent much time on the coast turning out canvases of Fécamp, Trouville, Dieppe, Étretat and Pourville. One day, on a train trip from Vernon to Gasny, Monet glimpsed the charming little village of Giverny. He found a house and, in 1883, he, Alice and a combined total of six children from their respective marriages moved in.

Monet travelled widely throughout France in the 1880s and his financial situation improved markedly from the sale of his paintings. By 1890 he was finally prosperous enough to buy the house and enter a new phase of his creative life. Rather than seek out new motifs for his paintings, Monet returned to the idea of painting the same subject in subtly varied lighting, a concept he explored years earlier in the Gare St-Lazare series. His first series was of haystacks, which he followed by paintings of poplars along the River Epte. The paintings were hugely successful and, in 1892, he took a room on the rue Grand-Pont in Rouen to paint the venerable cathedral. By now, Monet was moving away from quickly executed 'impressions' of objects and, in fact, away from reality altogether. The Gothic building became the basis for a gorgeous flight of fantasy rendered in layers of carefully applied paint. Twenty views of the cathedral went up for sale in 1895 and each one sold for 15,000FF, a substantial sum at the time.

Monet used his wealth to turn Giverny into the exact setting he required for his art. He planted his property with a variety of flowers, designed to insure he would have something to paint nearly all year. He dammed a branch of the Epte to create an artificial pond, planted it with waterlilies and installed a Japanese footbridge. With the first morning light, Monet was before his lily pond with an easel capturing the reflection of sun and sky in the water. He worked on a dozen canvases at a time, attempting to portray the fleeting light by day and pondering them in his studio at night. Beginning in a recognisably figural style, over the years Monet abandoned perspective, space and detail, edging ever closer to abstraction.

The first exhibition of his water-garden paintings was held in 1900 and brought Monet immediate renown both among critics and with the public. His house at Giverny became a pilgrimage point for painters and students. Pissarro, Sisley, Rodin, Mary Cassatt and Prime Minister Clemenceau were regular visitors as Monet continued to work on his waterlily series *Nymphéas*. Although Monet continued to travel in his earlier years at Giverny, failing eyesight and a long depression brought about by the death of his wife Alice in 1911 kept his later life centred around Giverny. In 1914 he began work on the mural-size versions of *Nymphéas* and constructed a third studio to accommodate them. Work on the *Décorations des Nymphéas* continued almost until his death in 1926. They now hang in the Musée de l'Orangerie in Paris.

larly appealing, inviting his American friend Whistler to stay with him at the Hôtel des Roches Noires in 1866. Renoir set up his easel in Pourville where he painted *Madame Charpentier et ses Enfants*, while Manet headed for Cherbourg. Camille Pissarro chose Rouen where he took a room overlooking the Seine in 1883, executing a series of river scenes. Degas 'discovered' Dieppe in the 1880s, attracting his admirers, including Whistler, to the port. Fécamp, Varengeville, Ste-Adresse and Le Havre also welcomed a succession of artists.

By the end of the century, a school of painters, pupils of Zacharie at the École des Beaux-Arts, arose in Rouen. The École de Rouen (so baptised by a Parisian critic in 1902) was dominated by Albert Lebourg (1849–1928). Born in Montfort-sur-Risle, the young painter came to Rouen to paint and sold his first painting to an Algerian. After painting in Algeria, Auvergne, Brittany and Holland, he returned to Rouen relatively successful, with paintings hanging in several Parisian museums. In his later years, he executed a number of paintings of the Seine in an Impressionistic style. His paintings are on view in the fine arts museums of Caen and Rouen.

**20th Century** The century opened with another revolution in painting. The Fauvists (wild beasts) rejected the Impressionist's use of soft colours and turned to a harsh, almost violent palette of ochre, green and vermilion. The short-lived movement was begun in 1898 by Matisse and was promulgated by a group of three painters from Le Havre: Othon Friesz, Raoul Dufy and Georges Braque. The three painters met in Paris in 1900 and turned out a number of paintings in the style, but by 1908 they had taken separate stylistic paths and the movement died out.

Braque (1882–1963) was raised in Le Havre and returned to the Normandy coast in 1905 before leaving to study painting with Cézanne. He became fascinated with the geometrical forms underlying conventional perspective and, after meeting Picasso in 1907, began to paint in a Cubist style. For a time the two artists were closely intertwined, rendering scenes in a multitude of dimensions. After returning from service in WWI, Braque moved in other directions, turning to still life and birds in paintings and lithographs. At the end of his life he set up a studio in Varengeville where he created stained glass windows for the local church and painted Norman landscapes. The museum in Dieppe has several of his lithographs.

When Raoul Dufy (1877–1953) abandoned Fauvism, he turned to colours that were vigorous without being strident and applied them to paintings and watercolours dominated by a rigorous use of line. His subjects were outdoor scenes at Normandy's resorts and ports, especially sailing and horse racing, rendered in a light, happy style. The museum in Le Havre has a selection of Dufy's paintings.

The Duchamp brothers had a huge influence on contemporary art although their connection with Normandy lies only in having been born and raised in Blainville, near Coutances. The oldest brother, Gaston Duchamp (1875–1963) was an early adherent of Cubism and, under the pseudonym Jacques Villon, created a provocative new style based upon neo-Impressionism and Cubism from his studio outside Paris. Raymond Duchamp-Villon (1876–1918) was a sculptor who, before dying in WWI, worked in a modernistic, abstract style. Marcel Duchamp (1887–1968) was a radical who rejected so-called 'retinal' art that only appealed to the eyes. Beginning with Fauvism and Cubism, Duchamp experimented with Dadaism and kinetic art. His work foreshadowed pop art, conceptual art and body art.

## Cinema
Normandy is the birthplace of a number of directors largely unknown outside France. The silent-film director René Le Somptier was born in Caen; André Berthomieur was born in Rouen, and another director of comedies, Serge Pénard, was born in Le Havre. Jean Grémillon, a director of the 1930s and 1940s, produced a moving documentary about D-Day near his home town of Bayeux. The New Wave director Jacques Rivette was born in 1928 in Rouen and worked with François Truffaut and Eric Rohmer before striking out on his own, becoming a leading figure of French cinema. In 1994 he made what is probably the best modern film of Joan of Arc, *Jeanne la Pucelle*, with Sandrine Bonnaire, which has unfortunately been overshadowed by Luc Besson's much inferior version.

One of France's finest actors, the ethereally handsome Jean Marais, was born in Cherbourg in 1913. In 1937 he met director Jean Cocteau, launching a personal and professional collaboration that lasted until the director's death. Marais went on to star in Cocteau's *La Belle et la Bête*, *Les Parents Terribles* and *Orpheus* before starting a new career as a painter sculptor in his later years. He died in 1998.

Many film celebrities have chosen a secondary residence in Normandy. Actor, writer and director Sacha Guitry had a villa along the Seine in Duclair. Actors Simone Signoret and Yves Montand had a house in

Autheuil in the Eure Valley. Actor Jean Gabin had a villa in Deauville and a vast domain in the Orne Valley at Moulins-la-Marche where he kept horses.

## SOCIETY & CONDUCT

Some visitors to France conclude that it would be a lovely country if it weren't for the French. As in other countries, however, the more tourists a particular town or area attracts, the less patience the locals tend to have for them. As in many other destinations, you'll probably find that people are more relaxed and welcoming in the small towns and villages than in the cities.

### Dos & Don'ts

By following a number of simple guidelines, you can usually win people over and avoid offending anyone. Here are a few dos:

- The easiest way to improve the quality of your relations with the French is always to say *'Bonjour, monsieur/madame/mademoiselle'* when you walk into a shop, and *'Merci, monsieur...au revoir'* when you leave. 'Monsieur' means 'sir' and can be used with any male person who isn't a child. 'Madame' is used where 'Mrs' would apply in English, whereas 'mademoiselle' is used when talking to unmarried or young women. When in doubt, use 'madame'.
- It is customary for people who know each other to exchange kisses *(bises)* as a greeting, though rarely between two men unless they are related. The usual ritual is one glancing peck on each cheek, but some people go for three or even four kisses. People who don't kiss each other will almost always shake hands.
- If invited to someone's home or a party, always bring some sort of gift, such as good wine (not some 10FF *vin de table*). Flowers are another good stand-by, but chrysanthemums are only brought to cemeteries.
- Many French people seem to feel that 'going Dutch' (ie, splitting the bill) at restaurants is an uncivilised custom. In general, the person who did the inviting pays for dinner, though close friends and colleagues will sometimes share the cost.

And a few don'ts:

- When buying fruit, vegetables or flowers anywhere except at supermarkets, do not touch the produce or blossoms unless invited to do so.

Show the shopkeeper what you want and they will choose for you.
- In a restaurant, do not summon the waiter by shouting *'garçon'*, which means 'boy'. Saying *'s'il vous plaît'* (please) is the way it's done nowadays.
- When you're being served cheese (for example, as the final course for dinner), remember two cardinal rules: never cut off the tip of the pie-shaped soft cheeses (such as Brie or Camembert); and cut cheese whose middle is the best part (for example, blue cheese) in such a way as to take your fair share of the crust.
- Money, particularly income, is a subject that is simply not discussed in France.
- In general, lawns in France are meant to be looked at and praised for their greenness, not sat upon; watch out for *pelouse interdite* (Keep off the Grass!) signs. But this has been changing in recent years, with signs being removed and replaced with *pelouse autorisée*, meaning tourists and locals alike are permitted to sit, eat, play and walk on the grass of certain parks

## RELIGION
### Catholics

Some 80% of French people identify themselves as Catholic but, although most have been baptised, very few ever attend church. The Catholic Church in France is generally very progressive and ecumenically minded. When Monsignor Jacques Gaillot was dismissed from his post in Évreux for advocating gay rights he became the world's first 'virtual bishop'. (For more details see the boxed text 'An Unlikely Saint?' in the Évreux section of the Eure chapter.)

### Protestants

France's Protestants (Huguenots), who were severely persecuted during much of the 16th and 17th centuries, now number about one million. In Normandy they are concentrated along the Atlantic coast from Le Havre to Dieppe.

### Muslims

France has between four and five million nominally Muslim residents, and they now make up the country's second-largest religious group. The vast majority are immigrants or their offspring who came from North Africa during the 1950s and 1960s. In recent years, France's Muslim community

## As They Say in Normandy...

It's not just the sea and salt air that draws writers to Normandy. Normans have a particularly colourful way of expressing themselves, with observations and images drawn from everyday Norman life.

The changeable weather and its meanings are a popular subject for comment: *Brouillards d'octobre et pluvieux novembre font bon décembre.* (Clouds in October and a rainy November make a good December.) Meteorologists may disagree, but who could argue with the perils of a warm November? *Chaleur de novembre pique fort, et cause de bien des gens la mort.* (November warmth stings strongly, and brings death to many.) Think it rains too much in Normandy? Oh no. *Même si tout mars il pleuvait, et que tout le monde criait: 'Tout est noyé, tout est perdu,' Il n'aurait encore pas assez plu.* (Even if all March it rains, and everyone complains: 'Everything is drowned, all is lost,' it still hasn't rained enough.)

Rain is good for apples and apples are good for Normandy. *La Normandie est un pays qui donne au paysan deux récoltes sans travailler: l'herbe et les pommes.* (Normandy is a country that gives the peasants two harvests without working: grass and apples.) But remember: *La fleur ne fait pas la pomme et la pomme ne fait pas le cidre.* (The flower doesn't make the apple and the apple doesn't make the cider.) Chew on that!

While on the subject of philosophy, ever notice that: *Tout le monde se plaint de sa memoire, jamais de son jugement*? (Everyone complains about their memory, never about their judgement.) Maybe they've been drinking too much Calvados, for: *L'abus de calva éteint l'homme et allume la bête.* (The abuse of Calvados extinguishes the man and awakens the beast.) But don't avoid Calvados completely: *Une fête sans calva, c'est une mare sans eau.* (A party without Calvados is a pond without water.)

Normans are also full of culinary advice, because: *Un Normand de bon goût bâtit sa maison autour de sa cuisine.* (A Norman with good taste builds their house around the kitchen.) And remember: *dans le cochon tout est bon* (in the pig, everything is good); *manger des huitres les mois en r; manger des moules les mois sans r* (eat oysters in months with an r; eat mussels in months without an r); and *il faut abbattre la truie à la lune vielle, et le verrat à la lune nouvelle* (slaughter a sow at the full moon, and a boar at the new moon). And if your Camembert is particularly good, you can exclaim, in the words of the poet Léon Paul Fargue: *'Les pieds de Dieu!'* (The feet of God!)

On the other hand, you may be lucky if you can get a Norman to say anything at all, for: *Un bon Normand tourne sept fois sa langue dans sa bouche avant de causer…quelquefois même il va jusqu'à huit.* (A good Norman turns his tongue seven times in his mouth before chatting…sometimes he even goes until eight.) And you'll know you're in Normandy because: *Un Normand se reconnaît vite: il n'a qu'une parole et il s'y tient.* (A Norman is easily recognised: he has only one word and he's keeping it.)

●●●●●●●●●●●●●●●●●●●●●●●●●●●●●●●●

has been the object of racist agitation by right-wing parties and extremist groups. The so-called Muslim scarf affair of 1994, when pupils were expelled from school for wearing scarves (considered 'ostentatious religious signs') brought the matter to the forefront but was more or less resolved two years later when the Constitutional Council ruled that schools may not suspend pupils who wear scarves if no overt religious proselytising is involved. Many from North Africa complain of discrimination.

### Jews

There has been a Jewish community in France for most of the time since the Roman period. During the Middle Ages, the community suffered persecution and there were a number of mass expulsions. French Jews, the first within Europe to achieve emancipation, were granted full citizenship in 1790–1. Since 1808, the French Jewish community has had an umbrella organisation known as the Consistoire based in Paris.

The country's Jewish community, which now numbers some 650,000 (the largest in Europe), grew substantially during the 1960s as a result of immigration from Algeria, Tunisia and Morocco. France generally enjoys a favourable standing with the Jewish community, and there have been relatively few incidents of anti-Semitism reported in recent years. The national Jewish community's Web site is www.col.fr.

A recent study published by the Matteoli Commission in April 2000, caused a stir by claiming that Nazi and French collaborators stole far more from Jews during WWII than had been previously assumed. Headed by Jean Matteoli, a Resistance fighter, the report found that $1.3 billion worth of assets was taken in the form of frozen bank accounts, fines, businesses and other property. Some 90% had been repaid within a decade after the war, but the French government still holds unclaimed funds estimated to be worth $2 billion.

## LANGUAGE

People speak French in Normandy although English is widely spoken, especially by young people. The Norman dialect died out several centuries ago and remains in only a few words that you may hear older people using. They may refer to a *cheval* (horse) as a *qu'va*, or a *coq* (rooster) as a *cô*. Unlike regions such as Brittany or Provence, there is no movement to revive the dialect.

# Facts for the Visitor

## HIGHLIGHTS
Normandy has a wealth of wonderful places to visit, but some aspects of the region are so outstanding that they deserve special mention:

### Art & Architecture
- Mont St-Michel at high tide
- Rouen's 'Big Three': the cathedral, Église St-Ouen and Église St-Maclou
- The cathedral of Coutances
- Rouen's Musée des Beaux-Arts
- The Bayeux Tapestry with its 'living scenes' from history

### Activities & Culture
- Cruising from Vernon to Les Andelys
- Taking the waters in the spa town of Bagnoles de l'Orne
- Walking the Mont St-Michel bay from Bec d'Andaine
- Walking the Cap de la Hague from Baie d'Écalgrain to Nez de Jobourg
- Star-watching at the Deauville Film Festival
- Listening to Gregorian chants at Le Bec-Hellouin abbey

### Beauty Spots
- Monet's gardens at Giverny in full blossom
- The River Seine seen from Château Gaillard
- The Suisse Normande
- The port of Honfleur
- The cliffs of Étretat

### D-Day Memorials
- Le Mémorial de Caen
- The American Military Cemetery at Colleville-sur-Mer
- Pointe du Hoc
- The British Cemetery and Memorial at Bayeux

## SUGGESTED ITINERARIES
Mont St-Michel is the great highlight of the region. It's worth juggling your schedule to see it at high tide, if at all possible.

One week
   Visit Rouen – the most beautiful city in Normandy – and Caen for a visit to Le Mémorial de Caen, Bayeux and the D-Day beaches, then Mont St-Michel.

Two weeks
   As above, plus Étretat, Honfleur, Monet's gardens at Giverny, Les Andelys, the Suisse Normande and Coutances.
One month
   As above but spending more time in each place and visiting the Côte d'Albâtre, the Côte Fleurie, the Cap de la Hague, the Seine Valley, the sights around Bernay and the Orne.

## PLANNING
### When to Go
Normandy is at its best in late spring, especially in May when the apple trees blossom. Early autumn is pleasant too, but the days are fairly short and it gets a bit cool for sunbathing. Winters are rainy and obviously less crowded. Beach resorts shut down but the dramatic coastline retains a lonely, windswept beauty.

In July and August, the weather is warm, but at least rainy days are at a minimum, making it a good time to plan outdoor pursuits. Museums, chateaux and abbeys are open longer in July and August and often present various cultural programs. The beach resorts are packed in August whilst the best restaurants and nightspots in the cities may be closed.

It's important to remember that small villages virtually shut down from midday on Saturday to Tuesday morning. Even in the larger cities most stores are closed Sunday and Monday. Sundays are particularly desolate with nothing open but a morning-only bakery. Regional public transport is likely to be limited or suspended. Even during the week there is nothing to do anywhere in Normandy between noon and 2 pm but sit down and eat. Stores, banks, museums, monuments, tourist offices and post offices are closed at lunchtime.

**Domestic Tourism** By law, French wage-earners get five weeks of *congés payés* (paid holiday) each year. Most of them take advantage of their time off between mid-July and the end of August, when France's city dwellers descend like a locust storm on the coasts, mountains and other areas.

Normandy's coasts are jammed during this period as Parisians, Brits and Normandy's city-dwellers head to the sea. Meanwhile, in the half-deserted cities of the interior – only partly refilled by foreign tourists – many shops, restaurants, cinemas, cultural institutions and even hotels simply shut down so the proprietors can head out of town along with their customers. Normandy enjoys a small burst of activity in the week following Easter but nothing like the summer vacation period.

**Weather Forecasts** If you understand French (or know someone who does), you can find out the *météo* (weather forecast) by calling the following numbers:

| | |
|---|---|
| National forecast | ☎ 08 36 70 12 34 |
| Regional forecasts | ☎ 08 36 68 00 00 |
| Mountain area & snow forecasts | ☎ 08 36 68 04 04 |
| Marine forecast | ☎ 08 36 68 08 08 |

For departmental forecasts dial ☎ 08 36 68 02 plus the two digit departmental number (76 for Seine-Maritime, 27 for Eure, 14 for Calvados, 50 for Manche and 61 for Orne). Each call costs five *télécarte* (phonecard) units or 2.23FF per minute. By Minitel, key in 3615 MET or 3617 METPLUS (for information on Minitel see Telephone later in the chapter).

## Maps

Road maps and city maps are available at Maisons de la Presse (large newsagencies found all over Normandy), bookshops and even some newspaper kiosks. Where relevant, advice on maps and where to buy them is given under Orientation in a city or town listing.

**Road Maps** A variety of *cartes routières* (road maps) are available, but if you're driving a lot, the best road atlas to have in the car is Michelin's yellow-jacketed 1:200,000 scale fold-out map number 231. It costs 35FF.

**City Maps** Rare is the town or village whose tourist office doesn't issue a free map. They can be of surprisingly good quality and quite detailed. Blay issues a number of orange-jacketed town maps (23FF) with helpful street indexes. With a scale of 1:10,000 the maps are easy to read and also cover the town's outskirts. Abbreviations commonly used on city maps include: *R* for *rue* (street); *Bd*, *Boul* or *Bould* for boulevard; *Av* for *avenue*; *Q* for *quai* (quay); *Cr* for *cours* (avenue); *Pl* for *place* (square); *Pte* for *porte* (gate); *Imp* for *impasse* (dead-end street); *St* for *saint* (masculine) and *Ste* for *sainte* (feminine).

**Walking & Cycling Maps** The IGN Blue Series covers dozens of walking trails throughout Normandy at a 1:25,000 scale (46FF). The recent Top 25 series (58FF) covers more ambitious walks and includes information about tourist offices, camping and horse trails. There's also an IGN Green Series at a 1:100,000 scale with suggested horse, car and bike routes roughly covering the five departments of Normandy (32FF). IGN No 906, known as *France – VTT & Randonnées Cyclos*, indicates dozens of suggested bicycle tours of rural France and includes Normandy (29FF).

The Fédération Française de la Randonnée Pédestre publishes six topoguides covering some of the major walks throughout Normandy. Prices range from 77FF to 99FF .

Didier et Richard publishes a series of

1:50,000 scale trail maps, which are perfect for hoofing it or cycling (67FF).

## What to Bring

The cardinal rule in packing is to bring as little as possible. It's better to start off with too little rather than too much, as virtually anything you could possibly need will be available locally.

If you'll be doing any walking with your gear, a backpack is the only way to go. One of the most flexible models is an internal-frame travel pack whose straps can be zipped inside a flap, turning it into a nylon suitcase. Some have an exterior pouch that zips off to become a daypack. Wheeled suitcases are a popular alternative if you're not walking, easy on the back and shoulders but a nuisance to drag up stairs. Look for inset wheels that won't fall off and a strong zip, preferably metal.

If you're hostelling, pack or buy a towel and a plastic soap container when you arrive. Bedding is always provided or available for hire, though you might want to take along your own sheet bag. You'll sleep easier with a padlock on your storage locker, which are usually provided at hostels.

Other optional items you might need include a torch (flashlight), an adapter plug for electrical appliances (such as a cup or coil immersion heater to make your own tea or instant coffee), a universal bath/sink plug (a plastic film canister sometimes works), sunglasses and a hat, a few clothes pegs and premoistened towelettes or a large cotton handkerchief, which you can soak in fountains and use to cool off while touring cities and towns in the warmer months.

For a checklist of first-aid and pharmaceutical items, see the Health section later in this chapter.

## RESPONSIBLE TOURISM

In Normandy's nature reserves and regional parks, be sure to follow the local code of ethics and common decency and pack up your litter. Minimise the waste you must carry out by taking minimal packaging and taking no more food than you will need.

Don't use detergents or toothpaste in or near watercourses, even if they are biodegradable. Bear in mind that sensitive biospheres, both for flora and fauna, may be seriously damaged if you depart from designated paths in protected areas. When camping in the wild (checking first with the landowners or a park ranger to see that it's allowed), bury human waste in holes at least 15cm (6 inches) deep and at least 100m (320 feet) from any watercourse.

For further tips on how you can reduce your impact on the environment, contact Les Amis de la Nature (☎ 01 46 27 53 56), 197 rue Championnet, 75018 Paris.

## TOURIST OFFICES
### Local Tourist Offices

Every city, town, village and hamlet seems to have either an *office de tourisme* (a tourist office run by some unit of local government) or a *syndicat d'initiative* (a tourist office run by an organisation of local merchants). Both are excellent resources and can almost always provide a local map at the very least. Some will also change foreign currency, especially when banks are closed, though the rate is rarely good. Some tourist offices will make local hotel reservations, usually for a small fee.

Details on local tourist offices appear under Information at the beginning of each city, town or area listing.

There are also departmental tourist offices that are an invaluable source of information when planning your trip. A lot of trees have died to produce the massive documentation issued by Normandy's tourist offices and it pays to take advantage of their sacrifice. Tourist offices have compiled lists of companies and individuals offering outdoor activities, off-the-beaten-track accommodation and special tours. They list parks, gardens, museums, chateaux, cultural highlights and special local events. Most of the more general brochures are in English but the brochures in French are also helpful in locating addresses. If you have a special interest – fishing, kayaking, D-Day monuments, cheese tasting, staying on farms – it pays to contact the relevant department or departments ahead of time since whatever information you're looking for undoubtedly appears in one of the region's countless brochures. Address your request to the Comité Départental de Tourisme:

**Seine-Maritime** (☎ 02 35 12 10 10, fax 02 35 59 86 04, ✉ seine.maritime.tourisme@ wanadoo.fr) 6 rue Couronné, BP 60, 76420 Bihorel-les-Rouen
**Eure** (☎ 02 32 62 04 27, fax 02 32 31 05 98, ✉ cdt-eure@wanadoo.fr) Hôtel du Département, boulevard Georges-Chauvin, BP 367, 27003 Évreux
**Calvados** (☎ 02 31 27 90 30, fax 02 31 27 90 35, ✉ calvatour@mail.cpod.fr) place du Canada, 14000 Caen
**Manche** (☎ 02 33 05 98 70, fax 02 33 56 07 03, ✉ manchetourisme@cg50.fr) Maison du Département, 50008 St-Lô Cedex
**Orne** (☎ 02 33 28 88 71, fax 02 33 29 81 60) 88 rue St-Blaise, BP 50, 61002 Alençon Cedex

For information on the entire Normandy region, contact Comité Régional de Tourisme (☎ 02 32 33 79 00, fax 02 32 31 19 04, ✉ normandy@imaginet.fr), Le Doyenné, 14 rue Charles-Corbeau, 27000 Évreux, or visit its Web site at www.normandy-tourism.org.

## Tourist Offices Abroad

French government tourist offices (usually called Maisons de la France) can provide brochures on Normandy but you'll get more information by contacting the regional, departmental or local tourist offices directly. French government tourist offices include:

**Australia**
(☎ 02-9231 5244, fax 9221 8682, ✉ ifrance@ internetezy.com.au) 25 Bligh St, 22nd floor, Sydney, NSW 2000. Open weekdays from 9 am to 5 pm.
**Belgium**
(☎ 02-513 5886, fax 514 3375, ✉ maisondela france@pophost.eunet.be) 21 avenue de la Toison d'Or, 1050 Brussels. Open weekdays from 10 am to 5 pm.
**Canada**
(☎ 514-288 4264, fax 845 4868, ✉ mfrance@ mtl.net) 1981 McGill College Ave, Suite 490,

Montreal, Que H3A 2W9. Open weekdays from 9 am to 4 pm.
**Germany**
(☎ 069-580 131, fax 069-745 556, ✉ maison_ de_la_France@t-online.de) Westendstrasse 47, D-60325 Frankfurt. Open weekdays from 9 am to 4.30 pm.
**Ireland**
(☎ 01-679 0813, fax 679 0814, ✉ french touristoffice@tinet.ie) 10 Suffolk St, Dublin 2. Open weekdays from 9.30 am to 1.30 pm and 2 to 5 pm.
**Italy**
(☎ 02 584 8657, fax 02 584 86222, ✉ info@ turismofrancese.it) Via Larga 7, 20122 Milan. Open weekdays from 9.30 am to 5.30 pm.
**Netherlands**
(☎ 0900 112 2332, fax 020-620 3339, ✉ inform atie@fransverkeersbureau.nl) Prinsengracht 670, 1017 KX Amsterdam. Open weekdays from 10 am to 5 pm.
**Spain**
(☎ 91-541 8808; fax 541 2412; ✉ maisonde lafrance@mad.sericom.es) Alcalá 63, 28014 Madrid. Open weekdays from 9 am to 1.30 pm and 4 to 7 pm (8 am to 3 pm in summer).
**Switzerland**
*Zürich* (☎ 01-211 3085, fax 212 1644, ✉ tourismefrance@bluewin.ch) Löwenstrasse 59, 8023 Zürich. Open weekdays from 10 am to 1 pm and 2 to 5.30 pm.
*Geneva* (☎ 022-90 8977, fax 909 8971, ✉ mdlfva@bluewin.ch) 2 rue Thalberg, 1201 Geneva. Open weekdays from 9 am to noon and 1 to 5.45 pm (to 5 pm on Friday).
**UK** (☎ 020-7399 3500, fax 7493 6594, ✉ piccadilly@mdlf.demon.co.uk) 178 Piccadilly, London W1V 0AL. Open daily from 10 am to 6 pm (to 5pm on Saturday; it is closed on Sunday).
**USA**
*New York* (☎ 212-838 7800, fax 838 7855, ✉ info@francetourism.com) 444 Madison Ave, 16th floor, New York, NY 10022-6903. Open weekdays 9 am to 5 pm.
*Los Angeles* (☎ 310-271 6665, fax 276 2835, ✉ fgto@gte.net) 9454 Wiltshire Blvd, Suite 715, Beverly Hills, CA 90212-2967. Open weekdays from 9 am to 5 pm.

## VISAS & DOCUMENTS
### Passport
By law, everyone in France, including tourists, must carry some sort of ID on them at all times. For foreign visitors, this means a passport (if you don't want to carry your

passport for security reasons a photocopy should do, although you may be required to report to a police station later to verify your identity) or, for citizens of the EU, your national ID card.

## Visas

**Tourist Visas** EU nationals have no entry requirements, and citizens of Australia, the USA, Canada, New Zealand and Israel do not need visas to visit France as tourists for up to three months. Except for people from a handful of other European countries (including Switzerland and Poland), everyone else needs a so-called Schengen Visa, named after the Schengen Agreement that abolished passport controls among Austria, Belgium, France, Germany, Greece, Italy, Luxembourg, the Netherlands and Portugal. A visa for any of these countries should, in theory, be valid throughout the area, but it pays to double-check with the embassy or consulate of the countries you intend to visit.

Visa fees depend on the current exchange rate, but a transit visa should cost about US$9, a visa valid for stays of up to 30 days is around US$23, and a single or multiple entry visa of up to three months costs about US$32. You will need your passport (valid for a period of three months beyond the date of your departure from France), a return ticket, proof of sufficient funds to support yourself, proof of pre-arranged accommodation (possibly), two passport-sized photos and the visa fee in cash. South African visas take two days to process.

If all the forms are in order, your visa will be issued on the spot. You can also apply for a French visa after arriving in Europe – the fee is the same, but you may not have to produce a return ticket. If you enter France overland, your visa may not be checked at the border, but major problems can arise if you don't have one later on (for example, at the airport as you leave the country).

**Long-Stay & Student Visas** If you'd like to work or study in Normandy or stay for over three months, apply to the French embassy or consulate nearest where you live for the appropriate sort of *long séjour* (long-stay) visa. Unless you live in the EU, it's extremely difficult to get a visa that will allow you to work in France. For any sort of long-stay visa, begin the paperwork in your home country several months before you plan to leave. Applications cannot usually be made in a third country nor can tourist visas be turned into student visas after you arrive in France. People with student visas can apply for permission to work part-time (enquire at your place of study).

If you are serious about living and working in France on a long-term basis, it pays to consult a qualified immigration attorney in France who can advise you on surmounting some of the hurdles. Your consulate may be able to provide a list of names.

**Au Pair Visas** For details on au pair visas, which must be arranged *before* you leave home (unless you're an EU resident), see Au Pair under Work later in this chapter.

**Carte de Séjour** If you are issued a long-stay visa valid for six or more months, you'll probably have to apply for a *carte de séjour* (residence permit) within eight days of arrival in France. For details, enquire at your place of study or the local *préfecture* (prefecture), *sous-préfecture* (subprefecture), *hôtel de ville* (city hall), *mairie* (town hall) or *commissariat* (police station).

**Visa Extensions** Tourist visas *cannot* be extended except in emergencies (such as medical problems). If you have an urgent problem, you should get in touch with the local prefecture.

If you don't need a visa to visit France, you'll almost certainly qualify for another automatic three-month stay if you take the train to Geneva or Brussels, say, and then re-enter France. The fewer recent French entry stamps you have in your passport the easier this is likely to be. If you needed a visa the first time around, one way to extend your stay is to go to a French consulate in a neighbouring country and apply for another one there.

People entering France by rail or road

often don't have their passports checked, much less stamped, and even at airports don't be surprised if the official just glances at your passport and hands it back without stamping the date of entry. Fear not: you're in France legally, whether or not you had to apply for a visa before arriving (though at some point, to show your date of entry, you may be asked to produce the plane, train or ferry ticket you arrived with). If you prefer to have your passport stamped (for example, because you expect to have to prove when you last entered the country), it may take a bit of running around to find the right border official.

## Travel Insurance

You should seriously consider taking out travel insurance. This not only covers you for medical expenses and luggage theft or loss but also for cancellation or delays in your travel arrangements. Cover depends on your insurance and type of airline ticket, so ask both your insurer and your ticket-issuing agency to explain where you stand. Ticket loss is also covered by travel insurance. EU citizens on public health insurance schemes should note that they're generally covered by reciprocal arrangements in France (see the Health section later in this chapter for more details).

Paying for your airline ticket with a credit card often provides limited travel accident insurance, and you may be able to reclaim the payment if the operator doesn't deliver. In the UK, for instance, institutions issuing credit cards are required by law to reimburse consumers if a company goes into liquidation and the amount in contention is more than UK£100. Ask your credit card company what it's prepared to cover.

## Diving Licence & Permits

Many non-European drivers' licences are valid in France, but it's still a good idea to bring along an International Driving Permit (IDP), which can make life much simpler, especially when hiring cars and motorbikes. Basically a multilingual translation of the vehicle class and personal details noted on your local driving licence; an IDP is not valid unless accompanied by your original licence. An IDP can be obtained for a small fee from your local automobile association – bring along a passport photo and a valid licence.

## Hostel Cards

A Hostelling International (HI) card is necessary only at official *auberges de jeunesse* (youth hostels), but it may get you small discounts at other hostels. If you don't pick one up before leaving home, you can buy one at almost any official French hostel for 70/100FF if you're under 26 years of age/26 or older. One night's membership (where available) costs 19FF, and a family card costs 150FF. See the HI Web site at www.iyhf.org for further details.

## Student, Youth & Teachers Cards

An International Student Identity Card (ISIC) can pay for itself through half-price admissions, discounted air and ferry tickets, and cheap meals in student cafeterias. Many places stipulate a maximum age, usually 24 or 25. In Caen, ISIC cards are issued by the Centre Régional d'Information Jeunesse (CRIJ). Visit its Web site at ww.istc.org.

If you're under 26 but not a student, you can apply for a GO25 card issued by the Federation of International Youth Travel Organisations (FIYTO), which entitles you to much the same discounts as an ISIC. It is also issued by student unions or student travel agencies and costs 60FF.

Teachers, professional artists, museum conservators and certain categories of students are admitted to some museums free. Bring along proof of affiliation, for example an International Teacher Identity Card (ITIC; 60FF).

## Seniors Cards

Reduced admission prices are charged for people aged over 60 at most cultural centres, including museums, galleries and public theatres. SNCF issues the Carte Senior (which replaces the Carte Vermeil) to those aged over 60, which gives reductions of 20 to 50% on train tickets. It costs 140FF for a card valid for purchasing four train tickets or 285FF for a card valid for one year.

## Camping Card International

The Camping Card International (CCI; formerly the Camping Carnet; issued by the Geneva-based Alliance Internationale de Tourisme) is a camping ground ID that can be used instead of a passport when checking into a camp site and includes third-party insurance (up to Sfr 2.5 million) for any damage you may cause. As a result, many camping grounds offer a small discount if you sign in with one. CCIs are issued by automobile associations, camping federations and, sometimes, on the spot at camping grounds. In the UK, the RAC issues them to its members for UK£4.

## Copies

The hassles brought on by losing your passport can be considerably reduced if you have a record of its number and issue date. All important documents (passport data page and visa page, credit cards, travel insurance policy, air/bus/train tickets, driving licence and so on) should be photocopied before you leave home. Leave one copy with someone at home and keep another with you, separate from the originals. A photocopy of your birth certificate can also be useful.

There is another option for storing details of your vital travel documents before you leave – Lonely Planet's on-line Travel Vault. Storing details of your important documents in the vault is safer than carrying photocopies. It's the best option if you travel in a country with easy Internet access. Your password-protected travel vault is accessible on-line at anytime. You can create your own travel vault for free at www.ekno.lonelyplanet.com. For further details on eKno services, see that section under Post & Communications later in the chapter.

If you do lose your passport, notify the police immediately to get a statement, and contact your nearest consulate.

## EMBASSIES & CONSULATES
### French Embassies & Consulates

Don't expect France's diplomatic and consular representatives abroad to be helpful or even civil at times, though you do come across the odd exception. Almost all of them have information posted at www.france.diplomatie.fr. Addresses include the following:

**Australia**
*Embassy:* (☎ 02-621 60100, fax 621 60127, e embassy@france.net.au) 6 Perth Ave, Yarralumla, ACT 2600
*Consulate:* (☎ 03-982 00921, fax 982 09363, e cgmelb@france.net.au) 492 St Kilda Rd, Level 4, Melbourne, Vic 3004
*Consulate:* (☎ 02-926 25779, fax 928 31210, e cgsydney@france.net.au) St Martin's Tower, 20th floor, 31 Market St, Sydney, NSW 2000

**Belgium**
*Embassy:* (☎ 02-548 8711, fax 513 6871, e amba@ambafrance.be) 65 rue Ducale, 1000 Brussels
*Consulate:* (☎ 02-229 8500, fax 229 8510, e consulat.france@skynet.bruxelles.be) 12a place de Louvain, 1000 Brussels

**Canada**
*Embassy:* (☎ 613-789 1795, fax 562 3735, e res@amba-ottowa.fr) 42 Sussex Drive, Ottawa, Ont K1M 2C9
*Consulate:* (☎ 514-878 4385, fax 878 3981, e fsltmral@cam.org) 1 place Ville Marie, 26th floor, Montreal, Que H3B 4S3
*Consulate:* (☎ 416-925 8041, fax 925 3076, e fsltto@idirect.com) 130 Bloor St West, Suite 400, Toronto, Ont M5S 1N5

**Germany**
*Embassy:* (☎ 030-20 639 000, fax 20 639 010) Kochstrasse 6–7, D-10969 Berlin
*Consulate:* (☎ 030-885 90243, fax 885 5295) Kurfürstendamm 211, 10719 Berlin
*Consulate:* (☎ 089-419 4110, fax 419 41141) Möhlstrasse 5, 81675 Munich

**Ireland**
*Consulate:* (☎ 01-260 1666, fax 283 0178, e consul@ambafrance.ie) 36 Ailesbury Rd, Ballsbridge, Dublin 4

**Italy**
*Embassy:* (☎ 06 686 011, fax 06 860 1360, e france-italia@france-italia.it) Piazza Farnese 67, 00186 Rome
*Consulate:* (☎ 06 6880 6437, fax 06 6860 1260, e consulfrance-rome@iol.it) Via Giulia 251, 00186 Rome

**Netherlands**
*Embassy:* (☎ 070-312 5800, fax 312 5854) Smidsplein 1, 2514 BT The Hague
*Consulate:* (☎ 020-624 8346, fax 626 0841, e consulfr@euronet.nl) Vijzelgracht 2, 1000 HA Amsterdam

**New Zealand**
*Consulate:* (☎ 04-384 2555, fax 384 2577,

e consulfrance@actrix.gen.nz) Rural Bank Building, 34–42 Manners Street, Wellington

**Spain**
*Embassy:* (☎ 91-423 8900, fax 423 8901) Calle de Salustiano Olozaga 9, 28001 Madrid
*Consulate:* (☎ 91-700 7800, fax 700 7801, e creire@ConsulFrance-Madrid.org) Calle Marques de la Enseñada 10, 28004 Madrid
*Consulate:* (☎ 93-270 3000, fax 270 0349, e info@consulat-france.org) Ronda Universitat 22, 08007 Barcelona

**Switzerland**
*Embassy:* (☎ 031-359 2111, fax 352 2191, e ambassade.fr@iprolink.ch) Schosshaldenstrasse 46, 3006 Berne
*Consulate:* (☎ 022-319 0000, fax 319 0072, e consualt.France@ties.itu.int), 11 rue Imbert Galloix, 1205 Geneva
*Consulate:* (☎ 01-268 8585, fax 268 8500, e consulat.france.zurich@swissonline.ch), Mühlebachstrasse 7, 8008 Zürich

**UK**
*Embassy:* (☎ 020-7201 1000, fax 7201 1004, e press@ambafrance.org) 58 Knightsbridge, London SW1X 7JT
*Consulate:* (☎ 020-7838 2000, fax 7838 2018) 21 Cromwell Rd, London SW7 2DQ
The visa section is at 6a Cromwell Place, London SW7 2EW (☎ 020-7838 2051).

**USA**
*Embassy:* (☎ 202-944 6000, fax 944 6166, e visas-washington@amb-wash.fr) 4101 Reservoir Rd NW, Washington, DC 20007
*Consulate:* (☎ 212-606 3688, fax 606 3620, e visa@franceconsulatny.org) 934 Fifth Ave, New York, NY 10021
*Consulate:* (☎ 415-397 4330, fax 433 8357, consul-general@accueil-sfo.org) 540 Bush St, San Francisco, CA 94108
Other consulates are located in Atlanta, Boston, Chicago, Houston, Los Angeles, Miami and New Orleans.

## Embassies & Consulates in France

All foreign embassies are in Paris but Germany and Spain have consulates in Rouen. To find an embassy or consulate not listed here, consult the *Yellow Pages* (look under Ambassades et Consulats) in Paris. Countries with representation in Paris or Rouen include the following:

**Australia**
(☎ 01 40 59 33 00, metro Bir Hakeim) 4 rue Jean Rey, 15e Paris

**Belgium**
(☎ 01 44 09 39 39, metro Charles de Gaulle-Étoile) 9 rue de Tilsitt, 17e Paris

**Canada**
(☎ 01 44 43 29 00, metro Franklin D Roosevelt) 35 avenue Montaigne, 8e Paris

**Germany**
*Embassy:* (☎ 01 53 83 45 00, e ambassade@amb-allemagne.fr, metro Franklin D Roosevelt) 13 avenue Franklin D Roosevelt, 8e Paris
*Consulate:* (☎ 02 35 88 16 52) 43 rue Jean Lecanuet, Rouen

**Ireland**
(☎ 01 44 17 67 00, ☎ 01 44 17 67 67 after hours, Minitel 3615 IRLANDE, metro Argentine) 4 rue Rude, 16e Paris

**Italy**
*Embassy:* (☎ 01 49 54 03 00, metro Rue du Bac) 51 rue de Varenne, 7e Paris
*Consulate:* (☎ 01 44 30 47 00, metro La Muette) 5 boulevard Émile Augier, 16e Paris

**Netherlands**
(☎ 01 40 62 33 00, metro St-François Xavier) 7 rue Eblé, 7e Paris

**New Zealand**
(☎ 01 45 01 43 43, metro Victor Hugo) 7 ter rue Léonard de Vinci, 16e Paris

**South Africa**
(☎ 01 53 59 23 23, metro Invalides) 59 quai d'Orsay, 7e Paris

**Spain**
*Embassy:* (☎ 01 44 43 18 00, metro Alma Marceau) 22 avenue Marceau, 8e Paris
*Consulate:* (☎ 02 32 10 28 10) 22 rue Mustel, Rouen

**Switzerland**
(☎ 01 49 55 67 00, metro Varenne), 142 rue de Grenelle, 7e

**UK**
*Embassy:* (☎ 01 44 51 31 00, e ambassade@amb-grandebretagne.fr, metro Concorde) 35 rue du Faubourg St-Honoré, 8e Paris
*Consulate:* (☎ 01 44 51 31 02, metro Concorde) 18 bis rue d'Anjou, 8e Paris

**USA**
*Embassy:* (☎ 01 43 12 22 22, e ambassade@amb-usa.fr, metro Concorde) 2 avenue Gabriel, 8e Paris
*Consulate:* (☎ 01 43 12 23 47, metro Concorde) 2 rue St-Florentin, 1er Paris

It's important to realise what your own embassy – the embassy of the country of which you are a citizen – can and can't do to help you if you get into trouble. Generally speaking, it won't be much help in emergencies if the trouble you're in is remotely your own fault. Remember that you are bound by the laws of the country you are in. Your embassy will not be sympathetic if you end up in jail after committing a crime locally, even if such actions are legal in your own country.

In genuine emergencies you might get some assistance, but only if other channels have been exhausted. For example, if you need to get home urgently, a free ticket home is exceedingly unlikely – the embassy would expect you to have insurance. If you have all your money and documents stolen, it might assist with getting a new passport, but a loan for onward travel is out of the question.

Some embassies used to keep letters for travellers or have a small reading room with home newspapers, but these days the mail holding service has usually been stopped and even newspapers tend to be out of date.

## CUSTOMS

The usual allowances apply to duty-free goods purchased at airports or on ferries outside the EU (from June 1999): tobacco (200 cigarettes, 50 cigars, or 250g of loose tobacco), alcohol (1L of strong liquor or 2L of less than 22% alcohol by volume *and* 2L of wine), coffee (500g or 200g of extracts), tea (100g or 40g of extracts) and perfume (50g of perfume and 0.25L of eau de toilette).

Do not confuse these with duty-paid items (including alcohol and tobacco) bought at normal shops and supermarkets in another EU country and brought into France, where certain goods might be more expensive. Then the allowances are more than generous: 800 cigarettes, 200 cigars, or 1kg of loose tobacco, 10L of spirits (more than 22% alcohol by volume), 20L of fortified wine or aperitif, 90L of wine or 110L of beer.

Note that duty-free shopping within the EU was abolished in mid-1999. This means that you can still enter an EU country with duty-free items from countries outside the EU; but you can't buy duty-free goods in, say, France and go to the UK.

## MONEY
### Currency

Until the euro is introduced (see the boxed text 'Adieu Franc, Bonjour Euro') the national currency is the French franc, abbreviated in this book by the letters 'FF'. One franc is divided into 100 centimes. French coins come in denominations of 5, 10, 20 and 50 centimes (0.5FF) and 1, 2, 5, 10 and 20FF; the two highest denominations have silvery centres and brass edges. It's a good idea to keep a supply of coins of various denominations for parking meters, road tolls, laundrettes and so on.

Banknotes are issued in denominations of 20FF (Claude Debussy), 50FF (the Little Prince and his creator, Antoine de St-Exupéry), 100FF (Paul Cézanne, who now replaces Eugène Delacroix), 200FF (Gustave Eiffel, replacing Montesquieu) and 500FF (Marie and Pierre Curie). It is often difficult to get change for a 500FF bill.

### Exchange Rates

| country | unit | euro | franc |
| --- | --- | --- | --- |
| Australia | A$1 | €0.58 | 3.79FF |
| Canada | C$1 | €0.71 | 4.66FF |
| EU | €1 | €1 | 6.55FF |
| Germany | DM1 | €0.51 | 3.35FF |
| Japan | ¥100 | €0.94 | 6.19FF |
| New Zealand | NZ$1 | €0.47 | 3.08FF |
| Spain | 100ptas | €0.60 | 3.94FF |
| UK | UK£1 | €1.58 | 10.37FF |
| USA | US$1 | €1.09 | 7.17FF |

### Exchanging Money

Wherever you change money, you can tell how good the rate is by checking the spread between the rates for *achat* (buy rates, that is, what they'll give you for foreign cash or travellers cheques) and *vente* (sell rates, that is, the rate at which they sell foreign currency to people going abroad) – the greater the difference, the further each is from the inter-bank rate (printed daily in newspapers, including the *International Herald Tribune*).

Banks, post offices and exchange bureaux often give a better rate for travellers cheques than for cash. Major train stations and fancy hotels have exchange facilities,

## Adieu Franc, Bonjour Euro

Increasingly you'll come across two sets of prices for goods and services across France. Since 1999 both the franc and Europe's new currency – the euro (€) – are legal tender. Along with national border controls, the currencies of various EU members are being phased out to complete Europe's monetary union.

Not all EU members have agreed to adopt the euro, but the franc, Deutschmark and lira will be among the first of 11 currencies to go the way of the dodo. The euro will end the 650-year reign of the franc, which began in 1360 when King Jean le Bon struck coins to signify that his part of France was *franc des anglois* (free of English domination). The timetable for the introduction of the euro runs as follows:

- On 1 January 1999 the exchange rates of the participating countries were irrevocably fixed to the euro. The euro came into force for non-cash transactions and prices could be displayed in both local currency and in euros.
- On 1 January 2002 euro banknotes and coins will be introduced. This ushers in a period of dual use of euros and existing local notes and coins.
- By 28 February 2002 local currencies will be withdrawn. Only euro notes and coins will remain in circulation and prices will be displayed in euros only.

The €5 note in France will be the same €5 note you will use in Italy and Portugal. There will be seven euro notes in different colours and sizes; they come in denominations of 500, 200, 100, 50, 20, 10 and five euros. There are eight euro coins, in denominations of two and one euros, then 50, 20, 10, five, two and one cents. Each participating state will be able to decorate the reverse side of the coins with their own designs, but all euro coins can be used in any country that accepts euros.

So, what does all this mean for the traveller? Until 2002, degrees of 'euro-readiness' will vary between countries, between different towns in the same country, or between different establishments in the same town. You may be given the option of paying in euros by credit card. Thomas Cook, American Express and other banks have started issuing travellers cheques in euros, but their usefulness is debatable: until cash euros come into circulation in 2002, travellers will still have to convert their euro travellers cheques into the local currency of each country.

Be forewarned that the scheme is open to abuse. For instance, a restaurant might print euro prices larger and more prominently on the menu. Check your bill carefully, too – your total might have the amount in francs, but a credit card company may bill you in the euro equivalent. Things will probably get worse during the first half of 2002, when countries can use both their old currency and the newly-issued euro notes and coins.

Fortunately, the euro has many benefits – cross-border travel will become easier, and prices in the 11 'euro-zone' countries will be immediately comparable. Also, once euro notes and coins are issued, you won't need to change money when travelling to other euro-zone members. Even EU countries not participating may price goods in euros and accept euros over shop counters.

The EU has a dedicated euro Web site, http://europa.eu.int/euro, and you can also check the currency converter at www.oanda.com for the latest rates.

which usually operate in the evening, at the weekend and during holidays, but the rates are usually poor.

**Cash** In general, cash is not a very good way to carry money. Not only can it be stolen, but in France you don't get an optimal exchange rate. The Banque de France, for instance, usually pays about 2.5% *more* for travellers cheques, more than making up for the 1% commission usually involved in buying cheques.

Bring along the equivalent of about US$100 in low-denomination notes, which makes it easier to change small sums of money if necessary (for example, at the end of your stay). Because of the risk of counterfeiting it may be difficult to change US$100 notes, even the new ones with the oversized picture of Benjamin Franklin.

Post offices often offer the best exchange rates in town, and accept banknotes in a variety of currencies as well as travellers cheques issued by American Express or Visa. The commission for French franc travellers cheques is 1.2% (minimum 16FF); ones in US dollars are cashed for free.

The Banque de France, France's central bank, used to offer the country's best exchange rates but nowadays the post offices are a better deal. Branches open Monday to Friday but only offer walk-in currency services in the morning.

Commercial banks usually charge a stiff 20FF to 35FF per foreign currency transaction. The rates offered vary, so it pays to compare. Hours are usually from 8 or 9 am to sometime between 11.30 am and 1 pm, and 1.30 or 2 to 4.30 or 5 pm, Monday to Friday or Tuesday to Saturday. Exchange services may end half an hour before closing time. See the Business Hours section later in this chapter for details of other standard opening times.

All major train stations have exchange bureaux – some run by Thomas Cook – but their rates are less than stellar.

**Travellers Cheques & Eurocheques**
Commercial banks charge something like 22FF to 35FF to cash travellers cheques. The post office will cash US-dollar travellers cheques for free, but charges 1.5% for ones in other currencies (usually a minimum fee of 15FF). American Express offices don't charge commission on their own travellers cheques (but 3% or at least 40FF on other brands).

The most flexible travellers cheques are issued by American Express (in US dollars or French francs) and Visa (in French francs) because they can be changed at many post offices.

Keep a record of cheque numbers, where they were purchased and which ones were cashed, separate from the cheques themselves. If your American Express travellers cheques are lost or stolen in France, call ☎ 08 00 90 86 00, a 24-hour toll-free number. In Rouen, reimbursements can be made at the American Express office (☎ 02 35 89 48 60) in the tourist office at 25 place de la Cathédrale.

If you lose your Thomas Cook cheques, contact any Thomas Cook bureau – for example in a major train station. Their customer service bureau can be contacted toll-free by dialling ☎ 08 00 90 83 30.

Eurocheques, available if you have a European bank account, are guaranteed up to a certain limit. When cashing them (for example, at post offices), you'll be asked to show your Eurocheque card, and perhaps a passport or ID card. Eurocheques are relatively unpopular with merchants and hotels because of the bank charges attached.

**ATMs** Known in French as DABs *(distributeurs automatiques de billets)* or *points d'argent*, ATMs can draw on your home account at a superior exchange rate. Most ATMs will also give you a cash advance through your Visa or MasterCard (see the following Credit Cards section). You must have a four-digit PIN code. There are plenty of ATMs linked to the international Cirrus, Plus and Maestro networks. If you normally remember your PIN code as a string of letters, translate it back into numbers, as keyboards may not have letters indicated. ATMs are a convenient solution for getting cash since they are in every village, town and city as well as most train stations.

**Credit Cards** Overall, the cheapest way to pay during your France trip is by credit or debit card. Visa (Carte Bleue) is the most widely accepted, followed by MasterCard (Access or Eurocard). American Express cards are only useful at more upmarket establishments.

When you get a cash advance against your Visa or MasterCard credit card account, your issuer charges a transaction fee which can be as high as US$10 *plus* interest – check with your card issuer before leaving home. Also, many banks charge a commission of 30FF or more. But you can deposit funds into your account ahead of time, effectively turning your credit card into an interest-bearing bank account – this method usually incurs the lowest fees.

It may be impossible to get a lost Visa or MasterCard reissued until you get home, so two different credit cards are safer than one. If your Visa card is lost or stolen, call Carte Bleue at ☎ 01 42 77 11 90 in Paris or ☎ 02 54 42 12 12 in the provinces, 24 hours a day. To get a replacement card you'll have to deal with the issuer.

Report a lost MasterCard, Eurocard or Access to Eurocard France (☎ 01 45 67 53 53) and, if you can, to your credit card issuer back home (for cards from the USA, call ☎ 314-275 6690).

If your American Express card is lost or stolen, call ☎ 01 47 77 70 00 or ☎ 01 47 77 72 00; both are staffed 24 hours a day. In an emergency, American Express card holders from the USA can call collect on ☎ 202-783 7474 or ☎ 202-677 2442. On-the-spot replacements can be arranged at any American Express office (see Travellers Cheques & Eurocheques earlier in this chapter).

Report lost Diners Club cards on ☎ 01 47 62 75 75.

**International Transfers** Telegraphic transfers are not very expensive but, despite their name, can be quite slow. Be sure to specify the name of the bank and the name and address of the branch where you'd like to pick it up.

It's quicker and easier to have money wired via American Express (US$50 for US$1000). Western Union's Money Transfer system (☎ 01 43 54 46 12) and Thomas Cook's MoneyGram service (☎ 01 47 58 21 00) are also popular.

## Security
Normandy is pretty safe but pick-pocketing, especially in the major cities, can be a real problem. Don't carry more money than you need, and keep your credit cards, passport

and other documents in a concealed pouch or a hotel safe. Cars with foreign plates are popular targets for smash-and-grab theft, so be sure to remove wallets, money and other valuables when you park. Always keep some spare travellers cheques or cash on hand for an emergency.

## Costs
By staying in hostels or showerless, toilet-less rooms in budget hotels and having picnics rather than dining out, you can travel around Normandy for about US$25 a day per person. A couple staying in a two-star hotel and eating one cheap restaurant meal each day should count on spending at least US$45 a day per person, not including car rental. Lots of moving from place to place, eating in restaurants, drinking wine or treating yourself to France's many little luxuries can increase these figures considerably.

**Discounts** Some museums and cinemas, the SNCF, ferry companies and other institutions offer all sorts of price breaks to people under the age of either 25 or 26, students with ISIC cards (age limits may apply) and *le troisième age* (seniors), that is, people aged over 60 or, in some cases, 65. Look for the words *demi-tarif* or *tarif réduit* (half-price tariff or reduced rate) on rate charts and then ask if you qualify. Those aged under 18 years get an even wider range of discounts, especially in museums.

Upper Normandy (the departments of Seine-Maritime and Eure) has recently instituted a special two-for-the-price-of-one museum discount program from June to October. The extra ticket can be used either by a companion or to visit another museum. There are 26 participating museums, including Musée des Beaux-Arts in Rouen.

**Ways to Save Money** There are lots of things you can do to shave francs off your daily expenditures. A few suggestions:

• Travel with someone else – single rooms usually cost only marginally less than doubles. Triples and quads (often with only two beds) are even cheaper per person. Budget hotel rooms often cost less per person than hostel beds.

• You'll get the best exchange rate and low commissions at post offices and by using a credit card (see Exchanging Money earlier in this chapter).
• Avoid travel in high season, when accommodation prices often go up.
• Avail yourself of Normandy's many free sights: bustling marketplaces, tree-lined avenues, cathedrals, churches, nature reserves and so on.
• When calling home, avoid France's pricey International Direct Dial (IDD) services – use a phonecard and ask to be rung back.
• Bring along a pocketknife and eating utensils so you can have picnics instead of restaurant meals. Supermarkets are cheaper than bakeries or outdoor markets, although the quality is not as good.
• Make lunch the main meal of the day. The lunch *menus* (set-price menus) are astoundingly good value and often cheaper than buying your own food.
• Carry a water bottle so you don't have to pay for a pricey cold drink each time you're thirsty (there are few public drinking fountains in France).
• In restaurants, order the *menu* and ask for tap water *(eau robinet)* rather than soft drinks, mineral water or wine.
• Avoid taking trains that incur supplements or reservation fees. For information on reduced-rate train tickets, see the Train section in the Getting Around chapter.
• If you'll be hiring a car, arrange rental before you leave home. If you'll be staying at least a month, hire a purchase-repurchase car (see Purchase-Repurchase Plans under Car in the Getting Around chapter).
• Buy discount bus/metro passes or carnets of reduced-price tickets rather than single tickets if you'll be staying in a city any length of time.
• It's cheaper to have coffee or a drink standing at the bar rather than sitting at a table, which usually incurs surcharges.
• If you're travelling around by car, fill it up with petrol in town rather than at service stations on the autoroutes, which are considerably more expensive.

## Tipping & Bargaining

French law requires that restaurant, cafe and hotel bills include the service charge (usually 10 to 15%), so a *pourboire* (tip) is neither necessary nor expected in most cases. However, most people leave a few francs in restaurants, unless the service was bad. They rarely tip in cafes and bars when they've just had a coffee or a drink.

In taxis, the usual tip is 2FF no matter what the fare, with the maximum about 5FF. People in France rarely bargain, except at flea markets.

## Taxes & Refunds

France's VAT is 20.6% on most goods except food, medicine and books, for which it's 5.5%; it is as high as 33% on items such as watches, cameras and video cassettes. Prices that include VAT are often marked TTC (*toutes taxes comprises*, or 'all taxes included').

If you're not an EU resident, you can get a refund of most of the VAT (TVA in French) provided that: you're over 15; you'll be spending less than six months in France; you purchase goods (not more than 10 of the same item) worth at least 1200FF (tax included) at a single shop; and the shop offers *vente en détaxe* (duty-free sales).

Present a passport at the time of purchase and ask for a *bordereau de détaxe* (export sales invoice). Some shops may refund less than the 17.1% of the purchase price you are entitled to in order to cover expenses involved in the refund procedure.

As you leave France, or another EU country, have all three pages (two pink and one green) of the bordereau validated by the country's customs officials at the airport or at the border. Customs officials will take the two pink sheets and the stamped self-addressed envelope provided by the store; the green sheet is your receipt. You mail one of the stamped pink sheets to the shop where you made your purchase, which will then send you a *virement* (transfer of funds) in the form you have requested, such as by French franc cheque, or directly into your account. Be prepared for a long wait. Some shops will let you charge the VAT separately, debit the card immediately for the untaxed portion and allow a reasonable amount of time to receive the stamped pink sheet.

**Instant Refunds** If you're flying out of Orly or Roissy Charles de Gaulle airports, certain stores can arrange for you to receive your refund as you're leaving the country.

You must make such arrangements at the time of purchase.

When you arrive at the airport you have to do three things:

- Up to three hours before your flight leaves, you need to take your bordereau, passport, air ticket and the things you purchased (don't put them in your checked luggage) to the *douane* (customs) office so they can stamp the three copies of the bordereau (one of which they'll keep).
- Go to an Aéroports de Paris (ADP) information counter, where they will check the figures and put another stamp on the documents.
- Go to the customs refund window *(douane de détaxe)* or the exchange bureau indicated on your bordereau to pick up your refund.

## POST & COMMUNICATIONS

Postal services in France are fast, reliable, bureaucratic and expensive. About three-quarters of domestic letters arrive the day after they've been mailed.

Each of France's 17,000 post offices is marked with a yellow or brown sign reading 'La Poste'; older branches may also be marked with the letters PTT. To mail things, go to the postal window marked *toutes opérations*.

Hours are generally 8.30 or 9 am to noon and 2 to 5 or 6 pm on weekdays, and Saturday mornings. See the Business Hours section later in this chapter for details of other standard opening times.

### Postal Rates

Domestic letters up to 20g cost 3FF. Postcards and letters up to 20g cost 3FF within the EU; 3.80FF to most of the remainder of Europe as well as Africa; 4.40FF to the USA, Canada and the Middle East; and 5.20FF to Australasia. Aerograms cost 5FF to all destinations.

Worldwide express mail delivery, called Chronopost (☎ 01 46 48 10 00, Minitel 3614 CHRONOPOST for information), costs a fortune.

Sea-mail services have been discontinued, so sending packages overseas sometimes costs almost as much as the exorbitant overweight fees charged by airlines, even if you use *économique* (discount) air mail.

Packages weighing over 2kg may not be accepted at branch post offices. Post offices sell smallish boxes in four different sizes for 6.50FF to 12.50FF.

### Sending Mail

All mail to France *must* include the five digit postcode, which begins with the two digit number of the department. The local postcode is listed under the main heading of each city or town in this book. The notation 'Cedex' after a town name simply means that mail sent to that address is collected at the post office, rather than delivered to the door.

### Receiving Mail

**Poste Restante** To have mail sent to you via poste restante (general delivery), available at all French post offices, it should be addressed as follows:

> SMITH, John
> Poste Restante
> Recette Principale
> 76000 Rouen
> FRANCE

Write your *nom de famille* (surname or family name) first and in capital letters. In case your friends back home forget, always check under the first letter of your *prénom* (first name). There's a 3FF charge for every piece of poste restante mail you pick up weighing less than 20g; for anything between 20g and 100g, the fee is 4FF. It's usually possible to forward *(faire suivre)* mail from one poste restante address to another. You'll need to present your passport or national ID card when you pick up your mail.

Poste restante mail not addressed to a particular branch goes to the city's *recette principale* (main post office) whether or not you include the words Recette Principale in the address. If you want it sent to a specific branch post office mentioned in this book (most of which are generally centrally located and marked on the maps), write the street address mentioned in the text.

You can also receive mail (but not parcels or envelopes larger than an A4 sheet of paper) in care of American Express. If you don't have an American Express card or their travellers cheques, there's a 5FF charge each time you check to see if you've received something (some offices waive the fee if there's nothing for you). The office will hold mail for 30 days before returning it to the sender. After that, having them forward it to another American Express office costs 15FF for two months.

## Telephone

A quarter of a century ago, France had one of the worst telephone systems in Western Europe. But thanks to massive investment in the late 1970s and early '80s, the country now has one of the most modern and sophisticated telecommunications systems in the world.

**International Dialling** To call from outside France, first dial your country's international access code, then 33 (France's country code), then omit the 0 at the beginning of the 10-digit local number.

To call someone outside France, dial the international access code (00), the country code, the area code (without the initial zero if there is one) and the local number. International Direct Dial (IDD) calls to almost anywhere in the world can be made from public telephones. Useful country codes include:

| | |
|---|---|
| Australia | ☎ 61 |
| Canada | ☎ 1 |
| Hong Kong | ☎ 852 |
| Germany | ☎ 49 |
| Japan | ☎ 81 |
| India | ☎ 91 |
| Ireland | ☎ 353 |
| Italy | ☎ 39 |
| Monaco | ☎ 377 |
| New Zealand | ☎ 64 |
| Singapore | ☎ 65 |
| South Africa | ☎ 27 |
| UK | ☎ 44 |
| USA | ☎ 1 |

If you don't know the country code *(indicatif pays)* and it's not posted in the telephone cabin, consult a telephone book or dial ☎ 12 (directory inquiries).

To make a reverse-charge (collect) call *(en PCV*, pronounced 'pey-sey-vey') or a person-to-person call *(avec préavis*, pronounced 'ah-vek preh-ah-vee'), dial 00, and then dial 33 plus the country code of the place you're calling (for the USA and Canada, dial 11 instead of 1). Don't be surprised if you get a recording and have to wait a while. If you're using a public phone, you must insert a phonecard (or, in the case of public coin telephones, 1FF) to place operator-assisted calls through the international operator.

For directory inquiries for numbers outside France, dial 00 then 3312 and finally the relevant country code (again, 11 instead of 1 for the USA and Canada). You may be put on hold for quite a while. In public phones, you can access this service without a phonecard, but from private lines the charge is 7.30FF per inquiry.

Toll-free 1-800 numbers in the USA and Canada are not toll-free when you call from France. You pay at the normal international rate.

**International Rates** Daytime calls to other parts of Europe cost from 1.64FF to 3.22FF a minute. Reduced tariffs (0.99FF to 2.28FF) generally apply on weekdays from 7 pm to 8 am, during weekends and on public holidays.

Non-discount calls to continental USA and Canada cost 1.64FF a minute on weekdays from 1 to 7 pm. The price then drops to 0.99FF. The rate to Alaska, Hawaii and the Caribbean is a whopping 9.22FF a minute (7.34FF discount rate).

Full-price calls to Australia, Japan, New Zealand, Hong Kong and Singapore are 4.26FF a minute. A discount rate of 3.07FF a minute applies daily from 7 pm to 8 am, at weekends and on public holidays.

Calls to other parts of Asia, South America and non-Francophone Africa are generally 5.45FF to 9.22FF a minute, though to some countries a rate of 4.26FF to 7.34FF will apply at certain times.

**Country Direct Services** Country direct lets you phone home by billing the long-distance carrier you use at home. The numbers can be dialled from public phones without inserting a phonecard. Services include AT&T (☎ 08 00 99 00 11), MCI (☎ 08 00 99 00 19) and Sprint (☎ 08 00 99 00 87), all US-based; BT (☎ 08 00 99 02 44) and Mercury (☎ 08 00 99 09 44), both based in the UK; and Telstra (☎ 08 00 99 00 61) and Optus (☎ 08 00 99 20 61) in Australia. Note that the rates aren't likely to be brilliant – you'll do better using a French phonecard (see Telephone Cards later in the chapter).

**Domestic Dialling** France has five telephone dialling areas. To make calls within any region, just dial the 10-digit number. The same applies for calls between regions and from metropolitan France to French overseas departments and vice versa.

For France Telecom's directory inquiries *(services des renseignements)*, dial ☎ 12. Operators don't all speak English. The call is free from public phones but costs a breathtaking 11.13FF from private lines (for one or two numbers).

You can not make domestic reverse-charge calls. Instead, ask the person you're calling to ring you back.

**Domestic Tariffs** Local calls are quite cheap, even at the peak tariff: one calling unit (0.81FF with a télécarte) lasts for three minutes. For calls anywhere in the country outside your local zone, one unit lasts 39 seconds.

The regular rate for calls within France, known as the *tarif rouge* (red tariff), applies 8 am to 7 pm Monday to Friday. The rest of the time, you enjoy 50% off with the *tarif bleu* (blue tariff).

Note that numbers beginning with '08 36' (such as the SNCF's national information number) are always billed at 2.23FF per minute, regardless of the day or the time.

Two-digit emergency numbers (see the Emergency section later in the chapter), country direct numbers and *numéros verts* (toll-free numbers – literally, 'green numbers' – which have 10 digits and begin 08

00), can be dialled from public telephones without inserting a phonecard or coins.

Numbers that begin with 06 are to mobile phones. France has adopted a 'caller pays' system which means that calling a mobile phone can be expensive. Calls to a mobile phone cost from about 1.60FF a minute to nearly 4FF a minute, depending upon the company and the time of day.

**Public Phones** Almost all public telephones in France require a phonecard, which can be purchased at post offices, *tabacs* (tobacconists and anywhere you see a blue sticker reading *télécarte en vente ici*). Cards worth 50/120 calling units cost 40.60/97.50FF.

To make a domestic or international phone call with a phonecard, follow the instructions on the LCD display. Most public phones have a button displaying two flags which you push for explanations in English.

## Mobile Phones

France uses GSM 900/1800, which is compatible with the rest of Europe and Australia but not with the North American GSM 1900 or the totally different system in Japan (though some North Americans have GSM 1900/900 phones that do work here). If you have a GSM phone, check with your service provider about using it in France, and beware of calls being routed internationally (very expensive for a 'local' call).

A prepaid Mobicarte is a cheaper alternative. Sold by France Telecom, this package deal costs from 490FF for the cellular phone and 270FF for 30 minutes of included time. For more time you can buy a recharge card for 70FF, 140FF or 250FF (including 30FF extra talk time) from tobacconists and other places you'd buy a phonecard. Per-minute costs depend on which rate scheme you choose; the *classique* plan charges you 4.20FF per minute, 24 hours a day. There are also schemes geared towards heavy evening and weekend use. Check out the Web site at www.mobicarte.tm.fr.

🍎🍎🍎🍎🍎🍎🍎🍎🍎🍎🍎🍎

If not, insert the card chip-end first with the rectangle of electrical connectors facing upwards and dial when you hear the tone.

You occasionally run across phones that take coins (2FF for a local call) rather than phonecards, especially in restaurants or bars. Remember that coin phones don't give change.

**Telephone Cards** You can buy prepaid phonecards in France that make calling abroad cheaper than with a standard télé-carte. France Telecom's *Le Ticket de Téléphone*, the *Carte Intercall Monde* and *Carte Astuce* are among the more popular cards, and give up to 60% off standard French international call rates. They're available in 50FF and 100FF denominations from *tabacs* (tobacconists) and other sales points.

**Minitel** Minitel is a screen-based information service peculiar to France, set up in the 1980s. It's useful but can be expensive to use, and the growing popularity of the Internet is giving Minitel a run for its money. The most basic variety, with a B&W monitor and a clumsy keyboard, are free to telephone subscribers. Newer Minitel models have colour screens, and many people now access the system with a home computer and a modem.

Minitel numbers consist of four digits (such as 3611, 3614, 3615) and a string of letters. Home users pay a per-minute access charge, but consulting the *annuaire* (directory) is free. Most of the Minitels in post offices are also free for directory inquiries (though some require a 1FF or 2FF coin), and many of them can access pay-as-you-go on-line services.

### eKno Communication Service
Lonely Planet's eKno global communication service provides low-cost international calls – for local calls you're usually better off with a local phonecard. eKno also offers free messaging services, email, travel information and an on-line travel vault, where you can securely store all your important documents. You can join on-line at www .ekno.lonelyplanet.com, where you will find the local-access numbers for the 24-hour customer-service centre. Once you have joined, always check the eKno Web site for the latest access numbers for each country and updates on new features.

### Fax
Virtually all large offices can send and receive domestic and international faxes *(télé-copies* or *téléfaxes)*, telexes and telegrams. It costs about 60FF (12FF within France) to send a one-page fax.

### Email & Internet Access
Over the past few years, some 1000 post offices across France have been equipped with a Cyberposte, a modern, card-operated Internet terminal for public use. This is about the cheapest reliable way to check your email in France, and it allows you to set up a free email address. To use the Cyberposte – restricted to post office opening hours – buy a chip card at the counter for 50FF; an hour's connection time costs 30FF. When the card's exhausted you can recharge for 30FF, good for another hour. There's a list of post offices with a Cyberposte at www.cyberposte.com.

Otherwise you can seek out one of the growing ranks of cybercafes in French towns. They aren't cheap: expect to pay 20FF to 30FF for a half-hour of Web surfing (note that some places charge by the minute, which might be useful if you just want to check your email).

See the Post & Communications sections under individual towns in this book for details of the local Cyberposte and Internet cafes.

### INTERNET RESOURCES
The World Wide Web is a rich resource for travellers. You can research your trip, hunt down bargain air fares, book hotels, check on weather conditions or chat with locals and other travellers about the best places to visit (or avoid).

There's no better place to start your Web explorations than the Lonely Planet Web site (www.lonelyplanet.com). Here you'll find succinct summaries on travelling to most places on earth, postcards from other travellers and the Thorn Tree bulletin board, where you can ask questions before you go or dispense advice when you get back. You can also find travel news and updates to many of our most popular guidebooks, and the subWWWay section links you to the most useful travel resources elsewhere on the Web.

Useful Web sites about France in English include:

**Diplomatic & Visa Information**
www.france.diplomatie.fr
(includes lists of consulates and embassies with visa information)
**French Government Tourism Office**
www.francetourism.com
(official tourism site with all manner of information on and about travel in France)
**Gay & Lesbian**
www.france.qrd.org
('queer resources directory' for gay and lesbian travellers)
**Maison de la France**
www.maison-de-la-france.fr
(the main tourist office site)
**Normandy Tourism**
www.normandy-tourism.org
(practical and cultural information about Normandy and links to regional, departmental and local tourist offices)
**Weather**
www.meteo.fr
(two-day weather forecasts and current conditions)

## BOOKS
Most books are published in different editions by different publishers in different countries. As a result, a book might be a hardcover rarity in one country while it's readily available in paperback in another. Fortunately, bookshops and libraries search by title or author, so your local bookshop or library is best placed to advise you on the availability of the following recommendations.

## Lonely Planet
Lonely Planet's *France, Western Europe, Mediterranean Europe* and *Europe on a Shoestring* have chapters dealing with Normandy. It also publishes a *French phrasebook* and one for Europe as a whole.

For those that want to explore the great outdoors, *Walking in France* and *Cycling France* offer a wealth of lively description and practical information. First-time travellers shouldn't miss *Read This First Europe*, the essential predeparture tool for exploring the continent, whilst *World Food France* is an ideal companion.

## Guidebooks
Large travel bookshops carry hundreds of titles on virtually every aspect of visiting France.

Michelin, the huge rubber conglomerate, has been publishing guidebooks ever since the earliest days of motorcar touring, when the titles were intended to promote sales of its inflatable rubber tyres. Its *Guides Verts* (green guides) are full of historical and cultural information, although the editorial approach is conservative and uncritical. It publishes an English language guide to Normandy that's difficult to find in Normandy and two French guides: *Normandie Vallée de la Seine* covering Upper Normandy and *Normandie Cotentin* for Lower Normandy and the Channel Islands.

Among the French-language guides, the best overall guidebooks are those published by *Guide Bleu*. Its blue-jacketed Normandie guide (198FF) provide accurate, balanced information on matters historical, cultural and architectural.

## Restaurants & Accommodation Guides
Many people swear by Michelin's red-jacketed *Guide Rouge* to France (130FF), published each March, which has over 1200 pages of information on 6400 mid- and upper-range hotels and 3900 restaurants in every corner of the country. Accompanied by 521 detailed city maps, it's best known for rating France's greatest restaurants with one, two or three stars. Its reputation has suffered a bit in recent years and the ratings don't quite carry the weight they used to. The icons used instead of text are explained in English at the front of the book.

The *Guide Gault Millau France* (189FF),

published annually, awards up to four *toques rouges* (red chefs' caps) to restaurants with exceptionally good, creative cuisine; *toques blanches* (white chefs' caps) go to places with superb modern or traditional cuisine. *Gault Millau* is said to be quicker at picking up-and-coming restaurants than the *Guide Rouge*. The symbols used are explained in English and an English edition is also available. The *Food Lover's Guide to France*, by the Paris-based American food reviewer Patricia Wells, is informative and a good read. *Le Guide des Hôtels Restaurants Logis de France* (95FF) is a complete listing of Logis de France affiliates (see Mid-Range Hotels in the Accommodation section later in this chapter).

The French-language *Guide du Routard* series is popular with youngish French people travelling around their own country. The restaurant tips generally offer good value, but rock-bottom hotels rarely make an appearance and there are few maps. There are two Normandy books: *Basse Normandie* (Lower Normandy) and *Haute Normandie* (Upper Normandy). They cost 79FF each.

In Upper Normandy, look for the French-language *Le P'tit Normand* (48FF) which has an excellent listing of restaurants, nightlife and museums.

## Fiction

Foreign and French writers have chosen Normandy as the setting for diverse works with historical, psychological and philosophical themes.

*Flaubert's Parrot* by Julian Barnes. A highly entertaining novel that pays witty homage to the great French writer.

*The Last English King* by Julian Rathbone. Fictionalised account of the Norman Conquest with the Normans as unredeemed bad guys.

*The Longest Day* by Cornelius Ryan. The fictionalised account of the D-Day landings later made into a movie.

*Madame Bovary* by Gustav Flaubert. Based on a true story that took place in Ry, Flaubert chronicles Emma Bovary's downfall with chilling precision.

*Nausea* by Jean-Paul Sartre. Sartre's hero experiences overwhelming existential dread and despair in 1930s Le Havre.

*Odo's Hanging* by Peter Benson. Essential background reading before a visit to the Bayeux Tapestry, Benson creates a colourful tale around the tapestry's making.

*Pierre and Jean* by Guy de Maupassant. Another pessimistic story set in Le Havre, this time about sibling rivalry. What is it about that port?

## History & Politics

A wide variety of excellent works on Normandy's history, chief historical characters and politics are available in English.

*The Age of the Cathedrals* by Georges Duby. An authoritative study of the relations between art and society in medieval France.

*The Bayeux Tapestry* by David M Wilson. An excellent overview of the making of the Bayeux Tapestry with beautiful photographs.

*Cross Channel* by Julian Barnes. A witty collection of key moments in shared Anglo-French history – from Joan of Arc to Eurostar.

*Cultural Atlas of France* by John Ardagh. A superb illustrated synopsis of French culture and history with a short section on Normandy.

*A Distant Mirror* by Barbara Tuchman. A highly readable account of the vicissitudes of the 14th century with a special focus on the beginning of the Hundred Years' War.

*Eleanor of Aquitaine and the Four Kings* by Amy Kelly. Although concentrated on Eleanor's role in the Plantagenet empire, there's plenty of fascinating detail about Henry, Richard the Lion-Heart and their activities in Normandy.

*Feminism in France* by Claire Duchen. A work that charts the progress of feminism in France from 1968 to the mid-1980s.

*France Today* by John Ardagh. A good introduction to modern-day France, its politics, its people, and their idiosyncrasies.

*The French* by Theodore Zeldin. A highly acclaimed and very insightful survey of French passions, peculiarities and perspectives. It's intelligent, informative and humorous.

*The Identity of France* by Fernand Braudel. A comprehensive (two volumes) look at the country and its people.

*Joan of Arc* by Mary Gordon. Perhaps the most vividly imagined portrait of the Maid, Gordon conveys the immense mystery of her accomplishments.

*Joan of Arc* by Mark Twain. A confirmed atheist, Mark Twain nevertheless became fascinated by the 15th-century saint.

*Joan of Arc: The Image of Female Heroism* by Marina Warner. A psychohistorical account of

Joan of Arc's accomplishments by an author with a distinctly modern outlook.

*Saint Joan of Arc* by Vita Sackville-West. Drawing upon contemporary sources and the trial in Rouen, Sackville-West presents a convincing account of Joan of Arc's life.

*Mont St-Michel and Chartres* by Henry Adams. The turn-of-the-century writer and historian brings a fine sensibility to Normandy's most famous monument.

*The Norman Achievement* by David C Douglas. A lively, vivid account of the Norman Conquest of England.

*The Norman Conquest* by D J A Matthew. A scholarly book examining the political and cultural effect of the Norman Conquest on England.

## Battle of Normandy

There are countless books chronicling the events of WWII, D-Day and the Battle of Normandy. Some to look out for include:

*Decision in Normandy* by Carlo d'Este. A readable military history of the Battle of Normandy that criticises key decisions of Montgomery and Bradley.

*The Good War* by Studs Terkel. A collection of interviews presenting WWII from the point of view of the participants, civilians and military.

*Overlord* by Max Hastings. A critical look at the shortcomings of Allied forces waging the Battle of Normandy.

*Six Armies in Normandy* by John Keegan. A narration of the Battle of Normandy that examines the roles played by the English, Canadian, Scottish, German, Polish and French armies.

## FILMS

English-language films set in Normandy mostly deal with D-Day. *Saving Private Ryan* (1999) by Stephen Spielberg is the most recent. This chillingly realistic, Oscar-winning account of the American landing at Omaha Beach was filmed in Ireland except for the scenes at the American cemetery.

The star-studded *The Longest Day* (1962) was filmed in various locations around Normandy. Daryl Zanuck's epic lacks Spielberg's blood and guts battle scenes but it includes actual participants in the battle among the walk-ons.

There are a wealth of French language movies set in Normandy *Les Parapluies de Cherbourg* (The Umbrellas of Cherbourg), Jacques Demy's delightful musical, was filmed on location with Catherine Deneuve. Roman Polanski's *Tess* (1979) was filmed in the countryside south of Cherbourg as a substitute for the English countryside. *Un Homme et une Femme* (A Man and a Woman), Claude Lelouche's poignant romance, was filmed in Deauville in 1966, as was the recent sequel with the same stars, Trintignant and Anouk Aimée. Also filmed in Deauville was *Dentellière* with Isabelle Huppert and scenes from Bernard Tavernier's 1986 great jazz movie, *Auteur de Minuit* (Around Midnight). Bernard Blier filmed *Préparez vos Mouchoirs* (Get Out Your Hankerchiefs) in Tréport in 1976 and Dieppe was the location for the final scene of *Journal d'Une Femme de Chambre* (Diary of a Chambermaid), Luis Buñuel's 1963 classic.

Claude Chabrol filmed his 1990 adaptation of *Madame Bovary* in Lyons-la-Forêt and Luc Besson's recent *Jeanne d'Arc* was partly filmed in Sées. Louis Malle's *Le Voleur* (The Thief; 1967) was filmed in Évreux. François Truffaut filmed *Deux Anglaises et le Continent* (Two English Girls; 1971) in Auderville; scenes from *400 Coups* (400 Blows; 1958) were filmed around Criqueboeuf, and scenes from *Jules et Jim* (Jules and Jim; 1961) were shot outside Vernon.

## NEWSPAPERS & MAGAZINES

*Ouest-France* is Normandy's most widely dispersed and respectable daily newspaper with editions for each department. *Paris Normandie* is simple to read if your French is basic. Other weekly and biweekly local newspapers include *Liberté*, *L'Eveil de Lisieux*, *Le Pays d'Auge*, *La Renaissance*, *Les Nouvelles de Falaise*, *La Manche Libre* and *L'Orne Combattante*. The bimonthly *Normandie Magazine* (20FF) is in French and English and covers cultural, business, political and economic news.

In larger towns, larger newsagencies and those at railway stations usually carry English-language dailies including the *International Herald Tribune*, *Guardian*, *Financial Times*, *New York Times* and the colourful

*USA Today*. Also readily available are *Newsweek*, *Time* and the *Economist*.

## RADIO & TV
### Radio
You can pick up a mixture of the BBC World Service and BBC for Europe on 648 kHz AM. The Voice of America (VOA) is on 1197 kHz AM but reception is often poor. By law, at least 40% of musical variety broadcasts must consist of songs in French (stations can get fined if they don't comply). This helps explain why so many English-language hits are re-recorded in French (which can be a real hoot).

### TV
Some good French programmes include *Le Vrai Journal* on Canal+ on Sunday afternoons. It's a popular, hard-hitting program of investigative journalism hosted by one Karl Zéro (surely NOT his real name). Another great show is *Guignol* (with Spitting Image-type rubber puppets), which is part of the same channel's nightly *Nulle Part Ailleur* program.

Weekend-to-weekend TV listings (such as *Tél' 7 jours or Télérama*) are sold at newsstands. Foreign movies that haven't been dubbed and are shown with subtitles are marked 'VO' or 'v.o.' *(version originale)*.

Upmarket hotels often offer Canal+ and access to CNN, BBC Prime, Sky and other English-language networks.

## VIDEO SYSTEMS
Unlike the rest of Western Europe and Australia, which use PAL, and the USA, which uses NTSC, French TV broadcasts are in SECAM. Non-SECAM TVs won't work in France. French videotapes can't be played on video recorders and TVs that lack a SECAM capability.

## PHOTOGRAPHY & VIDEO
### Film & Equipment
Colour-print film produced by Kodak and Fuji is widely available in supermarkets, photo shops and FNAC stores. It's fairly expensive in France compared to a lot of other countries, so it pays to stock up ahead of time. At FNAC, a 36-exposure roll of Kodak Gold costs 35/44FF for 100/400 ASA (note that film is usually sold in packs of two). Developing costs 20FF per roll plus 2.50FF per photo. Note that many smaller photography shops may charge less (from 1FF to 1.50FF per photo). One-hour developing is widely available.

For slides *(diapositives)*, count on paying at least 46/54/68FF for a 36-exposure roll of Ektachrome rated at 100/200/400 ASA; developing costs 28/32FF for 24/36 exposures.

Stay away from Kodachrome; it's difficult to process quickly in France and can give you lots of headaches if not handled properly.

You can obtain video cartridges for your video camera easily in large towns, but make sure you buy the correct format. It's usually worth buying a few cartridges duty-free to start off your trip.

### Technical Tips
For handy hints on improving your snaps, try Lonely Planet's *Travel Photography: A Guide to Taking Better Pictures*, written by internationally renowned travel photographer Richard I'Anson. It's full colour throughout and designed to take on the road.

### Airport Security
Be prepared to have your camera and film run through X-ray machines at airports and the entrances to sensitive public buildings. The gadgets are ostensibly film-safe up to 1000 ASA, and laptops and computer disks appear to pass through without losing data, but there is always some degree of risk.

## TIME
France uses the 24-hour clock, with the hours separated from the minutes by a lower-case letter 'h'. Thus, 3.30 pm is 15h30, 9.50 pm is 21h50, 12.30 am is 00h30 and so on.

France is on Central European Time, which is one hour ahead of (or later than) GMT/UTC. During daylight-saving (or summer) time, which runs from the last Sunday in March to the last Sunday in October, France is two hours ahead of GMT/UTC.

Without taking daylight-savings time into account, when it's noon in Paris it's 11 am in London, 6 am in New York, 3 am in San Francisco, 8 pm in Tokyo, 9 pm in Sydney and 11 pm in Auckland.

## ELECTRICITY
### Voltages & Cycles
France runs on 220V at 50Hz AC. In the USA and Canada, the 120V electric supply is at 60Hz. While the usual travel transformers allow North American appliances to run in France without blowing out, they cannot change the Hz rate, which determines – among other things – the speed of electric motors. As a result, tape recorders not equipped with built-in adapters may function poorly. Make sure the adapter you buy can handle the wattage of your appliance.

### Plugs & Sockets
Old-type wall sockets, often rated at 600 watts, take two round prongs. The new kinds of sockets take fatter prongs and have a protruding earth (ground) prong.

Adapters to make new plugs fit into the old sockets are said to be illegal but are still available at electrical shops.

## WEIGHTS & MEASURES
### Metric System
France uses the metric system. For a conversion chart, see the inside back cover of this book.

### Numbers
For numbers with four or more digits, the French use full stops or spaces where writers in English would use commas: one million therefore appears as 1.000.000 or 1 000 000. For decimals, on the other hand, the French use commas so 1.75 comes out as 1,75.

## LAUNDRY
To find a *laverie libre-service* (an unstaffed, self-service laundrette) near where you're staying, see Laundry under Information at the beginning of each city listing, or ask at your hotel or hostel. Laundrettes open at 7 or 8 am and close at 8 or 9 pm.

French laundrettes are not cheap. They usually charge 18FF to 20FF for a 6kg or 7kg machine and 2/5FF for five/12 minutes of drying. Some laundrettes have self-service *nettoyage à sec* (dry cleaning) for about 60FF per 6kg.

## TOILETS
Public toilets, signposted *toilettes* or *w.c.* (pronounced 'vey-sey' or 'doo-bluh vey-sey') are few and far between, though small towns often have them near the *mairie* (town hall). You're more likely to come upon one of the tan, self-disinfecting toilet pods. Get your change ready: many public toilets cost 2FF or 2.50FF.

In the absence of public amenities, you can try ducking into a fast-food outlet or a major department store. Except in the most tourist-filled areas, cafe owners are usually amenable to your using their toilets provided you ask politely (and with just a hint of urgency): *'Est-ce que je peux utiliser les toilettes, s'il vous plaît?'* Some toilets are unisex: the washbasins and urinals are in a common area through which you pass to get to the closed toilet stalls.

### Bidets
In many hotel rooms – even those without toilets or showers – you will find a bidet, a porcelain fixture that looks like a shallow toilet with a pop-up stopper in the base. Originally conceived to improve the personal hygiene of aristocratic women, its primary purpose is for washing the genitals and anal area, though its uses have expanded to include everything from hand-washing laundry to soaking your feet.

## HEALTH
Normandy is a healthy place. Your main problem is likely to be the addition of unwanted kilos from all the rich food or an upset stomach if you're not used to copious amounts of cream sauces. If you're trying to adhere to a low-fat, low-cholesterol, low-calorie or vegetarian diet, your meals will require careful planning. Otherwise, watch out for sunburn, foot blisters and dehydration if you'll be engaging in outdoor activities.

## Predeparture Planning

**Immunisations** No jabs are required to travel to France. However, it is recommended that everyone keep up-to-date with diphtheria, tetanus and polio vaccinations. You should seek medical advice at least six weeks before travel; some vaccinations should not be given during pregnancy or to people with allergies – discuss with your doctor. Jabs may be necessary to visit other European countries if you're coming from an infected area – yellow fever is the most likely requirement. If you are travelling to France with stopovers in Africa, Latin America or Asia, check with your travel agent or the embassies of the countries you plan to visit at least six weeks before you depart.

**Health Insurance** Make sure that you have adequate health insurance. See Travel Insurance under Visas & Documents in the Facts for the Visitor chapter for details.

Citizens of EU countries are covered for emergency medical treatment in France on presentation of an E111 form, though charges are likely for medications, dental work and secondary examinations, including X-rays and laboratory tests. Ask about the E111 at your national health service or travel agent at least a few weeks before you go. In the UK you can get the forms at the post office. Claims must be submitted to a local *caisse primaire d'assurance-maladie* (sickness insurance office) before you leave France.

**Other Preparations** Ensure that you're healthy before you start travelling. If you're going on a long trip make sure your teeth are OK. If you wear glasses take a spare pair and your prescription.

If you require a particular medication take an adequate supply, as it may not be available locally. Take part of the packaging showing the generic name, rather than the brand, which will make getting replacements easier. It's a good idea to have a legible prescription or letter from your doctor to show that you legally use the medication to avoid any problems.

## Medical Kit Check List

Following is a list of items you should consider including in your medical kit – consult your pharmacist for brands available in your country.

☐ **Aspirin or paracetamol (acetaminophen in the USA)** – for pain or fever

☐ **Antihistamine** – for allergies, eg hay fever; to ease the itch from insect bites or stings; and to prevent motion sickness

☐ **Cold and flu tablets, throat lozenges and nasal decongestant**

☐ **Multivitamins** – consider for long trips, when dietary vitamin intake may be inadequate

☐ **Antibiotics** – consider including these if you're travelling well off the beaten track; see your doctor, as they must be prescribed, and carry the prescription with you

☐ **Loperamide or diphenoxylate** – 'blockers' for diarrhoea

☐ **Prochlorperazine or metaclopramide** – for nausea and vomiting

☐ **Rehydration mixture** – to prevent dehydration, which may occur, for example, during bouts of diarrhoea; particularly important when travelling with children

☐ **Insect repellent, sunscreen, lip balm and eye drops**

☐ **Calamine lotion, sting relief spray or aloe vera** – to ease irritation from sunburn and insect bites or stings

☐ **Antifungal cream or powder** – for fungal skin infections and thrush

☐ **Antiseptic (such as povidone-iodine)** – for cuts and grazes

☐ **Bandages, Band-Aids (plasters) and other wound dressings**

☐ **Water purification tablets or iodine**

☐ **Scissors, tweezers and a thermometer** – note that mercury thermometers are prohibited by airlines

## Basic Rules

**Food** Take great care with shellfish such as mussels, oysters and clams, and try to avoid undercooked meat. If a place looks clean and well run then the food is probably safe. In general, places that are packed with travellers or locals will be fine, while empty restaurants are questionable. The food in busy restaurants is cooked and eaten quite quickly, with little standing around and is probably not reheated.

**Water** Tap water all over Normandy is safe to drink. However, the water in most fountains is not drinkable and – like the taps in some public toilets – may have a sign reading *eau non potable* (undrinkable water).

Always beware of natural sources of water. A burbling stream may look crystal clear, but it's inadvisable to drink untreated water unless you're at the source and can see it coming out of the rocks.

It's very easy not to drink enough liquids, especially on hot days or at high altitudes – don't rely on feeling thirsty to indicate when you should drink. Not needing to urinate or very dark-yellow urine is a danger sign. France suffers from a singular lack of drinking fountains, so it's a good idea to carry a water bottle.

The simplest way to purify water is to boil it thoroughly. Simple filtering will not remove all dangerous organisms, so if you cannot boil water it should be treated chemically. Chlorine tablets (Puritabs, Steritabs or other brand names) will kill many pathogens, but not some parasites, like amoebic cysts and giardia. Iodine is more effective in purifying water and is available in tablet form (such as Potable Aqua). Follow the directions carefully and remember that too much iodine can be harmful.

## Medical Treatment

**Public Health System** France has an extensive public health care system. Anyone (including foreigners) who is sick, even mildly so, can receive treatment in the *service des urgences* (casualty ward or emergency room) of any public hospital. Hospitals try to have people who speak English in the casualty wards, but this is not done systematically. If necessary, the hospital will call in an interpreter. It's an

excellent idea to ask for a copy of the diagnosis – in English, if possible – in case your doctor back home is interested.

Getting treated for illness or injury in a public hospital costs much less in France than in many other western countries, especially the USA: being seen by a doctor (a *consultation*) costs about 150FF (235FF to 250FF on Sunday and holidays, 275FF to 350FF from 8 pm to 8 am). Seeing a specialist is a bit more expensive. Blood tests and other procedures, each of which has a standard fee, will increase this figure. Full hospitalisation costs from 3000FF a day. Hospitals usually ask that visitors from abroad settle accounts right after receiving treatment (residents of France are sent a bill in the mail). Credit cards are acceptable.

**Pharmacies** French pharmacies are almost always marked by a green cross, the neon components of which are lit when it's open. *Pharmaciens* (pharmacists) can often suggest treatments for minor ailments.

If you are prescribed medication, make sure you understand the dosage, and how often and when you should take it. It's a good idea to ask for a copy of the *ordonnance* (prescription) for your records.

French pharmacies coordinate their days and hours of closure so that a town or district isn't left without a place to buy medication. For details on the nearest *pharmacie de garde* (pharmacy on weekend/ night duty), consult the door of any pharmacy, which will have such information posted.

## Infectious Diseases

**Diarrhoea** Simple things like a change of water, food or climate can all cause a mild bout of diarrhoea, but a few rushed toilet trips with no other symptoms is not indicative of a major problem.

Dehydration is the main danger with any diarrhoea, particularly in children or the elderly as dehydration can occur quite quickly. Under all circumstances *fluid replacement* (at least equal to the volume being lost) is the most important thing to remember. Weak black tea with a little sugar, soda water, or soft drinks allowed to go flat and diluted 50% with clean water are all good. Keep drinking small amounts often. Stick to a bland diet as you recover.

**Fungal Infections**  Fungal infections occur more commonly in hot weather and are usually found on the scalp, between the toes or fingers, in the groin and on the body (ringworm). You get ringworm (which is a fungal infection, not a worm) from infected animals or other people. Moisture encourages these infections.

To prevent fungal infections wear loose, comfortable clothes, avoid artificial fibres, wash frequently and dry carefully. If you do get an infection, wash the infected area at least daily with a disinfectant or medicated soap and water, and rinse and dry well. Apply an antifungal cream or powder like tolnifate (Tinaderm). Try to expose the infected area to air or sunlight as much as possible and wash all towels and underwear in hot water, change them often and let them dry in the sun.

**HIV & AIDS**  The human immunodeficiency virus (HIV), may develop into acquired immune deficiency syndrome (AIDS; SIDA in French), which is a fatal disease. Any exposure to blood, blood products or body fluids may put an individual at risk. The disease is often transmitted through sexual contact or dirty needles – vaccinations, acupuncture, tattooing and body piercing can be potentially as dangerous as intravenous drug use. HIV/AIDS can also be spread through infected blood transfusions; some developing countries cannot afford to screen blood used for transfusions.

If you do need an injection, ask to see the syringe unwrapped in front of you, or take a needle and syringe pack with you. Fear of HIV infection should never prevent you from seeking treatment for serious medical conditions.

For free, anonymous testing in Rouen contact Centre de Dépistage Anonyme et Gratuit (CDAG; ☎ 02 32 88 80 40), Charles Nicolle Hospital, which opens 8.30 am to 5 pm Monday to Friday and from 9.30 am to 1 pm Saturday. In Caen, contact Centre de Prophylaxie et de Depistage du SIDA (☎ 02 31 94 84 22), 3 rue des Cultures, which provides free, anonymous testing from 8.30 am to 5 pm Monday to Thursday and 8.30 am to 4 pm on Friday. There's also a 24-hour hotline ☎ 08 00 84 08 00.

**Sexually Transmitted Diseases**  Gonorrhoea, herpes and syphilis are among these diseases; sores, blisters or rashes around the genitals, discharges or pain when urinating are common symptoms. In some STDs, such as wart virus or chlamydia, symptoms may be less marked or not observed at all, especially in women. Syphilis symptoms eventually disappear completely but the disease continues and can cause severe problems in later years. While abstinence from sexual contact is the only 100% effective prevention, using condoms is also effective. The treatment of gonorrhoea and syphilis is with antibiotics. The different sexually transmitted diseases each require specific antibiotics. There is no cure for herpes or AIDS.

All pharmacies carry *préservatifs* (condoms), and many have 24-hour automatic condom dispensers outside the door. Some brasseries, discos, metro stations and WCs in petrol stations and cafes are also equipped with condom machines. Condoms that conform to French government standards are always marked with the letters NF *(norme française)* in black on a white oval inside a red-and-blue rectangle.

## Less Common Diseases
**Rabies**  This is a fatal viral infection found in many countries. Many animals can be infected and it is their saliva that is infectious. Any bite, scratch or even lick from a warm-blooded, furry animal should be cleaned immediately and thoroughly. Scrub with soap and running water, and then apply alcohol or iodine solution. If you suspect the animal is rabid, seek medical help promptly to prevent the onset of symptoms and, potentially, death.

## Women's Health
**Pregnancy**  Pregnant women should take extra care when travelling, particularly in

the first three months of pregnancy. Generally, it's best to avoid all vaccinations in those first three months as there is a theoretical risk of harm to the foetus and miscarriage. The best time to travel is during the middle three months, when the risk of complications is less, the pregnancy is relatively well established and your energy levels are getting back to normal. Seek advice from your medical practitioner before travelling.

## WOMEN TRAVELLERS
### Attitudes Towards Women
Women were given the right to vote in 1945 by De Gaulle's short-lived postwar government, but until 1964 a woman needed her husband's permission to open a bank account or get a passport. Younger French women especially are quite outspoken and emancipated, but self-confidence has yet to translate into equality in the workplace, where they're often kept out of senior and management positions. Sexual harassment in the workplace is more commonplace and tolerated here than in countries such as the USA and Australia.

### Safety Precautions
Women tend to attract more unwanted attention than men, but female travellers need not walk around Normandy in fear: people are rarely assaulted on the street. However, many French men (and some women ) still think that to stare suavely at a passing woman is to pay her a flattering compliment.

Physical attack is very unlikely but, of course, it does happen. As in any country, the best way to avoid being assaulted is to be conscious of your surroundings and aware of situations that could be potentially dangerous: deserted streets, lonely beaches, dark corners of large train stations and so on. Be careful about inviting unknown men up to your hotel room as date rape is unlikely to be taken seriously.

France's national rape-crisis hotline (☎ 08 00 05 95 95) can be reached toll-free from any telephone without using a phonecard. Staffed by volunteers from 10 am to 6 pm Monday to Friday, it's run by the women's organisation Viols Femmes Informations. In an emergency, you can always call the police (☎ 17), who will take you to the hospital.

## GAY & LESBIAN TRAVELLERS
France is one of Europe's most liberal countries when it comes to homosexuality, in part because of the long French tradition of public tolerance towards groups of people who choose not to live by conventional social codes. Predictably, attitudes towards homosexuality tend to become more conservative in the countryside and villages than in the large cities. France's lesbian scene is much less public than its gay counterpart and is centred mainly around women's cafes and bars.

France's relatively liberal attitudes make for a thriving pub and club scene in the big cities. Most of the larger towns have at least a few such bars, clubs or discos, and the regional chapters attempt to list some of the better ones; not surprisingly, few such venues exist in small towns and villages.

*Têtu* is a monthly national magazine available at newsstands everywhere (30FF). Be on the lookout for *e.m@le*, which has interviews, gossip and articles (in French) and among the best listings of gay clubs, bars and associations and personal classifieds. It is available free at gay venues or for 5FF at newsagencies.

Guidebooks listing pubs, restaurants, discos, beaches, saunas, sex shops and cruising areas include *Spartacus International Gay Guide* – a male-only guide (190FF; US$34.95) to travelling the world with some information about Normandy.

The monthly national magazine, *Lesbia* (25FF), gives a rundown of what's happening around France. *Les Nanas*, a freebie appearing every other month, is for women only. *Women's Traveller* is an English language guide (109FF/US$17.95) for lesbians published by Damron.

## Organisations
In Caen, Les Enfants Terribles (☎ 02 31 38 25 89), 16 rue Froide, has an open house

every Wednesday from 7 to 9 pm at the bar L'Excuse on rue Vauquelin and is available for advice from 7 to 9.30 pm Monday, Tuesday and Thursday at their offices. They offer dances and outdoor activities and are open to gays and lesbians.

Écoute Gaie (☎ 01 44 93 01 02) is a hotline for gays and lesbians, staffed from 6 to 10 pm on weekdays and 6 to 8 pm on Saturday. SOS Homophobie (☎ 01 48 06 42 41) accepts anonymous calls concerning discriminatory acts against gay people; it opens 8 to 10 pm on weekdays.

## DISABLED TRAVELLERS

France is not particularly well equipped for *handicapés* (disabled people): kerb ramps are few and far between, older public facilities and budget hotels often lack lifts and cobblestone streets are a nightmare to navigate in a wheelchair. But people with mobility problems who would like to visit France can overcome these problems. Most hotels with two or more stars are equipped with lifts, and Michelin's *Guide Rouge* indicates hotels with lifts and facilities for disabled people.

In recent years the SNCF has made efforts to make its trains more accessible to people with physical disabilities. A traveller in a wheelchair *(fauteuil roulant)* can travel in the wheelchair in both TGV and regular trains provided they make a reservation by phone or at a train station at least a few hours before departure. Details are available in SNCF's booklet *Guide du Voyageur à Mobilité Réduite*. You can also contact SNCF Accessibilité on toll-free ☎ 08 00 15 47 53.

General publications you might look for include:

*Holidays and Travel Abroad: A Guide for Disabled People* An annual publication (UK£5) that gives a good overview of facilities available to disabled travellers in Europe. Published in even-numbered years by the Royal Association for Disability & Rehabilitation (☎ 020-7250 3222), 12 City Forum, 250 City Rd, London EC1V 8AF.
*Gîtes Accessibles aux Personnes Handicapés* A guide (60FF) to *gîtes ruraux* and *chambres*

*d'hôtes* with disabled access. It is published by Gîtes de France (see Gîtes Ruraux & B&Bs under Accommodation later in this chapter).
*Guide du Voyageur à Mobilité Réduite* An SNCF pamphlet that details services available to train travellers in wheelchairs. One page of the guide is in English.

## SENIOR TRAVELLERS

Seniors are entitled to discounts in France on things such as public transport and museum admission fees provided they show proof of their age. In some cases they might need a special pass. See Seniors Cards under Visas & Documents earlier for details.

## TRAVEL WITH CHILDREN

Successful travel with young children requires planning and effort. Don't try to overdo things; even for adults, packing too much into the time available can cause problems. Include the kids in the trip planning; if they've helped to work out where you will be going, they will be much more interested when they get there. Lonely Planet's *Travel with Children* is a good source of information.

Most car-rental firms in France have children's safety seats for hire at a nominal cost, but it is essential that you book them in advance. The same goes for highchairs and cots (cribs); they're standard in most restaurants and hotels but numbers are limited. The choice of baby food, infant formulas, soy and cow's milk, disposable nappies (diapers) and the like is as great in French supermarkets as it is back home, but the opening hours may be quite different. Run out of nappies on Saturday afternoon and you're facing a very long and messy weekend.

## DANGERS & ANNOYANCES

In general, Normandy is a pretty safe place in which to live and travel. Though property crime – especially theft involving vehicles – is a major problem, it is extremely unlikely that you will be physically assaulted while walking down the street.

### Theft

By far the biggest crime problem in Normandy for tourists is theft *(vol)*. Most thieves are after cash or valuables, but they often end up with passports, address books, personal mementos and other items and their loss is likely to put you in a long-term bad mood. You may also have to rush off to your nearest consulate to sort out the missing documents.

The problems you're most likely to encounter are thefts from – and of – cars, pickpocketing and the snatching of daypacks or women's handbags, particularly in dense crowds (such as at busy train stations, on rush-hour public transport, in fast-food joints and in cinemas). A common ploy is for one person to distract you while another zips through your pockets. Be especially careful in the big cities in port areas.

Although there's no need whatsoever to travel in fear, a few simple precautions will minimise your chances of being ripped off.

**Before Leaving Home** Photocopy your passport, credit cards, driving licence, plane ticket and other important documents, such as your address book and travellers cheques receipts – leave one copy of each document at home and keep another one with you, separate from the originals. Some people even bring along a photocopy of their birth certificate, which is useful if you have to replace a passport.

Write your name and address on the inside of your suitcase, backpack, daypack, address book, diary and so on. If such items are lost or stolen and later recovered, the police will have at least some chance of finding you.

**Documents & Money** Always keep your money, credit cards, tickets, passport, driving licence and other important documents in a money belt worn *inside* your trousers or skirt. Never carry them around in a daypack or waist pouches, which are easy for thieves to grab (or slice off) and sprint away with. The same goes for those little pouches that you wear around your neck.

Keep enough money for a day's travel separate from your money belt (for example, in your daypack or suitcase). That way, you'll be penniless only if everything gets taken at once.

While theft from hotel rooms is pretty rare, it's a bad idea to leave cash or important documents in your room. Hostels are a fair bit riskier, since so many people are always passing through. If you don't want to carry your documents with you, ask the hotel or hostel's front desk to put them in the *coffre* (safe).

When going swimming try to leave valuables in the hotel or hostel safe. And while you're in the water, have members of your party take turns sitting with everyone's packs and clothes.

**While on the Move** Be especially careful with your passport and important documents at airports: pickpockets and professional passport thieves know that people are often careless when they first arrive in a foreign country.

When travelling by train the safest place for small bags is under your seat. Large bags are best off in the overhead rack right above your head, and you may want to fasten them to the rack with the straps or even a small lock. Bags left in the luggage racks at the ends of the carriage are an easy target: as the train is pulling out of a station, a thief can grab your pack and hop off; the author of this guide has seen it happen. In sleeping compartments, make sure to lock the door at night.

Keep an eagle eye on your bags in train stations, airports, fast-food outlets, cinemas and at the beach. Anything you can do to make your equipment easy to watch and clumsy to carry will make it more difficult to snatch. Some people lock, zip or tie their daypack to their main pack. Affixing tiny locks to the zips will help keep out sticky fingers. When sitting in a cinema or outdoor cafe, you might also wrap one strap of your daypack around your leg (or the leg of your chair).

**While Travelling by Car** Parked cars and motorbikes, as well as the contents of vehicles (especially those cars with a rental company sticker or out-of-town, red-coloured purchase-repurchase or foreign plates) are favourite targets for thieves.

*Never, ever* leave anything valuable inside

your car. Like other Europeans, many French people often carry their removable car radios with them whenever they park their vehicles. In fact, never leave anything at all in a parked car. Even a few old clothes, a handkerchief or an umbrella left lying in the backseat may attract the attention of a passing thief, who won't think twice about breaking a window or smashing a lock to see if there's a camera hidden underneath. Hiding your bags in the trunk is considered very risky; indeed, French people with hatchbacks often remove the plastic panel that covers the boot (trunk) so passing thieves can see that it's empty.

When you arrive in a new city or town, find a hotel and unload your belongings *before* doing any sightseeing that will involve leaving the car unattended. And on your last day in town, ask the hotel manager to store your luggage until after you've done any local touring, shopping or errands.

### Racism

The rise in support for the extreme right-wing National Front in recent years reflects the growing racial intolerance in France, particularly against North African Muslims and, to a lesser extent, black people from sub-Saharan Africa and France's former colonies and territories in the Caribbean. From time to time the friction erupts into violent demonstrations which are accompanied just as often by reports of police brutality.

In many parts of Normandy places of entertainment such as bars and discotheques are, for all intents and purposes, segregated: owners and their bouncers make it abundantly clear what sort of people are 'invited' to use their nominally private facilities and what sort are not. Such activities are possible in the land of *liberté*, *égalité* and *fraternité* because there is little civil rights enforcement. If you feel you've been discriminated against, contact Movement Contre le Racism (☎ 02 35 98 45 97) in Rouen.

### Hunters

The hunting season usually runs from the end of September to the end of February. If you see signs reading *chasseurs* or *chasse gardé* strung up or tacked to trees, you might want to think twice about wandering into the area, especially if you're wearing anything that might make you resemble a deer. Unless the area is totally fenced off, it's not illegal to be there, but accidents do happen (50 French hunters die each year after being shot by other hunters).

### Natural Dangers

There are strong undertows and currents along the Atlantic coast, particularly in Cap de la Hague. Thunderstorms can be sudden, violent and dangerous. It's a good idea to check the weather report before you set out on a long hike.

### EMERGENCY

The following toll-free numbers can be dialled from any public phone in France without inserting a phonecard or coins:

| | |
|---|---|
| SAMU (medical treatment/ ambulance) | ☎ 15 |
| Police | ☎ 17 |
| Fire | ☎ 18 |
| Rape crisis hotline | ☎ 08 00 05 95 95 |

### SAMU

When you ring ☎ 15, the 24-hour dispatchers of the Service d'Aide Médicale d'Urgence (Emergency Medical Aid Service) will take down details of your problem (there's a duty person who speaks English) and then send out a private ambulance with a driver (250FF to 300FF) or, if necessary, a mobile intensive care unit.

For less serious problems, SAMU can also dispatch a doctor for a house call. If you prefer to be taken to a particular hospital, mention this to the ambulance crew, as the usual procedure is to take you to the nearest one. In emergency cases (those requiring intensive care units), billing will be taken care of later. Otherwise, you need to pay in cash at the time you receive assistance.

### Highway Emergencies

There are *postes d'appel d'urgence* (emergency phones), mounted on bright orange posts, about every 4km along the main highways and every 1.5km to 2km on the autoroutes.

## LEGAL MATTERS
### Police

Thanks to the Napoleonic Code (on which the French legal system is based), the police can pretty much search anyone they want to at any time – whether or not there is probable cause. They have been known to stop and search chartered coaches for drugs just because they are coming from Amsterdam.

If asked a question, cops are likely to be correct and helpful, but no more than that (though you may get a salute). If the police stop you for any reason, be polite and remain calm. They have wide powers of search and seizure and, if they take a dislike to you, they may choose to use them. The police can, without any particular reason, decide to examine your passport, visa, carte de séjour and so on.

French police are very strict about security, especially at airports. Do not leave baggage unattended: they're serious when they warn that suspicious objects will be blown up.

### Drinking & Driving

As elsewhere in the EU, the laws are very tough when it comes to drinking and driving, and for many years the slogan has been: *'Boire ou conduire, il faut choisir.'* (To drink or to drive, you have to choose.) The acceptable blood-alcohol limit is 0.05%, and drivers exceeding this amount face fines of up to 30,000FF plus up to two years in jail. Licences can be suspended immediately.

### Drugs

Importing or exporting drugs can lead to a 10- to 30-year jail sentence. The fine for possession of drugs for personal use can be as high as 500,000FF.

## BUSINESS HOURS

Most museums are closed on either Sunday or Monday and almost invariably close for a midday break. Many are closed or operate with greatly reduced hours from November through to March.

Small businesses are open daily, except Saturday afternoon, Sunday and often Monday. Hours are usually 9 or 10 am to 6.30 or 7 pm, with a midday break from noon or 1 pm to 2 or 3 pm.

Banks usually open 8 or 9 am to sometime between 11.30 and 1 pm, and 1.30 or 2 to 4.30 or 5 pm, Monday to Friday or Tuesday to Saturday. Exchange services may end half an hour before closing time.

Post offices generally open 8.30 or 9 am to 5 or 6 pm on weekdays, usually with a two-hour break at midday, and Saturday mornings.

Supermarkets and hypermarkets open Monday to Saturday; a few open on Sunday morning in July and August. Small food shops are mostly closed on Saturday afternoon, Sunday and Monday, so Saturday morning may be your last chance to stock up on provisions until Tuesday, unless you come across a supermarket. Most restaurants are closed on Sunday.

Since you can never tell which day of the week a certain merchant or restaurateur has chosen to take off, this book includes, where possible (summer times can be particularly unpredictable), details on weekly closures.

In July and August, loads of businesses tend to shut down: the owners and employees heading for the hills or the beaches for their annual vacation. Small family-run hotels may also close for a week or two in July and August and some close on Sunday night.

## PUBLIC HOLIDAYS & SPECIAL EVENTS

The following *jours fériés* (public holidays) are observed in France:

**New Year's Day** *(Jour de l'An)* 1 January – parties in larger cities, fireworks tend to be subdued by international standards
**Easter Sunday and Monday** *(Pâques & lundi de Pâques)* Late March/April
**May Day** *(Fête du Travail)* 1 May – traditional parades
**Victoire 1945** 8 May – celebrates the Allied victory in Europe that ended WWII

**Ascension Thursday** *(L'Ascension)* May – celebrated on the 40th day after Easter
**Pentecost/Whit Sunday and Whit Monday** *(Pentecôte & lundi de Pentecôte)* Mid-May to mid-June – celebrated on the 7th Sunday after Easter
**Bastille Day/National Day** *(Fête Nationale)* 14 July – *the* national holiday
**Assumption Day** *(L'Assomption)* 15 August
**All Saints' Day** *(La Toussaint)* 1 November
**Remembrance Day** *(Le onze Novembre)* 11 November – celebrates the WWI armistice
**Christmas** *(Noël)* 25 December

The following are *not* public holidays in France: Shrove Tuesday (Mardi Gras; the first day of Lent); Maundy (or Holy) Thursday *(jeudi saint)* and Good Friday *(vendredi saint)* just before Easter; and Boxing Day (26 December).

Most museums and shops (but not cinemas, restaurants or most bakeries) are closed on public holidays. When a holiday falls on a Tuesday or a Thursday, the French have a custom of making a *pont* (bridge) to the nearest weekend by taking off Monday or Friday as well. The doors of banks are a good place to look for announcements of upcoming long weekends.

France's national day, 14 July, commemorates the day in 1789 when defiant Parisians stormed the Bastille prison, beginning the French Revolution. Often called Bastille Day by English speakers, it is celebrated with great gusto and usually ends with a fireworks display.

On May Day, many people – including those marching in the traditional trade union parades – buy *muguets* (lilies of the valley), said to bring good luck, to give to friends.

Most Normandy cities have at least one major music, dance, theatre, cinema or art festival each year. Some villages hold *foires* (fairs) and *fêtes* (festivals) to honour anything from a local saint to the year's garlic crop, kites to blood sausage. In this book, important annual events are listed under Special Events in many city and town listings; for precise details about dates, which change from year to year, contact the local tourist office. Remember that the largest festivals can make it very difficult to find accommodation, so make reservations as far in advance as possible.

## Film Festivals

The most prestigious film event in the region is the annual Festival of American Film in Deauville. Begun in 1975, the festival presents some 30 American films each year for 10 days at the beginning of September and attracts an audience of international stars and cinemaphiles. The most recent festival attracted Samuel L Jackson, Tommy Lee Jones, Harrison Ford, Susan Sarandon and Clint Eastwood. Although the festival has long emphasised the first French release of American blockbusters, in 1995 the organisers added a special competitive section open to small, independent films.

As of 1998, Deauville has begun to host a yearly Festival of Asian Cinema at the beginning of March. Rouen began a Festival of Nordic Cinema in 1987 that introduced Gabriel Axel's *Babette's Feast* to the world. It has continued to seek out little-known Scandinavian directors. Cherbourg hosts a British Film Festival in the second week of October that introduces popular British films to France.

## ACTIVITIES

Normandy's varied geography makes it a superb place for a wide range of outdoor pursuits even though little of Normandy consists of pristine wilderness. Even the remotest regions are dotted with villages and crisscrossed by roads, power lines and hydroelectric projects. On the other hand, to many travellers coming from built-up Britain (which supports roughly the same population) or other parts of continental Europe, parts of France will look almost empty. The Comité Régional de Tourisme de Normandie publishes several free brochures on Normandy activities (some in English) including *Randonées* (in French) with many walking, horse-riding and cycling routes.

## Cycling

The French take their cycling very seriously, and whole parts of the country almost grind to a halt during the annual Tour de France.

## Special Outdoor Events

From April to October, Normandy's tourist offices and outdoor activity associations sponsor weekend get-togethers for cycling, walking, horse riding and boat enthusiasts. Participation is usually free but sometimes there is a fee of 40FF to 50FF. It's a great way to discover Normandy's parks and countryside along with the locals or weekending Parisians. Following are some of the more popular yearly events that take place on either Saturday, Sunday or the entire weekend:

### April to October
**Country walks around Giverny** (☎ 02 32 51 29 36) Held one weekend a month to discover local flora; 40FF fee includes cider tasting.

### April
**The Côte Fleurie** (☎ 02 31 93 91 73, ☎ 02 31 43 14 37) 20km to 50km walking or cycling between Caen and Villers-sur-Mer.
**9th Annual Trans-Andaine** (☎ 02 33 30 72 70, ☎ 02 33 37 85 66) 15km to 45km along mountain bike routes in the Andaine forest near Bagnoles de l'Orne.
**Normandy Walks** (☎ 02 32 67 25 23) Guided walks through Avre and the Iton Valley.

### May
**Vire Valley Mountain Biking** (☎ 02 33 55 65 31) Circuits from 20km to 120km.
**Fécamp's Annual Nature Day** (☎ 02 35 28 51 01) Walking, horse riding, cycling, sailing and sea kayaking in and around Fécamp.
**Yéres Valley Outdoors Festival** (☎ 02 35 86 25 65) Between Le Tréport and Eu on foot, on horseback, by bike or canoe.

### June
**Mont St-Michel Bay** (☎ 02 33 89 64 00) A weekend of events and activities including walking and cycling.
**King Richard's Ride** (☎ 02 32 44 86 31) A weekend crossing the Pays d'Ouche on horseback.
**Perche Ornais** (☎ 02 33 83 22 9) Organised walks in the Perche Ornais.
**Normandie-Maine Regional Nature Park** (☎ 02 33 81 75 75) A weekend of walking, horse riding and cycling.
**Outdoors in the Pays d'Auge** (☎ 02 31 61 12 35) Walking, horse riding and cycling around Orbec.
**Regional Nature Park of the Cotentin and Bessin Marshes** (☎ 02 33 71 61 90) A day of walking, cycling, horse riding and boating.

### September
**Brotonne Regional Nature Park** (☎ 02 35 37 23 16) Tours of the park on foot, bike, horseback or horse and carriage.
**The Licorne Race** (☎ 02 33 29 19 92) 100km in 24 hours from Ouistreham to Argentan.

### October
**Equidays Trekking in St-Pierre-sur-Dives** (☎ 02 31 85 52 72) Equestrian activities including racing and carriage driving.

A *vélo tout-terrain* (VTT; mountain bike) is a fantastic tool for exploring the countryside. Some GR and GRP trails (see the Walking section later in this chapter) are open to mountain bikes, but take care not to startle hikers. A *piste cyclable* is a bicycle path.

Mountain bike enthusiasts who can read French should look for *La France a Velo: Normandie* part of *Guide Franck Cyclotourisme* published by Franck Mercier Editions. The loose-leaf folder proposes 90 circuits, with estimated time and distance, and coordinates with the Michelin 231 and IGN 3 maps.

*euro currency converter  €1 = 6.56FF*

There are a wealth of cycling possibilities. Some of the most popular include the hilly Suisse Normande, the flat country around Falaise, the apple country of the Pays d'Auge, Mont St-Michel bay, the Côte d'Albâtre and the Seine Valley.

For information on road rules, cycling organisations, transporting your bicycle and bike rental, see Bicycle in the Getting Around chapter. Details on places that rent out bikes appear at the end of each city or town listing under Getting Around.

## Walking

France is crisscrossed by a staggering 120,000km of *sentiers balisés* (marked walking paths), which pass through every imaginable kind of terrain in every region of the country. No permits are needed for walking, but there are restrictions on where you can camp.

Probably the best known trails are the *sentiers de grande randonnée*, long-distance footpaths whose alphanumeric names begin with the letters GR and whose track indicators *(jalonnement* or *balisage)* consist of red and white stripes on trees, rocks, walls and posts. The principal *grande randonnées* in Normandy are the GR2 that runs along the northern bank of the Seine; the GR21 from Le Havre to Étretat, the GR22 from Paris to Mont St-Michel, the GR23 that runs along the southern bank of the Seine through the Forêt de Brotonne, the GR211 running from Caudebec-en-Caux to Fécamp, the GR222 that crosses Calvados to Deauville, the GR225 that passes through the Forêt de Lyons, Pays de Bray and ends near Dieppe.

The *grandes randonnées de pays* (GRP) trails, whose markings are yellow and red, usually go in some sort of loop. These 'country walks' are designed for intense exploration of one particular area and usually take from a few days to a week, though some are longer.

Other types of trails include *sentiers de promenade randonnée* (PR), walking paths whose trail markings are yellow; *drailles*, paths used by cattle to get to high-altitude summer pastures; and *chemins de halage*, towpaths built in the days when canal barges were pulled by animals walking along the shore. Shorter day-hike trails are often known as *sentiers de petites randonnées* or *sentiers de pays*; many of them are circular so that you end up where you started.

The Fédération Française de la Randonnée Pédestre (FFRP; French Ramblers' Association) has an information centre and bookshop in Paris at 14 rue Riquet, 14e (☎ 01 44 89 93 93, fax 01 40 35 85 67, Minitel 3615 RANDO, metro Pernety), which opens 10 am to 6 pm Monday to Saturday.

The FFRP publishes some 120 topoguides (77F to 99FF), map-equipped booklets on GR, GRP and PR trails. Local tourist offices also produce topoguides (15FF to 30FF) some of them in the form of a *pochette* (a folder filled with single-sheet itineraries). The information that topoguides provide – in French, of course – includes details on trail conditions, flora, fauna, villages en route, camping grounds, mountain shelters and so on. Each departmental tourist office publishes a free pamphlet *Randonnées* or *Guide des Randonnées* with maps and suggested routes.

The UK publisher Robertson McCarta has translated quite a few topoguides into English, including one on Normandy that's issued in book form as part of the Footpaths of Europe series. It's cheaper and easier to find in the UK than in France.

Hotel treks are unguided walks in which a trekking company arranges for accommodation, hearty dinners and transport for your pack so you can hike unencumbered from village to village. Headwater Holidays (☎ 01606-813 333), a company based in Cheshire (UK) that arranges such treks, is represented in Australia by Peregrine (☎ 03-9663 8611).

The Club Alpin Français (☎ 02 31 86 29 55), 92 rue de Geôle, 14000 Caen, generally provides services (such as courses and group walks) to members only, though the shelters it maintains are open to everyone. Membership costs 486FF per year (285FF for people aged 18 to 24) and includes various kinds of insurance. Its Web site is at www.clubalpin-idf.com.

For details on *refuges* (mountain shelters)

and other overnight accommodation for hikers, such as *gîtes d'étape*, see the Accommodation section later in this chapter.

## Mountaineering & Rock Climbing

If you're interested in *alpinisme* (mountaineering) or *escalade* (rock climbing), you can arrange climbs with professional guides through the Club Alpin Français (see the Walking section earlier in this chapter). The area around Clécy in the Suisse Normande is the most popular spot in Normandy for rock climbing.

## Swimming

Normandy has lovely beaches along all of the coast from the pebbly beaches of the Côte d'Albâtre to the sandy beaches along the Côte Fleurie. The water is cold most of the year but temperate in July and August when the beaches are at their most crowded. The public is free to use any beach not marked as private in France. Swimming conditions are rated by coloured flags: green for safe swimming on a beach with a lifeguard; orange for cautious swimming on a lifeguarded beach; red when swimming is forbidden; violet for polluted waters.

Topless bathing for women is pretty much the norm in France – if other people are doing it, you can assume it's OK.

## Kayaking & Canoeing

Canoeing and kayaking are practised on many Normandy rivers, but the rivers of the Suisse Normande are particularly fast-moving and popular with enthusiasts. There are centres at Condé-sur-Vire and Thury-Harcourt. On the coast, there are rentals at Yvetôt, Dieppe, Fécamp and Le Havre. The Fédération Française de Canoë-Kayak (FFCK; ☎ 01 45 11 08 50; fax 01 48 86 13 25), 87 quai de la Marne, 94340 Joinville-le-Pont, is a good general source of information. In Normandy, there's the Comité Départmental de Canoë-Kayak Calvados, State Nautique, avenue Albert-Sorel, 14016 Caen, and the Comité Départmental de Canoë-Kayak de la Manche, 4 rue Charles-Péguy, 50100 Cherbourg.

## Sailing

Normandy's long coastline offers a host of opportunities for sailboating including courses and rentals. Overall advice is available from Fédération Française de Voile (☎ 01 44 05 81 00, fax 01 47 04 90 12), 55 avenue Kléber, 75784 Paris Cedex 16. In Normandy you can rent sailboats at: Albâtre Plaisance (☎ 02 35 28 94 58) 2 rue du Commandant Riondel 76400 Fécamp; M. Prenveille (☎ 02 35 28 99 53) 15 rue de la Vicomté, 76400 Fécamp; Normandie Yachting (☎ 02 32 74 90 00) 10 rue Maréchal de Lattre de Tassigny, 76600 Le Havre; Loisirs Yachting (☎ 02 35 50 16 70) 4 avenue des Canadiens, 76470 Le Tréport; and École de Voile de Cherbourg (☎ 02 33 94 99 00) Centre Albert Livory, 50100 Cherbourg.

## Fishing

With 14,500km of waterways and a 600km coast, fishing is an important activity in Normandy. Some of the best fresh water fishing is found in the Risle, Iton, Charentonne, l'Huisne, Touques, Bresle and Arques rivers where you'll find abundant trout and carp. The best sea fishing is around Dieppe which is rich in mackerel, bass and pollack. Fishing requires not only the purchase of a licence but a familiarity with conservation rules that differ from department to department and even from river to river. Dates when fishing is permitted are strictly controlled and, during part of the year, may be limited to only certain days of the week. There are rules about the types of lures and hooks you can use, the minimum legal size for each species (that, too, can vary from stream to stream) and the number of fish you can catch in the course of a day.

Each department has a fishing organisation that publishes brochures (in French) with the best sites and local regulations:

**Fédération Départementale des APP de Seine-Maritime** (☎ 02 35 07 57 28) 10 rue d'Harcourt, 76000 Rouen
**Fédération Départementale des AAPPMA de l'Eure** (☎ 02 32 57 10 73) BP 411, 27504 Pont-Audemer Cedex
**Fédération du Calvados pour la Pêche** (☎ 02 33 46 96 50) 18 rue de la Girafe, 14000 Caen

**Fédération de la Manche pour la Pêche** (☎ 02 33 46 96 50) 16 rue du Pont l'Abbé, BP 89, 50189, Périers

**Fédération de l'Orne pour la Pêche** (☎ 02 33 26 10 66) 59 rue Julien, BP 91, 61103 Alençon Cedex

## Horse Riding

Normandy is horse country and *équitation* (horse riding) is hugely popular, especially in Lower Normandy. Count on spending about 80FF an hour, 300FF to 350FF a day and 200FF to 400FF for a day of lessons. It's also possible to stay in a horse farm which runs from 500FF to 1200FF a weekend including meals and riding. Virtually every destination in this book has a horse-riding centre in close proximity offering lessons and hacks through the countryside. Some of the loveliest rides are through the Forêt d'Eawy, Forêt de Brotonne, the Mont St-Michel bay, the Normandy Maine Regional Park and the Forêt de Lyons. The departmental tourist offices listed earlier in the chapter or local tourist offices have ample documentation on horse-riding centres, or contact the Ligue de Normandie des Sports Équestres (☎ 02 31 84 61 87), 10 place de la Demi-Lune BP 2018, 74089 Caen.

## Hang-Gliding, Parachuting & Parapente

*Deltaplane* (hang-gliding) and *parapente* (paragliding) are practised throughout Normandy. Paragliding involves running off the top of a mountain dragging a rectangular parachute behind you until it opens. The chute then fills with air and, acting like an aircraft wing, lifts you up off the ground. If the thermals are good you can stay up for hours, circling the area peacefully.

Newcomers can try out parapente with a *baptême de l'air* (tandem introductory flight) for 250FF to 500FF. A five-day *stage d'initiation* (beginners course) costs from 2000FF to 3500FF. Some of the main centres are Optivol (☎ 02 35 42 67 90), 9 rue du Perrey, 76600 Le Havre, for paragliding, the Aéro-Club de Dieppe (☎ 02 35 84 86 55) for parachuting, and Club Eur'Enciel (☎ 02 32 33 64 87), 1 avenue A Briand 27003 Évreux, for hang-gliding.

## Spas & Thalassotherapy

For over a century, the French have been keen fans of *thermalisme* (water cures), for which visitors with ailments ranging from rheumatism to serious internal disorders flock to hot spring resorts. The most popular thermalist centre in Normandy is at Bagnoles de l'Orne (☎ 02 33 30 38 00), rue Prof Louvel 61140, which offers daily, weekly and monthly packages. There's a water-cure centre at Forges-les-Eaux run by Club Med (☎ 02 32 89 50 44), which offers weekly and monthly packages.

A salty variant of thermalisme is *thalassothérapie* (sea-water therapy). Centres dot the coast. Try the Cures Marines de Trouville (☎ 02 31 87 72 00) promenade des Planches, 14360 Trouville; Thalasso-Deauville (☎ 02 31 87 72 00) 3 rue Sem, 14800 Deauville; and Prévithal Institut de Thalassothérapie (☎ 02 33 90 31 10) 3 rue Jules-Michelet, BP 618, 50406, Granville Cedex.

## COURSES
## Language

Learning the language is a great way to experience Normandy. French courses are not abundant but you can contact the following centres in Caen, Rouen or Lisieux:

**Alliance Française** (☎ 02 35 98 55 99, fax 02 35 89 98 58, ⓔ alliance.francaise.rouen@wanadoo.fr) 79 quai du Havre, 76000 Rouen. Courses are available all year and last 15 or 20 hours a week. Beginners start in January, July and October and accommodation is possible with private residences or rental of studios or rooms. The fees are 555FF for a 15-hour week, 700FF for 20 hours a week and 2000/2600FF a month. Less than 15 hours a week, the cost is 50FF per hour and there's a registration fee of 200FF.

**Centre d'Enseignement Universitaire International pour Étrangers, Université de Caen** (☎ 02 31 56 55 38, fax 02 31 56 66 40) BP 5186, 14032 Caen. Courses run from mid-June to the end of August and include all levels. Accommodation can be arranged in the university dormitory, in private residences or in hotels.

**Centre d'Études de Lisieux** (☎ 02 31 31 22 01, fax 02 31 31 22 21, ⓔ centre.normandie@wanadoo.fr) 14 boulevard Carnot BP 176, 14404 Lisieux. Courses are available spring through autumn and accommodation can be in private residences or a dormitory.

INLINGUA (☎ 02 35 69 81 61, fax 02 35 69 81 59, ℮ rouen@inlingua.fr) 75144 Le Petit Quevilly. Courses from March to October are either individual or in small groups and can focus on a cultural theme such as cooking. Accommodation can be arranged within private residences or in a hotel.

## Cooking

Private cooking lessons are available in several hotels and restaurants around Normandy including: Hôtel-Restaurant L'Auberge du Val au Cesne (☎ 02 35 56 63 06, fax 02 35 56 92 78) 76190 Yvetôt; Hôtel-Restaurant Le Donjon (☎ 02 35 27 08 23, fax 02 35 29 92 24, ℮ ledonjon@wanadoo.fr) Chemin de St-Clair, 76790 Étretat; Hôtel-Restaurant Le Manoir du Lys (☎ 02 33 37 80 69, fax 02 33 30 05 80) Route de Juvigny 61140 Bagnoles de l'Orne.

## Lace-making

La Maison de la Dentelle et du Point d'Argentan (☎ 02 33 67 40 56, fax 02 33 67 34 47, ℮ dentelles.argentan@wanadoo.fr), 34 rue de la Noë, offers courses in lace-making and embroidery. They cost 20/240/1300FF an hour/day/week with an additional 100FF registration fee.

## WORK

With an unemployment rate of nearly 10% and laws that forbid non-EU nationals from working in France, working 'in the black' (that is, without documents) is difficult. People without documents probably have their best chance of finding work as an au pair, which can be done by non-EU citizens. Another option is to look for work as a courier for one of the package tour companies bringing Brits to Normandy for a short holiday. The October apple harvest in Normandy is another possibility, but EU workers are preferred.

The national minimum wage for nonprofessionals (SMIC, or *salaire minimum interprofessionel de croissance*) is 40.72FF an hour. However, employers willing to hire people in contravention of France's employment laws are also likely to ignore the minimum wage law. For practical information on employment in France, you might want to pick up *Working in France* by Carol Pineau and Maureen Kelly.

## Residence Permits

To work legally in France you must have a residence permit known as a carte de séjour. Getting one is almost automatic for EU nationals and almost impossible for anyone else except full-time students (see the Visas & Documents section earlier in this chapter).

Non-EU nationals cannot work legally unless they obtain a work permit *(autorisation de travail)* before arriving in France. Obtaining a work permit is no easy matter, because a prospective employer has to convince the authorities that there is no French – and, increasingly these days, no EU – citizen who can do the job being offered to you.

## Employment Agencies

The CRIJ, which provides all sorts of information for young people on housing, professional training and educational options, have noticeboards with work possibilities and work with the Agence National pour l'Emploi (ANPE), France's national employment service. See Rouen in the Seine-Maritime chapter and Caen in the Calvados chapter for CRIJ contact information.

## Au Pair

Under the au pair system, single young people (aged 18 to about 27) who are studying in France, live with a French family and receive lodging, full board and a bit of pocket money in exchange for taking care of the kids, babysitting, doing light housework and perhaps teaching English to the children. Most families prefer young women, but a few positions are also available for young men. Many families want au pairs who are native English speakers, but knowing some French may be a prerequisite.

For practical information, pick up *The Au Pair and Nanny's Guide to Working Abroad* by Susan Griffith and Sharon Legg.

In general, the family provides room and board and gives the au pair 400FF to 500FF a week of pocket money in exchange for up to 30 hours of work and two or three evenings of babysitting each week. By law, au pairs must have one full day off a week (usually Sunday).

Non-EU nationals have to contact the placement agency from their home country at least three months in advance, but residents of the EU can apply after arriving in France. Contact the CRIJ centres in Caen or Rouen for information about organisations arranging au pair work.

## ACCOMMODATION

Normandy has accommodation of every sort and for every budget. For further details – and, in many cases, help with reservations – contact the nearest tourist office.

Local authorities impose a *taxe de séjour* (tourist tax) on each visitor in their jurisdiction. The prices charged at camping grounds, hotels and so on may therefore be as much as 1FF to 7FF per person higher than the posted rates.

### Reservations

Advance reservations save you the hassle of looking for a place to stay each time you pull into a new town. During periods of heavy domestic or foreign tourism (for example, around Easter and Christmas–New Year, during the February–March school holiday and in July and August), having a reservation can mean the difference between finding a room in your price range and moving on.

Some tourist offices will help travellers make local hotel reservations, usually for a small fee (2FF to 10FF). In some cases, you pay a deposit that is later deducted from the first night's bill. The staff may also have information on vacancies, but they will usually refuse to make specific recommendations. You cannot take advantage of reservation services by phone – you have to stop by the office.

Many hotels, particularly budget ones, accept reservations only if they are accompanied by *des arrhes* (pronounced 'dez **ar**'; a deposit) in French francs. Some places, especially those with two or more stars, don't ask for a deposit if you give them your credit card number or send them a confirmation of your plans by letter or fax in clear, simple English.

Even during the peak season, most hotels keep a few rooms unreserved, so that at least some of the people who happen by looking for a place can be accommodated. As a result, a hotel that was all booked up three days earlier may have space if you ring on the morning of your arrival.

Most places will hold a room only until a set hour, rarely later than 6 or 7 pm (and sometimes earlier). If you're running late, let them know or they're liable to rent out the room to someone else.

### Camping

Camping, either in tents or in caravans, is immensely popular in Normandy. As a result there are hundreds of camping grounds, many of them near streams, rivers, lakes or the ocean. Most them close from November to March and some are only open in summer. Hostels sometimes let travellers pitch tents in the back garden.

Rates are generally the same for tents and camping cars, except that the latter are charged an extra fee for electricity. Some places have *forfaits* (fixed-price deals) for two or three people. Children up to about age 12 enjoy significant discounts. Few camping grounds are near major sights, so campers without their own wheels may spend a fair bit of money (and time) commuting.

*Camping à la ferme* (camping on the farm) is coordinated by Gîtes de France (see the Gîtes Ruraux & B&Bs section later in this chapter), publisher of the annual guide *Camping à la Ferme* (75FF). The sites – of which there are more than 1100 all over the country – are generally accessible only if you have a car or bicycle.

For details on camping grounds not mentioned in the text, enquire at a local tourist office. If you'll be doing lots of car camping, pick up a copy of Michelin's *Camping-Caravanning France* (83FF), which lists 3500 camping grounds.

In July and especially August, when most camping grounds are completely packed, campers who arrive late in the day have a much better chance of getting a spot if they arrive on foot (that is, without a vehicle). Camping ground offices are often closed for most of the day – the best times to call for reservations are in the morning (before 10 or 11 am) and in the late afternoon or early evening.

**Freelance Camping** If you'll be doing overnight backpacking, remember that camping is generally permitted only at designated camp sites. Pitching your tent anywhere else (for example, in a road or trailside meadow), known as *camping sauvage* in French, is usually illegal, though it's often tolerated to varying degrees. You probably won't have any problems if you're not on private land and are at least 1500m from a camping ground.

If you camp out on the beach, you'll be an easy target for thieves, so be careful where you put your valuables when sleeping. In areas with especially high tidal variations sleeping on the beach is not a good idea.

## Hostels & Foyers

Official hostels that belong to one of the three hostel associations in France are known as *auberges de jeunesse* and are so indicated in this book. In university towns, you may also find *foyers* (pronounced 'fwayei') student dormitories converted for use by travellers during the summer school holidays. In certain cities and towns, young workers are accommodated in dormitories called either *foyers de jeunes travailleurs* or *travailleuses*, and despite the names, most are now mixed sex. These places, which often take *passagères* and *passagers* (female and male short-term guests) when they have space, are relatively unknown to most travellers and very frequently have space available when the other kinds of hostels are full. Information on hostels and foyers not mentioned in the text is available from local tourist offices.

Expect to pay 60FF to 100FF a night for a hostel bed, including breakfast.

**Hostel Organisations** Most of France's hostels belong to one of three major hostel associations:

**Fédération Unie des Auberges de Jeunesse** (FUAJ; ☎ 01 44 89 87 27, fax 01 44 89 87 10, Minitel 3615 FUAJ, metro La Chapelle) 27 rue Pajol, 75018 Paris
Web site: www.fuaj.org
**Ligue Française pour les Auberges de la Jeunesse** (LFAJ; ☎ 01 44 16 78 78, fax 01 44 16 78 80, metro Glacière) 67 rue Vergniaud, 75013 Paris
**Union des Centres de Rencontres Internationales de France** (UCRIF; ☎ 01 40 26 57 64, fax 01 40 26 58 20, Minitel 3615 UCRIF, ☎ ucrif@aol.com, metro Les Halles or Étienne Marcel) 27 rue de Turbigo, 75002 Paris

FUAJ and LFAJ affiliates will require HI or similar cards, available at any hostel for about 100FF (70FF if you're aged under 26). They also require that you either bring a sleeping sheet or rent one for 13FF to 17FF per stay.

## Gîtes d'Étape

*Gîtes d'étape*, is a comfortable form of accommodation geared to hikers and cyclists passing through the region. They cost around 60FF or 70FF per person and are listed in *Gîtes d'Étape et de Séjour*, published annually by Gîtes de France (70FF).

## Gîtes Ruraux & B&Bs

Several types of accommodation – often in charming, traditional-style houses with gardens – are available for people who would like to spend time in rural areas and have a vehicle. All are represented by Gîtes de France, an organisation that acts as a liaison between owners and renters.

A *gîte rural* is a holiday cottage (or part of a house) in a village or on a farm. Amenities always include a kitchenette and bathroom facilities.

A gîte rural owned by a *commune* (the smallest unit of local government) is known as a *gîte communal*. In most cases there is a minimum rental period of a week, and sometimes you must supply your own linen.

A *chambre d'hôte*, basically a B&B (bed and breakfast), is a room in a private house rented to travellers by the night. Breakfast is included. It's a much more intimate experience than staying in a hotel but usually more expensive. Prices run from 200FF to

250FF a night and most homes are outside town, making a car essential.

Details on how to contact the nearest Gîtes de France office are available at any local or departmental tourist office, which can usually supply a brochure listing gîtes and chambres d'hôtes.

You can also contact the Fédération Nationale des Gîtes de France (☎ 01 49 70 75 75, fax 01 42 81 28 53, Minitel 3615 GITES DE FRANCE, ⒠ information@gites-de-france.fr, metro Trinité) at 59 rue St-Lazare, 75009 Paris. It also publishes *Chambres et Tables d'Hôtes* (120FF) and *Nouveaux Gîtes Ruraux* (120FF).

## Hotels

Most French hotels have between one and four stars; the fanciest places have four stars plus an L (for 'luxury'). A hotel that has no stars (that has not been rated) is known as *non-homologué*, sometimes abbreviated as NH. The letters 'NN' after the rating mean that the establishment conforms to the *nouvelle norme* (new standards), introduced in 1992. Hotel ratings are based on certain objective criteria (such as the size of the entry hall), not the quality of the service, the decor or cleanliness, so a one-star establishment may be more pleasant than some two or three-star places. Prices often reflect these intangibles far more than they do the number of stars.

Most hotels offer a continental breakfast consisting of a croissant, French rolls, butter, jam and either coffee or hot chocolate. The charge is usually 20FF to 40FF per person, a bit more than you would pay at a cafe. Some places in tourist-heavy areas require guests to take breakfast, especially during the summer.

**Budget Hotels** In general, hotels listed under 'budget' have doubles that cost less than two hostel beds, that is, up to 180FF. Most are equipped with a washbasin (and, usually, a bidet) but lack private bath or toilet. Almost all these places also have more expensive rooms equipped with a shower, toilet and other amenities.

Most doubles, which generally cost only marginally more than singles, have only one double bed, though some places have rooms with two twin beds *(deux lits séparés)*; triples and quads usually have two or three beds. Taking a shower in the hall bathroom is sometimes free but is usually *payant*, which means there's a charge of 10FF to 25FF per person.

Some cheap hotels have the unpleasant habit of refusing to refund the unused part of your deposit when you switch hotels or leave town earlier than planned. The moral of the story is not to prepay for those nights where there's a chance you won't be staying. In any case, the sooner you tell the manager, the better your chances of being reimbursed.

If you're travelling by car, you'll be able to take advantage of the remarkably cheap hotel chains on the outskirts of France's cities and towns, usually on a main access route. The best known, Formule 1, charges from 120FF to 150FF for a clean but bland room for up to three people; toilets and showers are in the hall but there's a washbasin in the room. Until 7 pm, there's no penalty to cancel a reservation prepaid by credit card. You can reserve on www .hotelformule1.com or ☎ 08 36 68 56 85 (2.23FF a minute). Etap Hôtel is one step up, offering rooms with private facilities for 180FF to 220FF. Reserve on their Web site (www.etaphotel.com) or call ☎ 08 36 68 89 00 (2.23FF a minute).

**Mid-Range Hotels** Hotels with double rooms listed under 'mid-range' in this book come with showers and toilets (unless otherwise noted) and usually have doubles costing 170FF to about 350FF. Many places listed under 'budget' have rooms that, from the point of view of amenities and price, fall in the mid-range category.

Some hotels – many of them family-run places in the countryside, by the sea or in the mountains – belong to Logis de France, an organisation whose affiliated establishments meet strict standards of service and amenities. They generally offer very good value. The Fédération Nationale des Logis de France (☎ 01 45 84 70 00, fax 01 45 83 59 66, Minitel 3615 LOGIS DE FRANCE,

*euro currency converter  10FF = €1.52*

e info@logis-de-france.fr, metro Tolbiac), based at 83 avenue d'Italie, 75013 Paris, issues an annual guide with a detailed map of how to find each hotel.

**Top End Hotels** Staying in an 18th- or 19th-century manor surrounded by gardens can be a delightful accommodation option. The inheritors of Normandy's spacious chateaux often found that it made sense to turn their properties into inns for well-heeled guests. The rambling old houses are renovated and crammed with antiques and family memorabilia. Since the chateaux are family-owned, the service is usually warm and personal. You'll need your own car, however, since the inns are usually out in the country and rooms aren't cheap. Count on paying from 350FF to 1000FF a night for a double. Details are available at the Normandy tourist office Web site (www .normandy-tourism.org) or you can send for their free brochure *Bienvenue au Châteaux*.

## Homestays

Under an arrangement known as *hôtes payants* (literally, 'paying guests') or *hébergement chez l'habitant* (lodging with the owners or occupants of private homes), students, young people and tourists can stay with French families. In general you rent a room and have access (sometimes limited) to the family's kitchen and telephone. Many language schools (see the Courses section earlier in the chapter) arrange homestays for their students.

Students and tourists alike should count on paying around 3000FF to 5200FF a month, 1200FF to 1500FF a week, or 130FF to 300FF a day for a single room, including breakfast.

## Rental Accommodation

If you don't speak French or have a local person helping you, it may be very difficult to find a flat for long-term rental. Since it is costly and time-consuming to evict people in France, landlords usually require substantial proof of financial responsibility for three-year leases. One-year leases of furnished apartments entail less of a commitment from the landlord, making them more likely to take a chance on a foreigner. After you've exhausted your personal connections, places to look include the *petites annonces* (classified ads) in local newspapers. Each Wednesday free newspapers are dropped off in bundles at many bars, tabacs and residences. Named after the number of their department (76 in Seine Maritime, 27 in the Eure, 14 in Calvados, 50 in the Manche and 61 in the Orne) they contain hundreds of classifieds. Students may wish to try the CROUS office of the nearest university. Estate agents require lots of paperwork and can charge commissions of up to one month's rent.

## FOOD

Normandy is famous for the incredible richness and superior quality of its local produce. Dairy products are the 'white gold' of the region. Each Norman cow produces an average of five tonnes of milk annually, which is why the region supplies something like half of France's milk, butter, cream and cheese. Norman cuisine is based on butter and cream sauces, which are slathered over eggs, chicken, fish, veal, seafood, vegetables and desserts. If a dish is *à la normande*, it's bound to contain butter, cream or both.

The best Normandy butter comes from Isigny-sur-Mer on the border between the Calvados and Manche departments. It's an exceptionally flavourful butter, sought after by chefs around France, although the butter from Ste-Mère-Église is also very highly regarded.

Fish and seafood are also of superior quality in Normandy. Oysters from the Cotentin peninsula and turbot are major delicacies throughout France. Look for *lisettes* (little mackerel) and *coquilles St-Jacques* (scallops) from Dieppe, shrimp from Honfleur, cod from Fécamp and crabs, clams and mussels all along the coast.

Meat and poultry are menus staples in the interior. The savoury lamb *pre-salé* from Mont St-Michel needs no sauce, but Normandy's fine beef, chicken and veal are often served in cider or Calvados-based sauces. Some think it's heresy, but don't be surprised to see a meat dish topped with a sauce based on one of Normandy's fine cheeses.

*Charcuteries* (delicatessens) abound in Normandy, their windows displaying various terrines, pâtés and tripe. Also common are *galantine*, a cold dish of boned, stuffed, pressed meat (especially pork) that is presented in its own jelly, often with truffles and pistachio nuts.

## Regional Specialities

**Cheese** Normandy is renowned for its cheese, much of it produced in the Pays d'Auge region of Lower Normandy. It's the birthplace of France's most popular cheese, Camembert, a luscious, creamy cheese with a complex flavour. The area around Camembert village had long been renowned for its cheese but it wasn't until 1791 that a farmwoman, Marie Harel, developed the Camembert formula based upon certain tips from a renegade priest she was sheltering. It was a big success at the market of nearby Vimoutiers and eventually in the court of Napoleon III. Unfortunately, much commercially produced Camembert is bland and flavourless since it's made from pasteurised milk. Look for Camembert made from *lait cru* (raw milk) and then let it get soft and runny before eating it. Don't put it into the refrigerator. The best brands are Monsieur Mellon and the Lepetit family.

Pont l'Évêque is another popular cheese from Auge country and is Normandy's oldest cheese. The town lies between Deauville and Lisieux and it's said that the grass feeding the region's cows is particularly oily, which gives the cheese its unique flavour. The process differs from that of Camembert cheese, requiring a longer ageing process and more frequent turning. The best label is Briouze.

Livarot became the most sought after Norman cheese in the 19th century and is the most complicated to make. Called the 'colonel' because of the five imprinted stripes on its rind, Livarot sits in a cellar for a month and is periodically washed with fresh or lightly salted water. Look out for Livarot from the Graindorge cheesemaker.

The *petits suisses* cheese from the Bray region has pleased generations of French children. Merging *crème fraiche* with white cheese, this creamy cheese emerged in the 19th century as a dessert. An entrepreneur, Charles Gervais, hired Swiss workers to manufacture it in quantity and it is now produced in the Gervais-Danone factory near Gournay. Some 600,000 litres of milk are processed each day to make little containers of sweet, salty or herbed-cheese. Other popular Normandy cheeses include the heart-shaped Neufchâtel made near Neufchâtel-en-Bray, the pavé d'Auge, brillat-savarin made near Forges-les-Eau and la Bouille from the town of the same name. Most Norman cheeses are best in spring and autumn.

**Sole Normande** It may not have been invented in Normandy, but the shellfish-rich coastal waters of Normandy provided the raw materials to dress up dull sole filets. Based on a white butter and cream sauce, the dish varies from town to town. In Dieppe they add mussels, mushrooms and sometimes crab. In Fécamp the sauce is enhanced with shrimp butter and in Le Havre and Trouville shrimp replaces the mussels and mushrooms. Some restaurants only add scallops to the sauce.

**Caneton Rouennais** Rouen is famous for its duck dishes but the most extreme is Caneton Rouennais. The duckling is strangled in order to retain its blood, then roasted for only 20 minutes. A red wine sauce is prepared using the duck's heart and liver. At the table, the duck is put through a duck press (which every kitchen has) to release the blood, which is then combined with the sauce. The dish is so special that there's an association devoted to its preparation. L'Ordre des Canardiers (the Order of Canardiers) licenses chefs qualified to prepare the duckling, publishes a magazine and even has a Web site (www.canardiers.asso.fr) where you can find the recipe for the dish and a list of master *canardiers* around the world.

**Tripes á la mode de Caen** Cows intestines may not be to everyone's taste but when France was poor and rural, every part of the animal had to be eaten. In the 16th century a monk from the Abbaye aux Hommes in Caen came up with the idea of stewing the intestines with carrots, onions, leeks, herbs, spices, cider and Calvados. Many Caen restaurants still prepare the dish and there's another association, the Tripière d'Or, that awards yearly prizes for the best *tripes á la mode de Caen.*

**Andouille de Vire** More guts, this time from a pig. It's rolled into a sausage that is then seasoned and smoked for two months before being served cold and cut into small rounds. The technique has been perfected in Vire but the sausage is served throughout Normandy.

**Boudin** Blood sausage has its fans and the place to eat your *boudin* is Mortagne-au-Perche. It's made with one-third pig's blood, one-third onion and one-third pig fat and often served with baked or fried apple. The Knights of the Boudin Tasters *(Chevaliers du Goûte Boudin),* based in Mortagne-au-Perche, is an order of *boudin* lovers so devoted to their product, they must swear to eat it at least once a week.

**Omelette á la Mère Poulard** At the foot of the Mont St-Michel abbey, Grandma Poulard (long since deceased) created an extraordinarily fluffy omelette that is still made in the Mère Poulard restaurant as well as several other restaurants in town. There's no particular secret to the omelette; it's cooked over a wood fire in a long-handled pan and taken away from the heat from time to time during the process.

## Traditional Meals
As the pace of French life becomes more hectic, the three-hour midday meal is becoming increasingly rare, at least on weekdays. Dinners, however, are still turned into elaborate affairs whenever time and finances permit. For visitors, the occasional splurge can be the perfect end to a day of sightseeing.

A fully fledged, traditional French meal is an awesome event, often comprising six distinct courses and sometimes more. The meal is always served with wine (red, white or rosé, depending on what you're eating). The fare served at a traditional *déjeuner* (lunch), usually eaten around 1 pm, is largely indistinguishable from that served at *dîner* (dinner), usually begun around 8.30 pm.

**Breakfast** In the Continental tradition, the French start the day with a *petit déjeuner* (breakfast) usually consisting of a croissant and a light bread roll with butter and jam, followed by a *café au lait* (coffee with lots of hot milk), a small black coffee or hot chocolate. Buying rolls or pastries from a patisserie is quite a bit cheaper than eating at the hotel or a cafe.

**Lunch & Dinner** For many French people, especially in the provinces, lunch is still the main meal of the day. Restaurants will generally serve lunch between noon and 2 or 2.30 pm and dinner from 7 or 7.30 pm to sometime between 9.30 and 10.30 pm. Very few restaurants (except for brasseries, cafes and fast-food places) are open between lunch and dinner, and most are closed on Sunday.

**Desserts** The best-known Norman dessert is the scrumptious *tarte normande,* a kind of apple pie with no top crust. The apples are sometimes cooked in cider and the tart may be served with warm cream. In Yport, a similar dish called *tarte au sucre* is served. By all means try to sample *tergoule,* sometimes called *terrinée,* a delicious concoction made from rice, sugar, milk and cinnamon, subjected to a long bake in the oven. Sailors' wives invented the dish in Honfleur when their husbands brought back exotic cinnamon from their travels. The dessert is often enjoyed with *falue,* an egg-based bread. You also might find *bourdelots* or *douillons,* apples or pears encased in pastry, on the dessert menu. Other dessert delicacies include the *sablés* (a round, crumbly pastry) and *fouaces* (hearth cake) of Caen and the *sucre de pomme* (apple sweet) of Rouen.

## Menus

Most restaurants offer at least one fixed-price, multi-course meal known in French as a *menu*, *menu à prix fixe* or *menu du jour* (menu of the day). A *menu* (not to be confused with a *carte* – throughout this book we italicise *menu* to distinguish it from the English word 'menu') almost always costs much less than ordering a la carte. In some places, you may also be able to order a *formule*, which usually has fewer choices but allows you to pick two of three courses. In many restaurants, the cheapest lunch *menu* is a much better deal than the equivalent one available at dinner.

When you order a three-course *menu*, you usually get to choose an entree, such as salad, pâté or soup; a main dish (several meat, poultry or fish dishes, including the *plat du jour* (dish of the day), are generally on offer); and one or more final courses (usually cheese or dessert).

*Boissons* (drinks), including wine, cost extra unless the menu says *boisson comprise* (drink included), in which case you may get a beer or a glass of mineral water. If the *menu* says *vin compris* (wine included), you'll probably be served a small *pichet* (jug) of wine. The waiter will always ask if you would like coffee to end the meal, but this will almost always cost extra.

## Types of Eateries

**Restaurants & Brasseries** There are lots of restaurants in Normandy where you can get an excellent meal for 150FF to 200FF, but good, inexpensive French restaurants are in short supply. In this book, we have tried to include restaurants that offer what the French call a *bon rapport qualité-prix* (good value for money).

Some of the best French restaurants in the country are attached to hotels, and those on the ground floor of budget hotels often have some of the best deals in town. Almost all are open to non-guests.

*Routiers* (road-side restaurants), usually found on the outskirts of towns and along major roads, cater to truck drivers and can provide a quick, hearty break from cross-country driving.

Restaurants usually specialise in a particular variety of food (for example, regional, traditional, North African or Vietnamese), whereas brasseries – which look very much like cafes – serve more standard fare. This often includes *choucroute* (sauerkraut served with meat) because the brasserie, which actually means 'brewery', originated in Alsace. Unlike restaurants, which usually open only for lunch and dinner, brasseries keep going from morning until night and serve meals (or at least something solid) at all times of the day.

Don't count on eating in a smoke-free environment. French eateries are required to set aside a section for nonsmokers but the law is widely ignored, especially in small family-run establishments.

**Ethnic Restaurants** Ethnic restaurants are not particularly cheap or plentiful in Normandy. There's invariably a Chinese restaurant, usually with a strong Vietnamese influence, in most towns, and often a North African restaurant serving *couscous* (rolled semolina) with stewed vegetables and meat.

**Vegetarian Restaurants** Vegetarians form only a small minority in France and are not very well catered for; specialised vegetarian restaurants are few and far between. Only the cities are likely to have vegetarian establishments, and these may look more like laid-back cafes than restaurants. Other options include *saladeries*, casual restaurants that serve a long list of *salades composées* (mixed salads). Indian restaurants usually have a variety of the vegetarian options and it's possible to order the North African dish, *couscous* without the meat.

**Salons de Thé** *Salons de thé* (tearooms) are trendy and somewhat pricey establishments that usually offer quiches, salads, cakes, tarts, pies and pastries in addition to tea and coffee.

**Crêperies** *Crêperies* specialise in crepes, ultra-thin pancakes cooked on a flat surface and then folded or rolled over a filling. In some parts of France, the word 'crepe' is used to refer only to sweet crepes made with *farine de froment* (regular wheat flour), whereas savoury crepes, often made with *farine de sarrasin* (buckwheat flour) and filled with cheese, mushrooms and the like, are called *galettes*.

**Cafeterias** Many cities have cafeteria restaurants offering a good selection of dishes you can see before ordering, a factor that can make life easier if you're travelling with kids. Cafeteria chains include Flunch, Mélodine and Casino.

## Self-Catering

Most people buy a good part of their food from a series of small neighbourhood shops, each with its own speciality. At first, having to go to four shops and stand in four queues to fill the fridge (or assemble a picnic) may seem rather a waste of time, but the whole ritual is an important part of the way many French people live their daily lives. It's perfectly acceptable to purchase only meal-size amounts: a few *tranches* (slices) of meat to make a sandwich, perhaps, or a *petit bout* (small chunk) of sausage.

**Boulangeries** Fresh bread is baked and sold at *boulangeries* (bakeries), which supply three-quarters of the country's bread. All boulangeries have 250g baguettes, which are long and thin, and 400g fatter loaves of *pain* (bread), both of which should be eaten within four hours of baking. If you're not very hungry, ask for a *demi baguette* or *demi pain*. A *ficelle* is a thinner, crustier version of the baguette – really like very thick breadsticks.

Bread is baked at various times of the day, so fresh bread is readily available as early as 6 am and also in the afternoon. Most boulangeries close one day a week, but the days are staggered so that you'll always find one open somewhere (except, perhaps, on Sunday afternoon).

**Pâtisseries** Mouth-watering pastries are available at *pâtisseries*, which are often attached to bakeries. Some of the most common pastries include *tarte aux fruits* (fruit

tarts), *pain au chocolat* (similar to a croissant but filled with chocolate), *pain aux raisins* (a flat, spiral pastry made with custard and sultanas) and *religieuses* (eclairs with one cream puff perched on top of another to resemble a nun's headdress).

You can tell if a croissant has been made with margarine or butter by the shape: margarine croissants have their tips almost touching, while those made with butter have them pointing away from each other.

**Confiseries** Chocolate and other sweets made with the finest ingredients can be found at *confiseries*, which are sometimes combined with bakeries and patisseries.

**Fromageries** If you buy your cheese in a supermarket, you'll end up with unripe and relatively tasteless products unless you know your stuff. Here's where a *fromagcrie*, also known as a *crémerie*, comes in. The owners will advise you and usually let you taste before you decide what to buy. Just ask: *'Est-ce que je peux le goûter, s'il vous plaît?'* Most fromageries sell both whole and half-rounds of Camembert, so you don't have to buy more than you're likely to eat in a day or two.

**Charcuteries** A *charcuterie* is a delicatessen offering sliced meats, seafood salads, pâtés, terrines and so on. Most supermarkets have a charcuterie counter. If the word *traiteur* (trader) is written on a sign, it means that the establishment sells ready-to-eat takeaway dishes.

**Fruit & Vegetables** *Fruits* and *légumes* are sold by a *marchand de légumes et de fruits* (greengrocer) and at food markets and supermarkets. Most small groceries have only a limited selection. You can buy whatever quantity of produce suits you, even if it's just three carrots and a peach. *Biologique* means that it has been grown organically (without chemicals).

**Meat & Fish** A general butcher is a *boucherie*, but for specialised poultry you have to go to a *marchand de volaille*, where *poulet fermier* (free-range chicken) will cost much more than a regular chicken. A *boucherie chevaline*, easily identifiable by the gilded horse's head above the entrance, sells horse meat. Fresh fish and seafood are available from a *poissonnerie*.

**Épiceries & Alimentations** A small grocery store with a little bit of everything is known as an *épicerie* (literally, 'spice shop') or an *alimentation générale*. Most épiceries are more expensive than supermarkets, though some – such as those of the Casino chain – are more like minimarkets. Some épiceries open on days when other food shops are closed, and many family-run operations stay open until late at night.

**Supermarkets** City centres usually have at least one department store with a large *supermarché* (supermarket) section. Places to look for include Monoprix, Prisunic and Nouvelles Galeries. Most larger supermarkets have a delicatessen and cheese counters, and many also have in-house bakeries.

The cheapest place to buy food is a *hypermarché* (hypermarket), such as those of the Auchan, Carrefour, Intermarché, E Leclerc and Rallye chains, where you'll pay up to 40% less for staples than at an épicerie. Unfortunately, they are nearly always on the outskirts of town.

**Food Markets** In most towns and cities, many of the aforementioned products are available one or more days a week at *marchés en plein air* (open-air markets), also known as *marchés découverts*, and up to six days a week at *marchés couverts* (covered marketplaces), often known as *les halles*. Markets are cheaper than food shops and supermarkets and the merchandise, especially fruit and vegetables, is generally fresher and of better quality.

## DRINKS

Although alcohol consumption has dropped by more than 20% since the war, the French drink more than any other national group in the world, except the people of Luxembourg. On average each French adult consumes 11L of pure alcohol a year, compared to 8.3L in the USA and 8.2L in the UK (and with the 18L they drank in 1960).

### Nonalcoholic Drinks

**Water** All tap water in France is safe to drink, so there is no need to buy expensive bottled water. Tap water that is not drinkable (that from most public fountains and some streams) will usually have a sign reading *'eau non potable'*.

If you prefer tap water rather than a pricey soft drink or wine, make sure you ask for *de l'eau* (some water), *une carafe d'eau* (a jug of water) or *de l'eau du robinet* (tap water). Otherwise you'll most likely get *eau de source* (mineral water), which comes *plate* (flat or noncarbonated) or *gazeuse* (fizzy or carbonated).

**Soft Drinks** Soft drinks are expensive in France. Don't be surprised if you're charged 20FF for a little bottle of Gini or Pschitt. A beer may be cheaper than a Coke. Even in the supermarket, soft drinks are only just cheaper than beer, milk and even some kinds of wine.

One relatively inexpensive cafe drink is *sirop* (fruit syrup or squash), served either *à l'eau* (mixed with water), with *soda* (carbonated water) or Perrier. A *citron pressé* is a glass of iced water (either flat or carbonated) with freshly squeezed lemon juice and sugar. The French are not particularly fond of drinking very cold things, so if you'd like your drink with ice cubes, ask for *des glaçons*.

**Coffee** The most ubiquitous form is espresso, made by forcing steam through ground coffee beans. A small, black espresso is called *un café noir*, *un express* or simply *un café*. You can also ask for a *grand* (large) version.

*Un café crème* is espresso with steamed milk or cream. *Un café au lait* is lots of hot milk with a little coffee served in a large cup or, sometimes, a bowl. A small café crème is a *petit crème*. A *noisette* (literally, 'hazelnut') is an espresso with just a dash of milk. Decaffeinated coffee is *un café décaféiné* or *un déca*.

**Tea & Hot Chocolate** *Thé* (tea) is also widely available and will be served with milk if you ask for *un peu de lait frais* (a little cold milk). Herbal tea, popular as a treatment for minor ailments, is called *tisane* or *infusion*. French *chocolat chaud* (hot chocolate) can be either excellent or completely undrinkable.

## Alcoholic Drinks

**Cider** Normandy is the only region in France that doesn't produce wine. You'll find plenty of wine from neighbouring regions on local menus and in stores – wine from the Loire Valley is especially popular – but Normans traditionally down copious quantities of *cidre* (cider) with their meals. This *bon bère* (as the Normans call their apple drink) crept into Normandy in the middle of the 12th century and became the most popular drink in the region by the 15th century.

Normans say that cider is 'difficult to make but easy to drink'. The first step in making good cider is to choose the right kind of apples. Usually sweet, bitter and acidulous apples are combined to make product that will ferment and retain a balance between sweet and sharp flavours. Cider-makers prefer apples from certain regions and sometimes include pears. The plateau of Gonneville at the mouth of the Seine is a favourite spot as well as the border between Normandy and Brittany. The apples are harvested between September and December, then crushed and pressed in January. Winter cold slows down the fermentation process which can last up to three months. Large manufacturers filter, pasteurise and sometimes add carbon dioxide before putting the cider in bottles. The length of the fermentation process determines the sweetness of the cider. *Cidre doux* (sweet) has an alcohol level of 2.5 to 3%; *brut* (dry) has an alcohol level of about 4.5%. Most cider is bubbly and, like champagne, comes in corked bottles. Look for *sec* (at least a year old), *pur jus* (no added water), *mousseux* (naturally carbonated), or *bouché* (the cider is fermented in the bottle). The Pays d'Auge produces the most celebrated cider, benefiting from an AOC label (see below).

**Aperitifs** *Pommeau* is a refreshing Norman aperitif made from apple juice and Calvados. It's made by stopping the fermentation of freshly pressed apples and adding Calvados, which preserves the apple flavour, the natural sugars of the fruit and an agreeable acidity. It is then aged in an oak barrel for 18 months. Drink pommeau cool but without ice. The alcohol level is a moderate 16 to 18% and it's particularly good with oysters, foie gras or apple-based desserts.

### The AOC Label

The label *Appellation d'Origine Contrôlée* (AOC) is the highest honour that can be bestowed on a French product. It signals that the product comes from a specific region and is made according to specific standards. Although the label is most regularly applied to wine, in Normandy certain cheeses and ciders have also received the label. The 'made-in Normandy' *(fabriqué en Normandie)* label means little since the original milk or apples could have come from outside Normandy.

Camembert received its AOC label in 1983, which means that the cheese must have been made either in the Pays d'Auge, the Orne bocage or the Cotentin peninsula. Pont l'Évêque can be made anywhere in Normandy plus the Mayenne department of the Loire Valley. Livarot cheese must be produced in a narrow area confined to the south-east of Calvados and north-east of the Orne; Neufchâtel is limited to a 30km-radius of the town in Pays de Bray.

Cider and Calvados from the Pays d'Auge also benefit from the AOC quality-control label. No other cider has an AOC label but Calvados from 10 other areas in Normandy – Avranches, Cotentin, the Pays de Bray and the Orne Valley, among others – has achieved the lesser distinction of being *réglementée* (regulated). Calvados from the Pays d'Auge is made only from apples around the Deauville region and it is subject to a double distillation.

*Poiré* is good if you can find it but unfortunately it is becoming increasingly rare. Essentially a dry cider made from pears, *poiré* is a light drink that you may find in the Orne valley.

**Digestifs** Need stronger stuff? Calvados is the pride of Normandy and, with an alcohol level of 50 to 55%, this apple brandy takes the sting out of a rainy Norman winter. Simply, Calvados is cider that has been allowed to age for at least a year, but the process is even more complicated. Some 40 different kinds of apples can go into the making of a good Calvados, many of them cultivated specifically for the brandy. After a one or two step distillation process the brandy is aged for at least one year, first in a new oak barrel and then in a series of progressively older oak barrels that lend it a particular woody taste. Its quality derives from the length of time it passes in the oak barrels. Three-star Calvados has been aged two years, *vieux* Calvados has aged three years, *Vieille Réserve* or VSOP (Very Special Old Pale) has aged five years, and *Hors d'Age Extra* or Napoleon has aged at least six years.

Calvados can be drunk at the end of a meal with coffee or in the middle of a meal – the *trou normand* (Norman pause).

Bénédictine is a heady plant-based liqueur made in Fécamp, although it is not widely imbibed in Normandy. For details see Fécamp in the Seine-Maritime chapter.

## ENTERTAINMENT

Local tourist offices are generally the best source of information about what's going on in a town or city. In larger towns, they'll usually have a free brochure listing the cultural events and entertainment planned for each week, fortnight or month.

### Pubs, Bars & Cafes

Traditional cafes (the places that open from the morning) are an important focal point for social life in France. Sitting in a cafe to read, write, talk with friends or just daydream is an integral part of many people's day-to-day existence. Three factors determine how much you'll pay in a cafe: where the cafe is situated, where you are sitting within it, and what time of day it is. Ordering a cup of coffee (or anything else) earns you the right to sit there for as long as you like.

You usually pay the *addition* (bill) right before you leave, though if your waiter is going off duty you may be asked to pay up then and there.

In most towns you'll also come across slightly seedy bars that attract people for whom drinking is more of a full-time occupation than an occasional pastime. These places are typically glass-fronted and have lots of tall barstools occupied by swarthy, vaguely suspicious-looking locals slurping a brew or a Calvados.

Big cities have a wider selection of watering holes. Crowded, funky student bars are usually good places to get a cheap brew. There's at least one English-style pub in each port city and bars on Latino themes that serve expensive tropical cocktails are becoming increasingly popular.

### Clubs

In French, a club or *discotheque* (also called a *boîte*) is any sort of establishment where music (live or recorded) leads to dancing. The music on offer ranges from rock to Latino and techno, and the crowd may be gay, lesbian, straight or mixed. The sign *'tenue correcte exigée'*, which you may see

---

## The Norman Pause

With even everyday meals stretching to four courses, it's not surprising that Normans need to take a break in the middle of the meal. After the starter and main course, Normans typically down a little glass of Calvados – known as the *trou normand* (Norman pause) – to help their digestion.

According to nutritionists, Calvados actually dilates the stomach lining, eliminating the impression of satiety and encouraging the diner to eat more.

At the more elegant restaurants, the traditional shot has been replaced by a serving of sorbet topped with Calvados.

---

displayed at various venues, means 'appropriate dress required'. Most clubs only begin to warm up after midnight (and sometimes much later).

An unfortunate fixture at many big-city clubs is the bouncer – the *videur* (literally 'emptier') who eyes you at the entrance to clubs. In some places, bouncers are encouraged to keep out 'undesirables', which, depending on the place, can range from unaccompanied men who aren't dressed right to members of certain minority groups (for example North Africans and blacks). All discos, however, are very careful not to admit people who are drunk.

## Jazz, Rock & Pop
Caen and Rouen have huge stadiums that stage mega-events featuring some of the world's top rock and pop performers, from Sting to French pop stars and world music. There is very little jazz regularly presented in clubs throughout Normandy although clubs with a more eclectic program will occasionally present local bands. The most prestigious jazz event in Normandy is the 'Jazz Sous les Pommiers' staged in Coutances each May. Besides the ubiquitous sounds of techno, the most popular dance beat now in Normandy is Latino in all its variations.

## Opera & Classical Music
The two major cultural centres of Normandy are Caen and Rouen, both of which have concert halls presenting good-calibre classical music, dance and opera from October to May. Classical music concerts are also regularly presented in churches around Normandy and there are some regional orchestras. Your best bet for catching the latest on the French and international music scene is during the month-long 'October in Normandy' festival in the Seine-Maritime department, which presents many concerts throughout the region. Consult the local tourist offices or the Web site at www .octobre-en-normandie.com.

## Cinemas
If you don't want to hear your favourite actor dubbed into French, look in the film listings and on the cinema's billboard for the letters *VO* or *v.o. (version originale)* or *v.o.s.t. (version originale sous-titrée)*, all of which mean that the film has been given French subtitles. If v.o. is nowhere to be seen, or if you notice the letters *v.f. (version française)*, it means the film has been dubbed into French.

Film-going in France does not come cheap – count on paying 40FF to 50FF for a first-run film. Most French cinemas offer discounts to students, and people aged under 18 or over 60 usually get discounts of about 25% (but not on Friday, Saturday or Sunday nights). On Wednesday, and sometimes also on Monday, most cinemas give discounts to everyone.

## Theatre
The French theatre scene is dominated by the revival of old favourites and the translation of foreign hits, although occasionally you'll see some more experimental works. Almost all major theatre productions, including those written in other languages, are performed in French. Contemporary comedies are popular but you will need excellent French as the dialogue is often dominated by cultural references.

## SPECTATOR SPORTS
The most uniquely Norman spectator sport is horse racing. The most elegant spot to watch the races is in Deauville which has races almost daily in July and August. Caen also has a racetrack which is in highest gear in September and October. Cabourg has races in January, July, August, October and in December, while Lisieux has race meetings several times a month from March to November.

The world's most prestigious bicycle race, the Tour de France, frequently passes through Normandy. Caen has welcomed the pedallers 32 times since the first Tour de France in 1903, and Le Havre has been a stop 18 times. Rouen was a stop 15 times and served as the departure city in 1961. The race takes place for three weeks in July and, despite being marred by doping scandals, is still a major event across France.

There's also a Tour de Normandie reserved for first rate amateurs. Begun in 1980, the race is attracting increasing attention throughout Europe as a proving ground for amateurs on the way to becoming professionals. The race takes place in March and the itinerary changes every year. Details can be found by contacting Normandie Cyclisme (☎ 02 31 95 24 92), 3 rue Michel Cabieu, BP 274, 14013 Caen.

## SHOPPING
Normandy's famous drinks make good souvenirs or gifts. Cider, Calvados and pommeau are available everywhere but are best bought in the Pays d'Auge. Fécamp's herbal Bénédictine liquor is another good deal.

Cheese may tempt you but the best cheese is meant to be eaten promptly and you may have trouble getting it through customs. Instead, gourmands should look for *Planches de Deauville* biscuits in Deauville, *Caprices des Ursulines* boxed pastries in Évreux and *Caïques* nougats in Fécamp. Chocoholics will love the chocolate-covered nuts in Fécamp's *Calettes*, Le Havre's domino-shaped *Dominos du Pays*, and Rouen's mixture of apples, pommeau, Calvados and chocolate called *Les 100 Clochers*.

Normandy's traditional crafts also make good souvenirs. Ceramics *(faïence)* is a uniquely Norman craft and you can find good deals in Rouen and Forges-les-Eaux. Alençon lace is expensive and can only be found in the lace museum of Alençon. Villedieu-les-Poêles is famed for its high quality copper pans, on sale around town.

# Getting There & Away

## AIR
### Airports & Airlines

Paris is the closest airport with regular international flights. Normandy's airports have few international flights. Air France has daily flights (excluding Saturday) from London City Airport to Le Havre (UK£262 return, 45 minutes), but all other London flights pass through Paris. Call the general Air France number in the UK (☎ 0845 084 5111) for information.

Airports in Rouen, Caen, Cherbourg and Le Havre serve the local market. Air France (www.airfrance.com and www.airfrance .co.uk) also has three daily flights from Caen to Lyons (1916FF return, one hour) and three daily from Rouen to Lyons (1949FF return, 1½ hours).

There are two direct flights daily from Le Havre to Rennes (1010FF return, 35 minutes), Lyons (1918FF, 2½ hours), Clermont-Ferrand (1719FF return, one hour and 20 minutes) and Nantes (1670FF return, 50 minutes). In July and August there are daily flights from Deauville-Trouville to Nice (2707FF return, two hours). Air Liberté (☎ 08 03 80 58 05) operates two flights a day from Monday to Friday between Paris and Cherbourg (1133FF, 55 minutes).

The above fares assume a booking at least 15 days in advance. Late bookings are substantially more expensive. Significant discounts are available to:

- Children aged under 12
- Young people aged 12 to 24
- Couples who are either married, have proof of cohabitation (a French government-issued *certificat de concubinage*), or who are *pacsé* (in an official state of non-married couplehood)
- Families, defined as at least one parent or grandparent travelling with one or more children aged 24 or under
- People aged over 60

On many flights, everyone else can also fly for considerably less than the full fare. You can sometimes find last-minute promotional fares – travel agents can provide you with details.

### Buying Tickets

A bit of research – talking to recent travellers, perusing the ads in newspapers, checking Internet sites – can often save you quite a bit of money on your air ticket. Start early: some of the cheapest tickets have to be bought well in advance, and the most popular flights sell out early.

Cheap tickets are available in two distinct categories: official and unofficial. Official ones are sold under a variety of names, including advance purchase tickets, advance purchase excursion (Apex) and super-Apex. Unofficial tickets are released by the airlines through selected travel agents and are not usually sold directly by the airline's offices. Since only a few travel agents may be given access to a particular batch of discounted tickets, the best way to find the best deals is to phone around.

Return (round-trip) tickets are usually cheaper than two one-ways. In some cases, the return fare may actually cost *less* than a one-way ticket. The cheapest tickets often come with cumbersome restrictions: you may have to buy your ticket weeks in advance or pay heavy penalties for changing travel dates; the non-extendable period of validity may be very short; there may be a minimum stay, for example, you may be required to spend a Saturday night at your destination (this weeds out the business travellers); the routing may involve time-consuming stopovers; and cancellation penalties of up to 100% may apply.

As you phone around, you may discover that those impossibly cheap flights are 'fully booked, but we have another one that costs only a bit more…' Or that the flight is on an airline notorious for its poor safety record and will leave you for 14 hours in the world's least-favourite airport, where you'll be confined to the transit lounge unless you get an expensive visa…Or the agent may claim that the last two cheap seats until next autumn will be gone in two hours. Don't panic – keep ringing around.

If you are travelling from the USA or South-East Asia, you will sometimes find that the cheapest flights are being advertised by obscure agencies whose names have yet to reach the telephone directory. Many such firms are honest and solvent, but there are a few rogues who will take your money and run – only to reopen elsewhere a month or two later under a new name. If you feel suspicious about a firm, don't give them all the money at once – leave a deposit of 20% or so and pay the balance when you get the ticket. If they insist on cash in advance, go somewhere else or take a very big risk. And once you have the ticket, ring the airline to confirm that you are indeed booked on the flight.

You may decide that it's worthwhile to pay a bit more than the rock-bottom fare in return for the safety of a better known travel agent. We mention a number of such firms in this section under individual country headings.

In France, as elsewhere, the only way to find the best deal is to shop around. Prices and available dates vary greatly. Inexpensive flights offered by charter clearing houses can be booked through many regular travel agents – look in agency windows for posters and pamphlets advertising Go Voyages (☎ 01 53 40 44 29, ✉ infos@govoyages.com) or Look Voyages (☎ 01 55 49 49 60, ☎ 08 03 31 36 13). Their Web sites are at www.govoyages.com and www.look-voyages.fr, respectively.

Reliable travel agency chains include the French student travel company OTU (☎ 01 40 29 12 12, ☎ 02 31 56 60 93 in Caen), Nouvelles Frontières (☎ 08 03 33 33 33 at 1.09FF a minute, ✉ mailus@newfrontiers.com) and the Franco–Belgian company Wasteels (☎ 01 43 62 30 00). Visit their Web sites at www.otu.fr, www.newfrontiers.com and www.voyages-wasteels.fr, respectively.

Aventure du Bout du Monde (ABM; ☎ 01 45 45 29 29, fax 01 45 45 20 30), based in Paris at 11 rue de Coulmiers (metro Alésia), is a non-profit organisation that facilitates the exchange of practical travel information (such as advice on cheap flights) between travellers. Membership costs 190FF a year. Visit its Web site at www.abm.fr.

Use the fares quoted in this book as a guide only. They are based on the rates advertised by travel agents as we went to press and are likely to have changed somewhat by the time you read this.

## Travellers with Special Needs

If you have special needs of any sort – you're vegetarian or require a special diet, you are travelling in a wheelchair, taking a baby, terrified of flying – let the airline people know as soon as possible so that they can make the necessary arrangements. Remind them when you reconfirm your booking (at least 72 hours before departure) and again when you check in at the airport. It may also be worth calling several airlines before making your booking to find out how they can handle your particular needs.

In general, children under the age of two travel for 10% of the standard fare (or, on some carriers, for free) as long as they don't occupy a seat. They do not get a luggage allowance. Skycots, baby food, formula, nappies (diapers) and so on should be provided by the airline if requested in advance. Children aged between two and 12 can usually occupy a seat for half to two-thirds of the full fare and do get a luggage allowance.

## The UK

Increased deregulation has brought in new carriers whose fares are made all the more attractive by the small discounts available if you book on-line. Return fares on the London–Paris route can be as low as UK£50; with the larger companies expect to pay at least UK£88. For return travel from London to the south of France, UK£60 is the absolute minimum; most fares cost from UK£90 to UK£150.

Some of the best deals, especially to destinations in France other than Paris, are offered by Buzz (☎ 0870 240 7070), Ryanair (☎ 0870 333 1231), easyJet (☎ 0870 600 0000) and British Airway's Go (☎ 0870 607 6543). Visit

## Air Travel Glossary

**Alliances** Many of the world's leading airlines are now intimately involved with each other, sharing everything from reservations systems and check-in to aircraft and frequent flyer schemes. Opponents say that alliances restrict competition. Whatever the arguments, there is no doubt that big alliances are the way of the future.

**Cancelling or Changing Tickets** If you have to cancel or change a ticket, you need to contact the original travel agent who sold you the ticket. Airlines only issue refunds to the purchaser of a ticket – usually the travel agent who bought the ticket on your behalf. There are often heavy penalties involved; insurance can sometimes be taken out against these penalties.

**Courier Fares** Businesses often need to send urgent documents or freight securely and quickly. Courier companies hire people to accompany the package through customs and, in return, offer a discount ticket which is sometimes a bargain. However, you may have to surrender all your baggage allowance and take only carry-on luggage.

**Fares** Airlines traditionally offer 1st class (coded F), business class (coded J) and economy class (coded Y) tickets. These days there are so many promotional and discounted fares available that few passengers pay full fare.

**Lost Tickets** If you lose your airline ticket an airline will usually treat it like a travellers cheque and, after enquiries, issue you with another one. Legally, however, an airline is entitled to treat it like cash and if you lose it then it's gone forever. Take good care of your tickets.

**Onward Tickets** An entry requirement for many countries is that you have a ticket out of the country. If you're unsure of your next move, the easiest solution is to buy the cheapest onward ticket to a neighbouring country or a ticket from a reliable airline which can later be refunded if you do not use it.

**Open-Jaw Tickets** These are return tickets where you fly out to one place but return from another. If available, this can save you backtracking to your arrival point.

**Overbooking** Since every flight has some passengers who fail to show up, airlines often book more passengers than they have seats. Usually excess passengers make up for the no-shows, but occasionally somebody gets 'bumped' onto the next available flight. Guess who it is most likely to be? The passengers who check in late. If you do get 'bumped' you are normally offered some form of compensation.

**Reconfirmation** Some airlines require you to reconfirm your flight at least 72 hours prior to departure. Check your travel documents to see if this is the case.

**Restrictions** Discounted tickets often have various restrictions on them – such as needing to be paid for in advance and incurring a penalty to be altered or cancelled. Others are restrictions on the minimum and maximum period you must be away.

**Round-the-World Tickets** RTW tickets give you a limited period (usually a year) in which to circumnavigate the globe. You can go anywhere the carrying airlines go, as long as you don't backtrack. The number of stopovers or total number of separate flights is decided before you set off and they usually cost a bit more than a basic return flight.

**Ticketless Travel** Airlines are gradually waking up to the realisation that paper tickets are unnecessary encumbrances. On simple one-way or return trips, reservations details can be held on computer, and the passenger merely shows ID to claim his or her seat.

**Transferred Tickets** Airline tickets cannot be transferred from one person to another. Travellers sometimes try to sell the return half of their ticket, but officials can ask you to prove that you are the person named on the ticket. On an international flight tickets are always compared with passports.

their Web sites at www.buzzaway.com, www
.ryanair.ie, www.easyjet.co.uk and www.go-
fly.com, respectively, where there may be
discounts for booking on-line.

British Airways (☎ 0845 773 3377) and
Air France (☎ 0845 084 5111), whose fares
are often quite reasonable (especially for
young people), link London and a variety of
other British cities (such as Birmingham, Edinburgh and Manchester) with Paris and Le
Havre. Their Web sites are at www.british
airways.com and www.airfrance.co.uk.

Other airlines which may have decent
prices include British Midland (☎ 0870 607
0555), KLM uk (☎ 0870 507 4074) and
British European (☎ 0870 567 6676). Their
Web sites are at www.iflybritishmidland
.co.uk, www.klmuk.com and www.british
european.com, respectively.

Advertisements for travel agents appear
in the travel pages of the weekend broad-
sheet newspapers as well as in *Time Out*, the
*Evening Standard* and the free magazine
*TNT*.

Popular discount 'student' travel agencies include STA Travel (☎ 0870 160 0599),
whose offices around the UK include one at
86 Old Brompton Road, London SW7 3LQ,
and Campus Travel (☎ 0870 240 1010),
whose many branches include one at 52
Grosvenor Gardens, London SW1W 0AG.
Check out their Web sites at www.statravel
.co.uk and www.usitcampus.co.uk.

Other recommended travel agencies include: Trailfinders (☎ 020-7937 1234), 215
Kensington High Street, London W8 6BD;
Bridge the World (☎ 020-7911 0900, fax
7813 3350, ⓔ sales@bridgetheworld.com),
with offices at 4 Regent Place, London W1B
5EA, and 47 Chalk Farm Road, London
NW1 8AJ; and Flightbookers (☎ 0870 010
7000 from the UK, ☎ 020-7757 2626 outside the UK), 177–178 Tottenham Court
Road, London W1T 7LX. You can visit
their Web sites at www.trailfinders.co.uk,
www.b-t-w.co.uk and www.ebookers.com,
respectively.

## Ireland

usit Voyages (☎ 01-602 1600 in Dublin,
☎ 01 42 34 56 90 in Paris) has changeable

and refundable Dublin–Paris flights for
students and under 26s for IR£55/99 one-
way/return (a bit more in the summer).
Its Web site is at www.usitnow.ie, or,
for northern Ireland, www.usitnow.com.
Ryanair (☎ 01-609 7881 in Dublin) often
has cheap promotional fares to Beauvais
(80km north of Paris) and a number of
minor regional airports. Belfast–Paris youth
and student fares start at UK£50/92. Its Web
site is at www.ryanair.ie.

## Continental Europe

Fares on some routes have been dropping as
deregulation kicks in. Air France offers
many of the best youth and student rates,
available if you are either aged 25 or under
or a student (maximum age somewhere
between 29 and 32).

In Amsterdam, agencies with cheap tickets include the NBBS subsidiary Budget Air
(☎ 020-627 1251) at Rokin 34. Youth and
student flights to Paris cost f158/279 one-
way/return; adult return fares to Paris/Nice
start at about f380/440. Its Web site is at
www.nbbs.nl.

In Stockholm, agencies such as Kilroy
Travels (☎ 08-234 515), at Kungsgatan 4,
can get young people and students to Paris
for 1212/2406 kr one-way/return. Try its
Web site at www.kilroytravels.com.

In Copenhagen, STA Travel (☎ 33 141
501) is at Fiolstraede 18 and Kilroy Travels
(☎ 33 110 044) is at Skindergarde 28. For
young people under 26 and students under
32, the one-way/return fare to Paris is 740/
1480 kr with Air France; the cheapest adult
return is about 1800 kr.

In Oslo, STA Travel (☎ 23 01 02 90) is at
Karl Johans Gt 33, while Kilroy Travels
(☎ 23 10 23 10) is at Nedre Spottsgate 23.
Youth and student flights to Paris on Air
France cost 1416/2645 kr one-way/return.

In Berlin, STA Travel (☎ 030-311 0950)
has one of its many branches at Goethes-
trasse 73 (U2 stop: Ernst-Reuter-Platz).
Return flights to Paris on Air France or
Lufthansa start at DM460; students can get
one-way fares of DM280.

In Rome, recommended travel agents include CTS Viaggi, whose many offices

around Italy include one at 16 Via Genova (☎ 06 462 0431); and Passagi (☎ 06 474 0923), which is at Stazione Termini FS, Galleria Di Tesla. For one-way/return youth and student flights to Paris on Air France expect to pay L230,000/490,000. Adult returns sometimes become available for L350,000.

In Madrid, usit Unlimited (☎ 902 25 25 75) is at 3 Plaza de Callao; Barcelo Viajes (☎ 91 559 18 19) is at Princesa 3, and Nouvelles Frontières (☎ 91 547 42 00, fax 93 542 00 95) is at Plaza de España 18. Their Web sites are at www.unlimited.es and www.nouvelles-frontieres.es, respectively. A youth and student fare to Paris costs 16,000/31,000 ptas one-way/return; low-season adult return fares start at 25,000 ptas.

## The USA

The flight options across the North Atlantic, the world's busiest long-haul air corridor, are bewildering. The *New York Times, LA Times, Chicago Tribune* and *San Francisco Chronicle* all have weekly travel sections in which you'll find any number of travel agencies' ads. Independent periodicals such as the *San Francisco Guardian* and New York's *Village Voice* are another good place to check.

Reliable discount travel chains include Council Travel (☎ 800 226 8624, fax 617-528 2091) and STA Travel (☎ 800 781 4040). Their Web sites are at www.council travel.com and www.sta.com, respectively. San Francisco-based on-line agency Ticket Planet (☎ 800 799 8888) has an excellent reputation and lots of round-the-world (RTW) offerings (www.ticketplanet.com).

You should be able to fly from New York to Paris and back for about US$475 in the low season and US$800 in the high season; even lower promotional fares are sometimes on offer. Tickets from the west coast are US$150 to US$250 higher. In Paris, one-way, off-season discount flights to New York start at about 1400FF; return fares of 3000FF are sometimes available, but a more usual rock-bottom fare is 2600FF (7000FF to 9000FF return around Christmas and in July and August). Return fares

to the west coast are 600FF to 1000FF higher.

If your schedule is flexible, flying standby can work out to be very reasonable. Airhitch (☎ 800 326 2009 in New York, ☎ 310-574 0090 in Los Angeles, ☎ 01 47 00 16 30 in Paris, @ airhitch@airhitch.org) specialises in this sort of thing and can get you to/from Europe (but not necessarily Paris) for US$169/199/219/249 each way from the north-east/south-east/mid-west/west coast, plus taxes of US$16 to US$46. Its Web site is at www.airhitch.org.

Another very cheap option is a courier flight, which can cost as little as US$300 for a New York–Paris return arranged at the last minute. The drawbacks are that your stay in Europe may be limited to one or two weeks; your luggage is usually restricted to a carry-on; there is unlikely to be more than one courier ticket available for any given flight; and you may have to be a local resident and apply for an interview before they'll take you on.

You can find out more about courier flights and fares from the Colorado-based Air Courier Association (☎ 800 282 1202), which charges US$59 for a one-year membership; the International Association of Air Travel Couriers (☎ 561-582 8320, fax 582 1581, @ iaatc@courier.org), and Now Voyager Travel (☎ 212-431 1616, fax 334 5243). Their Web sites are at www.air courier.org, www.courier.org and www .nowvoyagertravel.com, respectively.

## Canada

Travel CUTS (☎ 604-659 2887, fax 659 2888 in Vancouver; ☎ 416-614 2887, fax 614 9670 in Toronto), known as Voyages Campus in Quebec, has offices in all major cities. Visit its Web site at www.travel cuts.com.

You might also scan the travel agents' ads in the *Globe & Mail, Toronto Star* and the *Vancouver Province.*

From Toronto or Montreal, return flights to Paris are available from about C$600 in the low season; prices are C$300 or C$400 more from Vancouver. From Paris, flights are often a bit cheaper to Montreal than to

Toronto, with one-way/return fares starting at an absolute minimum of 1700/3500FF (double that in high season).

## Australia

STA Travel (☎ 131 776 Australia-wide) and Flight Centre (☎ 131 600 Australia-wide) are major dealers in cheap air fares. Their Web sites are at www.statravel.com.au and www.flightcentre.com.au, respectively.

Smaller agencies often advertise in the Saturday travel sections of the *Sydney Morning Herald* and the Melbourne *Age*.

From Melbourne or Sydney, one-way/return tickets to Paris cost from A$990/1510 (low season) to A$1010/2450 (high season, that is, June to August and around Christmas). Fares from Perth are about A$200 cheaper. Airlines that are offering good deals include Kuwait Airways, Qantas Airways, Thai Airways International, Royal Jordanian and Malaysia Airlines.

## New Zealand

As in Australia, STA Travel (☎ 09-309 0458) and Flight Centre (☎ 09-309 6171) are popular travel agents. Ads for other agencies can be found in the travel section of the *New Zealand Herald*.

The cheapest fares to Europe are routed through Asia. With Thai Airways International, one-way/return fares from Auckland (via Bangkok) cost from NZ$1169/2015 (low season) to NZ$1315/2319 (high season). Other companies with attractive fares include Royal Jordanian, Kuwait Airways, Quantas Airways and Malaysia Airlines.

## LAND

Paris – France's main rail and road hub – is linked with every part of Europe. International rail travel to places in France outside Paris sometimes (though much less frequently than in the past) involves switching train stations in the French capital.

## The UK

The Channel Tunnel, inaugurated in 1994, is the first dry-land link between the UK and France since the last Ice Age. The three parallel tunnels – two for trains and one for service access – pass through a layer of impermeable chalk marl 25m to 45m below the floor of the English Channel.

**Bus** Eurolines (☎ 0870 514 3219 in the UK, ☎ 01 43 54 11 99 in Paris) has coach services from London's Victoria Coach Station to Paris via Dover and Calais costing UK£32/45 one-way/return (a bit less if you qualify for a discount, a bit more in July and August) It takes seven and a half hours.

There are Eurolines buses daily from London to Caen (UK£37/50 one-way/return, 11½ hours) and Le Havre (UK£22/40 one-way/return, 10¼ hours). Bookings can be made at any office of National Express, whose buses also link London and other parts of the UK with the Channel ports. Visit their Web sites at www.eurolines.co.uk and www.gobycoach.com.

Intercars (see the Continental Europe section under Land later in this chapter) has a Manchester–London–Paris bus service.

From April to October, Busabout (☎ 020-7950 1661, ✉ info@busabout.co.uk), based in London at 258 Vauxhall Bridge Road, offers the bus version of the Eurail pass. Electronic tickets (replaceable if lost), valid for a minimum of 15 days, let you travel around much of Western Europe (18 countries) for 30 to 40% less than Eurail pass, though with less flexibility. Stops in France are in Paris, Tours, Bordeaux, Lyons, Avignon and Nice. One/two-month passes, available through student travel agencies, cost UK£309/479 or UK£279/429 for those aged under 26, students and teachers; a Flexi Pass good for 21 days of travel over three months costs UK£479 or UK£429 for those aged under 26, students and teachers. Buses stop at each of the 70 cities served every two days. On-board guides can take care of hostel reservations. Visit its Web site at www.busabout.com.

**Eurostar** Taking the Eurostar is an extraordinary experience that has changed the way many British people see the Continent: you are on a sleek, ultra-modern train clickety-clicking through Kent, it's dark for about 20 minutes, and then you're whizzing silently across Flanders at 300km/h. The highly civilised Eurostar takes only three hours (not including the one hour time change) to get from London to Paris: 70 minutes from London's Waterloo station to Folkestone, 20 minutes inside the Channel Tunnel, and 1½ hours from Calais to Paris' Gare du Nord.

There are direct services from London and Ashford to Paris and the three other stations in France: Calais-Fréthun, Lille and Disneyland Paris. In winter, Ski Trains link London with Bourg St-Maurice in the Alps. In France, ticketing is handled by the SNCF.

A full-fare, 2nd-class one-way/return ticket from London to Paris costs a whopping UK£155/270, but prices for return travel drop precipitously if you stay over a Saturday night: UK£69/80 if you book 14/seven days ahead, UK£100 to UK£140 if you don't. Tickets for people aged 25 and under cost UK£45/75 one-way/return. Kids under 12 pay UK£29/58. Student travel agencies often have youth fares not available direct from Eurostar. With the cheapest tickets you cannot change your travel dates or get a reimbursement.

For information on Eurostar contact Eurostar UK (☎ 0870 518 6186), Rail Europe Direct (☎ 0870 584 8848) or Eurostar France (☎ 08 36 35 35 39 at 2.23FF a minute). Alternatively, have a look at the Web site at www.eurostar.com.

**Eurotunnel** High-speed Eurotunnel shuttle trains (☎ 0870 535 3535 in the UK, ☎ 03 21 00 61 00 in France) whisk cars, motorbikes and coaches from Folkestone through the Channel Tunnel to Coquelles, 5km south-west of Calais, in air-conditioned and soundproofed comfort. Shuttles run 24 hours a day, every day of the year, with up to five departures an hour during peak periods (one an hour from 1 to 5 am). Its Web site is at www.eurotunnel.com.

Prices vary with market demand, but the regular one-way fare for a passenger car, including all its passengers, costs from UK£109.50 (in February or March) to UK£174.50 (July or August); return passage costs twice as much. Return fares valid

for less than five days cost from UK£139 to UK£229. The fee for a bicycle, including its rider, is UK£15 return; advance reservations (☎ 01303-288 680) are mandatory. To take advantage of promotional fares you must book at least one day ahead. From Coquelles, count on a 2½-hour drive to Le Tréport, the first town in Normandy.

## Continental Europe
France serves as one of Europe's major land transport hubs.

**Bus** Eurolines (☎ 01 43 54 11 99 in Paris, or ☎ 08 36 69 52 52 at 2.23FF a minute), an association of 31 bus companies that serve destinations in 26 countries, links Paris with points all over Western and Central Europe, Scandinavia and Morocco. Buses are slower and less comfortable than trains, but they are cheaper, especially if you qualify for the 10% discount available to those aged 25 or under and over 60, or take advantage of the discount fares on offer from time to time.

Eurolines' direct buses link Paris with destinations including Amsterdam (195FF, 7½ hours), Barcelona (485FF, 15 hours), Berlin (450FF, 14 hours), Budapest (515FF, 23 hours), Madrid (530FF, 17 hours), Prague (400FF, 16 hours) and Rome (450FF, 23 hours). These are one-way fares for young people and seniors – adults pay about 10% more. Return tickets cost about 20% less than two one-way tickets. In summer, it's not a bad idea to make reservations at least two working days in advance.

The Eurolines Pass, the companies' answer to the Eurail pass, gives you unlimited coach travel between 48 major cities in 21 European countries (but not to other cities en route). Low/high-season tickets good for 30 days cost €264/338 (€214/282 for young people); tickets good for 60 days cost €327/386 (€264/354 for young people). High-season rates apply between June and September.

Eurolines-affiliated companies can be found across Europe, including:

Amsterdam  (☎ 020-560 8787)
Barcelona  (☎ 93 490 4000)

| Berlin | (☎ 030-86 0960) |
| Brussels | (☎ 02 203 0707) |
| Budapest | (☎ 1-11 72 562, ☎ 1-317 2562) |
| Copenhagen | (☎ 33 25 12 44, ☎ 99 34 44 88) |
| Göteborg | (☎ 031-100 240, ☎ 020-98 73 77) |
| Hamburg | (☎ 040-24 98 18, ☎ 040-24 71 06) |
| Istanbul | (☎ 212-696 9600) |
| Lisbon | (☎ 01-315 2644) |
| Madrid | (☎ 91 528 11 05, ☎ 91 327 1381) |
| Prague | (☎ 02-2421 3420, ☎ 02-231 2355) |
| Rome | (☎ 06-44 23 39 28) |
| Vienna | (☎ 01-712 0453) |
| Warsaw | (☎ 022-870 5940, ☎ 022-620 49 48) |

Eurolines' all-Europe Web site at www .eurolines.com has links to each national company's site. Its French Web site is at www.eurolines.fr.

Intercars (☎ 01 42 19 99 35 in Paris, ☎ 01582-404 311 in the UK), whose Paris office is at 139 bis rue de Vaugirard (metro Falguière), links Paris with Berlin and Eastern Europe. From southern France, the company's buses serve Eastern Europe, Italy, Spain, Portugal and Morocco. Check its Web site at www.intercars.fr.

**Train** Rail services link France with every country in Europe; schedules are available from major train stations in France and abroad. The closest hub to Normandy is Paris in the east and the Brittany cities of Le Mans and Rennes in the south.

The only international TGV service links Paris' Gare du Nord to Brussels-Midi (€54, one hour and 25 minutes, 20 a day), Amsterdam CS (€73, 4¼ hours, five a day) and Cologne's Hauptbahnhof (€67, four hours, seven a day). It is known as Thalys (www.thalys.com). Youth fares cost half (or less) of the regular adult fare; seniors also get discounts.

For details on discount rail passes and tickets, see Train in the Getting Around chapter.

## SEA

Tickets for ferry travel to/from the UK, Channel Islands and Ireland are available from most travel agencies in France and the countries served. Except where noted, the prices given below are for standard one-

way tickets; in some cases, return fares cost less than two one-way tickets. Children aged four to somewhere between 12 and 15 (depending on the company) travel for half to two-thirds of the cost of an adult fare.

Food is relatively expensive on ferries so you might want to bring your own. Note that if you're travelling with a vehicle, you are usually denied access to it during the voyage.

## The UK

Fares vary widely according to demand, which depends on the season (July and August are especially popular) and the time of day (a Friday night ferry can cost much more than a Sunday morning one); the most expensive tickets can cost almost three times as much as the cheapest ones. Three or five-day excursion (return) fares generally cost about the same as regular one-way tickets; special promotional return fares, often requiring advance booking, are sometimes cheaper than a one-way fare. On some overnight sailings you have to pay extra for a mandatory reclining seat or sleeping berth.

Ferry companies may try to make it hard on people who use super-cheap one-day return tickets for one-way passage – a huge backpack is a dead giveaway that you're not out for an afternoon outing.

Eurail passes are *not* valid for ferry travel between the UK and France. Transporting bicycles is often (but not always) free.

**To Normandy** The Newhaven–Dieppe route is handled by Hoverspeed's SeaCats (2¼ hours, one to three a day). Pedestrians pay UK£28 one-way; a car with up to nine occupants is charged UK£139 to UK£195 one-way.

Poole is linked to Cherbourg by Brittany Ferries' 4¼-hour crossing (one or two a day). Foot passengers pay from UK£19 to UK£41 one-way; a car with up to five passengers is charged UK£80 to UK£187 one-way. On overnight sailings you have to book either a reclining seat (UK£3) or a sleeping berth (UK£14 to UK£21 for the cheapest variety).

On the Portsmouth–Cherbourg route, P&O Portsmouth has three car ferries a day

## Ferry Companies

### Brittany Ferries

| | |
|---|---|
| UK Reservations | ☎ 0870 901 2400 |
| Ireland Reservations (Cork) | ☎ 021-277 801 |
| France Reservations (Roscoff) | ☎ 02 98 29 28 00 |
| Caen | ☎ 02 31 36 36 36 |
| Cherbourg | ☎ 02 33 88 44 44 |
| St-Malo | ☎ 02 99 82 80 80 |
| Web site: | www.brittany-ferries.com |

### Condor Ferries

| | |
|---|---|
| UK Reservations (Weymouth) | ☎ 0845 345 2000 |
| France Reservations (St-Malo) | ☎ 02 99 20 03 00 |
| Poole | ☎ 01202-207 215 |
| St-Helier | ☎ 01534-601 000 |
| St-Malo | ☎ 02 99 20 03 00 |
| St-Peter Port | ☎ 01481-729 666 |
| Web site: | www.condorferries.co.uk |

### Émeraude Lines

| | |
|---|---|
| General Reservations (Jersey) | ☎ 01534-766 566 |
| Carteret | ☎ 02 33 52 61 39 |
| Granville | ☎ 02 33 50 16 36 |
| Guernsey | ☎ 01481-711414 |
| St-Malo | ☎ 02 23 18 01 80 |
| Web site: | www.emeraude.co.uk |

### Hoverspeed

| | |
|---|---|
| UK Reservations (Dover) | ☎ 0870 240 8070 |
| France Reservations | ☎ 08 20 00 35 55 |
| Calais | ☎ 03 21 46 14 54 |
| Dieppe | ☎ 02 32 14 42 80 |
| Web site: | www.hoverspeed.co.uk |

### Irish Ferries

| | |
|---|---|
| Ireland Reservations | ☎ 01-638 3333 |
| UK Reservations | ☎ 0870 517 1717 |
| Cherbourg | ☎ 02 33 23 44 44 |
| Paris | ☎ 01 44 94 20 40 |
| Roscoff | ☎ 02 98 61 17 17 |
| Rosslare | ☎ 053-33 158 |
| Web site: | www.irish-ferries.com |

### P&O Irish Sea Ferries

| | |
|---|---|
| Northern Ireland Reservations | ☎ 0870 242 4777 |
| Cherbourg | ☎ 08 03 01 30 13 |
| Web site | www.poirishsea.com |

### P&O Portsmouth

| | |
|---|---|
| UK Reservations | ☎ 0870 598 0555 |
| France Reservations | ☎ 08 03 01 30 13 |
| Web site: | www.poportsmouth.com |

### P&O Stena Line

| | |
|---|---|
| UK Reservations (Dover) | ☎ 0870 600 0611 |
| | ☎ 0870 600 9009 |
| France Reservations | ☎ 08 02 01 00 20 |
| Calais | ☎ 03 21 46 04 40 |
| Web site: | www.posl.com |

### SeaFrance Sealink

| | |
|---|---|
| UK Reservations (Dover) | ☎ 0870 571 1711 |
| France Reservations | ☎ 08 04 04 40 45 |
| Web site: | www.seafrance.com |

(five hours by day, eight hours overnight) and, from mid-March to mid-October, two faster catamarans a day. Foot passengers pay UK£20 to UK£36 one-way; a non-mandatory overnight cabin for one or two people costs UK£32 to UK£46. Cars with up to eight passengers pay UK£148 to UK£187 one-way, not including a surcharge of up to UK£40 for some catamaran crossings.

The Portsmouth–Le Havre crossing is handled by P&O Portsmouth (5½ hours by day, 7¾ hours overnight, three car ferries a day, a bit less in winter). Passage costs about the same as for Portsmouth–Cherbourg.

Brittany Ferries also has car ferries from Portsmouth to Caen (Ouistreham, six hours, three a day). Tickets cost a bit more than for Poole–Cherbourg.

**Via Far Northern France** The fastest way to cross the English Channel is between Dover and Calais, served by Hoverspeed's SeaCats (Australian-designed catamarans), which take 50 minutes. For foot passengers, a one-way trip (or a return completed within five days) costs UK£24 (243FF). Depending on the season, a car with up to nine passengers pays UK£109 to UK£175 one-way, and UK£135 to UK£225 for a five-day return. All sorts of incredibly cheap promotional fares are often available, including return day trip fares for pedestrians for as little as UK£5 or UK£10. From Calais, there are five daily trains to Le Tréport, the northernmost town in Normandy, (133FF, 2½ to four hours) with a change at Abbeville.

The Dover–Calais crossing is also handled by car ferries, run by SeaFrance (1½ hours; 15 a day) and P&O Stena (one to 1¼ hours, 29 a day). With SeaFrance, foot passengers pay UK£15 for a one-way or five-day return ticket; day trips are sometimes available for just UK£5 or UK£10. A car with up to nine passengers pays UK£122.50 to UK£170 one-way, double that for return. A five-day return is UK£150 to UK£215. Prices are a bit cheaper if you book on the Internet. If you don't book ahead there's a surcharge at the port. With P&O Stena, foot passengers pay UK£24 for a one-way or five-day return ticket; a car with up to nine people pays a minimum of UK£122.50.

**Via Brittany** From mid-March to mid-November, Plymouth is linked to Roscoff (six hours for day crossings; one to three a day) by Brittany Ferries. The one-way fare for foot passengers is UK£24 to UK£41. Cars with up to five passengers pay from UK£106 to UK£179 one-way. On overnight sailings you have to book either a reclining seat (UK£3) or a sleeping berth (UK£14 to UK£21 for the cheapest type).

Brittany Ferries also links Portsmouth with St-Malo (8¾ hours for day crossing, once a day). All sailings *to* St-Malo are overnight and require that you book either a reclining seat (UK£3) or a sleeping berth (at least UK£14 to UK£21). Pedestrians pay

UK£21 to UK£44 one-way; a car with up to five passengers is charged UK£91 to UK£192 one-way.

From late May to mid-October, Condor Ferries has one catamaran a day linking Weymouth with St-Malo. The 4¼-hour crossing costs UK£26 one-way for pedestrians; cars, including two passengers, cost UK£95 to UK£187. The company also links Poole with St-Malo.

## The Channel Islands

From April to mid-October, Émeraude Lines' passenger-only catamarans link the Channel Islands with two small ports on the western coast of Normandy, Granville and Carteret (daily, with departures to/from the Channel Islands in the morning/evening). The one-way pedestrian fare is UK£28; one-day excursion fares are UK£24 to UK£29. Émeraude links Guernsey with Dielette and also runs express car ferries between Jersey and St-Malo (1¼ hours). A car, not including the passengers, costs around UK£100 one-way.

## Ireland

Eurail pass holders pay 50% of the adult pedestrian fare for crossings between Ireland and France on Irish Ferries (make sure you book ahead).

Irish Ferries has overnight runs from Rosslare to either Cherbourg (18 hours) or Roscoff (16 hours) every other day (three times a week from mid-September to October, with a possible break in service from November to February). Pedestrians pay IR£40 to IR£80 (IR£32 to IR£66 for students and seniors). A two-bed cabin costs IR£26 to IR£34. A car with two passengers costs from IR£130 to IR£320.

From April to September, Brittany Ferries runs a car ferry every Saturday from Cork (Ringaskiddy) to Roscoff (14 hours), and every Friday in the other direction. Foot passengers pay IR£35 to IR£69; a car with two adults costs IR£115 to IR£319 one-way.

Freight ferries run by P&O Irish Sea link Rosslare with Cherbourg (18 hours, three times a week). A car with two passengers pays IR£110 to IR£260 one-way. Foot passengers are not accepted.

## The USA & Canada

The days when you could earn your passage to Europe on a freighter have well and truly passed, but it's still possible to travel as a passenger on a cargo ship. Trips from New York or Montreal to Northern Europe, some stopping at Le Havre, cost around US$2880 return. Such vessels typically carry five to 12 passengers (more than 12 would require a doctor on board).

Details are available from the TravLtips Cruise & Freighter Travel Association (☎ 800 872 8584 in the USA, ℮ info@travltips.com), Freighter World Cruises (☎ 800 531 7774 in the USA) and The Cruise People Ltd (☎ 800 268 6523 in the USA, ☎ 0800 526 313 in the UK, ☎ 416-444 2410 in Canada, ℮ cruise@dial.pipex.com).

You can visit their Web sites at www.travltips.com, www.freighterworld.com and at http://members.aol.com/CruiseAZ/home.htm, respectively.

## Warning

The information in this chapter is particularly vulnerable to change: Prices for international travel are volatile, new routes are introduced and cancelled, schedules change, special deals come and go, and rules and visa requirements are amended. Airlines and governments seem to take a perverse pleasure in making price structures and regulations as complicated as possible. You should check directly with the airline or a travel agent to make sure you understand how a fare (and ticket you may buy) works. In addition, the travel industry is highly competitive and there are many lurks and perks.

The upshot of this is that you should get opinions, quotes and advice from as many airlines and travel agents as possible before you part with your hard-earned cash. The details given in this chapter should be regarded as pointers and are not a substitute for your own careful, up-to-date research.

# Getting Around

France's domestic transport network, much of it owned or subsidised by the government, tends to be monopolistic: the state-owned SNCF takes care of virtually all inter-departmental land transport, and short-haul bus companies are either run by the department or grouped so each local company handles a different set of destinations.

## BUS

Normandy has an extensive network of buses linking the major cities and many small towns, but schedules are mostly designed to accommodate the needs of students and workers. Some smaller villages in the interior are not served at all by bus links. The coast has a more reliable service than the interior, but services through the region are cut dramatically on Saturday and are often non-existent on Sunday. School holidays also involve a rearrangement of bus schedules.

The bus network is handled by companies within each department as follows:

**Autocars Gris** (☎ 02 35 28 19 88) 55–7 rue de Verdier, Fécamp. Serves the Côte d'Albâtre.
**Bus Verts** (☎ 02 31 44 77 44) 11 rue des Chanoines, Caen. Serves Calvados department.
**Cars Jaquemard** (☎ 02 32 33 09 66) rue Gay Lussac, Évreux. Serves the eastern Eure department.
**Cars Joffret** (☎ 02 32 81 62 62) 10 boulevard Industrial, Sotteville-les-Rouen. Links Rouen with Lisieux and Pont Audemer.
**Compagnie Normande d'Autobus (CNA)** (☎ 02 35 52 92 29) rue des Charettes, Rouen. Serves the Seine-Maritime.
**SCETA Normandie** (☎ 02 35 98 13 38) 34 rue Verte, Rouen. Serves the northern and western Eure, southern Manche.
**Société des Transports de Normandie (STN)** (☎ 02 33 88 51 00) rue Jean Bouin, Tourlaville. Serves the Manche.
**STAO (Tourisme Verney)** (☎ 02 33 29 11 11) rue Lazare-Carnot, Alençon. Serves the Orne.

In addition, SNCF has replaced some train services with buses, most notably from the train station at Serqueux to Dieppe and from Briouze to Bagnoles de l'Orne.

## TRAIN

Normandy is also crisscrossed with trains, run by France's national rail network, the SNCF (Société Nationale des Chemins de Fer Français). Most are linked to Paris and serve the schedules of commuters who work in Paris and live in Normandy. Some of the major lines are: Paris–Alençon, Paris–Cabourg, Paris–Caen, Paris–Cherbourg, Paris–Évreux, Paris–Granville, Paris–Le Havre, Paris–Rouen, Caen–Rennes, Caen–Pontorson, Rouen–Alençon, Rouen–Caen, Rouen–Dieppe and Rouen–Fécamp.

### Train Passes

Details on the countrywide rail passes available for Europeans and non-Europeans

---

### How to Find Train Information

From 7 am to 10 pm daily, you can get schedule and fare information and make reservations for the SNCF's domestic and international services in a number of languages (2.23FF a minute):

| | |
|---|---|
| English | ☎ 08 36 35 35 39 |
| French | ☎ 08 36 35 35 35 |
| German | ☎ 08 36 35 35 36 |
| Spanish | ☎ 08 36 35 35 37 |
| Italian | ☎ 08 36 35 35 38 |

| | |
|---|---|
| SNCF | www.sncf.com |
| Eurostar | www.eurostar.com |
| Rail Europe (North America) | |
| | www.raileurope.com |

If your French is up to it you can also call the local train stations for information. Where available, the telephone numbers are provided in each destination.

---

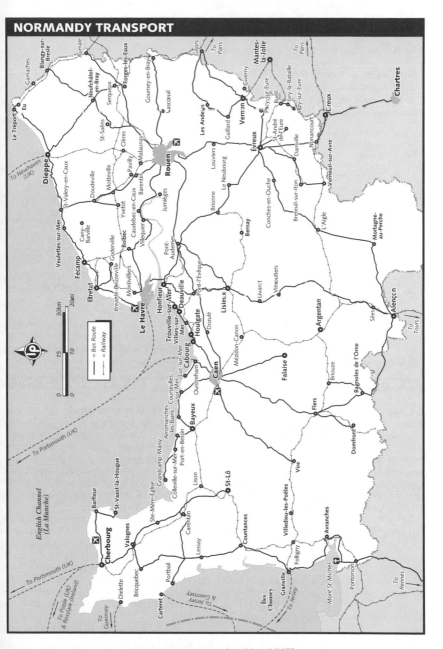

# NORMANDY TRANSPORT

= Bus Route
= Railway

English Channel
(La Manche)

To Newhaven (UK)
To Portsmouth (UK)
To Portsmouth (UK)
To Poole (UK) & Roslare (Ireland)
To Guernsey
To Guernsey & Jersey
To Jersey
To Rennes
To Tours
To Paris
To Paris

Le Tréport
Eu
Gamaches
Blangy-sur-Bresle
Aumale
Neufchâtel-en-Bray
Serqueux
Forges-les-Eaux
Gournay-en-Bray
Gisors
Giverny
Mantes-la-Jolie
Chartres
Dieppe
St-Saëns
St-Valéry-en-Caux
Doudeville
Motteville
Clères
Pavilly
Malaunay
Barentin
Rouen
Les Andelys
Gaillard
Pacy-sur-Eure
Bueil
Ivry-la-Bataille
Bréy-sur-Eure
Vernon
Évreux
St-André-de-l'Eure
Nonancourt
Évreux
Veulettes-sur-Mer
Cany-Barville
Goderville
Yvetot
Caudebec-en-Caux
Villequier
Jumièges
Louviers
Le Neubourg
Brionne
Conches-en-Ouche
Breteuil-sur-Iton
Damville
Verneuil-sur-Avre
Fécamp
Bréauté-Beuzeville
Montivilliers
Étretat
Pont-Audemer
Bernay
L'Aigle
Mortagne-au-Perche
Le Havre
Honfleur
Deauville
Trouville-sur-Mer
Villers-sur-Mer
Houlgate
Pont-l'Évêque
Lisieux
Livarot
Vimoutiers
Argentan
Sées
Alençon
Cabourg
Luc-sur-Mer
Ouistreham
Mézidon-Canon
Dozulé
Caen
Falaise
Bagnoles-de-l'Orne
Arromanches-les-Bains
Courseulles-sur-Mer
Bayeux
Briouze
Colleville-sur-Mer
Port-en-Bessin
Flers
Domfront
Grandcamp-Maisy
Lison
St-Lô
Vire
Ste-Mère-Église
Carentan
Coutances
Villedieu-les-Poêles
Avranches
Barfleur
St-Vaast-la-Hougue
Lessay
Valognes
Folligny
Cherbourg
Granville
Mont St-Michel
Pontorson
Dielette
Bricquebec
Portbail
Carteret
Îles Chausey

30km
20mi
15
10
0
0

euro currency converter €1 = 6.56FF

## Discount Train Tickets & Passes

The fares discussed below are available at all SNCF stations and there are no residency requirements.

**Reduced-Price Tickets** Discounts of 25% on one-way or return travel within France are available at train station ticket windows for certain groups of travellers, subject to availability. Just show the ticket agent proof of eligibility and you'll get the reduction on the spot.

- If you're aged 12 to 25, you are eligible for a Découverte 12/25 fare.
- One to four adults travelling with a child aged four to 11 qualify for the Découverte Enfant Plus fare.
- People aged over 60 enjoy a fare called Découverte Senior.
- Any two people who are travelling together qualify for a Découverte À Deux fare, which gives you a 25% reduction in 1st or 2nd class, but only on return travel.
- Internationally, young people aged 12 to 25 get significant discounts on the Eurostar.

**Découverte Séjour** No matter what age you are, you can get a 25% reduction for return travel within France if you meet two conditions: the total distance you'll be travelling is at least 200km; and you'll be spending a Saturday night at your destination.

**Découverte J30 & J8** You can save significant sums if you buy a ticket for a specific train well in advance. The Découverte J30, which must be purchased 30 to 60 days before the date of travel, offers savings of 45% to 55%. The Découverte J8, which you must buy at least eight days ahead, gets you 20% to 30% off. A refund of 70% is available up to four days before departure; after that, it's use it or lose it.

The Euro Domino and Inter-Rail passes are available to people of all ages and nationalities provided they have been resident in Europe for at least six months. However, you cannot purchase a pass for use in your country of residence. Holders of these passes also get discounts on the Eurostar, Thalys, SNCM ferries to Corsica, and SeaFrance ferries on the Dover–Calais route, but they must pay all

---

are outlined in the boxed text 'Discount Train Tickets & Passes', but if you'll be confining your travel to Normandy, it's unlikely that you'll rack up enough kilometres to make most passes worthwhile. In Lower Normandy there's a weekend pass, the *Carte Sillage Loisirs*, that offers a 50% reduction for the passholder and a second person and only a 1FF charge for additional people. The journey must be completed on either Saturday or Sunday; the pass costs 50FF and is valid for a year.

### Classes

Most French trains have both 1st- and 2nd-class sections. The 1st-class section is more spacious, but on the short hauls within Normandy it's not really worth the money.

### Tickets & Reservations

Some stations may have separate windows for *achat à l'avance* (advance purchase) and *départ du jour* (same-day departure). You can almost always use MasterCard, Visa, Diners Club, Aurore or Amex credit cards. Tickets bought with cash can be reimbursed for cash (by you or a thief), so keep them in a safe place.

If you buy your ticket with a credit card via the SNCF's Web site (see the boxed text 'How to Find Train Information'), you can either have it sent to you by post or pick it up at any SNCF ticket office using your *numéro de dossier* (reference number). As a safety precaution, you will also be asked to show the credit card used to purchase the ticket.

Almost every SNCF station in the region

## Discount Train Tickets & Passes

SNCF reservation fees (and, with Inter-Rail, supplements).

Several rail passes let people who are not residents of Europe take advantage of the French and European railway networks at a discount. These passes do *not* cover SNCF reservation fees or *couchette* (sleeping berth) charges, but they do get you discounts on the Eurostar and Thalys. Most of them come in half-price versions for children aged four to 11.

Contrary to popular belief, the Eurailpass and the other passes discussed below *can* be purchased at a limited number of places in Europe provided you're not a resident of any European country. However, prices are about 10% higher than they are overseas. In France, passes are available from the SNCF offices at Orly and Roissy Charles de Gaulle airports; in Paris at Gare du Nord, Gare de Lyon and Gare St-Lazare; and at the main train stations in Marseille and Nice.

**Eurailpass** The Eurailpass offers reasonable value if you plan to really clock up the kilometres and have not reached your 26th birthday on the first day of travel (people over that age can only get the pricey 1st-class versions). One/two months of unlimited travel with the Eurail Youthpass costs €665/941.

The Eurail Youth Flexipass, good for travel on any 10 or 15 days you select over a period of two months, costs €489/639. Eurailpasses are not valid in the UK or on cross-Channel ferries but they do get you half-off on Irish Ferries routes between the Irish Republic and France (note: these do not run between January and March).

**France Railpass** This flexipass entitles you to unlimited travel on the SNCF system for three to nine days over the course of a month. In 2nd class, the three-day version costs €192 (€155 each for two people travelling together); each additional day of travel costs €32.

The France Youthpass, available if you're 25 and under, costs €175 for four days of travel over two months; additional days (up to a maximum of 10) cost €21.

has at least one *billeterie automatique* (on-line ticket machine) that accepts credit cards for purchases of at least 10FF. Tickets *can* be purchased on board the train, but unless the ticket window where you boarded was closed, prohibitive surcharges apply: 50/100FF for journeys under/over 75km. If you search out the *contrôleur* (conductor) rather than letting yourself be discovered ticketless, the surcharge may be only 20/40FF.

Reserving in advance, at a cost of 20FF, is optional unless you're travelling by Eurostar or you'll be travelling during holiday periods (for example around Easter and 14 July) when trains may be full. Reservations can be made by telephone or via the SNCF's Web site.

Before departure time you can change

your reservation by telephone. To pick up your new tickets, go to a ticket counter with the reference number you've been given. Reservations can be changed for no charge up to one hour *after* your scheduled departure time, but only if you are actually at your departure station.

For full-fare SNCF tickets, getting a 90% reimbursement (100% before scheduled departure if you've got a reservation) is possible up to two months after purchase (up to six months for international tickets except for Eurostar). You can get a refund on the unused portion of a return ticket if it falls within the two- to six-month period. The process is pretty straightforward – just go to any train station ticket window or, in a mainline station, a Service Clientèle office. Tickets purchased from a travel agent or outside France can only be reimbursed at the issuing office.

## Schedules

SNCF's free, pocket-size *horaires* (time schedules) can be a bit complicated to read, especially if you don't understand French railway-speak.

The numbers at the top of each column are *notes à consulter* (footnote references). Often a particular train *circule* (runs) only on Friday or only on certain dates. Alternatively, it may operate *tous les jours* (every day) *sauf* (except) Saturday, Sunday and/or *fêtes* (holidays). Of 20 trains listed on the schedule, only a few may be running on the day you'd like to travel.

If you'll be doing a lot of travel in one region of France, ask at a train station for a *Guide Régional des Transports*, an easy-to-use booklet of SNCF schedules published by some regional governments. For national coverage, you can purchase an *Indicateur Horaires Ville à Ville* (60FF for a book or a Windows-compatible CD-ROM), sold in train stations at Relay newsagents.

Some people swear by the *Thomas Cook European Timetable* (150FF), useful for figuring out which domestic and international routings are feasible so you can use rail passes to their fullest. It is updated monthly and available from Thomas Cook bureaux de change.

## Validating Your Train Ticket

Before boarding the train you must validate your ticket by time-stamping it in a *composteur*, one of those orange posts situated somewhere between the ticket windows and the tracks. If you forget, find a conductor so they can punch it for you (if you wait for your crime to be discovered, you're likely to be fined).

Eurail and some other rail passes must be validated at a train station ticket window before you make your first journey to begin the period of validity.

## Costs

For 2nd-class travel, count on paying 50FF to 60FF per 100km for cross-country trips

and 70FF to 100FF per 100km for short hops. (In comparison, autoroute tolls come to 36FF to 46FF per 100km, while petrol adds another 44FF.) Full-fare return passage costs twice as much as one-way. Travel in 1st class is 50% more expensive than 2nd class. Children under four travel free; those aged four to 11 pay 50% of the adult fare.

On certain trains to/from Paris, passengers travelling during *heures de pointe* (peak periods) have to pay a supplement of up to 45FF to 90FF in 2nd class. Supplements do not generally apply to travel from one provincial station to another but may be levied if you take an international train on a domestic segment. Departure boards at train stations indicate which trains require supplements.

Where applicable, Eurailpass holders must pay reservation fees (20FF on all trains, including TGVs) but *not* supplements.

## Left-Luggage Services

A few larger SNCF stations have both a *consigne manuelle* (left-luggage office), where it costs 30FF or 35FF to store a bag, skis or a bicycle for 24 hours; and a *consigne automatique*, a computerised locker system that will issue you with a lock code or a magnetic ticket (good for 48 or 72 hours) in exchange for 15FF, 20FF or 30FF, depending on the size of the locker. At smaller stations you may be able to check your bag with the clerk at the ticket window (30FF). Some left-luggage facilities are open only for limited hours.

As we went to press most luggage lockers were out of service at part of a national program to prevent terrorist attacks.

## CAR & MOTORCYCLE

Having your own wheels gives you exceptional freedom and the ability to explore lovely, out-of-the-way places within Normandy's interior. Many of the small villages, chateaux and regional parks are totally inaccessible by public transport.

Motorcyclists will find Normandy great for touring, with winding roads of good quality and lots of stunning scenery. Just make sure your wet-weather gear is up to scratch.

There are four types of intercity roads:

**Autoroutes** These multilane divided motorways/highways, usually requiring the payment of tolls, have alphanumeric designations which begin with A. Marked by blue signs depicting a divided highway receding into the distance, they often have lovely *aires de repos* (rest areas), some with restaurants and pricey petrol stations.

**Routes Nationales** These are main highways, some of them divided for short stretches, whose names begin with N (or, on older maps and signs, RN).

**Routes Départmentales** These are local roads whose names begin with D.

**Routes Communales** These are minor rural roads whose names sometimes begin with C or V.

## Road Rules

All drivers must carry at all times a national ID card or passport; a valid driver's licence (*permis de conduire*; many foreign licences can be used in France for up to a year); car ownership papers, known as a *carte grise* (grey card); and proof of third-party (liability) insurance, known as a *carte verte* (green card). Never leave car ownership or insurance papers in your vehicle.

A right-hand drive vehicle brought to France from the UK or Ireland must have deflectors affixed to the headlights to avoid dazzling oncoming traffic. A motor vehicle entering a foreign country must display a sticker identifying its country of registration. In the UK, information on driving in France is available from the RAC (☎ 0800 550055) and the AA (☎ 0870 550 0600). *Motoring in Europe* (UK£4.99), published in the UK by the RAC, gives an excellent summary of road regulations in each European country, including parking rules.

French law requires that all passengers, including those in the back seat, wear seat belts, and children who weigh less than 18kg must travel in backward-facing child seats. A passenger car is permitted to carry a maximum of five people. North American drivers should remember that turning right on a red light is illegal in France.

Unless otherwise posted, a speed limit of 50km/h applies in *all* areas designated as built-up, no matter how rural they may appear. On intercity roads, you must slow to 50km/h the moment you pass a white sign with red borders on which a place name is written. This limit remains in force until you arrive at the other edge of town, where

## Road Distances (km)

| | Alençon | Avranches | Bayeux | Caen | Cherbourg | Coutances | Dieppe | Falaise | Le Havre | Mont St-Michel | Paris | Rouen |
|---|---|---|---|---|---|---|---|---|---|---|---|---|
| Alençon | --- | | | | | | | | | | | |
| Avranches | 125 | --- | | | | | | | | | | |
| Bayeux | 125 | 95 | --- | | | | | | | | | |
| Caen | 105 | 99 | 29 | --- | | | | | | | | |
| Cherbourg | 224 | 121 | 95 | 124 | --- | | | | | | | |
| Coutances | 155 | 44 | 59 | 81 | 75 | --- | | | | | | |
| Dieppe | 204 | 277 | 206 | 174 | 302 | 281 | --- | | | | | |
| Falaise | 23 | 130 | 64 | 36 | 158 | 135 | 208 | --- | | | | |
| Le Havre | 188 | 191 | 121 | 77 | 215 | 196 | 108 | 120 | --- | | | |
| Mont St-Michel | 134 | 19 | 119 | 100 | 155 | 68 | 302 | 152 | 190 | --- | | |
| Paris | 194 | 335 | 260 | 236 | 354 | 322 | 175 | 203 | 204 | 312 | --- | |
| Rouen | 147 | 223 | 153 | 104 | 247 | 214 | 56 | 152 | 71 | 233 | 139 | --- |

you'll pass an identical sign that has a red diagonal bar across the name.

Outside built-up areas, speed limits are:

- 90km/h (80km/h if it's raining) on undivided N and D highways
- 110km/h (100km/h if it's raining) on dual carriageways (divided highways) or short sections of highway with a divider strip
- 130km/h (110km/h in the rain, 60km/h in icy conditions) on autoroutes

Speed limits are generally not posted unless they deviate from those mentioned above. If you drive at the speed limit, expect to have lots of cars coming to within a few metres of your rear bumper, flashing their lights, and then overtaking at the first opportunity.

For overseas tourists, the most confusing – and dangerous – traffic law in France is the notorious *priorité à droite* (priority to the right) rule, under which any car entering an intersection (including a T-junction) from a road on your right has right-of-way. At most larger roundabouts (traffic circles) – French road engineers *love* roundabouts – priorité à droite has been suspended so that the cars already on the roundabout have right of way. Look for signs reading either *'vous n'avez pas la priorité'* (you do not have right of way) or *'cédez le passage'* (give way), or by yield signs displaying a circle made out of three curved arrows.

Priorité à droite is also suspended on priority roads, which are marked by an up-ended yellow square with a black square in the middle (see illustration). Such signs appear every few kilometres and at inter-

sections. Priorité à droite is reinstated if you see the same sign with a diagonal bar through it.

French law is very tough on drunk drivers. To find drivers whose blood-alcohol concentration (BAC) is over 0.05% (0.5 grams per litre of blood) – the equivalent of two glasses of wine for a 75kg adult – the police sometimes conduct random breathalyser tests. Fines start at 900FF; you can also be arrested on the spot.

Riders of any type of two-wheeled vehicle with a motor (except motor-assisted bicycles) must wear a helmet – if you're caught bareheaded, you can be fined and have your bike confiscated until you get one. Bikes of more than 125cc must have their headlights on during the day. No special licence is required to ride a motorbike whose engine is smaller than 50cc, which is why you often find places renting scooters rated at 49.9cc.

## Costs

The convenience of having your own vehicle does not come cheap, but for two or more people a car may cost less than going by train (this depends in part on what rail discounts you qualify for). Although petrol and tolls can add up, you'll be able to save money on accommodation by staying in super-cheap chain hotels such as Formule 1, camp sites and B&Bs that are often in the middle of nowhere.

*Essence* (petrol or gasoline), also known as *carburant* (fuel), is expensive in France, incredibly so if you're used to Australian or North American prices. At the time of writing, unleaded *(sans plomb)* petrol with an IOR octane rating of 98 cost 6.89FF to 7.89FF a litre (there are about 4L to a US gallon; about 4½L to a UK gallon). Diesel fuel *(gazole)* costs 5FF to 6FF per litre. Filling up *(faire le plein)* is most expensive at the rest stops along the autoroutes and cheapest at small rural petrol stations. Petrol is cheaper in all the countries that have borders with France (except, perhaps, Italy) than in France itself; Luxembourg is especially inexpensive.

Tolls are charged for travel on almost all

autoroutes (except around major cities) and many bridges. On autoroutes, you're essentially paying for the right to drive faster and thus save time – and to maintain the profit margins of the private companies that built and maintain the infrastructure.

At the *péages* (toll booth), count on paying 36FF to 46FF per 100km, by credit card if you prefer. Watch out for the A14 which is substantially more expensive than the A13. Rouen–Caen costs 42FF on the A13; Rouen–Le Havre on the A29 costs 21FF. Notice that the autoroute is mainly useful for the Rouen–Caen–Le Havre run; it does not connect many more cities.

The Web site www.autoroutes.fr is a useful source of information on autoroute driving.

### Dangers & Annoyances

Measured relative to the number of kilometres driven, the rate of fatalities on French roads – some 8000 a year – is almost double that of the UK or the USA.

Theft from and of cars is a *major* problem in all of France, including Normandy. For more details, see Dangers & Annoyances in the Facts for the Visitor chapter.

If you are involved in a minor accident with no injuries, the easiest way for the drivers to sort things out with their respective insurance companies is to fill out a Constat Aimable d'Accident Automobile, known in English as a European Accident Statement, which has a standardised way of recording important details about what happened. In rental cars it is usually included in the packet of documents you are given.

If your French is not fluent, find someone who can explain exactly what each word of traffic jargon means. Never sign anything you don't understand – insist on a translation and sign that only if it's acceptable. Make sure you can read the other driver's handwriting. If problems crop up, it's usually not very hard to find a police officer. To alert the police dial ☎ 17.

Make sure the report includes any information that will help you to prove that the accident was not your fault. For instance, if you were just sitting there and the other

---

### Parking

If you have a car and will be spending time in Normandy's cities, finding a place to park is likely to be the single greatest hassle you'll face. Your best bet is usually to ditch the car somewhere and then either walk or take public transport.

Parking in city centres requires paying up to 10FF an hour and is subject to a time limit, often two hours. This lamentable circumstance, which requires that you keep running to the car to feed the metre, is generally indicated either by the word *payant* written on the asphalt or by an upright sign in French.

Payment is made using kerbside *horodateurs* (parking meters), into which you feed coins according to how long you want to park. When you press the correct button (usually the green one – the other ones are for local residents), the machine spits out a little ticket listing the precise time after which you'll be illegally parked. Take the ticket and place it on the dashboard so it's visible from the pavement.

Horodateurs in most cities are programmed to take into account periods when parking is free, so you can pay the night before for the first two hours after 9 am.

Parking on some streets is governed by an arrangement called *stationnement alterné semi-mensuel*, which means you can park on one side of the street from the 1st of the month until the evening of the 15th and on the other side from the 16th until the end of the month. Your clue to this circumstance: a no parking sign with '1–15' (parking forbidden for the first half of the month) or '16–31' written on it.

---

person backed into you, mention this under Observations (No 14 on the Constat). Remember, if you *did* cause the accident (or can't prove that you didn't) you may end up paying a hefty excess (deductible), depending on your insurance policy or rental contract.

If your car is *en panne* (breaks down), you'll have to find a garage that handles your *marque* (make of car). There are Peugeot, Renault and Citroën garages all over the place, but if you have a non-French car you may have trouble finding someone to service it in more remote areas. Michelin's *Guide Rouge* lists garages at the end of each entry.

Note that service stations in many towns and villages are closed on Sunday. The local tourist office should be able to direct you to a service station that's open in off-hours but you'll have to pay by credit card.

Try not to be on the roads when the French are involved in their massive seasonal shift from home to holiday spot. On the first and last weekends of August, roads can be completely clogged, and the weekend around 15 August is also a time of heavy traffic. Tune into 107.7 MHz FM, which gives traffic reports in English every 30 minutes during the summer.

## Rental

**Car** The big international firms – Avis (☎ 08 02 05 05 05), Web site www.avis.com; Budget (☎ 08 00 10 00 01), Web site www.budget.com; Europcar (☎ 08 03 35 23 52), Web site www.europcar.com; Hertz (☎ 01 39 38 38 38), Web site www.hertz.com; and National-Citer (☎ 01 44 38 61 61 or ☎ 08 00 20 21 21), Web site www.citer.com – provide a very reliable service. Usually, you can arrange to return the car to a different outlet. Unfortunately, if you walk into an agency and ask for a car on the spot you'll pay a small fortune – up to 995FF for one day with Avis, about 40 to 50% of that with most of the others. Under SNCF's pricey Train + Auto plan, you can reserve an Avis car when you book your train ticket and it will be waiting for you when you arrive at any of 195 train stations.

Even the French-based chains such as ADA (☎ 01 55 46 19 99), Web site www.ada-sa.fr; Rent-a-Car Système (☎ 08 36 69 46 95), Web site www.rentacar.fr; and – for students – OTU Voyages (☎ 01 40 29 12 12), Web site www.otu.fr, are not really cheap, but you can generally get a small car for about 270FF for one day (including 100km) or 570/1500FF for a weekend/week. Weekly

rates with some of the big boys (such as Europcar or National-Citer) may be only marginally more expensive. It's a good idea to reserve a few days in advance, especially during tourist high seasons.

Prebooked and prepaid rates, arranged before you leave home, are often a *much* better deal than on-the-spot rentals. You can often get a car for US$200 a week (including collision damage and theft waivers); rentals in the countries bordering France, especially Belgium, can be up to 25% cheaper. Details of deals are available in newspaper travel sections, on the Internet, from local travel agents and from companies such as US-based Auto Europe (☎ 888 223 5555), Web site www.autoeurope.com, and UK-based Holiday Autos (☎ 0870 530 0400), whose US affiliate is Kemwel Holiday Autos (☎ 800 576 1590), Web site www.kemwel.com. If you'll be needing a car for more than three or four weeks, see the Purchase-Repurchase Plans section later in this chapter for details on some incredibly inexpensive options.

*Assurance au tiers* (third party/liability insurance) is mandatory, but things such as collision-damage waivers (CDW) vary greatly from company to company. The contract offered by some no-name, cut-rate firm may leave you liable for up to 8000FF – when comparing rates, the most important thing to check is the *franchise* (excess/deductible), which is usually 2000FF for a small car. If you're in an accident in which you're at fault, or the car is damaged and the party at fault is unknown (for example, someone dents your car while it's parked), or the car is stolen, this is the amount that you are liable for before the CDW kicks in. Some US credit card companies (such as Amex) have built-in CDW, but you may have to cover all expenses in the event of an accident and claim the damage back from the credit-card company later.

Most companies require that you be at least 21 (or, in some cases, over 25) and have had a driver's licence for a minimum of one year. Some may also require that you have a credit card. *Kilométrage illimité* means that there's no limit on how many kilometres you can drive. Airport tariffs may be higher than the rates charged in town.

The addresses of car rental companies appear in the Getting There & Away sections in individual city or town listings. Virtually all are closed on Sunday, and some are also closed on Saturday afternoon.

**Motorcycle** Moped and motorcycle rental is common in Normandy, especially in beach resorts, but it is all too common to see inexperienced riders leap on bikes and very quickly fall off them again. Where relevant, details on rental options appear under Getting There & Away at the end of city and town listings.

To rent a moped, scooter or motorcycle you usually have to leave a *caution* (deposit) of several thousand francs, which you forfeit – up to the value of the damage – if you're in an accident and it's your fault, or if the bike is in some way damaged. You'll also lose the deposit if the bike is stolen. Most places accept deposits made by credit card, travellers cheques or Eurocheques.

## Purchase-Repurchase Plans

If you'll be needing a car in Europe for 17 days to six months (one year if you're studying or teaching in France), by far your cheapest option is to 'purchase' a brand new one from Peugeot or Renault and then, at the end of your trip, 'sell' it back to them. In reality, you only pay for the number of days you use the vehicle.

The tax-free, purchase-repurchase *(achat-rachat)* aspect of the paperwork (none of which is your responsibility) makes this uniquely French type of leasing considerably cheaper than renting, especially for longer periods. Eligibility is restricted to people who are *not* residents of the EU (citizens of EU countries are eligible if they live outside the EU).

Everyone we know who's travelled with a purchase-repurchase car – including several Lonely Planet authors – has given Renault's Eurodrive and Peugeot's Vacation Plan (Sodexa) programs rave reviews. Prices include unlimited kilometrage, 24-hour towing

and breakdown service, and comprehensive insurance with – incredibly – no excess (deductible), so returning a damaged car is totally hassle-free. Both companies let you drive in about 30 countries in Western and Central Europe (not including Hungary and Poland for insurance reasons) as well as Morocco and Tunisia. The minimum age is 18. It's helpful but not obligatory to have a credit card. One minor problem: the red number plates announce to all passing thieves that the car is being driven by someone from abroad (see Dangers & Annoyances in the Facts for the Visitor chapter).

Payment for the period for which you would like the car must be made in advance. If you return it early, you can usually get a refund for the unused time (seven days minimum). Extending your contract is possible (using a credit card) but you'll end up paying about double the prepaid per-day rate, in part because of the added paperwork – call Peugeot (☎ 01 49 04 81 19) or Renault (☎ 01 40 40 33 68) at least four working days before your original return date so insurance coverage can be extended.

Cars can be picked up in cities all over Normandy and returned to any other purchase-repurchase centre. They can also be collected or dropped off in other parts of France and beyond (for example, in Amsterdam, Frankfurt, London, Madrid or Rome) but this involves a hefty surcharge (with Renault, from UK£122 to UK£229 each for pick-up and return).

**Renault** You can order a Eurodrive car either from a travel agent or through the company representatives – contact details are listed in the boxed text 'Purchase-Repurchase Contacts'. However, it might be cheaper to order a car in your home country or on the Internet, where special offers may be available. From abroad, allow at least three weeks to sort out paperwork.

From the USA, the cheapest model available – a 1.2L, three-door, five-speed Twingo (most people will want something a bit more muscular) – costs US$499 for the first 17 days and US$16 for each additional day. If arranged through Paris, a Twingo

## Purchase-Repurchase Contacts

### Renault Eurodrive Representatives
Have a look at the Web site at www.eurodrive.renault.com, or phone one of the following numbers:

| | | | |
|---|---|---|---|
| **France** | ☎ 01 40 40 32 32<br>fax 01 42 41 83 47 | **New Zealand** | ☎ 09-525 8800<br>fax 09-525 8818 |
| **Australia** | ☎ 02-9299 3344<br>fax 02-9262 4590 | **South Africa** | ☎ 011-325 2345<br>fax 011-325 2840 |
| **Canada** | ☎ 450-461 1149<br>fax 450-461 0207 | **USA** | ☎ 800 221 1052<br>☎ 212-532 1221<br>fax 212-725 5379 |

### Peugeot Vacation Plan Representatives
Take a look at the company Web Site at www.sodexa.com, phone one of the following numbers or check out one of the individual Web sites:

| | | | |
|---|---|---|---|
| **France** | ☎ 01 49 04 81 56<br>fax 01 49 04 82 50 | **USA**<br>Auto France | ☎ 800 572 9655<br>fax 201-934 75 01<br>www.auto-france.com |
| **Australia** | ☎ 02-9976 3000<br>fax 02-9905 5874<br>www.driveaway.com.au | | |
| **Canada** | ☎ 514-735 3083<br>fax 514-342 8802<br>www.europauto.qc.ca | Europe by Car | ☎ 800 223 1516<br>fax 212-246 1458<br>www.europebycar.com |
| **New Zealand** | ☎ 09-914 91 00<br>fax 09-379 41 11 | Kemwel | ☎ 914-825 30 00<br>fax 914-835 5449<br>www.kemwel.com |
| **South Africa** | ☎ 011-458 1600<br>fax 011-455 2818 | | |

costs 3700FF for the first 17 days and 60FF for each day thereafter. For 45/90 days, the prices – as we go to press – come out at US$947/1667 in the USA, US$759/1137 in Australia and US$787/1183 in France.

**Peugeot** The Vacation Plan, also known as Sodexa, is smaller than its counterpart at Renault. The company prefers for reservations to be made through its representatives abroad (see the boxed text 'Purchase-Repurchase Contacts' for details), which in any case is cheaper than going through the Sodexa office in Courbevoie (near Paris).

Arranged from the USA, the least expensive model on offer, a Peugeot 106 with a 1.0L engine (the 206 is much peppier), costs about US$490 for the first 17 days and US$13 or US$14 for each additional day. For 45/90 days, that comes to about US$860/1450 (including discounts); as we go to press, the cheapest 45/90-day rates, available in Australia, come to US$798/1230. Start the paperwork at least a month before your pick-up date (15 days if you deal directly with Sodexa's office in Paris).

## BICYCLE
Normandy is an eminently cycleable region, thanks in part to its extensive network of secondary and tertiary roads, many of which carry relatively light traffic. Indeed, some

connoisseurs consider such back roads – a good number of which date from the 19th century or earlier – the ideal vantage point from which to view Normandy's celebrated rural landscapes. One pitfall: they rarely have proper shoulders (verges). Some of the more popular routes include the hilly Suisse Normande and Cotentin peninsula, the winding, flat Seine Valley, Mont St-Michel bay and the orchards of the Pays d'Auge.

*Never* leave your bicycle locked up outside overnight if you want to see it or most of its parts again. You can store it in train station left-luggage offices for 35FF a day.

More information on map options and cyclists' topoguides can be found under Maps in the Facts for the Visitor chapter.

## Rental

Most large towns have at least one shop that hires out *vélos tout-terrains* (mountain bikes), popularly known as VTTs (60FF to 100FF per day), or cheaper touring bikes. In general, they require a deposit of 1000FF or 2000FF which you forfeit if the bike is damaged or stolen. Some cities have remarkably inexpensive rental agencies run by the municipality.

For details of rental shops, see Getting Around in many of the city and town listings.

## Bringing Your Own

It is relatively easy to take your bicycle with you on an aircraft. You can either take it apart and pack everything in a bike bag or box, or simply wheel it to the check-in desk, where it will be treated as a piece of baggage (you may have to supply your own box, available from bike shops). It may be necessary to remove the pedals and turn the handlebars sideways so that it takes up less space in the aircraft's hold. Check all this (and weight limits) with the airline well in advance, preferably before you pay for your ticket.

Transporting a bicycle is free on many trans-Channel ferries, though a fee of UK£5 or 50FF may apply, especially from April to September. On Eurotunnel, the cross-Channel fee for a bicycle, including its rider, is UK£15 return; reservations (☎ 01303-288 680) are mandatory. Bikes are sometimes free on ferries to and from Ireland but may cost up to IR£15.

European Bike Express (☎ 01642-251 440), Web site www.bike-express.co.uk, transports cyclists and their bikes from the UK to places all over France. Depending on your destination, return fares cost UK£139 to UK£169 (UK£10 less for members of the Cyclists' Touring Club).

Within France, a bicycle can be brought along free of charge as hand luggage on most trains, provided it is enclosed in a *housse* (cover) that measures no more than 1200cm by 90cm. You are responsible for loading and unloading your bicycle from the luggage section of your train car; the SNCF will accept no responsibility for its condition.

## Cycling Organisations

Fédération Française de Cyclisme (☎ 01 49 35 69 25, fax 01 49 35 69 92, @ ffc.desprez@ wanadoo.fr), 5 rue de Rome, 92561 Rosny-sous-Bois, is the national organisation devoted to cycling. They publish a leaflet in French on cycling routes with a few pages devoted to routes in Normandy. In Upper Normandy, contact the Ligue Régional de Cyclotourisme de la Haute-Normandie (☎ 02 32 45 35 06), 6 Le Clos Tiger, 27270 Beaumontel, for suggestions on routes throughout the Seine Valley and along the Côte d'Albâtre. In Lower Normandy, there's the CPIE (☎ 02 31 30 43 27), Vallée de l'Orne, Hôtel de Ville, 1402 Caen Cedex, and the Comité Départemental de Cyclotourisme de la Manche (☎ 02 33 05 98 70), Maison du Département, 50008 St-Lô Cedex.

## HITCHING

Hitching is never entirely safe in any country in the world, and we don't recommend it. Travellers who decide to hitch should understand that they are taking a small but potentially serious risk. However, many people do choose to hitch, and the advice that follows should help to make their journeys as fast and safe as is possible. Dedicated hitchers may wish to invest in Simon Calder's slightly outdated guide *Europe – A Manual for Hitch-Hikers*.

A woman hitching on her own is taking a risk, but two women should be reasonably safe. Two men together may have a harder time getting picked up than a man travelling alone. The best (and safest) combination is probably a man and a woman. In any case, never get in a car with someone you don't trust, even if you have no idea why. Keep your belongings with you on the seat rather than in the boot (trunk), and let someone know where you plan to go.

Hitching is as much a way to meet people as it is a way to get around. If you speak some French (few older people in rural areas know much English), thumbing it affords unmatched opportunities to meet French people from all walks of life. The less like a stereotypical tourist you look and feel, the better off you'll be.

Some of our readers report that it is more difficult to hitch in France than almost anywhere else in Europe, while others claim that France is one of the best places in Europe to thumb a ride. And some travellers have had luck getting rides from truck drivers at truck stops, while others find that passenger cars are more likely to pick them up, either on slip or access roads (highway entrances) or at petrol stations. In any case, hitching from city centres is pretty much hopeless: take public transport to the outskirts. It is illegal to hitch on autoroutes, but you can stand near the entrance ramps as long as you don't block traffic.

## BOAT

A few Normandy ports – Caen, Le Havre, Honfleur and Rouen – offer short sightseeing boat rides, or you can take a longer trip between Vernon and Les Andelys. For information on touring Normandy's waterways by boat, see Organised Tours at the end of this chapter.

## LOCAL TRANSPORT
### Public Transport

Normandy cities and larger towns usually have a bus system but schedules and routes are designed to take people back and forth to school or a market. Details of routes, fares, tourist passes, etc are available at

tourist offices and from local bus company information offices; in this book see Getting Around at the end of each city listing.

### Taxi

All large and medium-sized train stations – and many small ones – have a taxi stand (rank) out front. In big cities, look for the blue 'taxi' sign as taxis will normally not pick you up on the street. Fares vary slightly from department to department. Following is the schedule for taxi fares in the Seine-Maritime department:

**Tariff A** (about 3.90FF per kilometre). For return trips taken 7 am to 7 pm Monday to Saturday.
**Tariff B** (about 5.54FF per kilometre). For return trips taken 7 pm to 7 am and all day on Sunday and holidays.
**Tariff C** (about 7.80FF per kilometre). For one-way travel undertaken during the day from Monday to Saturday.
**Tariff D** (about 11.08FF per kilometre). For one-way travel at night and on Sunday and holidays.

Travel under 20km/h (or thereabouts) is calculated by time (about 95FF an hour) rather than distance. Since the *prise en charge* (flag fall) is about 11FF, a one-way, 4km trip taken on a weekday afternoon will cost about 42FF. There may be a surcharge of 5FF to get picked up at a train station or airport, a fee of 6FF per bag and a charge of 8FF for a fourth passenger.

## ORGANISED TOURS

Tailor-made tours of Normandy abound – the best way to find something that's your style is to ask an experienced travel agent or, better yet, to talk to people who have taken a tour themselves.

Some places are difficult to visit unless you have wheels, or are much more interesting with expert commentary. Where relevant (such as the D-Day Beaches in Normandy), your options are mentioned under Organised Tours in city listings and at the beginning of regional chapters.

**Cycling & Walking** In North America, CBT Tours (☎ 800 736-BIKE or ☎ 773-404 1710) runs cycling tours in many regions of

France. It has a Web site at www.bike trip.net. Upmarket cycling and walking holidays are a speciality of Butterfield & Robinson (☎ 800 678 1147 or ☎ 416-864 1354) based in Canada at 70 Bond St, Toronto M5B 1X3. In Normandy, it runs a week-long bicycle tour that covers Le Bec-Hellouin, Honfleur and the D-Day beaches for US$3850. See also the Web site at www.butterfieldandrobinson.com.

In the UK, Cycling for Softies (☎ 0161-248 8282) at 2–4 Birch Polygon, Manchester M14 5HX, arranges unescorted cycling trips through rural France including one that takes in the Sarthe Valley. See the Web site at www.cycling-for-softies.co.uk. Cycling and walking holidays for independent travellers, and guided group walking tours, are available from the Alternative Travel Group (☎ 01865-315 678) at 69–71 Banbury Road, Oxford OX2 6PE. It has a Web site at www.atg-oxford.co.uk.

**D-Day Tours** In addition to the D-Day tours organised by companies in Caen and Bayeux (see Organised Tours in the Caen and Bayeux chapters), several companies offer battlefield tours that include transport and accommodation. In the UK, Holt's Battlefield Tours (☎ 01304-612 248), 15 Market St, Sandwich, Kent CT13 9DA, offers five-day tours of the landing beaches for UK£524 including half-board. In the USA, Normandy Allies, Inc (☎ 716-387 9442, fax 716-387 9915, ⓔ normandyallies@worldnet.att.net),

PO Box 1332, Pittsford, NY 14534, offers an eleven-day tour open to adults and students aged 16 to 19. The tours begin in London and end in Paris, and include visits to war museums in London, landing beaches in Normandy and a city tour of Paris. The cost is US$1755 for adults, US$1580 for WWII veterans and US$1275 for students including the possibility of a travel grant for qualified student applicants. Tours include encounters with historians and eyewitnesses to the invasion.

**Boat Cruises** A number of companies offer the Seine cruise from Paris to Honfleur. In the USA, KD River Cruises of Europe (☎ 800 346 6525, fax 914-696 0833), 2500 Westchester Ave, Purchase, NY 10577, offers a seven-night cruise that stops at Vernon, Rouen and Caudebec-en-Caux. The cruises run from April to September, include half-board and shore excursions and cost from US$1498 to US$1978 depending on the type of cabin and the time of year. See the Web site at www.rivercruises.com.

There's also a French company, Croisi-Europe (☎ 01 44 32 06 60, fax 01 44 32 06 69, ⓔ info@croisieurope.com), 147 boulevard du Montparnasse, 75006, Paris, that offers a five-day return cruise from Paris to Honfleur, stopping at Caudebec-en-Caux and Rouen. It costs 2370FF including half-board but shore excursions are extra. See the Web site at www.croisiere.com.

# Seine-Maritime

To visit the Seine-Maritime department is to taste a little of everything that Normandy has to offer. From the fascinating city of Rouen, the River Seine winds sinuously along a valley dotted with ancient abbeys. The modern, almost futuristic, port of Le Havre stands sentinel over the Seine estuary on the Channel. As the coast curves north from Le Havre, fishing villages and rocky beaches cower under the white cliffs of the Côte d'Albâtre (Alabaster Coast). The coastal centres of Étretat, Fécamp and Dieppe supply Paris with seafood while Paris supplies them with a stream of seasonal and weekend visitors. A web of rivers laces the interior, watering the pastures that rise into forested hills and dip into lush valleys.

There's hours of good walking and cycling along the coast and through the interior, especially in the Forêt d'Eawy. From Gothic churches to the fine arts museums of Rouen and Le Havre, there are ample reminders of the region's rich cultural heritage that so inspired Normandy's luminaries and artists. Except for the deep interior, transportation connections allow you to see a good part of the department by public transport, whether you enter it by boat from the UK or by train from Paris.

## ROUEN
### postcode 76000 • pop 107,000
Half-timbered houses, craggy churches and lofty spires make the medieval centre of Rouen one of the most delightful in France. As the capital of Upper Normandy and the Seine-Maritime department, Rouen also has the political and economic muscle to support a thriving cultural scene, excellent restaurants, quirky bars and fashionable shops. Sprawled along the banks of the Seine 113km north-west of Paris, Rouen was badly damaged during the D-Day bombing campaigns but, with characteristic resilience, moved decisively to restore its most famous monuments and rebuild the ancient centre. The old city has around 2000

## Highlights

- Seeing the cathedral Monet loved in Rouen and his paintings in the Musée des Beaux-Arts
- Watching the sunset from the cliffs of Étretat
- Following the Seine west of Rouen taking in La Bouille and the abbeys of St-Georges de Boscherville, Jumièges and St-Wandrille
- Tackling a plate of fresh seafood in Dieppe; digging into a duck dish in Rouen
- Taking the boat tour from Fécamp to Étretat
- Strolling in the *Bois des Moutiers* park in Varengeville-sur-Mer

half-timbered houses, many with rough-hewn beams, posts and diagonals leaning this way and that. Some scars have not healed however. The rebuilt riverbanks are dreary and the part of the city that lies south of the Seine is a wasteland of tangled roads and haphazard development.

Fortunately, it's easy for a visitor to stay in the compact medieval centre. A wealth of sights recalls the history of a city that

## SEINE-MARITIME

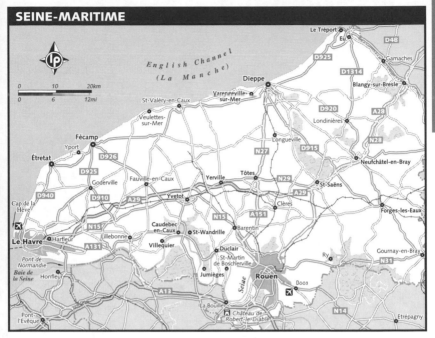

swung from Gothic glories to Joan of Arc's tragic martyrdom, and that produced Gustav Flaubert, Robert La Salle and nourished the genius of Claude Monet. With transportation links that stretch through all of Upper Normandy, Rouen is an excellent base for exploring the region.

### History

Rouen is one of the oldest towns in Normandy, originating around the time of the Roman conquest in 50 BC. St Mellon Christianised the town in the 3rd century but little is known about Rouen until the 9th century, when the Vikings arrived in a looting frenzy and pillaged the town repeatedly for 50 years. The great Viking leader Rollo was baptised here. He made Rouen his capital and it became an important religious, political and administrative centre. The city expanded in importance and gained a substantial degree of autonomy under King Henry II of England until the French king,

Philippe-Auguste, seized it in 1204 as the culmination of his conquest of Normandy. Once again, the city flourished, erecting its great cathedral with money earned from its flourishing textile business and its bustling port.

The 14th century brought a trio of troubles: famine, plague and the Hundred Years' War. Rouen fell into the hands of the English in 1419 and was, infamously, the place where Joan of Arc was tried, convicted and burned at the stake in 1431. The end of the Hundred Years' War in 1449 allowed the city to rebuild and resume its commercial activities. The 16th-century Renaissance brought a flurry of magnificent new construction, much of which still survives. The city reached a plateau in the latter half of the 17th century, but expanded again in the 19th century when the southern bank of the Seine was developed for manufacturing.

German troops set fire to the city in 1940 as part of their advance into France and the

SEINE-MARITIME

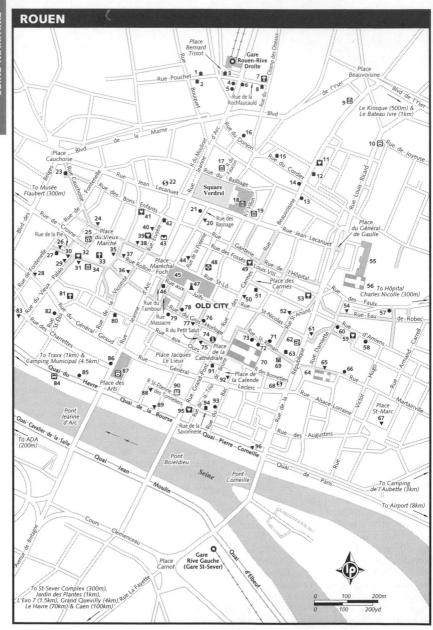

ROUEN

Place Bernard Tissot
Gare Rouen-Rive Droite
Place Beauvoisine
Rue Pouchet
Rue de la Rochfaucauld
Blvd
de l'Yser
Blvd de l'Yser

Le Kiosque (500m) &
Le Bateau Ivre (1km)

Rue de Joyeuse

Place Cauchoise
Blvd de la Marne
Rue du Donjon
Rue du Cordier
Rue Louis-Ricard

To Musée Flaubert (300m)
Square Verdrel
Place du Général de Gaulle

Place du Vieux Marché
Rue des Bons Enfants
Rue des Fossés
Place des Carmes

To Hôpital Charles Nicolle (300m)

Place Maréchal Foch
Rue St-Lô
OLD CITY

de Robec

Rue du Gros Horloge
Place de la Cathédrale

Place St-Marc

Place Jacques Le Lieur
Place des Arts

Place de la Calende

Quai du Havre
Quai de la Bourse
Rue de la Savonnerie
Quai Pierre-Corneille

To Traxx (1km) &
Camping Municipal (4.5km)

To ADA (200m)

Pont Jeanne d'Arc
Quai Cavalier-de-la-Salle

Pont Boieldieu
Seine
Pont Corneille

Quai Jean Moulin
Quai de Paris

To Camping de l'Aubette (3km)
To Airport (8km)

Cours Clemenceau

Place Carnot
Gare Rive Gauche (Gare St-Sever)
Quai d'Elbeuf

Avenue de Bretagne

To St-Sever Complex (300m),
Jardin des Plantes (1km),
L'Exo 7 (1.5km), Grand Quevilly (4km),
Le Havre (70km) & Caen (100km)

Rue La Fayette

0    100    200m
0    100    200yd

*euro currency converter  10FF = €1.52*

## ROUEN

**PLACES TO STAY**
1 Hôtel des Familles
2 Hôtel Beauséjour
3 Hôtel Dieppe; Avis
8 Hôtel de la Rochefaucauld
12 Hôtel Sphinx
15 Hôtel Normandya
23 Hôtel Dandy
27 Tulip Inn
42 Hôtel des Flandres
46 Hôtel Le Palais
51 Hôtel des Carmes
63 Hôtel de la Cathédrale
80 Hôtel de l'Europe
91 Hôtel Cardinal;
   Brasserie Paul
94 Hôtel de Lisieux

**PLACES TO EAT**
20 Au Temps Des Cerises
24 Le P'tit Zinc
26 L'Orangerie
28 Le Bistrot à Gillou
29 Kyoto
30 Le Rouennais
31 Les Maraîchers
35 Covered Food Market
36 Crêperie Tarte Tatin
37 Fromagerie du Vieux
   Marché
38 Jumbo
40 Le Bistrot de Panurge
44 Pascaline
50 Flunch
52 La Taverne St-Amand

54 Le P'tit Bec
61 Alimentation Générale
65 Auberge St-Maclou
67 Food Market
75 Gourmand'grain
77 Monoprix
83 Kashemir
88 La Vieille Auberge
89 Gill
92 Thé Majuscule
96 Highlands Cafe

**OTHER**
4 Voyages Wasteels
5 Budget
6 Hertz
7 Église St-Romain
9 Musée des Antiquités
10 Théâtre des Deux Rives
11 Bloc House
13 CRIJ
14 Laundrette
16 La Tour Jeanne d'Arc
17 Musée de la Céramique
18 Musée des Beaux-Arts
19 Musée Le Secq des Tournelles
21 L'Armitiere
22 Banque de France
25 Cybertechnics
32 L'Euro
33 Église Jeanne d'Arc
34 Musée Jeanne d'Arc
39 Le Buro
41 Le Guevara Cafe

43 Main Post Office
45 Palais de Justice
47 Monument Juif
48 Centre Commercial
49 Le Morrison Café
53 Le Café Curieux
55 Hôtel de Ville
56 Église St-Ouen
57 ABC Bookshop
58 Laundrette
59 Le Bistrot Parisien
60 Laundrette
62 PlaceNet
64 Église St-Maclou
66 Aître St-Maclou
68 Bureau de Change
69 Archbishop's Palace
70 Cathédrale Notre Dame
71 Fayencerie Augy
72 La Cour des Libraires
73 House at No 9/11
74 Tourist Office; American
   Express
76 Birthplace of Robert La Salle
78 Former Hôtel de Ville
79 Gros Horloge
81 Église St-Éloi
82 Rouen Cycles
84 Bus Station
85 Air France
86 Espace Métrobus
87 Théâtre des Arts
90 Cinéma Le Melville
93 Arts Diffusion Loisirs
95 XXL

Allies bombed it ferociously in 1944, but as the city was rebuilt its infrastructure was improved and modernised.

## Orientation

Rouen is a city with a dual character. Bisected by the Seine, the city is divided into the Rive Droite (right bank) on the northern bank and the Rive Gauche (left bank) on the southern bank. The Rive Droite is the oldest part of the city and contains almost all the churches, museums, hotels and restaurants. The main thoroughfare is rue Jeanne d'Arc, which runs from the main train station (Gare Rouen-Rive Droite) to the bank of the Seine. The old city is centred around rue du Gros Horloge between place du Vieux Marché and the cathedral. A long promenade filled with

skaters, strollers and cyclists runs along much of the Seine's right banks. Rive Gauche is primarily commercial, residential and industrial but has a shopping centre at St-Sever and a giant conference centre further south. All buses depart from the bus station along the quai du Havre and quai de la Bourse. The train station on the left bank (Gare St-Sever) mainly serves regional trains.

## Information

**Tourist Offices** The tourist office (☎ 02 32 08 32 40, fax 02 32 08 32 44, ⓔ otrouen@ mcom.fr) is in a lovely, early-16th-century building at 25 place de la Cathédrale, opposite the western facade of the cathedral. It opens 9 am to 7 pm Monday to Saturday, and 9.30 am to 12.30 pm and 2.30 to 6 pm on Sunday May to September. It opens 9 am to 6 pm Monday to Saturday, and 10 am to 1 pm on Sunday, during the rest of the year. Staff make hotel reservations in the area for 15FF. You can visit its Web site at www .mairie-rouen.fr.

Centre Régional d'Information Jeunesse (CRIJ; ☎ 02 35 98 38 75, fax 02 35 15 57 22, e crij.hn@wanadoo.fr), 84 rue Beau-voisine, has information on hostels and student accommodation throughout Normandy as well as information on student discounts, courses and jobs. It opens 11 am to 5 pm Monday to Friday.

**Money** The Banque de France at 32 rue Jean Lecanuet exchanges money 8.45 am to noon Monday to Friday. The Bureau de Change at 7–9 rue des Bonnetiers has decent exchange rates, no commission and opens from 10 am to 7 pm (closed Sunday). Banks line rue Jeanne d'Arc between the Théâtre des Arts and place Maréchal Foch, in front of the Palais de Justice.

American Express (☎ 02 35 89 48 60) has a branch in the tourist office at 25 place de la Cathédrale. It opens 9 am to 1 pm and 2 to 6 pm Monday to Saturday, and 9.30 am to 12.30 pm and 2.30 to 6 pm on Sunday. There are numerous ATMs, including one in the Rive-Droite train station.

**Post & Communications** The main post office, which also changes foreign currency, is at 45 rue Jeanne d'Arc and opens 8 am to 7 pm weekdays and to noon on Saturday. It has a Cyberposte terminal.

PlaceNet (☎ 02 32 76 02 22), 37 rue de la République, charges 32FF per hour of Internet use. It opens 1 to 9 pm on Monday, and 11 am to 9 pm Tuesday to Saturday. Cy-bertechnics (☎ 02 35 07 02 77), on place du Vieux Marché, opens 11 am to 7.30 pm Tuesday to Thursday and 11 am to midnight on Monday and Friday.

**Travel Agencies** Voyages Wasteels (☎ 02 35 71 92 56), 111 bis rue Jeanne d'Arc, sells discount air tickets. It opens 9 am to noon and 2 to 7 pm from Monday to Friday, and to 6 pm on Saturday.

**Bookshops** For English-language books try ABC Bookshop (☎ 02 35 71 08 67), 11 rue des Faulx; it opens 10 am to 6 pm Tuesday to Saturday. L'Armitiere (☎ 02 35 70 57 42), 5 rue des Basnage, is the local literary hang-out. In addition to books, guides and maps, there are frequent readings and discussion groups. It opens 9.30 am to 7 pm Monday to Saturday. Arts Diffusion Loisirs (☎ 02 32 08 67 29), 31 rue du Bac, has a good selection of books and magazines on Normandy. It opens 10 am to 7 pm Tuesday to Saturday and 2 pm to 7 pm on Monday.

**Laundry** Among several options, there are two laundrettes on rue d'Amiens and one at 75 rue Beauvoisine. They open from 7 am to 9 pm daily.

**Medical Services** SOS Médicins (☎ 02 35 03 03 30) will send a doctor to your hotel if necessary. For emergency medical treatment, go to Hôpital Charles Nicolle (☎ 02 35 08 81 81), 1 rue de Germont.

## Walking Tour

Begin your walk at place de la Cathédrale (for details on the cathedral see that section later in the chapter) and notice the **Bureau des Finances** – a striking Renaissance structure built in 1509 that now houses the tourist office. Turn onto rue St-Romain, the narrow street running along the northern side of the cathedral. Notice the house at **No 9–11**, a typical medieval structure of overhanging storeys, that dates from 1466. Across the street is **No 74**, a particularly handsome Gothic house from the 16th century, with niches showing St Nicolas reviving three children and St Romain crushing a gargoyle. Farther ahead on the right is **La Cour des Libraires** (the Booksellers Court) with a massive 15th-century gate carved with scenes from the Resurrection and Last Judgement above (unfinished), and scenes from Genesis below. Other figures include the Vices and Virtues, various professions and crafts, and a dragon with a human head.

Stretching from rue St-Romain to rue des Bonnetiers, the massive **archbishop's palace** is still where the archbishop resides.

On the rue St-Romain side, plaques remind you that Joan of Arc was tried here in 1431. Built in the 15th century it's possible to appreciate the majesty of the palace from the gate on rue des Bonnetiers. Before going up rue des Bonnetiers, cross rue de la République and visit **Église St-Maclou** and **Aître St-Maclou** (for further details see those sections later in the chapter).

Take a look at the 17th- and 18th-century houses on rue Damiette before returning to place de la Cathédrale via rue des Bonnetiers. Cross over the road and walk up rue du Gros Horloge – you'll see a plaque on the right, commemorating the **birthplace of Robert La Salle**; he claimed Louisiana for France. Notice the harmonious facade of the former **Hôtel de Ville** (city hall) on your right at Nos 60–66. Built by the prestigious architect Jacques Gabriel in 1607, the building was never finished and now houses a clothing store.

The **Gros Horloge** medieval clock – farther up the street on the left – is something of a mascot to the *Rouennais* (people of Rouen). The clock's mechanism dates from the 14th century when it was lodged in the adjacent belfry, but the citizens demanded a more conspicuous location. In 1529 the clock was given a flamboyant new facade in a Renaissance style and placed over its current arch. Its single hand points to the hour and, under the numeral VI, the day of the week appears in the form of the divinity associated with each day. On Monday, the moon is in a chariot drawn by deer; on Tuesday, Mars is drawn by wolves, and so on. Over the clock, a globe indicates the phases of the moon. The result was considered so admirable that the gender of the clock was 'elevated' from feminine to masculine. (In French, *horloge* is a feminine noun; the proper formulation should be 'grosse horloge'.) Once restoration of the 14th-century belfry is completed, it should be possible to visit the tower for a magnificent view over the city. Its bell still rings 'curfew' each night at 9 pm.

At the end of rue du Gros Horloge is **place du Vieux Marché**, bounded on the south by a striking ensemble of half-timbered buildings. It was here that Joan of Arc was burned alive in 1431; a towering cross and a plaque marks the spot where she was executed. At the time of her death, place du Vieux Marché was considerably smaller and contained several churches, a marketplace, a pillory and a stake. Scattered stones are all that remain of the old structures.

The centre piece of the square is the remarkable **Église Jeanne d'Arc**, constructed in 1979 after the designs of architect Louis Arretche. The church is meant to resemble an upturned boat and its roofs sprawl over most of the square. An older church, Église St-Vincent, once stood here but it was destroyed in the bombing of 1944. Fortunately, its 16th-century stained-glass windows were removed for safekeeping in 1939 and now they grace the surprisingly lofty interior of the new church. The church opens 10 am to 12.30 pm and 2 to 6 pm, except Friday and Sunday mornings.

Also on the square is the **Musée Jeanne d'Arc**, which recounts the life of La Pucelle (The Maid) in waxworks, documents and drawings. Kids like it, but the treatment is too superficial to interest most adults. The museum opens 9.30 am to 6.30 pm daily, June to September; and 10 am to noon and 2 to 6 pm the rest of the year. Admission costs 25FF (students 13FF).

### Palais de Justice

The ornate Palais de Justice (law courts) is a triumph of early 16th-century Gothic style.

JANE SMITH

**Gothic gargoyles of the Palais de Justice**

## The Warrior Saint

Of all the characters who have marched onto the stage of history, shaped events to their will and then disappeared, few have been as enduring a puzzle as Joan of Arc (Jeanne d'Arc). Who was this illiterate teenage peasant girl? How did she persuade a king to give her an army? How did she inspire an army to follow her? Was she a visionary, a madwoman, or a girl-genius blessed with a laser-like will and an incendiary charisma?

We have plenty of facts about 'la Pucelle' (the Maid) for she was a great celebrity in her day and much written about. The transcript of her trial in Rouen survives and paints a startlingly detailed portrait of her personality and motivations. Yet the facts only seem to deepen the mystery of her achievements and do little to unravel her complex, sometimes contradictory character.

She was born in Domrémy, a town in the Lorraine region, in 1412. The Hundred Years' War had been raging for over 70 years and a demoralised France was on the verge of becoming an English colony after a string of defeats. King Henry V of England assumed the French throne while the legitimacy of the French claimant, Charles, was called into question by his own mother.

When Joan was 12 years old, she began receiving visions of three saints: St Michael, St Catherine and St Margaret. At first their message was simple: be a good

JANE SMITH

**Unconventional Joan of Arc led France's armies against the English**

girl, stay a virgin and so on. Soon their message became more specific: she was to save France and put the Dauphin on the throne. When she was 17, she rode off to Chinon, Charles' court, to inform him of her plans. Although Charles had disguised himself, as a sort of test, Joan picked him out immediately and they retired for a private conversation. The substance of the conversation was never revealed (did she reassure him of his legitimacy?) but at the end of it Charles was under her spell. He placed the armies of France under her command.

---

Typical of the period, the architects move your eye upwards from a relatively sober ground floor to increasingly elaborate upper levels, topped by spires, gargoyles and statuary. The oldest part of the structure is the west wing, the Palais du Neuf Marché, begun in 1499. The section that faces rue Jeanne d'Arc dates from the 19th century. Seriously damaged at the end of WWII, the building has been painstakingly restored, though the 19th-century western facade still shows extensive bullet and shell damage. It was during construction of the city's underground (subway) system that archaeologists discovered a 3rd-century Gallo-Roman settlement.

### Monument Juif

Under the courtyard of the Palais de Justice is Rouen's only reminder of its ancient Jewish community. Until their expulsion from Rouen by Philippe Le Bel in 1306, Rouen's Jews lived between rue du Gros Horloge, rue des Carmes, rue St-Lô and rue Massacre. This impressive two-storey stone building was discovered by accident in 1976 as the courtyard was being repaved. Although the building is in the heart of the Jewish ghetto and the presence of Hebrew graffiti confirms that it belonged to the Jewish community, its exact function is unknown. It may have been used either as a

## The Warrior Saint

With a retinue of 4000 men Joan headed to Orléans, which the English had held under siege for six months. She chose the time if not the manner of the attack and fought alongside her men with strength and courage. Her example inspired others and led to a great victory on 8 May 1429. The English lifted the siege and, after several smaller defeats, left the Loire Valley.

Joan had now become quite a sensation and decided that it was time to lead the Dauphin to his coronation, even though the procession had to pass through territory held by the Burgundians, allies of the English. At the city of Troyes she personally commanded a siege that allowed the Dauphin to enter the city, paving the way to his coronation in Reims 17 July 1429.

Joan was at the height of her power after the coronation. Her victory inspired young French men to volunteer for a rapidly growing army and she decided to attack Paris. It was a mistake. She was wounded in battle, the English triumphed and her army (which Charles couldn't pay anyway) was disbanded.

She persuaded Charles to let her attack at Compiègne where, after a reckless assault, she was captured by the Burgundians. Charles could have ransomed her but chose not to, and the Burgundians sold her to the English.

The English put her on trial in Rouen on a menu of charges: witchcraft, heresy, idolatry and cross-dressing. The most serious was heresy, based upon her insistence on communicating with God directly rather than through the church. The panel of clerics who cross-examined her were deeply shocked by her refusal to wear women's clothing. Whether her adoption of male dress was a form of self-protection or a more deeply felt need, it was a habit she would not give up even at the cost of her life. Joan defended herself with panache, displaying tremendous stamina and mental agility, but unless she recanted her visions the result was a foregone conclusion.

Desperate to save her life, Joan put on a dress, signed a formal abjuration in exchange for life imprisonment and was brought back from the scaffold to her cell.

Over the next few days, she had a change of heart. Appearing again in men's clothes (although she may have been tricked into it) she formally renounced her abjuration and was pronounced a heretic. On 30 May 1431, she was led to place du Vieux Marché, tied to a stake and burned alive. She was 19 years old.

The rehabilitation of Joan of Arc began with a papal declaration of her innocence in 1456 and she was finally canonised in 1920. She is the patron saint of France and has recently become the mascot of the far-right Front National party. It seems unlikely that Joan would have approved.

synagogue or a yeshiva, or it may have belonged to a rich merchant. Dating from around 1100, it is the oldest Jewish monument in France. Hour-long guided visits (in French; reserve a day before at the tourist office) take place at 2.30 pm on Saturday. Admission costs 35FF (students 25FF).

## Cathédrale Notre Dame

The Impressionist artist Claude Monet was practically obsessed with Rouen's cathedral, devoting some 30 canvases to immortalising its glory. Begun in 1201 and completed in 1514, this masterful cathedral spans the entire period of French Gothic architecture, including its most recent let's-polish-up-the-old-monuments phase, which has left the cathedral gleaming white.

Like so many French churches, the Cathédrale Notre Dame was erected on the site of earlier churches. An early Christian sanctuary built by St Victrice was first on the spot at the end of the 4th century. A Romanesque cathedral followed, consecrated by William the Conqueror in 1063. In the mid-12th century, Archbishop Hugues d'Amiens undertook the expansion of the church, deciding to build the **Tour St-Romain** in what was considered a newfangled Gothic style. A fire in 1200 destroyed the entire church, leaving

## CATHÉDRALE NOTRE DAME

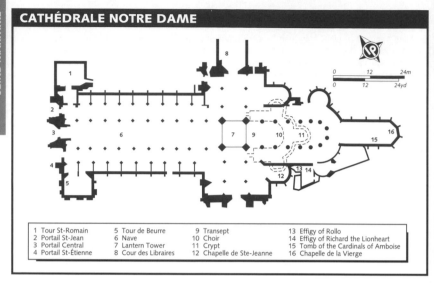

| | | | |
|---|---|---|---|
| 1 Tour St-Romain | 5 Tour de Beurre | 9 Transept | 13 Effigy of Rollo |
| 2 Portail St-Jean | 6 Nave | 10 Choir | 14 Effigy of Richard the Lionheart |
| 3 Portail Central | 7 Lantern Tower | 11 Crypt | 15 Tomb of the Cardinals of Amboise |
| 4 Portail St-Étienne | 8 Cour des Libraires | 12 Chapelle de Ste-Jeanne | 16 Chapelle de la Vierge |

only the Tour St-Romain, the two doors – Portes St-Jean and St-Etienne – and the **crypt**. Construction began almost immediately and much of the basic structure was finished by 1250. A period of expansion and embellishment followed that lasted for three centuries. Huguenots pillaged the cathedral in 1562 and 18th-century revolutionaries turned it into a Temple of Reason after destroying the tomb of Charles V. Bombs rained down on the cathedral the night of 19 April 1944 causing severe damage, which is still being repaired.

**Exterior** Notice the contrast between the austere and early-Gothic Tour St-Romain on the left and the Flamboyant Gothic **Tour de Beurre** on the right. Built from 1485 to 1506, the tower was paid for out of the alms donated by members of the congregation who wanted to eat butter during Lent. (Given the liberal use of butter in Norman cuisine, its absence must have been an intolerable hardship.) Within the tower is a carillon of 55 bells weighing 25 tons. The **central doorway** is surrounded by statues of patriarchs and prophets and topped by a sculpted Tree of Jesse. The central spire

dates from 1822, replacing an earlier one that was destroyed by lightning.

**Interior** The overall impression of the 135m-long interior is of grace and harmony. Over the entrance is a 16th-century **rose-window** that depicts God surrounded by angels. The transept is dominated by a majestic **lantern tower** and the aisles contain stained glass ranging from the 13th to 16th centuries. Notice the **Chapelle de Ste-Jeanne**, dedicated to Joan of Arc, in the south transept with a statue of the saint. The earliest part of the church is the **choir**. It dates from the 13th century and is notable for the simplicity and purity of its design. The recently restored **stalls** date from the 15th century and are decorated with ornate sculptures representing various professions.

On each side of the **altar**, which supports a lead sculpture of Christ, are angels that were rescued from the former Église St-Vincent on place du Vieux Marché. The **ambulatory** behind the choir has effigies of Rollo, his son and Richard the Lion-Heart, whose heart is in the cathedral treasury (the rest of him is in Fontevraud Abbey in the Loire Valley). Notice the size of the Rollo effigy. The nearby **Chapelle de la Vierge** is lit by original 14th-century windows representing the 24 archbishops of Rouen. Funerary art reached its apogee in the elaborate 16th-century **Tomb of the Cardinals of Amboise**. The kneeling cardinals are surrounded by a beautifully sculpted array of saints, apostles and allegorical figures.

There are several guided visits daily to the crypt, ambulatory and Chapelle de la Vierge during Easter, July and August, but only at the weekend during the rest of the year. Admission costs 15FF (students 10FF). The cathedral opens 8 am to 7 pm Monday to Saturday, and to 6 pm on Sunday. Access is restricted during Sunday morning masses.

### Église St-Ouen

In any other town Église St-Ouen would be a star attraction but, in Rouen, it's often overlooked by visitors rushing to the cathedral. However, this 14th-century church is a jewel of Rayonnant Gothic style. Its imposing size (137m long, 26m wide) and relative lack of decoration focuses the eye on its sweeping vertical lines and balanced proportions. Vast windows of 14th-, 15th- and 16th-century glass create an ethereal light that filters through a forest of slim columns. Notice the exceptional wrought-iron grill around the choir and the organ with its 3914 pipes.

The church was part of a powerful Benedictine abbey established in the mid-8th century on the site of St Ouen's grave. It was an active abbey until 1790 when it was sacked by revolutionaries. The entrance is through a lovely garden along rue des Faulx. It opens 10 am to 12.30 pm and 2 to 4.30 pm, and to 6.30 pm in summer (closed Tuesday). Admission is free.

### Église St-Maclou

This Flamboyant Gothic church was built between 1437 and 1521, displaying a remarkable unity of architectural style. The facade is an unusual arrangement of five pinnacled arches over a porch and three doors, richly decorated in Renaissance style. The left door recounts the parable of the Good Shepherd and the central door shows the circumcision and baptism of Christ. The

tympanum over the central door represents the Last Judgement. The interior of the church is as sober as the exterior is ornate. Notice the Flamboyant Gothic staircase, the 16th-century organ loft by Jean Goujon, the 18th-century confessional and oak doors from the mid-16th century. The 1944 bombing did a particularly nasty job on this church; most of the stained glass was destroyed and the church only reopened in 1980. It opens 10 am to noon and 2 to 6 pm (3 to 5.30 pm on Sunday). Admission is free.

### Aître St-Maclou

In 1348 Rouen was devastated by the plague; it took thousands of victims and provoked an urgent need for a new cemetery. Bodies were first buried near to the church in communal ditches. This curious ensemble of half-timbered buildings was built between 1526 and 1533 around the graveyard and is one of the few remaining examples of a medieval charnel house. The carvings of skulls, crossbones, grave-diggers' tools and hourglasses adorning the walls would seem macabre in any other location. The cat's carcass displayed in a case to the right of the entrance was discovered in a wall. It was probably an unlucky black cat, believed to embody the devil, that was entombed in order to keep evil spirits at bay. The courtyard was used as a burial ground for victims of the plague as late as 1781 and is now the municipal École des Beaux-Arts (School of Fine Arts). It can be visited 8 am to 8 pm; enter at 186 rue Martainville, behind Église St-Maclou. Admission is free.

### Musée des Beaux-Arts

Well-lit, well-organised and renovated in 1994, the Musée des Beaux-Arts (Fine Arts Museum; ☎ 02 35 71 28 40), 26 bis rue Jean Lecanuet, is one of the finest regional museums in France. With paintings from the 15th to 20th centuries, the major movements in European art are all present and accounted for.

The museum is organised chronologically, beginning in room one which contains one of the museum's highlights, *La Vierge Parmi les Vierges* by the 16th-century Flemish painter

Gérard David. Of the Italian school in rooms three and four, notice *St-Barnabé Guérissant les Malades* by Veronese. The painter Delacroix maintained that this alone justified a visit to Rouen. The Flemish school is represented by Marten De Vos, Van de Velde and a fine *Adoration des Bergers* by Pierre-Paul Rubens in room five. The superb *Flagellation du Christ* by Caravaggio in room six is another standout in the museum's collection.

The Fontainebleau school of painting that arose in 16th-century France is represented by Clouet's *Diane au Bain* in room 12, which also contains the 17th-century *Vénus armant Énée* by Poussin. Highlights of 18th-century French painting include Fragonard's *Les Blanchisseuses* (room 15) and David's *Portrait de son Geôlier* (room 20), an affectionate look at his jailer painted whilst he was imprisoned for counter-revolutionary activity in 1794.

Naturally the Rouennais school of painting is a major feature of the museum. Room 21 is entirely devoted to the works of Théodore Géricault, born in 1791 in Rouen and educated in Paris. Other French painters include the landscape painter Corot (room 22), Delacroix (room 25) and Monet (rooms 26, 27 and 28) although there is only one painting of the cathedral. Of the 20th-century painters in rooms 31 to 34, notice the works of Duchamp, Modigliani and the vast mural of the Seine painted by Raoul Dufy in 1937 for the Palais de Chaillot in Paris.

The museum opens 10 am to 6 pm, although the south wing closes between 1 and 2 pm. daily except Tuesday. Admission costs 20FF (students 13FF).

## Other Museums

The fascinating **Musée Le Secq des Tournelles** (☎ 02 35 71 28 40), 2 rue Jacques Villon, is in a desantified 16th-century church. The collection is devoted to the blacksmith's craft, displaying some 12,000 locks, keys, scissors, tongs and other wrought-iron utensils made between the 3rd and 19th centuries. Larger works, such as balconies, staircase ramps and grills, are found in the nave and transept of the church; the upstairs floor is devoted to fashion accessories such as jewellery, belt buckles and combs. There are also instruments from various professions such as gardening, dentistry, carpentry and surgery. The museum opens 10 am to noon and 2 to 5 pm. Admission costs 13FF (students 9FF).

The **Musée de la Céramique** (☎ 02 35 07 31 74), whose speciality is 16th- to 19th-century faïence (decorated crockery), is up a flight of steps at 1 rue du Faucon. Rouen is known for its fine ceramics, a speciality that dates back to the 16th century when fine Italian artisans were imported into the court of François I. A studio opened in 1645 in the St-Sever suburb of Rouen and the craft flourished until the end of the 18th century. Competition from English Wedgwood and a growing taste for porcelain sent Rouen's chinaware industry into decline. This museum has a fine collection of Rouen's ceramic crockery from the height of its artistry in the 17th and 18th centuries, earlier pieces from the Italian Renaissance, samples of Delft and oriental works. The museum is located in a 17th-century mansion with a fine courtyard. It opens 10 am to noon and 2 to 5 pm. Admission costs 15FF (students 10FF).

History and archaeology buffs will want to stop at the **Musée des Antiquités** (☎ 02 35 71 78 78), 198 rue Beauvoisine, to review Rouen's past life. A beautiful 3rd-century mosaic is the highlight of the Gallo-Roman exhibit; there are glasses and jewels from the Merovingien era, religious gold and silverwork from the 12th century, medieval and Renaissance wood sculpture and splendid tapestries. The museum is in a 17th-century convent and opens 9.30 am to noon and 1.30 to 6.30 pm daily except Tuesday. Admission costs 20FF (students 13FF).

The **Musée Flaubert et de l'Histoire de la Médicine** (☎ 02 35 15 59 95), 51 rue de Lecat, is in the former hospital where Flaubert's father worked as a surgeon. The tiny museum is organised around the apartment where the Flaubert family lived and displays numerous family mementos as well as surgical instruments, hospital furniture and ceramic pharmacy containers. One of the more interesting exhibits is a contraption designed to teach midwives how to better assist the delivery process, in the hope that a better understanding of the process would help reduce the era's appalling infant-mortality rate. The museum opens 10 am to noon and 2 to 6 pm daily except Sunday and Monday. Admission costs 12FF (students 8FF).

**La Tour Jeanne d'Arc** (☎ 02 35 98 16 21), rue du Donjon, is the sole survivor of eight towers that once ringed a huge chateau built by Philippe-Auguste in the 13th century. Joan of Arc was imprisoned and tortured here before her execution. A copy of her trial transcript is on the ground floor while upstairs there are exhibits about the chateau and Joan of Arc's life. The tower and its two exhibition rooms open 10 am to noon and 2 to 5 pm (to 5.30 pm in summer) daily except for Tuesday. Admission costs 10FF (students free).

## Jardin des Plantes
Rouen is a busy city and the Jardin des Plantes (☎ 02 32 18 21 30), between avenue de la Résistance and rue Lethuillier in the St-Sever neighbourhood, is a good place to take a breather, especially if you have kids. This 24-acre park is attractively landscaped with exotic plants and trees, including a giant Amazonian *Victoria regia* whose leaves can reach 1m in diameter. The park is also equipped with a shallow basin for kids to splash about or sail model boats. It opens 8 am to sunset and admission is free. By public transport, take bus line 12 to the Dufay or Jardin des Plantes stop.

## Organised Tours
The tourist office conducts two-hour guided tours of the city (in French only) daily in July and August, and at the weekend only during the rest of the year. The tour of east Rouen begins at 10.30 am and the tour of west Rouen begins at 3 pm. The cost is 35FF (children and seniors 25FF). On several Saturdays a month between April and September, the tourist office conducts boat rides along Rouen's port that last 1¼ hours and cost 41FF (children under 12, 30FF).

## Special Events
First organised in 1989, the Rouen Armada was such a spectacular success that it has become a regular feature every four years. The next Armada is in July, 2003 and is expected to draw at least 10 million visitors for the week-long festival that includes concerts, fireworks, boat rides and a parade of some 50 sailboats and warships. Accommodation is booked about a year in advance.

Other yearly events include the Festival of African Cinema in January, the antiques market in February, the Festival of Nordic Cinema in March, and the Joan of Arc Festival on the Sunday closest to 30 May. Joan of Arc's martyrdom is commemorated with parades and street events. The tourist office has exact dates and venues.

## Places to Stay
If you're staying over a weekend, ask the tourist office about its 'Bon Weekend' offer of two nights for the price of one in some hotels. You'll have to reserve eight days in advance to qualify.

**Camping** The *Camping Municipal* (☎ 02 35 74 07 59) is 5km north-west of the city in Déville-lès-Rouen on rue Jules Ferry. From the Théâtre des Arts or the bus station on quai du Havre, take bus No 2 (last bus at 11 pm) and get off at the *mairie* (town hall) of Déville-lès-Rouen. Open year round, it charges 25FF per adult with tent, 6FF per child and 8.50FF per car.

*Camping de l'Aubette* (☎ 02 35 08 47 69) is 3km east of Rouen at St-Léger-du-Bourg-Denis. It also opens year round, charging 31FF per person. Bus No 8 drops you off at the site.

**Hotels – Budget** Close to the Rive Droite train station, the welcoming *Hôtel de la Rochefaucauld* (☎ 02 35 71 86 58, 1 rue de la Rochefaucauld) offers simple single/double rooms for one or two people from 120/150FF, including breakfast. Showers cost 15FF.

The spotless *Hôtel Normandya* (☎ 02 35 71 46 15, 32 rue du Cordier) is a pleasant, family-run place. Singles (some with shower) cost 110FF to 140FF, doubles cost 10FF to 20FF more, and a hall shower costs 10FF.

The *Hôtel Sphinx* (☎ 02 35 71 35 86, 130 rue Beauvoisine) is a cosy, friendly place with some timbered rooms. Doubles cost from 100FF to 110FF; an extra bed is 60FF. Showers cost 10FF.

The *Hôtel des Flandres* (☎ 02 35 71 56 88, 5 rue des Bons Enfants) is probably the pick of the budget options, with comfy, newly renovated doubles for 150FF with shower (170FF with shower and toilet).

The *Hôtel Le Palais* (☎ 02 35 71 41 40, 12 rue du Tambour), well-situated near the Palais de Justice and the Gros Horloge, has rooms starting at 140FF.

**Hotels – Mid-Range** The two-star *Hôtel de la Cathédrale* (☎ 02 35 71 57 95, fax 02 35 70 15 54, 12 rue St-Romain) is a wonderfully atmospheric choice in a 17th-century house next to the cathedral. Rooms cost 210/250FF with hall facilities, 260/310FF with private shower and toilet. Ask for a room looking onto the inner courtyard. *Hôtel des Familles* (☎ 02 35 71 88 51, fax 02 35 07 54 65, 4 rue Pouchet), run by the friendly Mme Bretagnolle, has a number of bright, airy rooms that are surprisingly large and comfortable. Rooms with a private shower cost 240/280FF and 180/200FF without. The copious breakfast is an extra 35FF.

Across the street, the *Hôtel Beauséjour* (☎ 02 35 71 93 47, fax 02 35 98 01 24, ⒺⓉ beausejour@lerapporteur.fr, 9 rue Pouchet) is from the carpeted-wall school of decorating, but the rooms are comfortable and well fitted with telephone, cable TV and modern bathrooms that include hair dryers. Rooms with one/two beds cost 225/250FF. A continental breakfast costs 27FF. You can reserve a room on-line at www .lerapporteur.fr/beausejour.

*Hôtel Cardinal* (☎ 02 35 70 24 42, fax 02 35 89 75 14, 1 place de la Cathédrale) has many rooms with views of the nearby cathedral. Modern rooms with cable TV and telephone cost 260/300/315FF for a single/ double/twin with shower, and 285/330/ 350FF with a bath. A buffet breakfast costs 38FF and parking costs 31FF.

*Hôtel de l'Europe* (☎ 02 35 70 83 30, fax 02 35 15 50 65, 87–89 rue aux Ours) is on a quiet street and pleasant, well-appointed rooms with a shower cost 350/370FF and 390/450FF with a bath. *Hôtel de Lisieux* (☎ 02 35 71 87 73, fax 02 35 89 31 52, ⒺⓉ lisieux@hotel-rouen.com, 4 rue de la Savonnerie) is a well-kept establishment in a 15th-century building with rooms from 225/265FF and parking facilities.

*Hôtel des Carmes* (☎ 02 35 71 92 31, fax 02 35 71 76 96, ⒺⓉ h.des.carmes@mcom .mcom.fr, 33 place des Carmes) is the most romantic hotel in Rouen in this price range. Located on a quiet square and decorated with flair, the hotel has rooms costing 230/ 270FF.

**Hotels – Top End** The three-star *Hôtel Dieppe* (☎ 02 35 71 96 00, fax 02 35 89 65 21, ⒺⓉ hotel.dieppe@wanadoo.fr, place Bernard Tissot) is across the street from the Rive Droite train station and offers parking facilities at 20FF for the duration of your stay. This century-old hotel has been lovingly restored and offers smallish but plush rooms with all conveniences. Rooms cost 455/530FF. There's also a tiny single for 350FF. Twins cost 530/630FF with a private bathroom, but prices are less at the weekend. The buffet breakfast costs 50FF and the hotel has an excellent restaurant.

*Hotel Dandy* (☎ 02 35 15 48 82, fax 02 35 15 48 82, ⒺⓉ contact@hotels-rouen.net, 93 rue Cauchoise) also offers comfortable digs on a quiet street with the convenience of a coffee-maker in each room. Rooms cost 380/470FF. *Tulip Inn* (☎ 02 35 71 00 88, fax 02 35 70 75 94, ⒺⓉ tulip.inn@wanadoo .fr, 15 rue de la Pie) is a favourite with business people for its no-nonsense style and central location. Rooms with all comforts cost 440/650FF; there are secure parking facilities.

### Places to Eat
**Restaurants – Budget** The *Crêperie Tarte Tatin* (☎ 02 35 89 35 73, 99 rue de la Vicomté) does a good job with crepes and offers an excellent selection of salads. Come at lunch for the 55FF *menu* that includes a

crepe or salad with dessert and a drink. It serves food continuously from 11.30 am to 10.30 pm and is open year round.

Train stations are rarely dining destinations, but the 39FF salad bar at *Pub Station* (☎ *02 35 71 48 66)* has a tempting array of dishes and the 49FF *plat du jour* (dish of the day) is always fresh and bountiful. The long hours (6 am to midnight year round) are another plus. *Le Bistrot à Gillou* (☎ *02 35 88 89 10, 22 rue de Fontenelle)* doesn't look like much but the 49FF lunch *menu* is good value. It only serves weekday lunches.

It's hard to beat the 67FF lunch *menu* that includes wine and coffee at *Auberge St-Maclou* (☎ *02 35 71 06 67, 224–226 rue Martainville)*. It's rustic and even a little run-down, but still immensely popular for its simple, authentic dishes. It opens daily except Sunday dinner and Monday.

*Le P'tit Bec* (☎ *02 35 07 63 33, 182 rue Eau de Robec)* is a local institution for budget conscious diners. It's always crowded but try to squeeze in for the 75FF lunch *menu*. Vegetarians will like their *gratins* and vegetable terrines. Dinner is only served Friday or Saturday night and the restaurant becomes a tearoom in the afternoon. It opens daily except Sunday.

**Restaurants – Mid-Range** A popular spot, *Les Maraîchers* (☎ *02 35 71 57 73, 37 place du Vieux Marché)* has a lively pavement terrace and varied *menus* from 69FF for lunch (98FF for dinner). For a little more money, *Le Rouennais* (☎ *02 35 07 55 44, 5 rue de la Pie)* nearby offers a slightly more sophisticated cuisine as well as regional specialities. *Menus* cost 89FF (weekday lunches) and from 105FF for dinner. It opens daily except Sunday dinner and Monday.

*Gill, Le Bistrot du Chef...en gare* (☎ *02 35 71 41 15, Rive Droite train station)* – a lower-priced annex of top-end Gill (see Restaurants – Top End) – offers fine cooking with less-expensive ingredients than its sister establishment. The *menu* is small but includes such classics as *morue à la Lyonnaise* (cod cooked with onions) and a salad of *andouille* (tripe sausage). The 89FF

*menu* is a steal. It opens daily except for Saturday lunch, Sunday and Monday dinner.

*Brasserie Paul* (☎ *02 35 15 14 43, 1 place de la Cathédrale)*, next to Hôtel Cardinal, was a favourite of Rouen's artistic/ literary scene, attracting such notables as Simone de Beauvoir, Marcel Duchamp and Guillaume Apollinaire once upon a time. It's still popular, at least as much for its unbeatable view of the cathedral and cosy interior as for its well-produced bistro staples at reasonable prices. *Menus* start at 59FF for a hamburger and fries.

For hybrid Japanese/Korean/Chinese food, try *Kyoto* (☎ *02 35 07 76 77, 35 rue du Vieux Palais)*, open for lunch and dinner daily except Sunday and Monday lunch.

*Pascaline* (☎ *02 35 89 67 44, 5 rue de la Poterne)* is an old-time bistro with a player piano and some wonderful duck dishes. The chef is a master *canardier* who prepares the famous *caneton á la Rouennais* (see the Food section in the Facts for the Visitor chapter). It opens for lunch and dinner with two- and three-course *menus* for 69FF and 99FF. The same owners have recently taken over *L'Orangerie* (☎ *02 35 98 16 03, 2 rue Thomas Corneille)*, an 18th-century building with a terrace on a quiet pedestrian street. In addition to good three-course *menus* for 105FF, special *assiettes* (literally 'plates') are served at lunch for 55FF that are composed of either fish, vegetable, duck or dessert portions. It opens daily except Sunday dinner and Monday.

Cheese, cheese and more cheese is served at *Au Temps Des Cerises* (☎ *02 35 89 98 00, 4–6 rue des Basnage)*. Turkey breast with Camembert, *oeufs cocotte* (eggs cooked in ramekins and topped with a sauce) and of course fondue are well-prepared at reasonable prices. Lunch *menus* start at 60FF and dinner *menus* cost 90FF and 120FF. It opens daily except Monday lunch and Sunday.

The intimate *La Vieille Auberge* (☎ *02 35 70 56 65, 37 rue St-Étienne des Tonneliers)* has an enticing 98FF *menu* including fish dishes such as trout with almonds or fillet of whiting and duck with Calvados The dishes are traditional and the ambience is homely. It opens daily except Monday.

*euro currency converter €1 = 6.56FF*

*Le Bistrot de Panurge* (☎ 02 35 15 97 02, 91 rue Ecuyère) is the place to go for the best leg of lamb you'll ever taste. Everyone who's anyone makes a stop here. Lunch *menus* start at 85FF and dinner *menus* cost from 115FF to 145FF. It opens daily except Saturday lunch, Sunday and Monday.

**Restaurants – Top End** The finest restaurant in Rouen is *Gill* (☎ 02 35 71 16 14, 8 quai de la Bourse) run by Gilles and Sylvie Tournadre. Although expensive, the quality of the food makes it excellent value. Try the lobster with baby vegetables or foie gras in a fig compote. Lunch is the best deal of course. Light-lunchers will be satisfied with a two-course meal at 185FF, but heartier appetites will enjoy the 220FF four-course *menu* (served weekdays only). There are also 300FF and 420FF *menus* available in the evening. It is closed Sunday and Monday from May to October; and for Sunday dinner, Monday and Tuesday lunch from November to April.

*Le P'tit Zinc* (☎ 02 35 89 39 69, 20 place du Vieux Marché) has a more casual style than Gill but also serves superb, traditional dishes such as *sauté de veau* (sautéed veal) and lamb with tomatoes and baby vegetables. The wine list is first-rate. A two- or three-course meal without wine costs from 150FF to 250FF. It opens daily except Saturday dinner and Sunday.

**Vegetarian** Vegetarians have a tough time of it in Rouen but for lunch there's *Gourmand'grain* (☎ 02 35 98 15 74, 3 rue du Petit Salut) with good salads and healthfood *menus* for 45FF and 69FF. It opens daily apart from Sunday and Monday. For spicier fare, try *Kashemir* (☎ 02 35 71 85 89, 13 rue Anatole France), an Indian restaurant that offers competently prepared vegetarian lunch/dinner *menus* for 49/80FF.

**Cafes & Tearooms** A unique combination of a used bookshop and a tearoom, the literary ambience of *Thé Majuscule* (☎ 02 35 71 15 66, 8 place de la Calende) is supplemented by a selection of simple dishes including good salads and vegetable *gratins*

served for lunch only. It opens noon to 6.30 pm daily, except Sunday.

*Highlands Cafe* (☎ 02 35 70 38 78, 2 quai Pierre Corneille) is a trendy bar, cafe and brasserie, known for its wide selection of beer and anything-can-happen musical evenings. Its 90FF *menus* are served for lunch and dinner but it's a fun place to hang out at any time. It opens daily except Sunday.

*La Taverne St-Amand* (☎ 02 35 88 51 34, 11 rue St-Amand) is an old favourite in an 18th-century building. It has a 80FF/95FF weekday lunch/dinner *menu* but is a pleasant place to just have a drink. It opens noon to midnight daily except Saturday lunch and Sunday.

**Fast Food** A good self-service place, *Flunch* (☎ 02 35 71 81 81, 60 rue des Carmes) offers a range of salads, cheese and desserts, as well as main courses that start at 39FF. An even cheaper alternative is *Jumbo* (☎ 02 35 70 35 88, 11 rue Guillaume-le-Conquerant) which serves simple meals from 19.50FF and a *menu* for 40FF.

**Self-Catering** Dairy products, fish and fresh produce are on sale 6 am to 1.30 pm at the *covered market* at place du Vieux Marché daily except Monday. Thursday to Sunday, there's a more lively food and clothing *market* on place St-Marc. Rue Rollon has a number of good *fruit stalls*, *cake shops* and *bakeries* for prepared snacks and salads. *Fromagerie du Vieux Marché* (18 rue Rollon) has an excellent selection of cheeses (try the Camembert soaked in Calvados) as well as cider, pommeau and Calvados. It opens daily except Sunday.

The *Alimentation Générale* (78 rue de la République) is a grocery store that opens 8 am to 10.30 pm. The *Monoprix* supermarket (65 rue du Gros Horloge) opens 8.30 am to 9 pm daily except Sunday.

**Entertainment**
Rouen boasts a lively night scene with concerts, clubs, cinemas and theatres pulling in crowds from about October to May. The action quietens down during the summer and

comes to a complete halt in August when the locals go on holiday before swinging into gear again in September. The tourist office has information about concerts and shows but serious nightcrawlers should check out *Le P'tit Normand* (48FF), a yearly handbook with all the current venues. *Le Cyber Noctambule* is distributed free in most clubs and bars and is a good source of information about the late-night circuit. *L'Agenda Rouennais*, also free, covers a wide range of cultural events. Keep an eye on the daily *Paris-Normandie* as well, especially for the cinema schedule.

**Pubs & Bars** Latino music and style is popular in Rouen and *Le Guevara Cafe* (☎ 02 35 15 97 67, *31 rue des Bons Enfants*) is a colourful, relaxed venue to get in the salsa mood. Tropical cocktails are reasonably priced (18FF for a margarita) and there are even free salsa lessons every night at 8.30 pm when the music starts up in the downstairs bar.

You can nibble and sip the day away at *L'Euro* (☎ 02 35 07 55 66, *41 place du Vieux Marché*), sampling tapas, tropical cocktails, bistro dishes and pasta. When the sun goes down there are theme nights and DJs to keep you busy until the wee hours. It opens from 10.30 am to 2 am (Sunday from 3 pm).

*Le Bateau Ivre* (☎ 02 35 70 09 05, *17 rue des Sapins*) is an easy-going place to enjoy varied music that might include rock, rhythm & blues or French songs in the style of Jacques Brel. It opens 10 pm to 4 am except Tuesday and Wednesday when it closes at 2 am. It is closed completely on Sunday and Monday. To get there take bus T53 to the rue des Sapins stop.

*Le Morrison Café* (☎ 02 35 89 39 99, *18 rue des Fossés Louis VIII*), named after the deceased doe-eyed Doors idol, serves drinks to a leather and jeans crowd. It opens noon to 2 am. It is closed Sunday evening.

*Le Bistrot Parisien* (☎ 02 35 70 55 65, *77 rue d'Amiens*) has a Parisian Left Bank flavour, with plenty of students, artists and trendies browsing the racks of magazines and listening to unobtrusive music. It opens 8 am to midnight except Sunday.

**Discos & Nightclubs** The newest and hottest venue on Rouen's night-time circuit is *Le Café Curieux* (☎ 02 35 71 20 83, *rue des Fossés Louis VIII*). With an eclectic schedule that includes house, hip-hop and jazz, there's something for everyone. It opens 7 pm to 2 am Tuesday to Saturday and is as popular for early evening drinks (14FF for beer) as for its later activities. You have to become a member (10FF) but it is valid for a year.

*Le Kiosque* (☎ 02 35 88 54 50, *43 boulevard de Verdun*) is a popular dance club playing music in a variety of styles for a crowd aged 18 to 25. It opens 11 pm to 5 am Thursday to Saturday. *L'Exo 7* (☎ 02 35 03 32 30, *13 place des Chartreux*) is a dinosaur on Rouen's night scene but still going strong with its blend of classic rock, new rock and rock concerts. Take buses 7 or 14 to the Chartreux stop. Admission to both costs 40FF on Thursday, 50FF on Friday and 60FF on Saturday. On Friday and Saturday the admission cost includes a free drink.

**Gay & Lesbian Venues** Rouen's oldest gay bar, *Le Buro* (☎ 02 35 70 62 59, *81 rue Ecuyère*), is a good introduction to the city's gay scene. It opens 7 pm (10 pm on Sunday) to 2 am. *XXL* (☎ 02 35 88 84 00, *25 rue de la Savonnerie*) is a relaxed cafe during the day but the action heats up at night. It opens noon to 2 am. *Bloc House* (☎ 02 35 07 71 97, *138 rue Beauvoisine*) is a funky hang-out for the lesbian community. It opens 7 pm to 2 am Monday to Saturday.

Techno-phobes should avoid *Traxx* (☎ 02 32 70 72 02, *4 bis boulevard Ferdinand de Lesseps*), the city's foremost venue for the genre. It's young, hot and attracts a mixed gay and straight crowd. It opens from 10 pm to 4 am Wednesday to Saturday. To get there take any of bus Nos 9, 26, 29 or 30 to the Ango stop and then walk towards the river.

**Cinema** Undubbed English-language films are occasionally shown at *Cinéma Le Melville* (☎ 02 35 98 79 79, *12 rue St-Étienne des Tonneliers*). Tickets cost 30FF.

**Theatre** The *Théâtre des Deux Rives* (☎ 02 35 89 63 41, 48 rue Louis Ricard) offers a mixed bag of plays from classical and contemporary French theatre to more international works.

**Classical Music, Opera & Ballet** The *Théâtre des Arts* (☎ 02 35 71 41 36, place des Arts) is Rouen's premier music venue. Home to the Opéra de Normandie, the theatre also runs a series of concerts and ballets. Tickets cost from 85FF to 310FF and are on sale at the box office 11 am to 6 pm Tuesday to Saturday and one hour before the performance. *Théâtre Duchamp-Villon* (☎ 02 32 18 28 10), in the St-Sever complex, offers an adventurous program of contemporary music and dance from around the world. Farther south in Grand-Quevilly the *Théâtre Charles Dullin* (☎ 02 35 69 51 18, allée des Arcades) presents plays, variety acts, song-fests and dance.

There are also music concerts in Rouen's churches. From mid-July to mid-August, Église St-Maclou hosts a regular series of classical music concerts and there are organ concerts held each Sunday in September in Église St-Ouen. The tourist office will have details.

## Shopping

Rouen is an important centre for the antiques business in Upper Normandy. Whether you're in the market for a piece of furniture or not, it's interesting to stroll around the antique stores on place St-Marc. There's an antiques and bric-a-brac market on the square 8 am to 6.30 pm on Tuesday, Saturday and Sunday (to 1.30 pm on Sunday). There are also a number of shops selling antiques and decorative objects on rue Damiette and rue Eau de Robec. The latter street is particularly scenic with an artificial brook and cunningly restored houses.

The Centre Commercial is a new shopping centre with various boutiques and a FNAC, which sells CDs and books as well as audio-visual equipment. Rue du Gros Horloge and the surrounding streets are also filled with shops.

The St-Sever shopping centre, just south of the city centre on the Rive Gauche, is where most Rouen residents come to do their shopping. Prices are cheaper than in the city centre and there is a bric-a-brac market on place des Emmurées. It opens 8 am to 6.30 pm Tuesday, Thursday and Saturday.

Fayencerie Augy (☎ 02 35 88 77 47), 26 rue St-Romain, is a good place to buy Rouen ceramics. It sells reproductions of traditional designs as well as original creations. It opens 9 am to 7 pm Tuesday through Saturday.

## Getting There & Away

**Air** The Aéroport Rouen Valée du Seine (☎ 02 35 79 41 00) is 8km south-east of town at Boos. Air France (☎ 08 02 80 28 02), 15 quai du Havre, has weekday direct flights to Lyons (1261FF return) that connect with other cities in France as well as international destinations.

**Bus** Espace Métrobus (☎ 02 35 52 92 00), 9 rue Jeanne d'Arc, dispenses information on all regional buses including Dieppe (68FF, two hours, three daily) and towns along the coast west of Dieppe, including Fécamp (93FF, 3¼ hours, one daily) and Le Havre (84FF, three hours, five daily). The buses to Dieppe and Le Havre are much slower than the train and are more expensive.

Buses provide efficient connections to Évreux (one hour, nine daily), Louviers (35 minutes, 11 daily), Les Andelys (52FF, 1¼ hours, twice daily), Gisors and Forges-les-Eaux (1¼ hours, once daily), Lyon-la-Forêt and Caudebec-en-Caux (13 daily), Clères (one hour, nine daily) and Neufchâtel-en-Bray (1¼ hours, three daily). The frequency given here is for weekdays, there are far fewer connections at the weekend. Buses leave from quai du Havre and quai de la Bourse.

**Train** Trains to Paris and other far-flung destinations depart from the Gare Rouen-Rive Droite (☎ 02 35 52 13 13). Gare Rouen-Rive Gauche, south of the river, has mainly regional services.

From Gare Rouen-Rive Droite, there's a

frequent express train to/from Paris' Gare St-Lazare (124FF, 70 minutes). Other frequent services include Amiens (96FF, 1¼ hours), Bernay (79FF, one hour, six daily), Caen (116FF, two hours, four daily), Dieppe (55FF, 45 minutes, seven daily), Fécamp (69FF, one hour, seven daily), Le Havre (92FF, one hour, hourly), Lisieux (88FF, 1½ hours, five daily) and, via Paris, Lyons (392FF, four hours).

## Getting Around

**To/From the Airport** There is no public transport into town; a taxi will cost about 120FF.

**Bus & Metro** TCAR (also known as Espace Métrobus) operates Rouen's extensive local bus network as well as its metro line and a new line of high-tech buses in the process of construction. When the line is completed, the name will change from TCAR to TEOR (Transport Est Ouest Rouennais). The metro runs between 5 am (6 am on Sunday) and 11.30 pm. Tickets, valid for an hour of unlimited travel, cost 8FF, or 63FF for a magnetic card for 10 rides. A Carte Découverte, good for one/two/three days, is available at the tourist office for 20/30/40FF.

The public transportation system is designed to encourage residents of Rouen's suburbs to leave their car at home when they come into town to work. Since the town centre of Rouen is compact enough to explore on foot, it's unlikely you'll be taking too many buses or metros. For a visitor, the most convenient metro line runs from the train station to Palais de Justice in the town centre and then on to the Théâtre des Arts before continuing on to the St-Sever neighbourhood. Depending on the line, the buses stop running between 6.30 and 9.30 pm. The last metro leaves the station at 23.12 pm.

**Car & Motorcycle** For rental, try ADA (☎ 02 35 72 25 88), 34 avenue Jean Rondeaux, south of the town centre. Avis (☎ 02 35 88 60 94), place Bernard Tissot; Budget (☎ 02 35 98 64 38), 117 rue Jeanne d'Arc;

and Hertz (☎ 02 35 70 70 71), 130 rue Jeanne d'Arc, have offices near the train station.

**Taxi** To order a taxi 24 hours a day, ring Radio Taxi (☎ 02 35 88 50 50).

**Bicycle** Rouen Cycles (☎ 02 35 71 34 30), 45 rue St-Éloi, rents out mountain bikes for 120FF a day with a deposit of 2000FF to 3000FF, depending on the model. It opens 8.30 am to 12.15 pm and 2 to 7.15 pm from Tuesday to Saturday.

## AROUND ROUEN
### La Bouille
postcode 76530 • pop 791

This pretty riverside village 15km south of Rouen is a relaxing escape from the bustling city. Beneath high coastal cliffs, flower-bedecked houses form a tiny medieval centre and a promenade runs along the Seine. In the 15th century, it was an important port and, later on, painters and poets fell in love with the enchanting vistas along the river. If you bring a bike, you can pedal up the river about 6km to Beaulieu. Otherwise, there's not much to do except eat, stroll and eat again, which is not a hardship since there are some excellent restaurants. With frequent buses into Rouen, La Bouille makes a good alternative place to stay if you're not on a tight budget.

**Places to Stay & Eat** In an elegant white building on the main road along the river, *Hôtel Bellevue (☎ 02 35 18 05 05, fax 02 35 18 00 92, 13 quai Hector Malot)* has cheerful singles/doubles with satellite TV and telephone for 200/290FF (370FF for a room with a river view). Nearby is the stylish *Hôtel St-Pierre (☎ 02 35 18 01 01, fax 02 35 18 12 79)*, which has rooms for 280/350FF. Both hotels have fine restaurants which open daily except Sunday evening.

*Hôtel de la Poste (☎ 02 35 18 03 90, fax 02 35 18 18 91, 6 place du Bateau)* has two rooms for 230FF and a restaurant that is known for its classic, regional cooking. It opens daily except Monday dinner and Tuesday. There's also the *Restaurant de la*

*Maison-Blanche (☎ 02 35 18 01 90, 1 quai Hector Malot)*, which has *menus* costing from 110FF to 280FF.

**Getting There & Away** Bus No 31 connects Rouen with La Bouille (8FF, 20 minutes, departing every 30 minutes).

## Château de Robert-le-Diable

With a panoramic view over the Seine, this fortified castle is worth the dreary trip past Rouen's port installations. Robert the Devil was a mythical figure who reportedly had the ability to communicate with demons and ghosts. The character was probably inspired by William the Conqueror's father, Robert, and over the centuries his name became attached to the chateau.

Gallo-Roman wells in the courtyard indicate a long presence on the site, which clearly has a commanding and militarily useful view of Seine river traffic. The 11th-century chateau dates back to the earliest Norman dukes but it was destroyed by Robert Lackland in 1204. Rebuilt by King Philippe-Auguste, the Rouennais again destroyed it in the 15th century in order to prevent the English from occupying it during the Hundred Years' War. The reconstructed castle now has a moderately interesting **museum** that traces the history of the Viking conquerors with waxworks and a reconstruction of a *drakkar* (a Viking ship).

The chateau (☎ 02 35 18 02 36) opens 9 am to 7 pm from March to August, closes from December to February and closes Monday the rest of the year. Admission costs 22FF (children under 13, 13FF).

**Getting There & Away** Bus No 31 connects Rouen with Château de Robert-le-Diable (8FF, 20 minutes, every half-hour).

## The Abbey Route

Following the Seine Valley west of Rouen, the D982 road winds through little towns, occasionally following the banks of the Seine as it climbs and descends. Minor resort towns such as Duclair, Caudebec-en-Caux and Villequier are scenic places to have a snack or stroll along the river, but the real highlights of the route are the three extraordinary abbeys.

Only 8km west of Rouen, the first abbey downstream is **L'Abbaye St-Georges de Boscherville** (☎ 02 35 32 10 82) in the village of St-Martin de Boscherville. Founded in 1114 on a pagan sanctuary, this sober but elegant abbey shows Norman Romanesque architecture at its finest. Unlike other abbeys, St-Georges was never destroyed, substantially remodelled or allowed to fall into decay, leaving a remarkable unity of style throughout. The geometric motifs that adorn the church facade seem curiously modern, although it was built from 1080 to 1125. The light, bright nave is supported by massive pillars forming majestic arcades.

The restored chapterhouse is adorned with statue columns illustrating themes from monastic life.

The abbey is in continual restoration but you should be able to admire the arched ceilings of the monastery building, the 13th-century chamberlain chapel and scattered vestiges of Gallo-Roman temples. A promontory over the garden planted with medicinal herbs affords a splendid view of the abbey. The abbey opens 9 am to 7 pm June to September; 2 to 5 pm October to March and 9.30 am to noon and 2 to 7 pm during April and May. Admission costs 25FF.

With its ghostly white stone set off by a backdrop of trees, **Jumièges** (☎ 02 35 37 24 02) is one of the most evocative ruins in the region. Little remains of the church – its nave is now open to the sky – but its imposing facade is flanked by 46m-high towers. It's easy to imagine the majesty of the structure from the sheer size of the remaining fragments – a tribune here, a chapel there, a noble arch sustaining a damaged bell tower. The church was begun in 1020 on the site of a 7th-century abbey destroyed by the Viking invasion. William the Conqueror attended its consecration in 1067 and the abbey soon took its place at the forefront of the spiritual and intellectual development of the age. It declined during the Hundred Years' War and then enjoyed a renaissance under Charles VII who stayed there with his mistress

All is well in the colourful seaside town of Dieppe.

Dieppe originally prospered from the ivory trade.

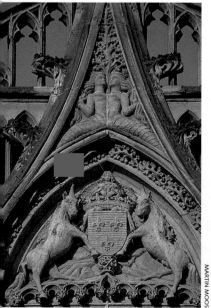

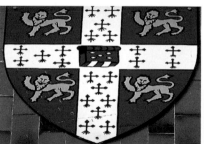

The Norman coat of arms

Take in Rouen's feast of Gothic architecture.

Stock up on delicacies at Rouen's street markets.

The dramatic chalky cliffs of the Côte d'Albâtre

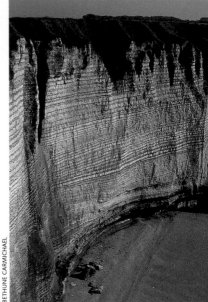

Étretat – a favourite of artists and tourists alike

Perched near the cliff edge, these rural farmhouses have changed little over the centuries.

Agnes Sorel. The abbey continued to flourish until revolutionaries systematically destroyed it in the 18th century.

It opens 9.30 am to 7 pm mid-April to mid-September; and 9.30 am to 1 pm and 2.30 to 5.30 pm the rest of the year. Admission costs 21FF (people aged 18 to 25, 15FF). To get to the abbey take the D65 south from the D982.

Returning to the D982, the next abbey you come to is **L'Abbaye St-Wandrille** (☎ 02 35 96 23 11), 19.5km west of Rouen, which harbours a community of 50 Benedictine monks. Founded in 649 by St Wandrille, the original structure was destroyed by the Vikings in the 9th century. A new abbey church was consecrated in 1031 and donations from William the Conqueror enlarged the abbey's property. The abbey flourished along with other Norman abbeys in the 11th century until the church was destroyed by fire in the mid-13th century. By the time a new church was completed, the Hundred Years' War ended the monastic life of St-Wandrille. The abbey reopened in the 16th century but, with little revenue, it wasn't until the 17th century that buildings were improved and expanded. Most of the structure dates from the 17th to 18th centuries, when the Revolution caused another suspension of monastic life. A Benedictine community moved in again in 1931 and began restoring the structure.

Visits are conducted by a monk and include the refectory, cloister, the new chapel of Notre Dame de Caillouville, and the ruins of the ancient abbey church. In accordance with the Benedictine tradition of hospitality, it's possible to stay at the monastery for a maximum of 10 days. Write well in advance to Père Hôtelier, Abbaye St-Wandrille, 76490 St-Wandrille.

The site opens 5.15 am to 9.15 pm but visits are only possible in summer at 11 am, 3.30 pm and 4 pm Tuesday to Saturday; and 11.30 am Sunday. In winter the schedule is limited to one tour at 3.30 pm Tuesday to Saturday, and 11.30 am and 3.30 pm on Sunday. Admission costs 20FF. It's worth timing a visit for a morning or evening mass when the monks sing Gregorian chants. If your image of monks is limited to prayers and chants, check out the superb abbey Web site at www.st-wandrille.com, which leaves no stone unturned.

CNA in Rouen (☎ 02 35 52 92 00) has bus connections to the abbeys. There are up to 15 buses daily to St-Georges de Boscherville (17FF, 20 minutes) and St-Wandrille (35FF, one hour). Two buses go to Jumièges daily (23FF, one hour).

## Ry
**postcode 76116 • pop 605**

Flaubert's *Madame Bovary* was based on a real-life drama that occurred in Ry in the mid-19th century. Emma Bovary's adulterous prototype was Delphine Couturier Delamare, wife of Eugène Delamare, who was a student of Flaubert's father when he was teaching at the medical school in Rouen. As in the novel, Madame Delamare committed suicide after running up enormous and unpayable debts. Her husband died shortly thereafter.

The pleasant but unremarkable town of Ry offers incessant reminders of its connection with Flaubert's groundbreaking novel, including a small museum, **Galerie Bovary Musée d'Automates** (☎ 02 35 23 61 44), that presents scenes from the novel animated by mannequins. An English translation of the scenes provides a good summary of the novel for those who haven't read it, can't remember it or haven't seen any of the Bovary movies. It also has a reconstruction of the pharmacy where Madame Delamare bought her lethal poison. The museum is on place Gustave Flaubert and opens 11 am to noon and 2 to 7 pm Saturday, Sunday and Monday from Easter to October, and also 3 to 6 pm Tuesday to Friday during July and August. Admission costs 30FF.

You can also visit the Delamare graves behind **Église St-Sulpice**, built from the 12th to 16th centuries. Notice the elaborately carved Renaissance wooden porch, unique in the region.

The tourist office (☎ 02 35 23 19 90) is across the street from the museum and has free maps of suggested scenic walking, cycling and driving routes through the region.

It opens 10 am to noon and 2.30 to 6 pm from Ascension (40 days after Easter) to October, but weekends only from Easter to Ascension.

Ry is 20km north-west of Rouen and an easy day trip by car, but there's only one bus daily from Rouen (one hour) and nowhere to stay in Ry if you must depend on public transport.

## Clères
**postcode 76690 • pop 1091**
The main attraction of Clères is its fascinating **zoo** (☎ 02 35 33 23 08) just steps away from the village marketplace. Established in 1920 around a Renaissance chateau, it has expanded to become a 32-acre park containing 200 mammals and 2000 birds of 250 different species. Antelopes, wallabies, deer, peacocks, flamingos, cranes and gibbons live together amid a wide variety of exotic trees and plants. There's also a 19th-century chateau on the premises. The park opens from 9.30 am to 6 pm Easter to September; 9.30 am to noon and 1.30 to 5.30 or 6 pm the rest of the year (closed December to March). Admission costs 30FF (children 20FF).

There are six trains daily between Clères and Rouen. The zoo is about 500m to the right when you leave the train station.

# Pays de Bray

North of the Forêt de Lyons and north-east of Rouen, the Pays de Bray includes the Béthune, Andelle and Epte Valleys in a formation known as the 'buttonhole'. When the Alps were formed in the Tertiary period (65 million to 1½ million years ago) a large dome of land arose that eroded to form a valley 70km long and 15km wide. This fertile 'buttonhole' of land is marked by rolling hills, lush vegetation, meandering rivers and many pastures. No big cities mar the tranquillity. Never over-populated, dairy farming has always been the region's mainstay. Neufchâtel cheese is on sale everywhere from local markets to family farms, while creamy Gervais-Danone dairy desserts invented near Gournay-en-Bray have pleased generations of French kids. The 16,000-acre Forêt d'Eawy, west of Neufchâtel-en-Bray, offers marvellous trails through giant beech trees.

## NEUFCHÂTEL-EN-BRAY
**postcode 76270 • pop 6140**
For a town that suffered badly in the German bombardments of 1940, Neufchâtel has regained its balance nicely. The 15th-, 16th- and 17th-century houses have been well reconstructed and the cheese industry has kept the town thriving. The cows-milk Neufchâtel cheese is the only heart-shaped French cheese (although it's sold in other shapes as well). The young cheese is chalk-white; the colour darkens as the cheese ages and develops a stronger flavour. Gervais-Danone 'petit suisse' dessert cheese is produced in a factory outside town. In addition to providing a good base for trips into the Forêt d'Eawy, Neufchâtel has a restored Renaissance church and an interesting town museum.

### Orientation & Information
The main road through town is Grande rue St-Pierre, which becomes Grande rue Fausse Porte, Grande rue Notre-Dame and Grande rue St-Jacques. The tourist office (☎ 02 35 93 22 96) is at 6 place Notre-Dame across from the church on Grande rue Notre-Dame. It opens 9 am to 12.30 pm and 2 to 6.30 pm Tuesday to Saturday year round; and 10.30 am to 12.30 pm Sunday mid-June to mid-September. The office has maps and brochures of the Forêt d'Eawy as well as a list of dairy farms available for visits and cheese tasting. The post office is on the corner of Grande rue St-Pierre and rue du Général de Gaulle.

### Things to See & Do
The **Église Notre Dame** is notable for its Flamboyant Gothic porch and 16th-century nave topped with Renaissance capitals. Notice also the wooden statue of the Virgin at the entrance to the choir. The **Musée Municipal Mathon-Durand** (☎ 02 35 93 06 55) is down the street from the church near the post office. Five rooms in this medieval

half-timbered house are devoted to illustrating daily rural life in Normandy. Tools for roasting coffee, making butter, washing, making pottery as well as blacksmithing, iron-working and cheese-making are on display. The museum opens 3 to 6 pm Tuesday to Sunday May to September (weekends only the rest of the year). Admission costs 30FF.

Market day is Saturday morning at place Notre-Dame; there's a *marché aux bestiaux* (livestock market) Wednesday morning in the Parc des Expositions, south-west of the town centre.

### Places to Stay & Eat
There's a camp site, *Camping de Ste-Claire* (☎ *02 35 93 03 93)*, less than 1km south of the town centre. The site is signed from the Parc des Expositions. It charges 18FF per adult and 18FF for a tent.

*Hôtel Les Airelles (☎ 02 35 93 14 60, fax 02 35 93 89 13, 2 passage Michu)* is a centrally located two-star hotel in a pleasant ivy-covered stone building. Rooms with telephone and satellite TV cost from 230FF to 300FF. Another alternative is *Hôtel du Grand Cerf (☎ 02 35 39 91 14, fax 02 35 38 47 08, 9 Grande rue Fausse Porte)*, also in the centre, which has rooms from 230FF to 350FF. Both hotels have good restaurants with 57FF lunch specials (except Sunday).

### Getting There & Away
All trains stop at Serqueux and are met by buses to Neufchâtel. There are three daily connections from Rouen to Neufchâtel (55FF, 1½ hours); three from Dieppe (34FF, one hour) and four from Paris (two hours). There are also four buses daily from Rouen to Neufchâtel (1¾ hours).

## FORGES-LES-EAUX
### postcode 76440 • pop 3700
Forges-les-Eaux, 40km north-east of Rouen, owes its existence to two precious commodities – iron and water. Iron has been mined from the region since antiquity, giving rise to forges powered by the River Andelle. The mineral-rich water spouting from La Chevrette spring developed a reputation for its curative powers in the 16th century, drawing such noble figures as Louis XIII, Anne of Austria and Cardinal Richelieu. It remained popular throughout the 19th century, even meriting a mention in Alexandre Dumas' *Les Trois Mousquetaires* (The Three Musketeers). Forges-les-Eaux is still very much a resort town, staid but relaxing. The wooded park around the Andelle lake is good for a healthy 5km stroll and its chic casino enlivens the nightlife.

### Orientation & Information
The main road through town is avenue des Sources, which becomes rue de la République, lined with stores and bakeries. The tourist office (☎ 02 35 90 52 10, fax 02 35 90 34 80) is at the bottom of rue de la République, behind the town hall on rue du Maréchal Leclerc, and has a useful Web site (www.ville-forges-les-eaux.fr). The tourist office opens 8.30 am to 12.30 pm and 2 to 6 pm Monday to Friday, 9 am to noon and 2 to 6 pm Saturday (10 am to noon Sunday mid-June to mid-September). The post office is on rue de la République across from place Charles de Gaulle.

### Things to See & Do
The unusual **Musée des Maquettes Hippomobiles et Outils Anciens** was put together by a retired couple and displays models of horse-drawn vehicles from the 19th century. The museum is in the park behind the town hall and opens 2 to 5 pm Tuesday to Sunday from Easter to October. Admission costs 10FF. The **Musée de la Faïence de Forges** displays examples of pottery forged in the region. Located in the town hall, visits (12FF) can be arranged through the tourist office Tuesday to Friday from Easter to October.

Market day is Thursday morning and you'll find it on place Charles de Gaulle. Cycles Vauquet (☎ 02 32 89 02 64), 23 rue de la Libération, rents out bicycles for 80FF per day.

### Places to Stay & Eat
Less than 1km south of the town centre on boulevard Nicolas Thiéssé is the camp

site, *La Minière* (☎ *02 35 90 53 91*), open April to October. It charges 14FF per adult and 21FF per tent for each night.

One of the region's most interesting places to stay if you have your own transport is *La Ferme de Bray* (☎ *02 35 90 57 27,* e *ferme.de.bray@wanadoo.fr),* 6km north-west of Forges-les-Eaux, outside Sommery on the road to Dieppe. The Perriers are the 18th generation to run this dairy farm, turning it into a combination museum/inn. The farm buildings now house exhibits devoted to such traditional Norman activities as pressing cider, baking bread and churning butter. There's a pond for trout fishing and equipment rental for those without tackle. The comfortable rooms of the inn are furnished in French country style with wooden furniture and Laura Ashley wallpaper. Single/double/triple/quad rooms cost 200/260/320/360FF. You can visit the farm 2 to 6 pm from Easter to Halloween (31 October), daily in July and August, but weekends only the rest of the season. Admission costs 20FF.

*La Paix* (☎ *02 35 90 51 22, fax 02 35 09 83 62, 15 rue de Neufchâtel),* in the town centre, has charmless but adequate rooms costing 256/370FF. Across from the casino is the grand *Hôtel Continental* (☎ *02 35 89 50 50, fax 02 35 90 26 14, 110 avenue des Sources)* in a restored half-timbered building. Rooms cost from 280FF to 650FF. The more expensive rooms have balconies.

### Getting There & Away
All trains stop at Serqueux and are met by buses to Forges-les-Eaux. There are three connections daily from Rouen (47FF, one hour) and three from Dieppe (47FF, one hour). There is also a daily bus from Rouen (1½ hours).

# Côte d'Albâtre

Stretching 120km from Le Tréport south to Cap de la Hève at Le Havre, the lofty white cliffs of the Côte d'Albâtre (Alabaster Coast) create the most dramatic coastal scenery in Normandy. Reminiscent of the southern coast of England, these chalky towers can reach 120m as they curve around stony beaches and crack open into dry valleys. The largest towns are built where rivers have been able to push their way to the sea: Le Havre at the mouth of the Seine, Dieppe on the River Arques, Fécamp on the Valmont and Le Tréport on the Bresle. Fishing ports and resorts complete the coastal picture while grain fields and pastures cap off the cliffs.

It's impossible to appreciate the Côte d'Albâtre by public transport, but hikers, bikers and motorists will be treated to a series of ever-changing panoramas. Walkers can follow the coastal GR21 from Dieppe to Le Havre. If you are driving, take the coastal road, which starts as the D75 west of Dieppe, and not the inland D925. Good biking routes include the D211 from Étretat, the D79 from Fécamp north-east to St-Valéry-en-Caux and the D68 and D75 from St-Valéry-en-Caux to Dieppe.

## LE HAVRE
**postcode 76600 • pop 193,000**
Le Havre, France's second most important port, is also a bustling gateway for ferries to Britain and Ireland. Like most gateways, people tend to pass through it on the way to someplace else.

All but obliterated by WWII bombing raids, Le Havre was rebuilt around its historical remains by Auguste Perret. With a pressing need to shelter 80,000 suddenly homeless residents and little money to work with, it's not surprising that efficiency triumphed over design. The short three-storey buildings are out of proportion to the wide boulevards, which results in a cold, uninviting urban landscape. Yet, the very newness of the city can be intriguing. There's plenty of modern architecture you can either admire or laugh at, and the sophisticated André Malraux fine arts museum is one of the finest in Normandy. Other positive points include a wide, rocky beach with cold but clean water, good seafood restaurants, lots of parking and a number of good-value hotels in case you want to use Le Havre as a base for exploring the Côte d'Albâtre.

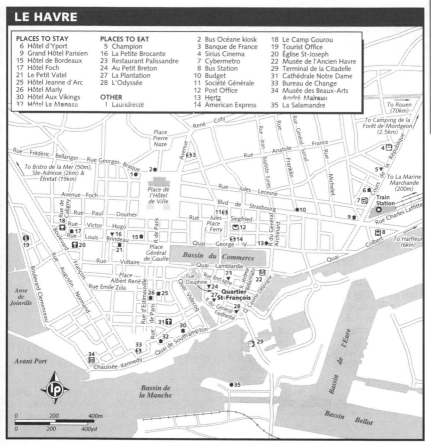

## LE HAVRE

**PLACES TO STAY**
6 Hôtel d'Yport
9 Grand Hôtel Parisien
15 Hôtel de Bordeaux
17 Hôtel Foch
21 Le Petit Vatel
25 Hôtel Jeanne d'Arc
26 Hôtel Marly
30 Hôtel Aux Vikings
32 Hôtel Le Monaco

**PLACES TO EAT**
5 Champion
16 La Petite Brocante
23 Restaurant Palissandre
24 Au Petit Breton
27 La Plantation
28 L'Odyssée

**OTHER**
1 Laundrette
2 Bus Océane kiosk
3 Banque de France
4 Sirius Cinema
7 Cybermetro
8 Bus Station
10 Budget
11 Société Générale
12 Post Office
13 Hertz
14 American Express
18 Le Camp Gourou
19 Tourist Office
20 Église St-Joseph
22 Musée de l'Ancien Havre
29 Terminal de la Citadelle
31 Cathédrale Notre Dame
33 Bureau de Change
34 Musée des Beaux-Arts André Malraux
35 La Salamandre

## History

Le Havre was created in 1517 by François I to replace the ports of Harfleur and Honfleur, which were silting up. The two-hour high tides made Le Havre attractive for maritime activities and the city quickly took its place as an important commercial centre. In the 17th century Cardinal Richelieu built a citadel and enlarged the ports just in time for the city to capitalise on emerging trade connections with the Americas. Ships loaded with cotton and coffee sailed into the port and, in the 18th century, sailed out with guns and supplies for American revolutionaries. The North American connection continued into the 20th century with the advent of luxury ocean liners that connected New York with Le Havre in 15 days.

Pre-war Le Havre was a teeming port city, although probably lacked graciousness. After all, the city inspired Jean-Paul Sartre to write *La Nausée* in the 1930s while teaching philosophy at a local high school. The Germans occupied Le Havre in 1940, turning it into an important garrison. The Allied response was fierce. From 2 to 12 September, the city was subjected to a furious bombing campaign while the Germans, in a desperate last stand, blew up the port installations. The city was 85% destroyed.

## Orientation

The main square is the enormous place de l'Hôtel de Ville. Avenue Foch runs westwards to the sea and the Port de Plaisance recreational area; boulevard de Strasbourg goes eastwards to the train and bus stations. Rue de Paris cuts southwards past Espace Oscar Niemeyer, a square named after the Brazilian who designed two peculiar cultural centre buildings (which have been compared to a truncated cooling tower and a toilet bowl).

Rue de Paris ends at the quai de Southampton and the Bassin de la Manche, from where ferries to Britain set sail out of the Terminal de la Citadelle, south-east of the central square. Within easy walking distance of the terminal is the Quartier St-François, Le Havre's restaurant-filled 'old city'.

## Information

**Tourist Offices** The tourist office (☎ 02 32 74 04 04, fax 02 35 42 38 39, ✉ office.du .tourisme.havre@wanadoo.fr), 186 boulevard Clemenceau, on the waterfront about 650m south-west of the city hall, opens 9 am to noon and 1.30 to 6 pm Monday to Saturday, and 10 am to 1 pm Sunday October to April; and 8.45 am to 7 pm Monday to Saturday and 10 am to 12.30 pm and 2.30 to 6 pm Sunday May to September. Staff reserve local accommodation for free. The city Web site is www.ville-lehavre.fr.

**Money** The Banque de France, 22 avenue René Coty, changes money 8.45 am to noon Monday to Friday. Société Générale is at 2 place Léon Meyer, and there are more banks on boulevard de Strasbourg. An exchange bureau opposite the old Irish Ferries terminal at 41 Chaussée Kennedy opens from 8 am to 12.30 pm and 1.30 to 7 pm Monday to Saturday (8 am to 7.30 pm in July and August).

American Express (☎ 02 32 74 75 76), 57 quai Georges V, opens 8.45 am to noon and 1.30 to 6 pm weekdays.

**Post & Communications** Le Havre's main post office, 62 rue Jules Siegfried,

opens 8 am to 7 pm weekdays and to noon on Saturday. It has Cyberposte. Cybermetro (☎ 02 32 73 04 28), 15 cours de la République, opposite the train station, charges 30/45FF (students 20/35FF) per half-hour/hour of Internet use. It opens from 9 am to midnight daily.

**Laundry** The laundrette at 5 rue Georges Braque, just west of the city hall, opens 8 am to 10 pm daily.

## Things to See & Do

The main highlight of Le Havre is the newly remodelled **Musée des Beaux-Arts André-Malraux** (☎ 02 35 19 62 62), 2 boulevard Clemenceau. Inaugurated in 1961 by former Minister of Culture André Malraux, this ultra-modern museum is marked by steel, glass and a cascade of light bathing a spacious interior. Le Havre native and long-term resident Eugène Boudin is represented by his many paintings of local beach scenes. Another large section is devoted to Fauvist Raoul Dufy who was also born in Le Havre. The city has more than a passing connection with Impressionism since Monet's *Impression Soleil Levant* portrayed the sunrise over Le Havre's port, lending a name to the new movement. Several works by Monet including a *Les Nymphéas* are displayed as well as paintings by Sisley, Renoir and Manet. The museum opens 11 am to 6 pm Monday to Friday, and 11 am to 7 pm at the weekend. Admission costs 25FF (students 15FF).

The **Musée de l'Ancien Havre** (☎ 02 35 42 27 90), 1 rue Jérôme Bellarmato, gives historical depth to a city that can seem as though it was built yesterday. The museum is in a 17th-century building that emerged unscathed from the WWII bombing and now has a moderately interesting collection of photos, models, posters, drawings and documents focusing on the maritime traditions of Le Havre. It opens from 1 am to noon and 2 to 6 pm Wednesday to Sunday. Admission costs 10FF.

**Cathédrale Notre Dame** on place du Vieux-Marché, is Le Havre's oldest sight. Although badly damaged in 1944, clever restoration has revealed the church's unusual mixture of Gothic and Renaissance styles. The magnificent 17th-century organ was a gift from Cardinal Richelieu.

The tallest building in Le Havre is **Église St-Joseph** at the corner of rue de Caligny and rue Louis Brindeau, designed by Auguste Perret. Visible all over the city, the 107m-high bell tower was intended to be the first thing ship passengers from the USA saw as they neared Le Havre. The angular lines wouldn't be out of place in New York but the interior is suffused with a soft light created by the stained-glass windows.

### Organised Tours
From June to September the tourist office operates walking tours of various monuments and neighbourhoods in Le Havre that last from 1½ to two hours and cost 30FF. From late July to August, there are daily 1½-hour boat rides around the port of Le Havre aboard *Le Salamandre*. The cost is 65FF (children aged four to 14, 50FF). Call ☎ 02 35 42 01 31 for details.

### Places to Stay
**Camping** The closest camp site is *Camping de la Forêt de Montgeon* (☎ 02 35 46 52 39), nearly 3km north of town in a 250-hectare forest. It opens April to September and charges 55FF for up to two people and 12FF per car. From the station, take bus No 11 and alight after the 700m-long Jenner Tunnel. Then walk north through the park another 1.5km.

**Hotels – Budget** Hidden down an alley opposite the train station is *Hôtel d'Yport* (☎ 02 35 25 21 08, fax 02 35 24 06 34, 27 cours de la République). It's a friendly place with a range of rooms including basic singles/doubles/triples costing from 120/170/210FF. A hall shower costs 25FF extra. Rooms with a shower cost 180/200/243FF. The hotel has a private garage (35FF).

Near the old Irish Ferries terminal, *Hôtel Le Monaco* (☎ 02 35 42 21 01, fax 02 35 42 01 01, 16 rue de Paris) has shipshape rooms costing from 150/190FF. Nearby, the tiny *Le Ferry Boat* (☎ 02 35 42 29 55, 11 quai de Southampton) has seven rooms costing from 160/180FF. Hall showers are free. *Hôtel Jeanne d'Arc* (☎ 02 35 21 67 27, fax 02 35 41 26 83, 91 rue Emile Zola) has small, well-kept rooms for 155FF with sink only and 210FF with a shower.

**Hotels – Mid-Range** Also close to the station is the *Grand Hôtel Parisien* (☎ 02 35 25 23 83, fax 02 35 25 05 06, 1 cours de la République). It is clean and pleasant and has rooms from 210/260FF with shower and TV. *Hôtel Aux Vikings* (☎ 02 35 42 51 67, fax 02 35 42 45 22, 27–29 quai de Southampton) is bland but the redecorated rooms have a phone, TV and hair dryer. Rooms cost from 255FF to 285FF and breakfast is 36FF. *Hôtel Foch* (☎ 02 35 42 50 69, fax 02 35 43 40 17, 4 rue de Caligny) is a friendly place with rooms of various sizes that cost from 310FF to 330FF. *Le Petit Vatel* (☎ 02 35 41 72 07, fax 02 35 22 37 86, 86 rue Louis Brindeau) is an excellent budget option with small bright rooms costing 220/250FF.

**Hotels – Top End** At the eastern end of the Bassin du Commerce is the Best Western *Hôtel de Bordeaux* (☎ 02 35 22 69 44, fax 02 35 42 09 27, 147 rue Louis Brindeau). Rooms cost 385/470FF with discounted rates at weekends. *Hôtel Marly* (☎ 02 35 41 72 48, fax 02 35 21 50 45, 121 rue de Paris) has large, functional rooms that are often filled with business travellers. Rooms cost from 385FF to 480FF.

### Places to Eat
All-you-can-eat buffets are a rarity in France but *La Marine Marchande* (☎ 02 35 25 11 77, 27 boulevard Amiral Mouchez) offers a full table of hors d'oeuvres, plus a main course, cheese, dessert and wine or cider for 60FF. It's closed Saturday lunch and Sunday. To get there take rue Charles Laffitte from the train station, follow it to the right as it becomes rue Marceau, and onto boulevard Amiral Mouchez.

*L'Odyssée* (☎ 02 35 21 32 42, 41 rue du Général Faidherbe) is one of Le Havre's best addresses for dipping into superb fish dishes. *Menus* at 125FF (weekday lunch), 155FF and 195FF (weekends) offer excellent value for money. It opens daily except Saturday lunch, Sunday evening and Monday. *La Plantation (☎ 02 35 41 75 68, 27 rue Général Faidherbe)* is a friendly, colourful establishment that serves up specialities from the Antilles. There are good tropical cocktails and a 70FF *menu*. It opens daily except Monday.

*La Petite Brocante (☎ 02 35 21 42 20, 75 rue Louis Brindeau)* is a chic bistro serving a variety of delicious meat and fish dishes. The wine list is excellent. *Menus* start at 130FF; it opens daily except Sunday.

Quartier St-François is the best place to eat, with creperies and couscous restaurants in abundance. If you're looking for the latter, try *Au Petit Breton (☎ 02 35 21 44 14, 11 rue Dauphine)*. Couscous starts at 60FF. The restaurant at the *Hôtel Le Monaco* (see Places to Stay earlier in the chapter) has excellent seafood *menus* from 69FF.

The seafood at the *Bistro de la Mer (☎ 02 35 42 24 24, 56 rue Guillemard)* is fresh, copious and served with panache either inside or on the outdoor terrace. Prices are reasonable (75/99FF *menus*) and there's continuous service throughout the day. To get there take boulevard Clemenceau to boulevard Albert 1er – it's on the right.

*Restaurant Palissandre (☎ 02 35 21 69 00, 33 rue de Bretagne)* attracts flocks of business diners at lunch to feast on the classic French cuisine. *Menus* cost from 65FF to 149FF. It opens daily except Wednesday dinner, Saturday lunch and Sunday.

*Champion* supermarket is on the corner of rue de la République and rue Turenne.

## Entertainment

*Le Camp Gourou (☎ 02 35 22 00 92, 163 rue Victor Hugo)* is a raucous student bar that attracts lots of Australians. *Sirius Cinema (5 rue Duguesclin)*, just off cours de la République, often has movies in English with French subtitles.

## Getting There & Away

**Air** The airport (☎ 02 35 54 65 00) is 6km north of town in Octeville-sur-Mer. There's no public transport to town; a taxi will cost about 100FF.

**Bus** Caen-based Bus Verts du Calvados (☎ 08 01 21 42 14) and Rouen's CNA (☎ 02 35 52 92 00) run frequent services from the bus station to Caen (102.50FF), Honfleur (42.40FF), Rouen (84FF) and Deauville-Trouville (59FF). Auto-Cars Gris (☎ 02 35 27 04 25) has 10 buses daily to Fécamp (45FF, 1½ hours) via Étretat (one hour) and five on Sunday.

**Train** Le Havre's train station (☎ 08 36 35 35 35) is east of the city centre on cours de la République. Chief destinations are Rouen (72FF, one hour, 15 daily) and Paris' Gare St-Lazare (151FF, 2¼ hours, 10 daily). A secondary line goes north to Fécamp (43FF, 1¼ hours, five daily) with a change at Bréauté-Beuzeville.

**Boat** P&O European Ferries (☎ 08 02 01 30 13), which links Le Havre with Portsmouth, uses the new Terminal de la Citadelle on avenue Lucien Corbeaux just over 1km south-west of the train station. The information desk opens 9 am to 7 pm. A bus (8FF) takes passengers from the terminal to the tourist office and the train station 15 minutes after each ferry arrives.

## Getting Around

**Bus** Bus Océane runs 14 lines in Le Havre; its information office (☎ 02 35 43 46 00), in a kiosk on place de l'Hôtel de Ville, opens 7 am to 7 pm Monday to Saturday. Single tickets cost 9FF and a carnet of 10 costs 56FF; a Ticket Ville costs 18FF and gives unlimited bus travel for that day.

**Car & Motorcycle** Avis (☎ 02 35 53 17 20) is in the train station. There's also Hertz (☎ 02 35 19 01 19) at 1 rue du Général Archinard and Budget (☎ 02 35 22 53 52) at 161 boulevard de Strasbourg.

**Taxi** To order a taxi, ring ☎ 02 35 25 81 81 or ☎ 02 35 25 81 00. A two-hour taxi tour (in English) of Le Havre costs 300FF (reserve on ☎ 02 35 25 81 81) for up to four people.

## AROUND LE HAVRE

Boulevard Albert leads along the sea 2km to the **Ste-Adresse** village, which survived WWII intact. Built in the 14th century, the village became a fashionable watering spot for writers and artists at the end of the 19th century. Sarah Bernhardt, Alexandre Dumas, Monet and Raoul Dufy all came here to take the waters and enjoy the sea vistas. During WWI the Belgian government relocated to Ste-Adresse. It's still a popular spot for residents of Le Havre and makes a welcome change from the modern city. Bus No 1 runs to Ste-Adresse.

**Harfleur** is a quiet little village 6km east of Le Havre with cobblestone streets surrounding the 15th-century Église St-Martin. Harfleur's original claim to fame was as a port before the creation of Le Havre in 1517 rendered it useless. In 1415 the English army under the command of Henry V landed at Harfleur and laid siege to the town before proceeding to Agincourt for their famous victory. The new tourist office (☎ 02 35 13 37 40) in the town centre is trying to capture some overflow business from Le Havre by playing up Harfleur's history and pretty village appeal. The bar/hotel *Le Moderne (☎ 02 35 51 44 30, 67 rue de la République)* offers extremely simple single/double/triple rooms for 120/140/165FF. Showers and toilets are in the hall; rooms at the front could be noisy. Bus Nos 9 and 13 from central Le Havre stop at the church.

## DIEPPE

postcode 76200 • pop 35,000

Dieppe is an ancient seaside town and long a favourite among British weekend visitors. It's not the prettiest place in Normandy, but its location – set between two limestone cliffs – and its medieval castle are dramatic. Dieppe also has the attractive, gritty appeal of an old-fashioned port; it's the closest Channel port to Paris (175km).

Like most Norman port cities, Dieppe was a coveted prize for invading armies throughout the centuries. The Vikings came in the 7th and 8th centuries, followed by Philippe-Auguste of France who seized it from Richard the Lion-Heart in the 12th century. It changed hands several times in the Hundred Years' War, and was invaded by Prussians in the war of 1870. The most recent incursion into Dieppe took place in 1942 when an Anglo-Canadian force of 6100 men landed in Dieppe in a show of force against the Germans. Although intended to demonstrate the British will and ability to launch a cross-Channel operation, the tragic loss of nearly two-thirds of the men in one day only demonstrated Allied military unpreparedness.

The port and wide sweep of beach has always defined Dieppe's culture and economy. Privateers made Dieppe their lair of choice as early as 1338 when they pillaged Southampton. Explorers launched expeditions from Dieppe, most notably Giovanni da Verrazano who sailed from here in 1524 to found New York. His enterprise was financed by the rich and powerful privateer, Jehan Ango, who became governor of Dieppe. From the 16th to 17th centuries, Dieppe flourished as the ivory and spice trade brought new wealth to its coffers. Protestants fleeing persecution left Dieppe's port in the 17th century when the Edict of Nantes was revoked, often on their way to Canada. A bout of plague and the bombardment of the city by the English and Dutch put an end to Dieppe's prosperity in the late 17th century.

It rebounded in the 19th century when aristocrats discovered the health benefits of sea bathing. With the construction of a railway link to Paris in 1848, fashionable Parisians began to spend weekends in Dieppe while the English came for longer periods. Parisians deserted Dieppe after WWII in favour of glamorous Deauville but Dieppe still keeps Paris well supplied with fish and seafood.

### Orientation

The town centre is largely surrounded by water. Boulevard de Verdun runs along the lawns – a favourite spot for kite-flyers – that border the beach. Most of the Grande rue and rue de la Barre has been turned into a pedestrian mall. Quai Duquesne and its continuation, quai Henri IV, follow the

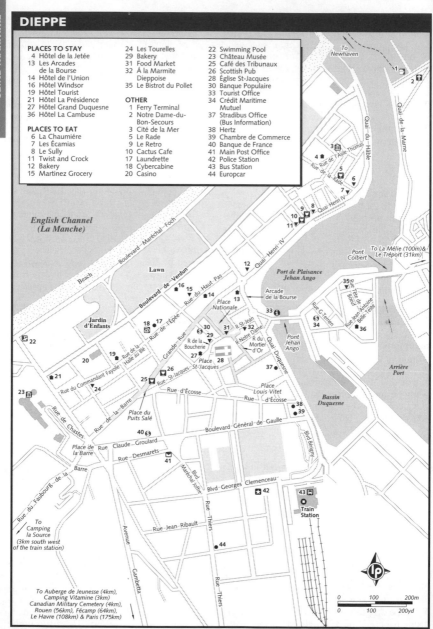

## DIEPPE

**PLACES TO STAY**
4 Hôtel de la Jetée
13 Les Arcades
de la Bourse
14 Hôtel de l'Union
16 Hôtel Windsor
19 Hôtel Tourist
21 Hôtel La Présidence
27 Hôtel Grand Duquesne
36 Hôtel La Cambuse

**PLACES TO EAT**
6 La Chaumière
7 Les Écamias
8 Le Sully
11 Twist and Crock
12 Bakery
15 Martinez Grocery

24 Les Tourelles
29 Bakery
31 Food Market
32 Á la Marmite
Dieppoise
35 Le Bistrot du Pollet

**OTHER**
1 Ferry Terminal
2 Notre Dame-du-
Bon-Secours
3 Cité de la Mer
5 Le Rade
9 Le Retro
10 Cactus Cafe
17 Laundrette
18 Cybercabine
20 Casino

22 Swimming Pool
23 Château Musée
25 Café des Tribunaux
26 Scottish Pub
28 Église St-Jacques
30 Banque Populaire
33 Tourist Office
34 Crédit Maritime
Mutuel
37 Stradibus Office
(Bus Information)
38 Hertz
39 Chambre de Commerce
40 Banque de France
41 Main Post Office
42 Police Station
43 Bus Station
44 Europcar

*euro currency converter* 10FF = €1.52

western and northern sides of the port area. The picturesque fishermen's quarter is on the eastern side of the canal. Roads lead up to the chapel Notre Dame-du-Bon-Secours from which there are stunning views.

Ferries dock at the terminal on the north-eastern side of the port, just under 1km on foot from the tourist office. The train station is south of the town centre, off boulevard Georges Clemenceau – the bus station is located in the same building. The police station is west of the train station on the same road.

## Information

**Tourist Offices** The tourist office (☎ 02 32 14 40 60, fax 02 32 14 40 61, e officetour-dieppe@wanadoo.fr) is on Pont Jehan Ango, on the western side of the port area. It opens 9 am to 1 pm and 2 to 7 pm Monday to Saturday from May to September (to 8 pm in July and August), 10 am to 1 pm and 3 to 6 pm Sunday; 9 am to noon and 2 to 6 pm, Monday to Saturday, the rest of the year. Hotel reservations in the Dieppe area cost 20FF. Visit the city Web site at www .mairie-dieppe.fr.

**Money** Banks in Dieppe are closed on Monday except the Crédit Maritime Mutuel, at 3 rue Guillaume Terrien. The Banque de France is at 4 rue Claude Groulard. Several other banks are around place Nationale, including a Banque Populaire at No 15.

**Post & Communications** The main post office, 2 boulevard Maréchal Joffre, opens 8.30 am to 6 pm on weekdays and until noon on Saturday. It has Cyberposte.

The Cybercabine (☎ 02 35 84 64 36), 46 rue de l'Épée, charges 60FF per hour of Web surfing. It opens noon to 7 pm Monday to Saturday, and 2 to 6 pm Sunday.

**Laundry** The laundrette at 44 rue de l'Épée opens 7 am to 9 pm.

## Things to See & Do

Though the white cliffs on either side of Dieppe have been compared to those at Dover, the **beach** is gravelly and at times very windy. The vast **lawns** between boule-vard de Verdun and the beach were laid out in the 1860s by that seashore-loving imperial duo, Napoleon III and his wife, Eugénie. **Église St-Jacques**, a Norman Gothic church at place St-Jacques, has been reconstructed several times since the early 13th century.

High over the city on a western cliff, the **Château Musée** (☎ 02 35 84 19 76), is Dieppe's most impressive landmark. The castle dates from the 15th century and served as a residence for the governors of Dieppe until the Revolution, receiving François I, Henri IV and Louis XIV as visitors. It was a prison and an army barracks before the city purchased it in 1906 and turned it into a museum. Damaged by the retreating German army in 1944, the structure has been restored and now offers sweeping views over the sea. The museum is devoted to Dieppe's maritime and artistic history, a large portion of which involved the dubious practice of separating African elephants from their tusks and shipping the ivory back to Dieppe.

The craft of ivory-carving reached extraordinary heights in Dieppe during the 17th century and the results are on display in a series of rooms. At one time, some 350 artisans were working ivory in the town, with skills so finely honed it was rumoured that they had found a way to soften the ivory before carving it.

Other highlights of the museum include prints by Georges Braque who periodically resided in Dieppe and memorabilia of composer Camille St-Saëns whose family was from Dieppe. To get to the museum on foot, take rue de la Barre and follow the signs up rue de Chastes. It opens 10 am to noon and 2 to 5 pm daily, except Tuesday, October to May; and 10 am to noon and 2 to 6 pm daily June to September. Admission costs 13FF (children 7.50FF).

If you want to learn more about what Dieppe takes from – and gives back to – the sea around it, visit the **Cité de la Mer** (☎ 02 35 06 93 20) at 37 rue de l'Asile Thomas. Those with an interest in boating will enjoy the first floor, which traces the history and evolution of boat building and navigation. Fishing techniques are the subject of the upper-floor exhibits with a glance at the processes of freezing and distribution. Curious about cliffs? The formation, erosion and utility of Dieppe's cliffs are explained in detail. The visit ends with five large aquariums filled with happy living examples of fish and shellfish that are usually found on French plates: octopus, sole, lobsters, turbot and cod. The museum opens 10 am to noon and 2 to 6 pm September to April, and 10 am to 7 pm May to August. Admission costs 28FF (children aged up to 16, 16FF).

The **Canadian Military Cemetery** is 4km towards Rouen. To get there, take avenue des Canadiens (the continuation of avenue Gambetta) southwards and follow the signs.

The **GR21 hiking trail** follows the Côte d'Albâtre south-westwards from Dieppe all the way to Le Havre. A map (35FF) is available at the tourist office. For easy walks in the surrounding areas ranging from one to three hours, pick up a copy of *Topo-Guide Côte d'Albâtre* for 90FF.

The sea may be cold but water in the Olympic-sized **swimming pool** is heated to 25° and there are diving boards.

### Special Events

Dieppe is kite-capital of the world for one week in September in even-numbered years. From all over the world kite-makers and kite-flyers come to show off their skills. One of the featured events is *l'Arche des Enfants* when 2500 kites fly over the beach, each one individually decorated by a child from Dieppe.

### Places to Stay

**Camping** The *Camping La Source* (*☎/fax 02 35 84 27 04*) is 3km south-west of Dieppe in a lovely creekside location just off the D925 (well-signposted). It charges 22FF per adult, 28FF per tent and 6FF per car. It opens mid-March to mid-October. Take bus No 4 to the Petit-Appeville train station (10 minutes), walk beneath the railway bridge and up the marked gravel drive.

*Camping Vitamine* (*☎ 02 35 82 11 11*) is about 3km west of the train station. Take bus No 2 to the Vazarely stop. It charges

24FF per adult and 25FF per tent; it opens April to mid-October.

**Hostels** The *Auberge de Jeunesse (☎ 02 35 84 85 73, fax 02 35 84 89 62, ⓔ dieppe@ fuaj.org, 48 rue Louis Fromager)*, about 4km south-west of the train station, opens mid-March to mid-October. A bed costs 48FF a night. There's a kitchen and laundry, and you can pitch a tent on the grounds for 25FF a night. From the train station, walk straight up boulevard Bérigny to the Chambre de Commerce from where you take bus No 2 (direction: Val Druel) to the Château Michel stop.

**Hotels** There are a number of popular small hotels along rue du Haut Pas and its continuation, rue de l'Épée, including *Hôtel de l'Union (☎ 02 35 84 35 52, 47–49 rue du Haut Pas)*. Basic singles/doubles with hall showers cost 110/150FF.

The *Hôtel de la Jetée (☎ 02 35 84 89 98, 5 rue de l'Asile Thomas)* has pleasant rooms from 150FF with washbasin and 220FF with shower. *Hôtel La Cambuse (☎ 02 35 84 19 46, 42 rue Jean-Antoine Belle-Teste)* has clean, no-nonsense doubles with washbasin for 180FF, and with shower from 200FF.

*Hôtel Tourist (☎ 02 35 06 10 10, fax 02 35 84 15 87, 16 rue de la Halle au Blé)* has no particular charm but the price is right. Bland rooms fitted with a shower only cost 135/165FF; doubles with full private facilities cost 245FF. *Hôtel Grand Duquesne (☎ 02 32 14 61 10, fax 02 35 84 29 83, 15 place St-Jacques)* is in an older building but the rooms have recently been polished up, adding more style and comfort. Rooms with private bath cost 243/298FF; 210/255FF with sink only. Prices include breakfast.

*Les Arcades de la Bourse (☎ 02 35 84 14 12, fax 02 35 40 22 29, 1–3 Arcade de la Bourse)* is an elegant, old-style hotel in the centre of town with views over the port. Rooms with private bath, TV and telephone cost 280/450FF depending on the size and the view.

Two-star *Hôtel Windsor (☎ 02 35 84 15 23; fax 02 35 84 74 52, 18 boulevard de*

*Verdun)* on the seafront (though a long way from the water across those lawns) has small, garishly decorated doubles with washbasin from 150FF and with full amenities from 290FF. Rooms with a sea view cost 50FF extra.

One of the more luxurious hotels is *Hôtel La Présidence (☎ 02 35 84 31 31, fax 02 35 84 86 70,  hotel-la-presidence.com, boulevard Verdun)* facing the sea. This sleek, modern hotel has all the comforts you would expect for the price including a restaurant with a view of the sea. Rooms cost from 280FF to 765FF.

## Places to Eat

**Restaurants** An inexpensive sandwich place, *Twist and Crock (67 quai Henri IV)* also serves brochettes and vegetarian salads that cost from 20FF to 25FF. Mussels with fries cost only 35FF.

One of the cheapest and least touristy restaurants in town is at the *Hôtel de l'Union* (see Places to Stay earlier in the chapter). It has 55FF and 89FF *menus* daily, except Wednesday. In summer it's only available for dinner.

*Les Écamias (☎ 02 35 84 67 67, 129 quai Henri IV)* is a simple, family-style place serving fresh, tasty seafood at reasonable prices. You can't go wrong with the mussels or *raie* (ray) with butter sauce. *Menus* cost 75FF, 105FF and 170FF. It opens daily except Monday. Also facing the port is the classic *Le Sully (☎ 02 35 84 23 13, 97 quai Henri IV)* offering a large selection of fish and shellfish simply or elaborately prepared. Vegetarians will enjoy the 75FF vegetarian *menu*. Other *menus* cost 65FF to 130FF. The *choucroute de la mer* (choucroute with seafood rather than ham and sausage) won't leave you hungry. It opens daily except Tuesday dinner and Wednesday.

Just behind the casino, *Les Tourelles (☎ 02 35 84 15 88, 43 rue du Commandant Fayolle)* serves good-value *menus* from 59FF and generous paellas from 85FF (which must be ordered 24 hours in advance).

The friendly *La Chaumiére (☎ 02 35 40 18 54, 1 quai du Hâble)* on the waterfront, has an excellent 68FF seafood *menu*, but if

### Marmite Dieppoise

This fish soup is the proud speciality of Dieppe although it can be found in many variations along the Côte d'Albâtre. Serve it with a sparkling dry cider.

4 servings

700g mussels
2 onions
5 tablespoons butter
1L cider
assorted fish heads and bones
2 leeks
2 celery stalks
1 bay leaf
3 stalks of fresh thyme or 1 teaspoon dried
900g firm-fleshed white fish (sole, turbot, monkfish) in fillets
250ml crème fraîche
2 tablespoons chopped fresh parsley
salt and pepper to taste

Scrub the mussels under cold running water to remove all sand, discarding any that do not close when firmly tapped. Peel and chop the onions. Put half of them in a large pot, add half the butter, 200ml of the cider and then the mussels. Cover and cook on high heat for a few minutes until the mussels open.

Shell the mussels, discarding any that have not opened, and set aside. Strain the cooking liquid and reserve.

Put the fish heads and bones in a pot. Add the washed, chopped leeks, the remaining chopped onions, the celery cut into rounds, the bay leaf and thyme. Add the remaining cider, 250ml of water and the cooking liquid from the mussels. Cook uncovered over medium heat for 30 minutes.

Season the white fish and put it into another pot. Pour the strained vegetable broth over it. Add the remaining butter, cut up into pieces, and the crème fraîche. Bring back to a simmer and cook over low heat for 15 minutes. Correct the seasoning.

Add the mussels and reheat for two minutes. Pour into a large serving bowl, garnish with the parsley and tuck in!

you really want to taste Dieppe's *fruits de la mer* at their best, head for the intimate *À la Marmite Dieppoise* (☎ 02 35 84 24 26, 8 rue St-Jean) in the old city. Their speciality is *marmite Dieppoise*, a delicious fish stew. *Menus* cost from 85FF to a whopping 215FF. It opens daily except on Sunday evening and Monday.

*Le Bistrot du Pollet* (☎ 02 35 84 68 57, 23 rue Tête de Boeuf) is away from the tourist crowds in the old fishermen's quarter. The daily *menu* (68FF) is written on a blackboard and offers an excellent deal. The a la carte offerings include *lotte* (monkfish) marinated in wine and *daurade* (sea bream) with herbs. It opens daily except Sunday and Monday. A more expensive alternative in the fishermen's quarter is *La Mélie* (☎ 02 35 84 21 19, 2–4 Grande rue du Pollet). The chef knows how to pick the very best fish, which he cooks to perfection in typically Dieppe style. *Menus* cost 180FF and there's a 230FF *menu* that includes wine. It is closed Sunday dinner and Monday.

**Self-Catering** The *food market* between place St-Jacques and place Nationale opens Tuesday and Thursday mornings and all day Saturday. The *bakery* at 15 quai Henri IV opens daily from 7 am to 7.30 pm (closed Monday). There's another bakery at 14 rue de la Boucherie (closed Wednesday). The *Martinez Grocery*, 44 rue du Haut Pas, opens 7.30 am to 8.30 pm (closed Monday).

## Entertainment

Dieppe has loads of pubs and bars full of interesting characters, but don't be surprised if you have to buzz to be let in. The *Scottish Pub* (12 rue St-Jacques) is a good place to start a crawl, and the friendly bar staff will point you in the right direction. *Café des Tribunaux* (place du Puits Salé) is an inviting place in a sprawling 18th-century building that harboured the crowd of Impressionist painters in the late 19th century.

On the port, *Cactus Cafe* (71 quai Henri IV) has a wide selection of beer and cocktails, snacks and tapas. Decor is in the ever-popular Latin theme (closed Sunday in winter). Across the road is *Le Retro* at No

73, which is also a popular hang-out. *Le Rade* (12 rue de la Rade) is where fishermen come to throw back a drink or two and discuss the day's catch (closed Monday).

## Getting There & Away

**Bus** The bus station is in the same cavernous building as the train station. CNA (☎ 02 35 52 92 00) has services to Fécamp (75FF, 2¼ hours, at least two daily), Le Tréport (41FF, 1¼ hours, four daily) and Rouen (72FF, two hours, three daily). No buses run on Saturday or Sunday afternoon.

**Train** The paucity of direct trains to Paris' Gare St-Lazare (126FF, 2¼ hours, four daily) is offset by frequent services to Rouen (55FF, 45–60 minutes, 10 daily), where there is a connecting service to Le Havre (110FF, two hours from Dieppe). The last train from Dieppe to Paris (via Rouen) leaves just before 7 pm daily.

**Boat** The first ferry service from Dieppe to the UK (Brighton, to be exact) began in 1790. These days Hoverspeed (☎ 08 20 00 35 55) runs car and pedestrian ferries between Dieppe and Newhaven. Boats depart from the ferry terminal on the north-eastern side of the port area at the end of quai de la Marne. For details on prices and times see Sea in the Getting There & Away chapter.

## Getting Around

**Bus** The local bus network, Stradibus, runs 13 lines that run to either 6 or 8 pm. All buses stop at either the train station or the nearby Chambre de Commerce, on quai Duquesne. It has an information office on this road. A single ticket costs 6.40FF, a 10-ticket carnet 42FF.

Buses are timed to meet incoming and outgoing ferries and shuttle foot passengers between the terminal and the tourist office (12FF).

**Car & Motorcycle** ADA car rental (☎ 02 35 84 32 28) has an office in the train station. Hertz (☎ 02 32 14 01 70) is at 5 rue d'Écosse and Europcar (☎ 02 35 04 97 10) is at 33 rue Thiers.

**Taxi** Taxis can be called on ☎ 02 35 84 20 05. The fare from the ferry pier to the city centre is about 35FF.

## AROUND DIEPPE

**Varengeville-sur-Mer**, a country village 8km west of Dieppe, is so small you don't know you've been there until you leave it. Little more than a cluster of houses along the side of the road, Varengeville charmed painters such as Monet, Dufy, Miró and Braque. Miró included two paintings of Varengeville in his cycle, *Constellations*, and Braque had a studio here at the end of his life. Braque is buried in Varengeville outside a cliff-top **church** for which he designed several vividly coloured stained-glass windows. His tomb is beneath a mosaic of a white dove on a blue background and there are bracing coastal views from the cemetery. The cemetery opens 8 am to 9 pm in summer and from 9 am to 6 pm in winter.

Next door is the splendid garden-park **Bois des Moutiers** (☎ 02 35 85 10 02), a wonderland of flowers and trees from China, North America, Chile and Japan as well as France. The gardens are an extension of a country house built for Guillaume Mallet at the turn of the century. The British architect Sir Edwin Lutyens designed the house in the popular Arts and Crafts style and the English landscape gardener Gertrude Jekyll collaborated with him on the gardens, which are one of the finest in France. Designed as a series of walled spaces, the gardens lead you to a 30-acre park that winds down to the sea. Come in March and April for the flowering magnolias, in May and June for the azaleas and rhododendrons (some of which are 10m high), in the summer for roses and hydrangeas and in October and November for the Japanese maples. The house is also highly original but can only be visited by appointment (100FF per person for a group of eight). The park opens 10 am to noon and 2 to 6 pm daily from mid-March to mid-November. You can stay through lunch and until 8 pm from May to September. Admission costs 35FF in March and April and July to November, and 40FF in May and June. Bus No

60/61 from Dieppe stops at the park (17FF, 25 minutes, twice daily except Sunday).

Since the cemetery and park are on a cliff high above town, it makes sense to visit them first if you're coming by bus and then walk down the hill to the town centre to visit **Le Manoir d'Ango** (☎ 02 35 85 14 80). Built by the shipbuilder and privateer Jehan Ango in the 16th century, this manor has a stunning *colombier* (dovecote) with an unusual domed top and an Italian loggia decorated with frescos from the school of Leonardo da Vinci. The manor is fit for a king and, in fact, Ango received François I here in 1523. Despite his successful expeditions on behalf of the crown, Ango died in his manor almost penniless still waiting for repayment of money he had lent to the Treasury years earlier. The manor opens 10 am to 12.30 pm and 2 to 6.30 pm daily mid-March to mid-November. Admission costs 30FF (students 20FF).

## LE TRÉPORT
**postcode 76470 • pop 6500**

Lying 30km north of Dieppe, Le Tréport is the northernmost point of the Côte d'Albâtre. Like many towns along the coast, Le Tréport was once a fishing port that became fashionable in the 19th century. It's not particularly fashionable now, only very crowded in the summer season. The beachfront has been developed to death but the wide, pebbly beach has its charms and the towering cliffs rising at the south-western end provide a dramatic setting. If the summertime craziness gets too much, the quieter Mers-les-Bains resort lies just north-east of the port.

### Orientation & Information

Le Tréport is separated from Mers-les-Bains by the canalised River Bresle, which opens onto a port at the opening to the Channel. The restaurant-packed quai François 1er runs along the port to the seafront. The most interesting part of town is the old rope-makers quarter wedged between the port and the beach. From rue de l'Hôtel de Ville on quai François 1er, 350 steps lead to the top of the cliff.

The train and bus station are shared with

Mers-les-Bains, north-east of the town centre on the other side of the port. The tourist office (☎ 02 35 86 05 69, fax 02 35 86 73 96, ⓔ officetourismeletreport@wanadoo.fr, quai Sadi Carnot) is east of quai François 1er. It opens 9 am to noon and 2 to 6 .30 pm April to June and September, 9 am to 1 pm and 2 to 7 pm July and August and 9 am to noon and 2 to 6 pm Monday to Saturday the rest of the year.

## Things to See & Do

On your way to the top of the cliffs, stop at **Église St-Jacques**. Built in the 15th century to replace a much earlier church that collapsed in a storm, the church has several Renaissance highlights including its main door and a polychrome Madonna from the 16th century. Notice the scallop decoration in the interior. Pilgrims on the way to Santiago de Compostella in Spain adopted the scallop as their emblem and it eventually took on a religious connotation.

The view from the top of the cliff is worth the climb and you can recuperate with a drink on the terrace of the Hôtel Le Trianon located here. The tourist office has a map and suggestions for walking and cycling in the region.

## Places to Stay & Eat

*Camping Les Boucaniers* (☎ *02 35 86 35 47)* is in a quiet location on the road to Mers-les-Bains.

*Le St-Yves* (☎ *02 35 86 34 66, fax 02 35 86 53 73, 7 quai Albert Cauët)* is near the train station, offering access both to Le Tréport and Mers-les-Bains, 500m up the road. Rooms cost from 260FF to 320FF depending on size and whether there's a view of the sea.

Le Tréport is known for its giant plates of fresh seafood and you'll find a dozen equally good places on the quai François 1er. Count on spending about 150FF. For a simpler meal there's *Pizzeria de la Tour* (☎ *02 35 50 12 17, 1 rue de la Tour)*, with meals from 64FF to 85FF, which opens daily except Monday and *La Crêperie du Musoir* (☎ *02 35 86 69 41, 2 rue de Paris)* that serves light meals for 59FF to 75FF.

## Getting There & Away

The best way to reach Le Tréport is by bus from Dieppe. CNA has at least four buses daily (41FF, 1¼ hours). There are also trains from Rouen (95FF, 2¼ hours, three daily) and Paris (163FF, three hours, five daily).

## FÉCAMP

**postcode 76400 • pop 21,000**

At the foot of the highest cliffs in Normandy (126m), Fécamp is a sturdy fishing town 41km north of Le Havre. Fishing boats and pleasure boats crowd its port and a promenade runs along an exhilarating stretch of rocky beach. Until the mid-1970s, Fécamp was the fourth largest fishing port in France with fishermen setting sail for the cod-filled waters of Newfoundland. In recent decades, fishing boats stay closer to home, bringing the daily catch to nearby freezing, drying and salting factories. Ship repair and net-making are also important industries in Fécamp.

Fécamp's dramatic setting and neat rows of brick houses has made it a popular summer resort and there are fascinating reminders of its history scattered through the town. Fécamp was little more than a fishing village until the 6th century, when a few drops of Christ's blood miraculously found their way here and it became a pilgrimage centre. The first dukes of Normandy built a fortified chateau here in the 10th century that remained a ducal residence for over 100 years. The dukes also encouraged the formation of a Bénédictine abbey, which remained influential until the Revolution. In the early 16th century a Bénédictine monk concocted a 'medicinal elixir' from a variety of plants. Although the recipe was lost during the Revolution, it was re-discovered in the 19th century and the after-dinner liqueur was produced commercially. Today, Bénédictine is one of the most widely-marketed *digestifs* in the world. Visits to the abbey, the Bénédictine distillery and cod-fishing museum cover the main axes of Fécamp's development and the narrow streets remain much as they were in the 19th century when they served as a backdrop for the evocative tales of Guy de Maupassant.

## Orientation

The town centre lies south-west of a series of ports and basins. Quai de la Vicomté and quai Bérigny along the Port de Plaisance and Bassin Bérigny form a busy commercial road packed with shops and restaurants. The pedestrianised streets between the St-Étienne church and place Charles de Gaulle are also good for shopping. The oldest part of town lies east of rue du Président René Coty, which is where you'll find most places of interest.

## Information

The tourist office (☎ 02 35 28 51 01, fax 02 35 27 07 77, ⓔ fecamp-tourisime@wanadoo .fr) is at 113 rue Alexandre Le Grand. It opens 9 am to 12.15 pm and 1.45 to 6 pm daily (10 am to 6 pm in July and August). Check out its Web site at www.fecamp.com. There's another, smaller tourist office (☎ 02 35 29 16 94) on quai de la Vicomté, open in summer only from 10.30 am to 1 pm and 2.30 to 7 pm.

You can change money at Crédit Fécampois, 23 rue Alexandre Legros, which opens 9 am to noon and 2 to 6.30 pm Tuesday

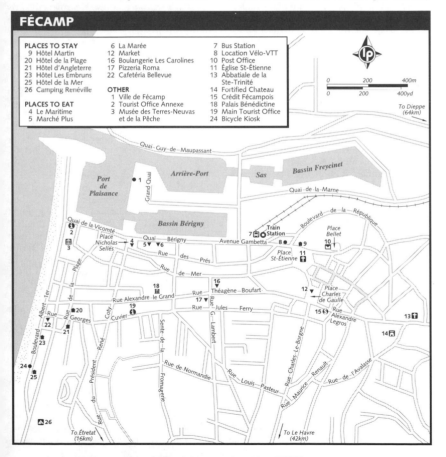

### FÉCAMP

**PLACES TO STAY**
9 Hôtel Martin
20 Hôtel de la Plage
21 Hôtel d'Angleterre
23 Hôtel Les Embruns
25 Hôtel de la Mer
26 Camping Renéville

**PLACES TO EAT**
4 Le Maritime
5 Marché Plus

6 La Marée
12 Market
16 Boulangerie Les Carolines
17 Pizzeria Roma
22 Cafétéria Bellevue

**OTHER**
1 Ville de Fécamp
2 Tourist Office Annexe
3 Musée des Terres-Neuvas et de la Pêche

7 Bus Station
8 Location Vélo-VTT
10 Post Office
11 Église St-Étienne
13 Abbatiale de la Ste-Trinité
14 Fortified Chateau
15 Crédit Fécampois
18 Palais Bénédictine
19 Main Tourist Office
24 Bicycle Kiosk

to Friday, and 9 am to 12.30 pm and 2 to 3.15 pm on Saturday.

The main post office is on place Bellet and opens 8.30 am to 12.30 pm and 1.30 to 5.30 pm Monday to Friday, and Saturday morning. It has Cyberposte.

## Things to See & Do

The **Palais Bénédictine** (☎ 02 35 10 26 10) is at 110 rue Alexandre Le Grand in an ornate building (1900) mixing Flamboyant Gothic and eclectic styles, inspired by the 15th-century Hôtel de Cluny in Paris. It's geared up to tell you everything about the history and making of its aromatic liqueur – except the exact recipe. We do know that it involves the prettily named melissa, angelica and hyssop plants, and 24 other herbs and spices.

Tours start in the art museum, which houses the private collection of founder Alexandre Le Grand. This rich merchant loved medieval art and the display includes carved ivory and wood, 15th- and 16th-century statues, manuscripts, wrought iron and a stained-glass window of Alexandre Le Grand commissioned by his son. The visit continues through a hall where hundreds of bottles of bootlegged Bénédictine are proudly displayed. In the fragrant Plant & Spice Room, you can smell a handful of some of the ingredients used to make the potent drink and then see the oak vats where it is fermented.

The Palais opens 10 am to noon and 2 to 5.30 pm, mid-March to June, and early September to mid-November; 9.30 am to 6 pm, July to early September; and 10 to 11.15 am and 2 to 5 pm, mid-November to mid-March. Admission costs 29FF (students 22FF, children 14.50FF) and includes a free shot of Bénédictine.

Fortified by the Bénédictine, proceed to the **Abbatiale de la Ste-Trinité** (☎ 02 35 28 84 39), place des Ducs Richard. Built from 1175 to 1220 under the instigation of Richard the Lion-Heart, this Benedictine abbey was the most important pilgrimage site in Normandy until the construction of Mont St-Michel. Its primary draw for pilgrims has been the drop of holy blood that

miraculously floated to Fécamp in the trunk of a fig tree. A fountain sprouted from the spot where the trunk landed and eventually the holy blood was placed in the custody of the abbey monks.

The exterior is a combination of primitive Gothic and a classical style dating from an 18th-century reconstruction. The spacious interior is 127m long and 23m high, which compares favourably with many of France's finest cathedrals. Among the many treasures inside is the late-15th-century *Dormition de la Vierge* – a polychrome bas relief of remarkably lifelike faces crowding around a weeping Virgin. Nearby is the *Pas de l'Ange* sculpture, which represents the footprint of the angel that allegedly descended upon the church during its consecration, demanding that it be named after the Holy Trinity. The abbey opens 9 am to 6 pm daily. Admission is free.

Across from the abbey are the remains of the **fortified chateau** built by the earliest dukes of Normandy in the 10th and 11th centuries.

The **Musée des Terres-Neuvas et de la Pêche** (☎ 02 35 29 76 22), 27 boulevard Albert 1er, evokes a typical life of a cod fisherman with extraordinary verve. For centuries the men of Fécamp boarded sailing ships to Newfoundland where they caught, cleaned and salted cod to be brought back to Spain and Portugal. The practice began in the 16th century and the last boat to make the crossing was in 1987. While some displays show fishing techniques, the emphasis is on men's relationship with the sea and their capacity for brutal, dangerous work.

The museum opens 10 am to noon and 2 to 5.30 pm Wednesday to Monday (Tuesdays also in July and August). Admission costs 20FF (students 10FF).

## Organised Tours

The boat *Ville de Fécamp* runs daily 1½-hour trips to Étretat (65FF) and 45 minute trips to Yport (50FF). There are also four-hour fishing trips (170FF, equipment included). Trips take place April to October depending on the weather and boats leave from the Grand Quai. Call ☎ 02 35 28 99 53 for further information.

## Places to Stay

Dramatically situated on the western cliffs, **Camping Renéville** (☎ 02 35 28 20 97, Côte de Renéville) charges 38FF per person and 25FF per tent.

The cheapest hotel in town is **Hôtel Martin** (☎ 02 35 28 23 82, fax 02 35 28 61 21, 18 place St-Étienne), above a restaurant. Basic rooms cost 150FF, those with a shower only cost 175FF, and rooms with a full bathroom cost 200FF.

Hotels across from the beach are an appealing choice but, since they are on a busy boulevard, the front rooms can be noisy. The best is **Hôtel de la Mer** (☎ 02 35 28 24 64, fax 02 35 28 27 67, 89 boulevard Albert 1er), a modern establishment of no particular charm, where many of the comfortable rooms have balconies with sea views. Rooms with sink only cost 180FF; rooms with private facilities cost 320FF.

Nearby is the **Hôtel Les Embruns** (☎ 02 35 28 31 31, fax 02 35 28 45 17, 73 boulevard Albert 1er), which is smaller but also has rooms with balconies facing the sea costing 295/310FF a single/double, and 280FF for rooms with no sea view.

**Hôtel de la Plage** (☎ 02 35 29 76 51, fax 02 35 28 68 30, 87 rue de la Plage) is set back a block from the sea, offering stylish, well-furnished rooms that are freshly renovated. There's one small room with a toilet in the hall for 260FF but others cost from 300FF to 400FF depending on the size of the room. The **Hôtel d'Angleterre** (☎ 02 35 28 01 60, fax 02 35 28 62 95, 93 rue de la Plage) nearby also offers cheery rooms that cost from 250FF to 390FF.

## Places to Eat

An extension of a fish shop, **La Marée** (☎ 02 35 29 39 15, 75 quai Bérigny) offers the freshest, tastiest fish in town. The choucroute de la mer has just the right touch of tang but all the fish and seafood is prepared with a minimum of fuss. Finish off with crème brûlée à la Bénédictine. Weekday menus start at 98FF but rise to 135FF at the

weekend. It opens daily except for Sunday dinner and on Monday.

There's a lot to choose from at **Le Maritime** (☎ 02 35 28 21 71, 2 place Nicolas Selles), most of it from the sea, as the name would imply. The seafood platters are copious and can be ordered take-away. Menus start from 89FF on weekdays and 128FF at the weekend.

The restaurant at the **Hôtel Martin** (see Places to Stay earlier in the chapter) is one of the better value restaurants in town. In a cosy dining room, waiters bring out Norman dishes cooked with flair. Mussels with cider and fresh cod are standouts. Weekday menus start at 75FF; at the weekend the cheapest menu is 95FF. It opens daily except Monday.

For a change of pace from seafood try **Pizzeria Roma** (☎ 02 35 29 46 36, 51 rue Théagène Boufart), which has pizzas that cost from 49FF to 66FF.

**Cafétéria Bellevue** (☎ 02 35 29 22 92, 63 boulevard Albert 1er) serves a buffet of vegetables for 27FF, a vegetable plate for 18FF and a plat du jour for 42FF, as well as a selection of standard French dishes.

Bread lovers will revel in the chewy loaves at **Boulangerie Les Carolines** (☎ 02 35 27 33 45, 44 rue Théagène Boufart). Look for an old brick house with murals on bread-making themes. It opens daily except Sunday afternoon and Wednesday.

There's a **Marché Plus** (83 quai Bérigny) supermarket and a **market** all day Saturday on place Charles de Gaulle.

## Getting There & Away

Fécamp is accessible by bus from Dieppe, Le Havre and Rouen, and by train from Le Havre. See the Getting There & Away sections for those towns for more information. The train station (☎ 02 35 28 24 82) opens 9.15 (10.15 Saturday) to 11.50 am and 1.40 to 6 pm daily (10.10 am to 12.20 pm and 3.15 to 7 pm Sunday). The bus between Fécamp (30 minutes, seven daily) and Le Havre also connects Fécamp with Étretat.

## Getting Around

Fécamp has a city bus line mainly to serve students. For a visitor, bus No 6 that runs from place St-Étienne to the beach, via the Palais Bénédictine would be the most useful, but there are only five buses daily. Tickets cost 4.90FF.

Mountain bikes and 10-speeds (80FF per day) are available for rent from Location Vélo-VTT (☎ 02 35 28 45 09), 2 avenue Gambetta, and in a kiosk (☎ 02 35 28 51 01) across the street from Hôtel de la Mer.

For a taxi call ☎ 02 35 28 17 50.

## AROUND FÉCAMP

Quiet **Yport** makes Fécamp, 6km to the west, look like a major metropolis. Also squeezed between giant cliffs, Yport has a rocky beach sadly marred by wooden bathhouses and an ugly casino. Yet, there's an endearing simplicity to Yport, which seems as though it's been left behind in the rush towards tourism along the coast. The tourist office (☎ 02 35 29 77 31) is in the town centre on place JP Laurens. It opens 10 am to noon and 3 to 7 pm mid-May to mid-September. The post office is across the street.

Places to stay are sparse but the tourist office has a list of *chambres d'hôtes* (B&Bs). The *Hôtel Normand (☎ 02 35 27 30 76, place JP Laurens)* has singles/doubles with shower only for 170/215FF and rooms with a private bathroom for 280FF. There are no cheap restaurants but you won't be disappointed by the food at friendly *Les Embruns (☎ 02 35 27 31 32, 2 rue Emmanuel Foy)*, which has weekday *menus* for 75FF and opens daily except Monday. Yport is accessible by bus from Fécamp (15 minutes, eight daily).

## ÉTRETAT

**postcode 76280 • pop 1600**

Étretat, a small village 20km south-west of Fécamp, is renowned for its two cliffs: the Falaise d'Amont and the Falaise d'Aval. Featuring the most unusual rock formations in the area, you'll see them long before you arrive, appearing somewhat deceivingly to be one rock. Unlike other coastal towns, Étretat has no port and never amounted to much until painters and writers discovered its beauty in the 19th century. Guy de Maupassant spent part of his youth here and the

stunning scenery made it a favourite of painters Camille Corot, Eugène Boudin, Gustav Courbet and Claude Monet. With the vogue for sea air at the end of the 19th century, fashionable Parisians came and built villas. Étretat has never gone out of style and swells to bursting point with visitors in summer and on long weekends. Count on huge traffic jams and overbooked hotels if you come in peak periods.

### Orientation

The main road into town is avenue de Verdun, which takes you down to the tourist office. Follow rue Monge eastwards and you'll come to busy boulevard du Président René Coty and the seaside promenade. Most hotels, shops and restaurants are in the compact town centre.

### Information

**Tourist Offices** The tourist office (☎ 02 35 27 05 21, fax 02 35 29 39 79, e ot.etretat@ wanadoo.fr), in the centre of the village on place Maurice Guillard, has accommodation lists for the area posted on the door for inspection outside opening hours. It opens 10 am till noon and 2 to 6 pm daily in spring and autumn but without interruption in the summer. In winter, it opens Friday and Saturday only. It has a map of the cliff trails and rents out bicycles for 100FF a day. Visit its Web site at www.etretat.net.

**Money** You can change money at Crédit Agricole, 20 rue Prospero, across from the tourist office. It opens daily except Sunday and Monday.

**Post & Communications** The main post office is at 25 rue George V. It opens 8.30 am to noon and 2 to 6 pm Monday to Friday and Saturday morning. There's no Cyberposte.

**Laundry** There's a laundrette at 78 avenue de Verdun. It opens 7 am to 9 pm daily.

### Things to See & Do

The big attraction of Étretat are the stony white cliffs that press in the town, the **Falaise d'Amont** to the north-east and the

**Falaise d'Aval** to the south-west. The Falaise d'Aval is accessible via signposted stairs from place du Général de Gaulle. The cliff descends to the water in a delicate arch, the **Porte d'Aval**, that reminded writer Guy de Maupassant of an elephant dipping its trunk into the water. Behind the arch is the 70m-high **L'Aiguille** (Needle), which arises from the water like an obelisk. **Le Trou à l'Homme** grotto lies on the other side of the arch and can be reached on foot at low tide. Beyond the grotto is the stunning **La Manneporte** rock arch. The Falaise d'Amont is accessible by car, taking rue Jules Gerbeau, or on foot from the signposted path at the north-eastern end of the promenade. At the top is a monument and little museum commemorating the spot where two aviators, Charles Nungesser and François Coli, were last seen before their attempt to cross the Atlantic in 1927. Count on about 1½ hours for each walk.

Serious walkers might enjoy continuing north along the GR21 from the Falaise d'Amont to the **Aiguille de Belval** and Benouville for the splendid coastal views. Do *not* try to explore the base of the cliffs outside low tide. Ask the tourist office for the schedule.

You can't miss the **old covered market** in the centre of town. This handsome wooden structure looks more like a church but was built in 1926 as a covered marketplace. It now houses various arts and crafts shops.

## Special Events

The *Bénédiction de la Mer* (blessing of the sea) on Ascension Thursday commemorates a legend whereby fishermen were caught in a terrible storm. A monk prayed on bended knee for the winds to stop and they did, sparing the lives of all. The ceremony dates from the Middle Ages and includes music, a fair, a mass and, of course, a blessing of the sea.

## Places to Stay

About 1km east of the town centre, taking rue Guy de Maupassant, is *Camping Municipal* (☎ 02 35 27 07 67). It charges 17FF per person and 14FF per tent. A prettier site is *Camping Les Tilleuls* (☎ 02 35 27 11 67)

about 4km south-west of Étretat in the village of Tilleuls.

The cheaper hotels are in from the sea along avenue George V or place Foch. *Hôtel de la Poste* (☎ 02 35 27 01 34, fax 02 35 27 76 28, 6 avenue George V) offers singles/doubles with shower, toilet and TV for 180/220FF. A pet parrot livens up the cosy breakfast room. *Hôtel des Falaises* (☎ 02 35 27 02 77, 1 boulevard du Président René Coty) has polished, new rooms costing 340FF with bath and 280FF with shower only.

The most interesting hotel in town is the nearby *Hôtel La Résidence* (☎ 02 35 27 02 87, 4 boulevard du Président René Coty). This 14th-century building with an appealingly dilapidated facade once belonged to an alchemist who adorned the windows with alchemy signs. Renovation of the interior has added modern bathrooms (some with a Jacuzzi) but left intact the creaky stairway, wooden floors and doors and overhanging beams. Rooms vary considerably in size and comfort but all are well-maintained. Count on spending 170FF for a small room with a toilet in the hall and up to 690FF for a large, comfortable room with a Jacuzzi.

For a room with a sea view, head to *Hôtel Le Corsaire* (☎ 02 35 10 38 90, fax 02 35 28 89 74, rue Général Le Clerc) where you can have memorable views of the cliffs at prices ranging from 275FF to 590FF. And to really wallow in luxury, there's the turreted *Hôtel Le Donjon* (☎ 02 35 27 08 23, fax 02 35 29 92 24, @ ledonjon@wanadoo.fr, Chemin de St-Clair) about 1km north-east of the town centre. The rooms are decorated with striking originality, some with sea views and others with Jacuzzis. There's an excellent restaurant and a swimming pool. Rates from Sunday to Friday cost from 880FF to 1280FF and are considerably more expensive at the weekend.

## Places to Eat

The dining scene in Étretat has few standouts, but there are some good seafood places where you can feast well if you want to pay the price. The best is *Le Galion*

(☎ 02 35 29 48 74, boulevard du Président René Coty), which offers such specialities as *médaillon de lotte* (a cut of monkfish) and salmon with saffron sauce in a romantic beamed dining room. *Menus* cost from 120FF to 240FF. It opens daily except for Tuesday and Wednesday.

On a less exalted level, *L'Huitrière* (☎ 02 35 27 02 82, rue de Traz Perier) offers *menus* that begin at an affordable 98FF and climb to 239FF for an elaborate array of seafood. The round dining room has a panoramic view of the Falaise d'Aval.

The hotels *Le Corsaire* and *Le Donjon* turn out good food and there are a number of inexpensive *creperies*, *pizzerias* and *brasseries* on rue Alphonse Karr, boulevard du Président René Coty and place Foch. The *Point Coop* supermarket (*40 rue Notre Dame*) is open daily except for Sunday afternoons.

The *market* is held 9 am to 1 pm on Thursday around the old covered market.

## Getting There & Away
The only way to reach Étretat is on the bus line that runs from Fécamp to Le Havre, stopping at Yport. For information, see the Getting There and Away sections for those towns.

# Eure

Since it doesn't have a beach, the land-locked Eure department is untrampled by throngs of sun-worshippers. Tourists flock by the busload to Monet's luxuriant garden at Giverny, but fewer make it to the plains, valleys and forests of the interior. Yet the rewards are many. The magnificent Forêt de Lyons in the north-east offers a wide choice of walks and drives through the beech trees that reveal forgotten chateaux and obscure old villages. The mighty fortresses of Gisors and Château Gaillard recall the turbulent time when the kings of England and France battled furiously to gain control of this department.

Riversides are a large part of the Eure's appeal. Vernon and Les Andelys on the Seine, Évreux on the Iton and Bernay on the Charentonne have carefully groomed riverbanks that make the town centres gentle and relaxing. You'll need a car to do full justice to the department since public transport is infrequent to non-existent, especially to the circle of attractions – Bec-Helluoin and the chateaux of Beaumesnil and Champ de Bataille – around Bernay.

## Pays d'Ouche

Capital of the Eure department, picturesque Évreux gives way to forested vales in the north-west and the humid hills of the Ouche country in the south-west.

### ÉVREUX

**postcode 27000 • pop 51,000**

Around 50km south of Rouen, Évreux is a tranquil provincial city on the River Iton. A fine cathedral and archaeological museum recall its turbulent history, which began around the 1st century AD when it was known as Mediolanum. Throughout the Middle Ages, Évreux was a battleground for every conquering army in Normandy. The Vandals destroyed the ancient city in the 5th century, the Normans destroyed it

EURE

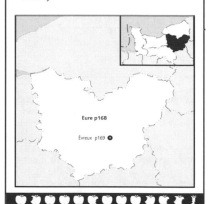

Eure p168

Évreux p169

again in the 9th century and Henry I burned it in the 12th century. It was burned again by King Philippe-Auguste later in the 12th century after John Lackland (brother of Richard the Lion-Heart) invited 300 French soldiers garrisoned in Évreux for a nice dinner and then massacred them. During the 14th century Évreux was caught in the struggle between the French and English and burned again, this time losing its Episcopal palace and priceless archives. It became part of France in 1441 but suffered again in 1791 when Revolutionaries razed

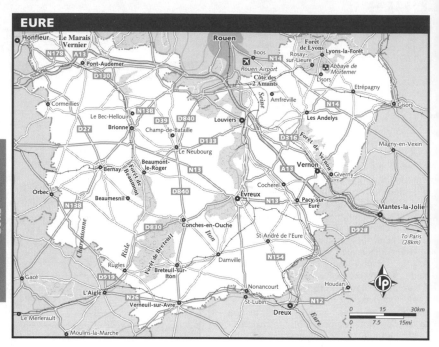

six churches, two convents and two abbeys. German bombs devastated the town in 1940 and Allied bombs rained down on it in 1944. Phoenix-like, Évreux has risen again. Careful reconstruction has created a warm, liveable town centre with plenty of green spaces. The banks of the Iton are graced with tree-lined promenades, and old half-timbered houses are being restored. Although there's not enough in Évreux to keep anyone engrossed for more than an afternoon, it makes a relaxing overnight stop or base for exploring other towns in the Eure.

## Orientation

The adjacent train and bus stations are about 1km south of the town centre. The Tour de l'Horloge is the most conspicuous landmark in the centre. Shops, restaurants and cafes are clustered on and around rue Joséphine and rue du Docteur Oursel. The riverbank, promenade des Remparts and promenade Robert de Floques, runs from the tourist office to the cathedral and museum. Rue Chatraine and rue de la Harpe are also lively streets, full of shops, banks and cafes.

## Information

The tourist office (☎ 02 32 24 04 43, fax 02 32 31 28 45, e information@evreux-tourisme.org) is in the centre of town at 3 place du Général de Gaulle. It opens from 9.30 am to 12.30 pm and 1.30 to 6.15 pm Monday to Saturday and 10 am to 12.30 pm Sunday (closed on Sunday in winter). The office has maps of five proposed cycle routes in the area. See the Web site at www.evreux-tourisme.org.

You can change money at the Banque de France on 26 rue Victor Hugo. It opens Monday to Friday.

The main post office is at 25 rue du Docteur Oursel and opens 8 am to 7 pm Monday to Friday and also in the mornings

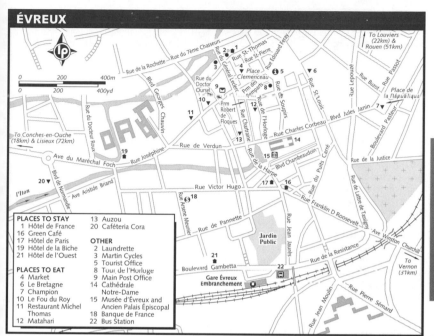

**ÉVREUX**

0   200   400m
0   200   400yd

To Louviers
(22km) &
Rouen (51km)

To Conches-en-Ouche
(18km) & Lisieux (72km)

Place de
la République

l'Iton

Jardin
Public

To
Vernon
(31km)

Gare Évreux
Embranchement

EURE

**PLACES TO STAY**
1  Hôtel de France
16  Green Café
17  Hôtel de Paris
19  Hôtel de la Biche
21  Hôtel de l'Ouest

**PLACES TO EAT**
4  Market
6  Le Bretagne
7  Champion
10  Le Fou du Roy
11  Restaurant Michel
    Thomas
12  Matahari

13  Auzou
20  Cafétéria Cora

**OTHER**
2  Laundrette
3  Martin Cycles
5  Tourist Office
8  Tour de l'Horloge
9  Main Post Office
14  Cathédrale
    Notre-Dame
15  Musée d'Évreux and
    Ancien Palais Épiscopal
18  Banque de France
22  Bus Station

on Saturday. It has Cyberposte facilities for
Internet connection.

There's a laundrette at 27 rue St-Thomas
open 7 am to 9 pm daily.

## Things to See & Do

The **Cathédrale Notre-Dame** has been destroyed and rebuilt so many times it has become a temple to changing architectural
styles. The Romanesque arcades in the nave
date from the late 12th century, and survived
when the church went up in flames in 1194
as part of Philippe-Auguste's attack on the
city. Reconstruction of the cathedral was
slow but by the end of the 13th century the
choir was completed in an elegant Rayonnant Gothic style. Notice the fine 14th-
century windows around the choir. The
cathedral burned again in 1356 and 1378 in
assaults by the Count of Évreux and Charles
V respectively. Under Louis XI in the 15th
century, the transept, the lantern tower and a
wonderful north door were built in a Flam-

boyant Gothic style. The end of the Gothic
era is marked by the *Mère de Dieu* (Mother
of Christ) chapel ornamented by a splendid
series of stained-glass windows. The church
wasn't finished until the western facade was
remodelled by a Parisian architect, and it
was to suffer yet more indignities. All its
statues were destroyed in the Revolution and
a 1940 bombing caused terrible damage to
its towers and the *clocher d'argent* (bell
tower). As if it hadn't suffered enough, a
hurricane in 1983 tore through the venerable
old structure. Restorations are continuing
and the church can be visited from 8 am to
noon and 2 to 7 pm daily.

Next to the church is the **Ancien Palais
Épiscopal** built on the vestiges of a Gallo-
Roman rampart that surrounded the city in
the 3rd century AD.

The **Musée d'Évreux** (☎ 02 32 31 52 29),
6 rue Charles Corbeau, presents an excellent overview of Évreux's history. In addition to costumes, paintings and tapestries

there's an impressive segment of the 1700-year-old Gallo-Roman ramparts in the basement. Amidst a display of prehistoric and Merovingian antiquities is a remarkable 1st-century bronze-and-silver statue of Jupiter and a later statue of Apollo. The exhibits are well-presented but captioned only in French. The museum opens 10 am to noon and 2 to 6 pm from Tuesday to Sunday. Admission is free.

The noble **Tour de l'Horloge** is 44m high and was built between 1490 and 1497, on the former site of the city gates. The two-ton bell, cast in 1406, strikes on the hour and two chimes strike on the half-hour.

## Places to Stay

The cheapest lodging in town is the *Green Café* (☎ 02 32 39 05 46, *1 rue Franklin D Roosevelt*) which is little more than 10 rooms over a brasserie. Small rooms with a sink and toilet are 115FF. Singles/doubles with private bath, telephone and TV are 180/200FF. If it is closed (as it is for two weeks in August), try nearby *Hôtel de Paris* (☎ 02 32 39 12 97, *32 rue de la Harpe*), which has six rooms over a bar that cost 125FF with a sink only and 160FF to 190FF for rooms with a shower.

Across from the train station, *Hôtel de France* (☎ 02 32 39 09 25, fax 02 32 38 38 56, *29 rue St-Thomas*) has pretty, old-fashioned rooms of different sizes on a quiet street. Rooms cost 275FF to 345FF.

The most interesting hotel in town is the *Hôtel de la Biche* (☎ 02 32 38 66 00, fax 02 32 33 54 05, *9 rue Joséphine*) which was a hunting lodge under François I and then a chic bordello. The theatrical interior lobby is topped by a *belle époque* skylight and ornamented in beige and cherry-toned wood. The rooms are somewhat faded but some overlook the river and all have private showers. En suite rooms cost 240FF and 260FF, and rooms with a shower only cost 195FF.

Across the street from the train station, *Hôtel de l'Ouest* (☎ 02 32 39 20 39, fax 02 32 62 37 19, *47–49 boulevard Gambetta*) offers plain but adequate rooms with private bath and television for 200FF.

### An Unlikely Saint?

'Will no one rid me of this turbulent priest?' cried Henry II about the rebellious Thomas Becket. The phrase may also have echoed around the Vatican in the early 1990s. Jacques Gaillot was named Bishop of Évreux in 1982 and ran into immediate difficulty with the Church. The Vatican's stand on homosexuality, the use of condoms to prevent the spread of HIV, birth control and the ordination of married men are unpopular in France and particularly with Bishop Gaillot. His espousal of a more open and inclusive church resonated beyond his see and attracted the attention of media outlets around the country. After Gaillot's declaration to a gay magazine that 'homosexuals will go to heaven before us' the Vatican began to ponder his more immediate earthly future within the Catholic church. In a 1992 ceremony the Pope murmured to him 'you have to sing inside the choir as well as outside it'.

When his song didn't change, the Vatican dismissed him from his see in 1995 and appointed him head of the obsolete diocese of Partenia in Mauritania. If they thought they were going to silence the outspoken priest, they were wrong. Thousands of people turned out for his last mass and Monseigneur Gaillot became an even bigger celebrity. Rather than disappear, he turned to cyberspace and set up the world's first virtual bishopric. He is now on-line at www.partenia.org where he ministers to the faithful in French and English via email and remains an outspoken advocate for the rights of immigrants and the downtrodden.

## Places to Eat

Several of the hotels listed above have good restaurants. Try the restaurants at Hôtel de la Biche (open daily except Sunday) or Hôtel de France (open daily except Sunday for dinner and Monday) for *menus* starting at about 150FF. *Le Fou du Roy* (☎ 02 32 39 33 41, *3 bis rue du Docteur Oursel*) serves inexpensive crepes, galettes and salads. It opens daily except Monday evening and

Sunday. For a three-course meal with coffee, you can't beat the *Caféteria Cora* (☎ 02 32 29 50 00, boulevard de Normandie) which fills you up for only 35FF. It opens daily except Sunday.

The trendiest dining spot in town is *Matahari* (☎ 02 32 38 49 88, 15 rue de la Petite Cité). The terrace on the river is a peaceful spot for a snack and the interior often has exhibitions by local artists within its African-inspired decor. *Menus* start at 60FF and it opens all day from 11 am (from 4 pm Saturday and Sunday). *Le Bretagne* (☎ 02 32 39 27 38, 3 rue St-Louis) is a friendly place, often crowded with regulars who come for the fresh fish, seafood or chicken with Camembert sauce. The 61FF weekday lunch *menu* includes an hors d'oeuvres buffet. Other *menus* cost from 78FF to 159FF. It opens daily except Wednesday evening and Monday. *Restaurant Michel Thomas* (☎ 02 32 33 05 70, 87 rue Joséphine) has a creative chef who turns out Normandy dishes with a twist. *Menus*, available in the elegant upstairs restaurant, start at 115FF, but a simple *plat du jour* costs 50FF to 65FF and there's a weekday lunch *menu* for 105FF. It opens daily except Sunday.

Self-caterers can try the *Champion* supermarket at place de la République and anyone with a sweet tooth should go to *Auzou (31 rue Chartraine)*. It sells boxes of scrumptious, almond-based pastries called *Les Caprices des Ursulines* which was supposedly first developed by bored conscripts at the Ursuline convent. Congratulate yourself if you manage not to finish the entire box of 16 in one sitting. It opens daily except Sunday afternoon and Monday. There's a *market* on Saturday morning on place Clemenceau.

## Getting There & Away

**Bus** Effia Voyageurs (☎ 02 35 98 13 38) runs buses from L'Aigle (66FF, one hour, three daily), Conches, (24FF, 40 minutes, three daily), Honfleur (102FF, two hours, Friday, Saturday and Sunday), and Le Bec-Hellouin (55FF, one hour, twice daily). Cars Jacquemard (☎ 02 32 33 09 66) connects Évreux with Les Andelys (40FF, one hour, twice daily) and Gisors (55FF, one hour 40 minutes, twice daily), Pacy-sur-Eure (22FF, 25 minutes, nine daily) and Vernon (31FF, 45 minutes, seven daily). CNA (☎ 02 35 52 92 00) connects Évreux with Rouen (65FF, one hour, 10 daily). Call the bus station (☎ 02 32 39 40 60) for further information on schedules.

**Train** The train station (☎ 02 32 78 32 12) is open 8 am to 10 pm. Évreux connects with Paris (104FF, one hour, up to 16 daily) via Caen (118FF, 1½ hours, up to 15 daily); Lisieux (69FF, one hour, up to five daily); Conches (20FF, 10 minutes, up to five daily); and Bernay (28FF, 45minutes, up to 10 daily).

## Getting Around

Trans Urbain (☎ 02 32 31 34 36) runs the local bus system. All buses from the train station go to the town centre. Tickets cost 5.60FF. You can rent mountain bikes for 80FF per day at Martin Cycles (☎ 02 32 39 17 08), 13 rue du Général LeClerc. For a taxi call ☎ 02 32 33 43 33.

## AROUND ÉVREUX
## Conches-en-Ouche
postcode 27190 • pop 4000

Conches-en-Ouche, 16km south-west of Évreux, is the capital of the Pays d'Ouche, a sparsely populated, forested plateau well-watered by rivers. With harsh winters and chalky soil, neither industry nor agriculture has taken root but mysteries and tales of sorcerers have flourished in the evocative mists wafting through the valleys. Conches is perched on a spur above the River Rouloir and was once a prestigious stop on the road to Santiago de Compostella in Spain. The town was tossed back and forth during the Hundred Years' War, with fighting centred around its 12th-century chateau. These days, the only fighting is likely to be for rooms in Conche's only hotel. With fresh air, half-timbered houses and valley views, the little town is a popular destination for weekending Parisians, many of whom have second residences in the region.

**EURE**

An interesting feature of Conches's terrain is the network of passages and caves carved out of the subterranean rock.

**Orientation & Information** The main road running through town is the rue Ste-Foy, which contains almost all local businesses, as well as the church, museum and hotels. The tourist office (☎ 02 32 30 76 42, fax 02 32 60 22 35) is on place Aristide-Briand in the town centre at the top of the hill. It opens 10 am to 12.30 pm and 2 to 6 pm Tuesday to Saturday. The office rents bikes and organises cycling and walking trips. The post office and several banks are downhill from place Aristide-Briand on rue Ste-Foy. The bus from Évreux stops at the place Aristide-Briand and the train station is at the bottom of the hill.

**Things to See & Do** The **Église Ste-Foy** is the town's proudest monument. Built at the end of the 15th century, the church is notable for its stunning ensemble of 22 Renaissance glass windows and some well-carved interior and exterior statues. Admission is free. Across the street is the **Maison du Fer Forgé** (☎ 02 32 30 20 50), 12 rue Ste-Foy, which displays metalwork in a room that was once the local jail. Torture beams, cells and prison graffiti make a chilling visit. The museum opens from 9 am to noon and 2.30 to 7 pm Wednesday to Saturday, and 4 to 7 pm on Sunday.

Not much is left of the 12th-century **chateau** that was a stronghold of Bertrand du Guesclin, except the keep and the wells that provided water during the castle's many sieges. The interior can't be visited but the surrounding park is agreeable and a woodsy path circles down around it.

**Places to Stay & Eat** About 2km south of the town centre next to a swimming pool is *Camping Municipal* (☎ 02 32 30 22 49). *Hôtel-Restaurant Le Cygne* (☎ 02 32 30 20 60, fax 02 32 30 45 73, 2 rue Paul Guilbaud) is in a rustic old manor and offers traditional rooms for 145FF with toilet only and 270FF to 320FF with bathroom. The restaurant is excellent and half-board can be

arranged for 275FF per person. *Menus* at the restaurant start at 95FF (closed Sunday dinner and Monday).

There are a few *boulangeries* and cafes around place Aristide-Briand; they close about 2 pm on Sunday. *Restaurant Galettes & Crêpes de Bretagne* (☎ 02 32 60 15 10, 43 rue Ste-Foy) serves decent small meals for 45FF to 58FF. It opens daily except on Saturday evening, Sunday and Monday.

**Getting There & Away** Conches is an easy day trip from Évreux by bus or train. See Getting There & Away in the previous Évreux section for details.

## Louviers
postcode 27400 • pop 19,400

Halfway between Rouen and Évreux, Louviers has preserved much of its original grace, despite a ruinous bombardment in 1940. Several branches of the Eure cut through the town centre, softening the landscape and allowing quiet riverside walks. A number of carefully restored half-timbered houses survive from the days when Louviers was renowned for the manufacture of woollen cloth. The wool industry that developed in the 13th century has been replaced by the manufacture of batteries and TV antennae but the factories are mercifully far from town. Even if there's an unavoidably artificial quality to much of the reconstruction, the gaily decorated facades make for an eye-pleasing stroll.

**Orientation & Information** The main street in town is Rue Maréchal Foch, leading from the south to the church, L'Église Notre-Dame, and most businesses. North of the church it becomes rue Pierre Mendès-France; the oldest part of town is north-east of the church. The Eure runs parallel to the main street.

The tourist office (☎ 02 32 40 04 47) at 10 rue du Maréchal Foch opens 10 am to noon and 2.30 to 6 pm Monday to Saturday, June to August and 2.30 to 5.30 pm Tuesday to Friday, April, May and September. The post office is at 2 rue de la Poste and there's Cyberposte.

**Things to See & Do** The **Musée Munici-pal** (☎ 02 32 09 58 55), place Ernest Thorel on rue Pierre Mendès-France, focuses on Louviers's cloth-making history with displays of various tools involved in the process. The collection of ceramics, paintings and furniture from the 16th to 19th century is also interesting and there are regular temporary exhibits of contemporary art. The museum opens 10 am to noon and 2 to 6 pm Wednesday to Monday. Admission is free. **L'Église Notre-Dame** dominates the town centre with its Flamboyant Gothic facade that was a 16th-century overlay on the 13th-century structure. The best part is the exterior, particularly the extravagantly decorated southern door.

**La Maison en Vaisselle Cassée** (☎ 02 32 40 22 71), 80 rue du Bal-Champêtre, is one of the most eccentric residences in Normandy. For over 40 years the owner, Robert Vasseur, has been amassing pieces of broken crockery and arranging them in whimsical, swirling designs on his house, garage, wall, in his garden and even on his dog's kennel. All the flowers, plants and seashells composed of coloured and mirrored ceramics create an almost hallucinatory effect, that alone is worth the trip to Louviers. Mr Vasseur is happy to give 30-minute tours when he's available which seems to be irregularly. If he's not around, you can still admire the exterior and peek over the gate for a look at the garden. To find the house, take the boulevard Maréchal Joffre from the place Ernest Thorel, turn left at the end and continue on rue de la Citadelle to rue du Bal-Champêtre.

**Places to Stay & Eat** There's a limited choice of accommodation in Louviers. *Hôtel de Rouen* (☎ 02 32 40 40 02, fax 02 32 50 73 41, 11 place Ernest Thorel) is the most reasonable with rooms that run from 200FF to 350FF depending on whether there's a bath or a shower.

There are several brasseries and inexpensive cafes around the church. One of the better ones is *Le Jardin de Bigard* (☎ 02 32 40 02 45, 39 rue du Quai), behind the church, which offers typically Norman

dishes such as trout with Camembert. Weekday lunch *menus* start at 60FF but you'll pay at least 80FF for an evening *menu*. It opens daily except Wednesday evening.

**Getting There & Away** CNA runs up to six buses daily from Rouen and Évreux to Louviers, they take about an hour.

# North-Eastern Eure

## LES ANDELYS
postcode 27700 • pop 8500

Some 39km south-east of Rouen, Les Andelys is set like a jewel at the confluence of the mighty Seine and modest Gambon rivers. From 12th-century Château Gaillard, a breathtaking panorama takes in the bend of the grassy riverbanks that rise to forested hills and high, white bluffs.

As the name indicates, there are two Andelys: modern Grand Andely, the commercial heart of the duo, and the older, more scenic Petit Andely, on the banks of the Seine. Most visitors gravitate to the riverside Andely for the winding streets of half-timbered houses or to scramble up the hill to the chateau.

Les Andelys developed as an extension of the Château Gaillard. By 1196, Richard the Lion-Heart's Norman territory was coming under increasing pressure from the French king Philippe-Auguste, who was pushing west from Paris along the Seine. Sensing that Rouen, his prize possession, was under threat, Richard looked for a position that would definitively close the door on Upper Normandy. On the promontory rising over 100m above the Seine, Richard built the magnificent Château Gaillard, intending it to be an impenetrable bulwark against French expansion. The fortress only lasted seven years before falling to Philippe Auguste but the little village of Petit Andely took root and expanded north-east to Grand Andely. It is the birthplace of the neoclassical painter, Nicolas Poussin, who was born in 1594 and it became the residence of French dramatists Thomas and Pierre Corneille in the 17th century. The bombs

EURE

that fell on Grand Andely in 1940 destroyed a large chunk of the town but it is still worth visiting for 13th-century Église Notre Dame.

## Orientation & Information

The Andelys are connected by avenue de la République, in Petit Andely, which becomes avenue du Général de Gaulle in Grand Andely. The centre of Grand Andely is place Nicolas Poussin which is over 1km northeast of Petit Andely. The bus station is situated across from the town hall near place Nicolas Poussin.

The tiny tourist office (☎ 02 32 54 41 93) is at 24 rue Philippe-Auguste in Petit Andely, at the foot of the cliffs which form the base of the chateau. The office opens from 9.30 am to noon and 2 to 6 pm, Monday to Saturday (to 5.30 pm on Sunday), June to September; and 2 to 5.30 pm daily, the rest of the year. The post office is at 9 avenue de la République and there are numerous banks on place Nicolas Poussin.

## Château Gaillard

The chateau was built with extraordinary speed between 1196–7 and according to the latest ideas in military architecture and engineering. His workers rerouted tributaries of the Seine leaving the mammoth cliff-top structure tenuously connected to the plateau by a narrow and easily defensible ridge. It was divided into two parts separated by a deep moat. The northern structure was the *châtelet* (the heart of the castle) protected by five towers, while the *fort principal* opposite features a three-storey keep at its heart protected by concentric circles of 4m walls. Richard the Lion-Heart's defensive system included iron chains that reached from the chateau across the Seine, literally blocking all river traffic. Richard merrily pronounced it *gaillard*, a word that translates as saucy or gallant, reflecting its impregnability to mock French pretensions on the region. It's said that Philippe-Auguste defiantly shouted 'If its walls were made of solid iron, yet would I take them!', to which Richard cried back 'By the throat of God, if its walls were made of butter, yet would I hold them!'

After Richard's death in 1199, Philippe-Auguste laid siege to the chateau. A population of about 400 terrified civilians joined the English garrison but when supplies dwindled they were abruptly ejected into the winter snow, resorting to cannibalism in a desperate attempt to survive. The siege dragged on for eight months until a cavalryman noticed that the mighty fortress had one unprotected opening: the latrine. The French soldiers squirmed in and the battle for Château Gaillard – and Normandy – was over in hours.

Unfortunately the chateau is now mostly in ruins thanks to Henry IV who ordered its destruction in 1603, but the ghostly white walls still cut a dramatic silhouette against the sky and enough remains to give a reasonably good idea of its former majesty. More impressive than the ruins is the fantastic view over the Seine, whose white cliffs are best seen from the viewing platform just north of the castle. You're free to wander about year round, but guided tours (in French) of the stark interior are held 9 am to noon and 2 to 6 pm mid-March to mid-November, and cost 18FF (children 9FF).

The chateau is a stiff 20-minute climb via a signposted path, Chemin de Château Gaillard, which begins about 100m north of the tourist office. By car, take the turn-off opposite the Église Notre Dame in Grand Andelys and follow the signs.

## Places to Stay & Eat

The *Camping Municipal* (☎ 02 32 54 23 79) is conveniently located along the river in Petit Andely, but it's not particularly well-maintained. A better bet is to head to *Camping Château Gaillard* (☎ 02 32 54 18 20, fax 02 32 54 32 66, route de la Mare), 800m south-east of the chateau and 200m from the Seine. It charges 28/26FF per adult/tent site, including use of the pool. It's closed in January.

Hotels are expensive in Les Andelys, but the tourist office has a list of *chambres d'hotes* with doubles from about 130FF. The *Hôtel Normandie* (☎ 02 32 54 10 52, fax 02 32 54 11 28, 1 rue Grande) has nicely equipped doubles with shower from 220FF. You can find regal luxury and prices at the three-star *Hôtel de la Chaine d'Or* (☎ 02 32 54 00 31, fax 02 32 54 05 68, *27 rue Grande*) in Petit Andely which has a renowned restaurant. Rooms run from 420FF to 760FF and the restaurant has *menus* at 150FF and 330FF. Both the hotel and restaurant are open daily except Sunday evening and Monday.

In Petit Andelys, the *Villa du Vieux Château* (☎ 02 32 54 30 10, *78 rue G Nicolle*) does excellent fish *menus* for 89FF. It opens daily except Monday and Tuesday. There are *restaurants* around place Nicolas Poussin in Grand Andely and a *market* on Saturday morning.

### Getting There & Away
There's no train station in Les Andelys. SATAR buses link Grand Andely and Rouen at least twice a day (52FF, 1¼ hours). Cars Jacquemard (☎ 02 32 33 09 66) connects Grand Andely with Évreux (40FF, one hour, twice daily) and with Vernon (23FF, one hour, three daily).

### Getting Around
Local buses link Grand and Petit Andelys. From the bus station, take line C to reach the waterfront in Petit Andely. Tickets cost 5.50FF (44.60FF for a booklet of 10). Bikes can be rented at the Hôtel Modern (☎ 02 32 54 10 41), behind the town hall on 10 rue Clémenceau, for 120FF per day.

## GISORS
postcode 27140 • pop 9000
Gisors, situated 50km north-east of Évreux, is a lively town at the confluence of the Rivers Epte, Troësne and Révillon. It is the capital of the Vexin Normand region, a vast plateau bordered by the Epte and Andelle Valleys. Although badly damaged in WWII, Gisors has restored its town centre to highlight the manicured banks of the Epte and its two most famous monuments: the chateau, built by the son of William the Conqueror, and the Église St-Gervais-St-Protais. The views from the chateau's tower are without match.

### Orientation & Information
The train station is at the end of avenue de la Gare, about 1km north-east of the town centre. The tourist office (☎ 02 32 27 60 63, fax 02 32 27 60 75) is in the large place des Carmélites next to the river. It opens 9 am to noon and 2 to 6 pm on Monday and 8.45 am to noon and 2 to 6 pm Wednesday to Friday. Outside those hours, you can get information at the chateau. The post office, on rue Général de Gaulle, is at the other end of the place des Carmélites. The main commercial street in town is rue Vienne which runs from the chateau to the place des Carmélites. There are a number of shops, *boulangeries* and banks on rue Vienne; you can change money at Crédit Agricole, 18 rue Général de Gaulle.

### Things to See & Do
Because of its strategic position at the eastern limit of the Norman duchy, the chateau (☎ 02 32 27 60 63) was at the centre of five centuries of Anglo-Norman conflict. To the east lay Paris and the perpetually ambitious French kings. The castle was begun by Guillaume le Roux (William the Redhead), son of William the Conqueror, in 1097. He began his fortress with a mound topped by a two-storey timbered keep. His successor, Henry I of England, added a large masonry keep, enlarged the interior and then added towers.

Henry II of England took over in 1181, raising the keep and reinforcing the exterior fortifications. After his death, the castle passed to Richard the Lion-Heart, who left it alone, but when Philippe-Auguste seized the castle in 1193 he immediately enlarged and expanded it. Up went the round Prisoner's Tower that is the current castle's most outstanding feature, as well as other towers and expanded residential quarters. Despite its strength the castle was taken by the English during the Hundred Years' War, returned to the French when hostilities ceased, and seized by Henri IV during the Religious Wars. It was finally abandoned in the 16th century and slowly fell into disrepair.

The most impressive part of the chateau is the Prisoner's Tower, so called because of the ancient graffiti on the walls scribbled by the prisoners incarcerated here, and Henry II's keep. Notice also the remains of the chapel Henry II built in commemoration of Thomas Becket, whom he had murdered.

The chateau is open for unguided visits 10 am to noon and 2 to 6 pm Wednesday to Monday, October to March. There are tours (in French with English translations) at 10 am, 11 am, 2.30 pm, 3.45 pm and 5 pm Wednesday to Monday, April to September. Admission costs 25FF (students 18FF). The park around the castle opens from 8 am to 7.30 pm daily.

The church on rue Vienne, **L'Église St-Gervais-St-Protais**, is a remarkable combination of Gothic and Renaissance style. Begun in 1119 and rebuilt from 1240 to 1249, the serious work on it took place at the height of the Renaissance in the 16th century. The pure Renaissance facade has a noble arch and a rich profusion of carvings flanked by classic Gothic towers. Inside, the purity of the Gothic structure sets off a series of fine Renaissance chapels. Notice the *Chapelle du Rosaire* with a lavishly sculpted bas-relief of the Tree of Jesse, sculpted between 1585 and 1593, and the *Chapelle de l'Assumption* north of the choir with a bas-relief of the Assumption.

### Places to Stay & Eat
In a pretty location on a lake near the Epte is *Camping Municipal (☎ 02 32 55 43 42)*, 5km south-west of Gisors. One adult with a tent pays 30FF.

*Hôtel Moderne (☎ 02 32 55 23 51, fax 02 32 55 08 75, place de la Gare)* offers comfortable rooms with private facilities that cost from 210FF to 385FF. The restaurant turns out simple Norman dishes and has *menus* that run from 68FF to 140FF. It opens daily except Sunday evening and Monday.

*Hôtel Restaurant de Paris (☎ 02 32 55 44 50, 58 rue Libération)*, south of the town centre, has basic, showerless rooms for 150FF, a weekday lunch *menu* for 60FF and other *menus* that range from 75FF to 165FF. It opens daily except Sunday evening and Monday. Should you develop the bizarre yearning for a meal on Sunday night or

Monday, there's Chinese, Vietnamese and Thai food at *Le Mirama (☎ 02 32 27 27 17, 72 rue de Vienne)* with lunch *menus* that start at 59FF. It opens daily except Wednesday. There's a **market** all day Monday and on Friday morning on place des Carmélites.

### Getting There & Away
The train station (☎ 02 32 55 01 30) opens from 6.30 am to 10 pm. There are 11 trains daily between Paris and Gisors (62FF, 1¼ hours), up to four from Forges-les-Eaux (45FF, 45 minutes), and three trains from Rouen (79FF, two hours) with a change at Serqueux.

There are two buses daily from Évreux (55FF, two hours, twice daily), one daily evening bus from Rouen (64FF, 1½ hours), two from Les Andelys (one hour 10 minutes) and up to three daily from Dieppe (79FF, 1½ to two hours).

### Getting Around
Vexin Bus (☎ 02 32 27 41 00) runs three buses a morning and three buses in the early evening between place Blanmont, next to the chateau, and the train station.

## FORÊT DE LYONS
Between Gisors and Rouen lies the Lyons-Andelle region whose most outstanding feature is the Forêt de Lyons. This splendid old beech forest spreads over some 26,000 acres and offers excellent opportunities for walks, as well as a number of interesting chateaux. The forest has been a regional centre for centuries, ever since it was favourite hunting turf for the Merovingian kings.

In the Middle Ages, monks from the Abbaye de Mortemer began clearing the terrain, creating hamlets that were quickly occupied by the kind of artisans that badly needed a supply of wood for their craft. The wood-gobbling glass industry took off and lasted until the 18th century. Even though the forest was exploited for heating-wood until the last century, careful planting and management has left it an extraordinary place in which to wander. A lack of undergrowth has left it a compara-

Monet set out to make his home and garden at Giverny as dreamy and colourful as his canvases.

Pretty as a picture – Monet's idyllic water gardens and Japanese bridge are still an inspiration.

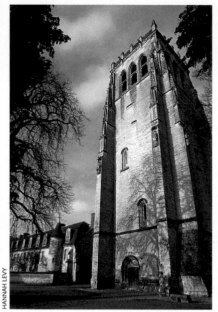

HANNAH LEVY

The abbey at Le Bec-Hellouin, founded in 1035

HANNAH LEVY

Even a water tower gets artistic treatment here!

BARBARA VAN ZANTEN

Reminders of the region's seafaring tradition

BARBARA VAN ZANTEN

Honfleur's old harbour is still irresistible to artists.

DIANA MAYFIELD

Sample the superior seafood at Honfleur's quay.

## Pigeon Houses

The unique cylindrical *colombiers* (pigeon houses, or dovecotes) dotting the Normandy countryside were once a major status symbol for Norman nobility. In pre-revolutionary France the right to erect a *colombier* was a rare privilege that the law awarded to the most important landholders. With only one *colombier* permitted for each fiefdom, the lords of the lands tried to outdo each other in building elaborate pigeon houses. Brick and stone were often arranged in geometrical patterns and half way up the cylinder a stone band prevented rodents from reaching the top cone. The cone is usually topped with a small ornament in shiny metal or ceramic that pigeons on the wing could easily spot. Inside, a ladder led to the pigeon loft where the birds lived in thousands of niches.

The *colombiers* were a bitter source of grievance for the local peasantry who watched in fury as pigeons ate their freshly sowed grain. For decades they agitated to close the *colombiers* at least during the sowing season. It's significant that one of the Revolutionaries' first acts was to abolish the right to *colombiers* in a law dated 4 August 1789.

JANE SMITH

**The pretty brickwork of *colombiers* makes a fine house for our feathered friends!**

tively bright forest where the sun filters down through 20m-tall beech and oak trees.

### Orientation & Information
The main centre for information is the tourist office at Lyons-la-Forêt (see that section later in the chapter) which has maps of the region and suggestions for walks to do on your own. They also provide a schedule of guided walks that take place Friday, Saturday and Sunday, July to September.

### Things to See & Do
In addition to Lyons-la-Forêt, other highlights of the forest include the traditional villages of **Rosay-sur-Lieure**, **Ménesqueville** and **Lisors**. About 6km south of Lyons-la-Forêt and near Lisors, **L'Abbaye de Mortemer** (☎ 02 32 49 54 34) is a Cistercian abbey convent founded in 1134 by Henry I Beauclerc, son of William the Conqueror. After the Revolution, stones from the abbey were removed and used to construct the village of Lisors. In the midst of a vast park, the abbey is falling to pieces but a remarkable pigeonnier is still standing. The *colombier* (pigeon loft, or dovecote) has 934 niches which once sheltered the birds until they were caught and eaten. There is also an 18th-century chateau in the grounds which has been transformed into a museum. Audiovisual equipment and wax figures are used to vividly re-create scenes from the monastic life and there's also a small doll museum.

It's said that the abbey is haunted. Mathilde, wife of the German emperor Henry V, was imprisoned here and cries out her anguish whenever there's a full moon. Other ghosts include the last four monks of the abbey, whose throats were cut by Revolutionaries. You might catch them floating around the pigeon loft.

In addition to visitations from beyond, the abbey hosts son et lumière shows on Saturday nights in August and a medieval fair on 15 August. Admission to the show costs 70FF (children aged 6 to 16, 40FF).

The park, ruins and pigeon loft are open 1 to 6 pm. Admission costs 35FF (children aged 6 to 16, 15FF). Guided visits of the museum take place 2 to 6 pm daily, May to August; 2 to 5.30 pm weekends and holidays during the rest of the year. They cost an additional 10FF.

On a limestone spur, 150m above the Seine and Andelle Valleys, is the **Côte des Deux Amants**, 2km north of Amreville-sous-les-Monts. The view is simply breathtaking and an indicator table lets you know what you're looking at. According to legend, the 'Two Lovers' hill got its name from the tragic tale of Edmond and Calliste. They fell in love when Edmond rescued her from a wild boar, but her father wouldn't consent to the marriage until Edmond proved his strength by running to the top of the hill with Calliste in his arms. He tried but collapsed and died at the summit and Calliste immediately expired from a broken heart.

### Getting There & Away

The only public transport within the Forêt de Lyons is the once-a-day bus No 28 that runs from Rouen to Lyons-la-Forêt. You'll need wheels (four or two) and the nearest place to rent them is in Rouen.

## LYONS-LA-FORÊT
### postcode 27480 • pop 795

In the middle of Forêt de Lyons and along the left bank of the River Lieure, Lyons-la-Forêt is the most postcard-perfect village in Upper Normandy. The brick and half-timbered houses clustered around the central square have survived nearly intact since the 17th century, giving the impression of a film set. In fact, it was a film set, for Jean Renoir's and Claude Chabrol's film versions of *Madame Bovary*. It's easy enough to imagine women in long dresses sweeping down the streets to meet their illicit lovers even though you're more likely to meet Parisians on their way to weekend mansions in the woods. The composer Maurice Ravel found the village a peaceful spot, coming here to reflect and compose.

Once the site of a Gallo-Roman settlement 31km south-east of Rouen, Lyons-la-Forêt coalesced around the castle built by Henry I of England in the 12th century. The king died in his fortified castle in 1135 (supposedly from eating eels fished from the Lieure), but the village thrived until it was destroyed by a fire in 1590. Fortunately, the WWII bombing campaigns spared the town, making it a scenic base to launch excursions into the surrounding Forêt de Lyons and nearby Abbaye Mortemer. The town is classified as a national historic monument.

### Orientation & Information

The centre of town is place Benserade, marked by the 18th-century thatch-roofed Halles, which sometimes hosts art exhibitions. The tourist office (☎ 02 32 40 04 41, fax 02 32 49 29 79) is near the main square at 20 rue de l'Hôtel de Ville. It opens 10 am to noon and 2 to 6 pm Tuesday to Saturday (to 4 pm on Sunday) June to August, and can give you information about walks into the forest. There are guided walks at the weekend in July and August.

### Things to See & Do

On the right bank of the Lieure just west of the town centre, the 12th-century **Église St-Denis** is built of silex (flint) and contains a 16th-century wooden statue of St Christopher. Opening hours are irregular; check with the tourist office. From the Halles take the rue d'Enfer to the house called 'Le Fresne' on the left which is where Ravel stayed to orchestrate Moussorgski's 'Pictures at an Exhibition' and to compose the 'Tombeau de Couperin'. The **town hall** near the main square is a handsome 18th-century brick building.

Although the region is great for cycling, you'll have to bring your own bike as there are no rental shops in town.

### Places to Stay & Eat

Lyons-la-Forêt is not a cheap town in which to stay or eat but there is a camp site, *Camping St-Paul* (☎ *02 32 49 42 02*), roughly 2km north-east of the town centre. The cheapest hotel is *Le Grand Cerf* (☎ *02 32 49 60 44, place Benserade)*, which has rooms with sink only for 220F. Rooms with en-suite facilities cost 320FF to 500FF. The ivy-covered, three-star *Hôtel La Licorne* (☎ 02 32 49 62 02, fax 02 32 49 80 09, place Benserade) is in a 400-year-old building with extensive grounds, with a courtyard behind the hotel. Rooms cost from 405FF to 800FF depending on the size. Both hotels have restaurants, or you could try the *Café de Commerce* (☎ 02 32 49 60 39, place Benserade) which offers a 57FF lunch *menu*. It has a pleasant pavement terrace from which you can contemplate the town square.

## VERNON
**postcode 27200 • pop 23,000**
Some 80km from Paris, Vernon's main draw is as a jumping-off point to visit Monet's house and gardens at Giverny. There's little reason to make a special journey to see Vernon alone but the transport connections are good, making it a convenient stop on your way into or out of Normandy.

Although Vernon is an ancient city, with roots stretching back to the earliest Vikings, WWII bombings destroyed most of its medieval centre. The city has lavished attention on the few crooked streets and half-timbered houses that remain, creating an agreeably cosy feeling. With the Seine only steps away from the town centre, Vernon is also the easiest place in Normandy to board a boat for a river cruise.

## Orientation
The town centre lies on the south-western bank of the Seine. Both the train station on rue Emile Loubert and the bus station on place de la République are only a few hundred metres from the town centre which is marked by the Notre Dame church.

The main street is rue Albuféra which runs from place d'Évreux to the Seine. Most shops, restaurants and services lie between avenue Pierre Mendès and rue Albuféra; the oldest part of town is around the tourist office.

## Information
**Tourist Office** The tourist office (☎ 02 32 51 39 60, fax 02 32 51 86 55, ⓔ tourisme .vernon@wanadoo.fr) is at 36 rue Carnot in a 15th-century house called *Le Temps Jadis*. It opens 2.30 to 6.30 pm Monday, 9.30 am to noon and 2.30 to 6.30 pm Tuesday to Saturday in summer; and 2.30 to 5.30 pm Monday, 10 am to noon and 2.30 to 5.30 pm Tuesday to Saturday in winter. The office has maps of suggested hikes in the region, walks in the town and cycle routes that take in Giverny.

**Money** There are a number of banks on rue Albuféra. Try Crédit Mutual at No 37 which opens 9 am to 12.30 pm and 2 to 5.30 pm Tuesday to Friday (to 4.30 pm on Saturday).

**Post & Communications** The post office is at 2 place d'Évreux and there's Cyber-poste. It opens 8 am to 6.30 pm Monday to Friday and 8 am to noon on Saturday.

**Laundry** There is a laundrette at 5 rue Pontonniers, open 8 am to 9 pm.

## Things to See & Do
The **Église Collégiale Notre Dame** is a stately gothic structure dating from the 12th century but incessantly restored throughout the centuries. The 15th-century facade contains an exceptional rose window and the central tower dates from the 13th century. Highlights of the interior include a 15th-century sculptured organ-loft, a main altar in the style of Louis XVI, and a number of 16th-century glass windows.

The **Musée AG Poulain** (☎ 02 32 21 28 09), 12 rue du Pont, is a grab-bag of antiquities, sculpture and paintings amassed by the collector AG Poulain and displayed in a 16th-century mansion. Among the works of painters Pierre Bonnard, Rosa Bonheur and Alfred Sisley, the highlights are two works by Monet, *Falaises à Pourville* (Cliffs at Pourville) and *Nympheas* (Waterlilies). The museum opens 11 am to 1 pm and 2 to 6 pm Tuesday to Friday in summer (afternoons only the rest of the year).

## Organised Tours
Fleuves et Réceptions (☎ 01 30 74 43 39), 6 avenue Fernand Lefebvre, Poissy, organises

EURE

EURE

a number of river cruises from Vernon. Every Sunday from mid-May to mid-September there's a 1¼-hour cruise down the Seine to Pressagny l'Orgueilleux and back. In July and August, there are also departures Wednesday, Thursday, Saturday and Sunday. It leaves at 3.30 pm and costs 50FF. There are 2½-hour cruises to Les Andelys that leave at 9.30 am and 4 pm on Friday in July and August and cost 90FF. Occasionally there are special cruises that include lunch and guided visits. All boats leave from Mail Anatole France between the bridge and the swimming pool.

## Places to Stay & Eat

There are only two hotels in Vernon, although the tourist office can provide a list of *chambres d'hotes* in the region. A cheap hotel is *Hôtel d'Évreux-Le Relais Normand* (☎ 02 32 21 16 12, fax 02 32 21 32 73, 11 place d'Évreux), which has serviceable rooms with shower from 210FF and rooms with full bath for 350FF. One of the nicest in town is *L'Oeuf et la Plume* (☎ 02 32 51 38 62, e ch.regentete@libertysurf.fr, 10 rue St-Saveur) which has spare but artfully decorated rooms full of beams and angles in a 17th-century building. Singles/doubles/triples cost 250/300/350FF with shared bath.

*Hôtel Normandy* (☎ 02 32 51 97 97, fax 02 32 21 01 66, 1 avenue Pierre Mendès) is in a classic building and offers three-star comfort in standardised but somewhat small rooms which run from 370FF to 390FF for a single or double.

Whether you bite into a pizza, munch on a salad or go for a full meal, *La Halle aux Grains* (☎ 02 32 21 31 99, 31 rue de Gamilly) won't disappoint. Main courses run from 42FF to 75FF but there's no *menu*. It opens daily except Sunday evening and Monday. *Le Bistro des Fleurs* (☎ 02 32 21 29 19, 73 rue Carnot) is the bistro annex of the more expensive restaurant next door. The 88FF *menu* is a great deal and even ordering a la carte offers good value for money. It opens daily except Monday night and Sunday. For a meal on Sunday or Monday, try *Pizzeria del Teatro* (☎ 02 32 21 35

49, 34 rue d'Albuféra) which is open daily. There's a *market* on Wednesday morning and all day on Saturday, and a *Monoprix* supermarket on place de la République.

## Getting There & Away

The train station (☎ 02 32 51 01 72) opens 5.30 am to 8.30 pm.

From Paris' Gare St Lazare (66FF, 50 minutes), there are two early-morning trains to Vernon. For the return trip there's roughly one train an hour between 5 and 9 pm. From Rouen (54FF, 40 minutes), four trains leave before noon; the other way, there's about one train every hour between 5 and 10 pm.

There's a bus twice daily to Gisors (29FF, one hour) and Évreux (55FF, two hours) and three to Les Andelys (27FF, one hour).

## Getting Around

You can rent bikes at the Café de Chemin de Fer (☎ 02 32 21 16 01) next to the train station for 60FF a day.

## GIVERNY
### postcode 27620 • pop 548

Situated between Paris and Rouen and an ideal day trip from either, this small village contains the Musée Claude Monet, the home and flower-filled garden from 1883 to 1926 of one of France's leading Impressionist painters. Here Monet painted some of his most famous series of works, including *Décorations des Nymphéas* (Water Lilies). Upon Monet's death in 1926, his son, Jean Monet, took possession of the property which he left to the Académie des Beaux-Arts in 1966. In 1980, the property opened to the public with Monet's house, studio, garden, waterlily pond and Japanese footbridge gloriously restored. The only missing elements are Monet's paintings, although reproductions can be viewed in his studio. The garden-museum attracts almost 500,000 visitors a year, many of whom also come to view the fine Impressionist collection of the Musée Américain.

## Musée Claude Monet

The hectare of land that Claude Monet owned has become two distinct areas, cut by the Chemin du Roy, a small railway line that, unfortunately, was converted into what is now the busy D5 road. These days the **studio** where Monet painted his *Nymphéas* murals is the entrance hall, adorned with precise reproductions of his works and ringing with cash-register bells. Books about Monet are on sale for the same price you would pay anywhere else.

A few steps from the studio is Monet's pretty pink **house**. The painter's love of colour is evident in the sunny yellow kitchen and sky-blue upstairs rooms furnished in their original cosy, warm style. Monet's collection of Japanese prints are on display as well as photos and paintings by some of the many houseguests who came to pay homage to the master.

In front of the house is the **Clos Normand** garden that Monet planted soon after he moved into the house in 1883. He constructed an arbour of climbing roses to replace the tree-lined path that once led to an orchard. A lawn is on the site of the former orchard, planted with Japanese cherry and flowering crab-apple trees with irises and poppies scattered about. Surrounding the arbour are French-style symmetrical gardens with beds of gladioli, larkspur, daisies, asters and a lush profusion of other flowers.

From the Clos Normand's far corner, a tunnel leads under the D5 to the **Jardin d'Eau** (Water Garden). Having bought this piece of land in 1895 after his reputation had been established, Monet dug a pool (fed by the Epte, a tributary of the nearby Seine), planted water lilies and constructed the Japanese bridge, which has since been rebuilt. In contrast to the orderly Clos Normand, the Jardin d'Eau has a dreamy, mysterious ambience. Draped with purple wisteria, the bridge blends into the asymmetrical foreground and background, creating the intimate atmosphere for which the 'Painter of Light' was famous.

The seasons have an enormous effect on the gardens at Giverny. From early to late spring, daffodils, tulips, rhododendrons, wisteria and irises appear, followed by poppies and lilies. By June, nasturtiums, roses and sweet peas are in flower. Around Sep-

tember, there are dahlias, sunflowers and hollyhocks.

Monet's home (☎ 02 32 51 28 21) opens 10 am to 6 pm daily except Monday, April to October. Avoiding the camera-clicking crowds isn't easy but here are some tips: be at the ticket window when it opens at 10 am; visit between noon and 2 pm when others are at lunch; and hold off until 4.30 pm and visit until closing time at 6 pm. Admission to the house and gardens costs 35FF (students/children 25/20FF).

## Musée Américain

The American Impressionist Museum (☎ 02 32 51 94 65) contains works of American Impressionist painters who flocked to France in the late 19th and early 20th centuries. Opened in 1992, the museum is intended to provide a link between Giverny and the Americans who briefly turned the village into an artists' colony and were involved in the Impressionist movement.

Highlights of the collection include *La Tasse de Chocolat* (A Cup of Chocolate) by Mary Cassatt, *Une Averse, rue Bonaparte* (A Shower, rue Bonaparte) by Frederick Childe Hassam and *Automne à Giverny, la Nouvelle Lune* (Autumn in Giverny, the New Moon) by John Leslie Breck. It is housed in a garish building at 99 rue Claude Monet, 100m down the road from Musée Claude Monet. It opens 10 am to 6 pm daily except Monday from April to October. Admission costs 35FF (students 20FF; children aged seven to 12, 15FF).

## Getting There & Away

Giverny is 76km north-west of Paris and 66km south-east of Rouen. The nearest town is Vernon, nearly 7km to the north-west on the Paris–Rouen train line. There are two early morning trains from Paris' Gare St Lazare to Vernon (66FF, 50 minutes). Once you reach Vernon it is still quite a hike to Giverny. Buses (☎ 02 35 71 32 99) meet most trains and cost 14/22FF for a single/return fare. It is usually possible to get a taxi from the train station; alternatively call one on: ☎ 06 09 31 08 99. The fare between Vernon and Giverny is around 40FF.

EURE

# Western Eure

## BERNAY
postcode 27300 • pop 11,000

With so many towns in Normandy bombed to rubble in WWII, it seems almost miraculous that Bernay was spared. The town is a thriving regional centre, 42km north-west of Évreux, at the confluence of the Rivers Charentonne and Cosnier. Branches of the rivers meander through a town centre composed of ancient half-timbered houses and cobblestone streets, creating an extraordinarily attractive landscape of stone, water and wood, just as the tourist brochures boast. Bernay coalesced around an 11th-century abbey and owed its early prosperity to a now-defunct textile industry. As capital of the bucolic Risle-Charentonne region, Bernay keeps the local economy humming by manufacturing small planes as well as marketing the region's cattle. If you have your own transport, Bernay makes an excellent base to explore several fine chateaux or the nearby village, Le Bec-Hellouin.

### Orientation & Information

Rue Thiers is the main street in town and where you'll find most shops and businesses. The most colourful part of town is around rue Folloppe which leads to the river. The tourist office (☎ 02 32 43 32 08, fax 02 32 45 82 68) is at 29 rue Thiers in the centre of town. It opens from 9.30 am to 12.30 pm and 2 to 6 pm Monday to Saturday year round, and on Sunday mid-May to mid-September. The main post office is at place Paul Derou and there's Cyberposte. It opens 8 am to noon and 1 to 6 pm Monday to Friday but morning only on Saturday. You can change money at the Crédit Lyonnais, 2 rue Gambetta, which opens 8.30 am to noon and 1.30 to 5.30 pm Tuesday to Friday, and 8.30 am to 12.15 pm and 1.45 to 4.30 pm on Saturday.

### Things to See & Do

Strolling the streets of the **old town**, especially for the extensive Saturday morning market, is one of the most agreeable activities in Bernay. The tourist office has a helpful map pointing out various historic buildings. The **Église Abbatiale** (☎ 02 32 46 63 23), is the oldest Romanesque church in Normandy, constructed somewhere between 1017 and 1075 as part of an abbey. The abbey has been ravaged over the years, even becoming a warehouse and a granary. Part of it now houses the mayor's office and the courthouse. The church is under continuous restoration but the great columned arcades of the nave and high windows recall its ancient majesty. Part of the abbey is devoted to the **Musée Municipal** which displays private collections that were bequeathed to the city. There's a collection of ceramics from Rouen, objects from Egypt and Mesopotamia gathered by a local archaeologist, 18th-century furniture and French, Dutch, English and Italian paintings from the 17th to 20th centuries.

Entrance to the abbey is through the museum on place de la République. The abbey and museum open 10 am to noon and 2 to 5.30 pm (to 7 pm June to September) Wednesday to Monday. Admission costs 19.50FF, including the museum and abbey.

### Places to Stay & Eat

About 2km south-west of the town centre is **Camping Municipal** (☎ 02 32 43 30 47, rue des Canadiens), which charges 14.50FF per person and per tent.

There are only two hotels in the town centre. **Hôtel d'Angleterre et du Cheval Blanc** (☎ 02 32 43 12 59, fax 02 32 43 63 26, 10 rue du Général de Gaulle) is in a lovely old building that's getting a little rundown. The old-fashioned rooms are a good size but could use some sprucing up. Singles/doubles with sink only are 105/130FF and en-suite rooms with TV are 230FF. For that price you're better off at **Le Lion d'Or** (☎ 02 32 43 12 06, fax 02 32 46 60 58, 48 rue du Général de Gaulle) which has singles with/without bath for 200/170FF and doubles from 230FF with bath. Both hotels have decent restaurants.

Rue Folloppe has several modestly priced eateries. Between **Au Lapin Gourmand** (☎ 02 32 43 42 32, 10 rue Folloppe), open daily except Sunday and Wednesday, and *Crêperie du Roy* (☎ 02 32 46 05 32, 9 rue Folloppe), open daily except Sunday and Monday, you'll find everything you could want if what you want is pizza, salad, crepes, grilled meat or brasserie food. Crêperie du Roy is slightly more expensive but still manageable at under 60FF for a copious salad.

A prime spot for people-watching on busy rue Thiers and a good place to relax over a drink or enjoy a light meal is *Brasserie Le Commerce* (☎ 02 32 43 00 90, 1 rue Thiers). *Le Piano* (☎ 02 32 43 68 00, 32 rue Folloppe) is a large bar with a vast choice of beers and occasional live concerts. It opens daily except Monday.

### Getting There & Away
The train station (☎ 02 32 43 01 25) opens 6 am to 9 pm and connections from Bernay are good. There are trains to Évreux (28FF, 45minutes, up to 10 daily), Rouen (69FF, one hour, four daily), Caen (66FF, 45 minutes, 15 daily), Lisieux (32FF, 20 minutes, 12 daily) and Conches-en-Ouche (35FF, 20 minutes, once daily).

### Getting Around
You can rent bikes at Cycles Gitane (☎ 02 32 43 46 14), 10 rue Albert Glatigny, for 70FF a day. It opens daily except Sunday and Monday. There are buses every half-hour between the train station and place Paul Derou as well as several other points in the town centre. Tickets cost 2FF.

## AROUND BERNAY
### Château de Beaumesnil
Dubbed the 'Normandy Versailles', the exterior of the Château de Beaumesnil (☎ 02 32 44 40 09) is almost as marvellous as that other chateau outside Paris. The Baroque castle seems to float in the middle of an artificial pond that opens onto a magnificent 80-hectare landscaped park. Built by an obscure architect between 1633 and 1640, the ornate brick-and-stone facade is decorated with a profusion of sculpted heads, making it one of the finest examples of Baroque style in Normandy. Don't miss the maze of privet bushes alongside the castle and take time to appreciate the park designed by a student of Le Nôtre, the landscaper of Versailles. The interior contains a museum of bookbinding displaying hundreds of intricately decorated leather-bound books and an unusual staircase suspended between two floors, but is not as interesting as the castle's exterior. The chateau opens 10 am to noon and 2 to 6 pm Wednesday to Monday in July and August, and 2 to 6 pm Friday to Monday, April to June and September. Admission costs 35FF for the garden and the museum and 15FF for the garden alone. The chateau is 13km south of Bernay in a little village on the D140; there is no public transport.

### Le Bec-Hellouin
**postcode 27800**
This peaceful little village buried in the lush Becquet Valley, 17 km north-east of Bernay, seems predestined to rest the eyes of weary tourists. Ivy-covered half-timbered houses cluster around an ancient abbey and a little river bubbles between tree-shaded banks. Except for paved roads, cars and a few art galleries, everything looks about the same as it must have around 900 years ago when the abbey was built. After soaking up the scenery, a visit to **L'Abbaye** (☎ 02 32 43 72 60) is most worthwhile. It was founded in 1035 and soon became a highly influential intellectual centre. Its first abbot, Lanfranc, was one of the most learned men of the age and was summoned by William the Conqueror to straighten out the Pope's opposition to his marriage to Mathilde. Lanfranc and his successor, Anselm, became archbishops of Canterbury. The monastery remained a powerful force until the Revolution when the monks were chased out and the invaluable library vandalised.

It remained empty until 1948, when a new community of monks moved in and began restoring the church, cloister, chapter room and convent buildings. The abbey is open 7 am to 7 pm daily and there are five tours a day from June to September, which cost 25FF guided by monks. Try to time a visit for daily mass (11.45 am weekdays,

10.30 am on Sunday), when the monks sing Gregorian chants. If mechanical pianos and barrel organs are your passion, there's the **Musée de la Musique Mécanique** (☎ 02 32 46 16 19) which offers guided visits of its collection at 3, 4 and 5 pm, April to September. They cost 30FF.

There is no tourist office in Le Bec-Hellouin but the tourist office in neighbouring Brionne (☎ 02 32 45 70 51, fax 02 32 45 70 51, 1 rue du Général de Gaulle) can give you some information about accommodation in and around the village. *Camping Municipal* (☎ 02 32 44 83 55), 1km north of the town centre, charges 44FF for one or two people with a tent or car. The only hotel in town is the pricey *Auberge de L'Abbaye* (☎ 02 32 44 86 02, fax 02 32 46 32 23) which has rustic but extremely comfortable rooms for 480FF per person including obligatory half-board. The restaurant is a gourmet delight; it opens daily except Monday and Tuesday off-season. There are a few creperies around the abbey and a little grocery store across from the church on rue Lanfranc but nothing is cheap in Le Bec-Hellouin.

The only public transport to Le Bec-Hellouin is the bus from Évreux. See Getting There & Away in the Évreux section for details. Another option is to take the train to Brionne from Bernay, Rouen or Évreux and take a taxi 5km north to Le Bec-Hellouin. Call a taxi on ☎ 02 32 45 50 00; the fare will cost about 50FF.

## Château du Champ de Bataille

This sumptuous chateau at Ste-Opportune du Bosc, 20km north-east of Bernay, contains an exquisite collection of 17th- and 18th-century furniture and *objets d'art*. Built in the 17th century, the chateau was recently purchased by French designer Jacques Garcia who decorated the interior in opulent 18th-century style. Some of the items on display belonged to the royal family of Louis XVI before the Revolutionaries looted the palaces at Versailles and Tuileries. Panelled walls, chandeliers, Flemish tapestries, Chinese porcelain, portraits, busts and vases have been arranged with impeccable taste to evoke the royal lifestyle in pre-Revolutionary France. The gardens are also in a French classical style, with Italian statuary, lawns and a maze. The overall effect of the visit is eye-popping but it's a shame that admission at 80FF is almost twice as expensive as admission to Versailles. Included is a one-hour guided tour of the chateau (with a written translation in English) and admission to the gardens. Visiting the gardens and chateau kitchen alone costs 35FF. Tours are given hourly between 2 and 6 pm daily, Easter to September (weekends only March, October and November). There's no direct public transport to the chateau but it's possible to take a morning bus from Évreux to Le Neubourg and then a taxi from the train station 2km to the chateau. Call a taxi on ☎ 02 32 35 09 34; the fare is around 40FF.

# Calvados

The department of Calvados stretches from Honfleur in the east to Isigny-sur-Mer in the west and is famed for its rich pastures and farm products: butter, cheese, cider and an apple-flavoured brandy called Calvados. The name of the department and the brandy dates from 1588 when a Spanish ship, *El Salvador*, ran aground on the coastal rocks and sank. The ship had been sent to battle Protestant England and the Protestant-leaning Normans were so pleased with the ship's fate that they applied its name, somewhat corrupted, to their department.

The D-Day beaches extend along almost the entire coast of Calvados while much of the interior is given over to the vast cereal plains extending from Caen to Falaise. Of all departments in Normandy, Calvados suffered the worst destruction during the Battle of Normandy. Only a handful of towns and villages survived unscathed, poignant reminders of a lost heritage.

## CAEN
### postcode 14000 • pop 114,000
Caen, the capital of Basse Normandie, is a bustling university city with several fine museums, two historic abbeys and a massive 11th-century chateau. Unfortunately, there's little else in Caen to hold a visitor's attention. The city burned for over a week in the Battle of Normandy and has been rebuilt in a utilitarian, although not entirely unpleasing, style. Only a nugget of medieval streets remains as a sad reminder of all that was lost. At least the wide boulevards have been able to accommodate the traffic that accompanied the city's rapid postwar expansion. Caen makes a good base from which to explore Normandy's D-Day beaches and has good transport connections to other towns in the region. It is also the gateway for Ouistreham, a minor passenger port for ferries to England.

## History
Until the 11th century Caen was little more than a ragtag collection of villages scattered

## Highlights

- Comparing Boudin's depiction of Honfleur in the Boudin Museum to a boat tour of the real thing
- Spending a day at the races in Deauville
- Honouring the fallen of WWII at Le Mémorial de Caen, Pointe du Hoc and the American Cemetery at Omaha Beach
- Witnessing William's conquest of England on the Bayeux Tapestry
- Walking across the Pont de Normandie
- Exploring the Suisse Normande

around the confluence of the Rivers Orne and Odon. Its fortunes changed upon the marriage of William the Conqueror and his cousin, Matilda of Flanders, in 1050. A marriage between cousins displeased the pope and in order to receive a dispensation each spouse promised to build an abbey in Caen. William built the Abbaye aux Hommes or Men's Abbey and Matilda the Abbaye aux Dames or Ladies' Abbey. The town apparently pleased William and, after becoming king of England in 1066, he made Caen his secondary residence, building a massive fortified castle on a rocky spur.

Caen flourished under William's rule.

CALVADOS

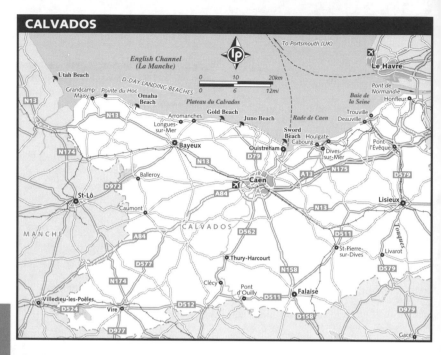

CALVADOS

The city's intellectual tradition was born in its abbeys and creamy Caen limestone was used to build Westminster Abbey and Canterbury Cathedral in England. Caen's prosperity attracted the attention of England's King Edward III who sacked the city in 1346, during the Hundred Years' War.

The city had hardly recovered when the English returned under Henry V in 1417 for another bout of looting and pillage. This time the English stayed for a 33-year occupation that turned out rather well for Caen. The monarchy established a university in 1432 that long outlasted the occupation, currently attracting some 30,000 students.

In 1850 Caen was linked to the sea by a canal running parallel to the River Orne, which aided the growth of the steel industry that is now at the heart of its economy. It was a thriving industrial, commercial and intellectual centre when on 6 June 1944 the first Allied bombs began raining down on the city. The bombing was intended to block

German Panzers from reinforcing their divisions on the Cotentin beaches. Caen went up in flames and burned for 11 days, reducing the medieval quarters of St-Pierre and St-Jean to ruins. Having been told to evacuate the city, many residents had fled south to the quarries of Fleury-sur-Orne; others took refuge in the ancient Abbaye aux Hommes but thousands more were entombed in the rubble. Although planning had called for a rapid occupation of the city, the Germans quickly launched a counter-offensive that blocked Allied troops just outside the city. The stalemate continued for three weeks but Caen had to be wrested from the Germans in order to allow a clear advance south along the vast plains. On 7 July the northern part of the city was targeted but the actual bombing pushed farther into the centre, which received 2500 tons of explosives. More than 80% of the city was destroyed and some observers felt that the operation achieved dubious results. The heaps of rubble impeded the

Allied advance through the city and it did not delay the transfer of German divisions from the British to the American sectors as was originally intended. Caen's role in the Battle of Normandy is evoked in the outstanding museum, Le Mémorial de Caen.

## Orientation
Caen's modern heart is made up of a few pedestrianised shopping streets and some busy boulevards. The largest, avenue du 6 Juin, links the centre, which is based around the southern end of the chateau, with the canal and train station to the south-east. Bassin St-Pierre is the city's pleasure port, its quays serving as favourite promenades in mild weather.

## Information
**Tourist Office** The modern tourist office (☎ 02 31 27 14 14, fax 02 31 27 14 18, ⓔ tourisminfo@ville-caen.fr), place St-Pierre, opens 10 am to 1 pm and 2 to 6 pm Monday to Saturday, and 10 am to 1 pm on Sunday, September to June; 10 am to 7 pm Monday to Saturday, and 10 am to 1 pm and 2 to 5 pm on Sunday, July and August. Hotel reservations within the city cost 10FF. The office sells various maps including one of the D-Day beaches (39FF). The city's Web site, www.ville-caen.fr, offers up-to-date information on Caen life including extensive entertainment listings. The Centre Regional d'Information Jeunesse (CRIJ; ☎ 02 31 27 80 80, fax 02 31 27 80 89, ⓔ crij.bn@wanadoo.fr), 6 rue Neuve St-Jean, has a wealth of information for students including available discounts, lodging referrals and courses. It also sells ISIC cards (60FF) and hostel cards (70/100FF under/over 26).

**Travel Agencies** The student travel agency, OTU (☎ 02 31 56 60 93), on esplanade de la Paix, north of Château de Caen, can help book cheap flights and is a good source of information on transportation discounts.

**Money** Banque de France, 14 avenue de Verdun, exchanges money from 8.45 am to 12.15 pm. There's an exchange bureau run by Crédit Agricole at 1 boulevard Maréchal Leclerc. From May to September the tourist office also offers exchange services.

**Post & Communications** The main post office, place Gambetta, opens 8 am to 7 pm weekdays and to noon on Saturday. It has Cyberposte. There is Internet access at the tourist office, Musée de Normandie and Le Mémorial de Caen.

**Laundry** The laundrette at 127 rue St-Jean opens 7 am to 8 pm daily.

## Le Mémorial de Caen
Le Mémorial de Caen (☎ 02 31 06 06 44) is the most vivid and comprehensive treatment of the Battle of Normandy in the region – possibly in the world. The exhibits use lights, sound, video, film footage, documents, photos and animated maps to trace the rise of Nazi Germany, the world's descent into war, the occupation of France and the preparations, execution and aftermath of D-Day.

The museum is intended not merely to commemorate the liberation of Europe but to promote peace. A concluding section dealing with the establishment of the United Nations and global conflicts since WWII ends on a note of cautious optimism without glossing over some of the major obstacles to world peace. The museum packs a powerful punch, although the emotional effect can be diluted by the hordes of noisy French school children swarming through the rooms. Try to visit at the weekend or during school holidays.

Built over the command post of the German General Richter and inaugurated on 6 June 1988, the museum was financed by various governmental committees as well as American, Canadian, British and other Allied organisations. Visitors enter through a jagged crack in the stark white facade, meant to symbolise the broken city of Caen and the Allied breach of the German juggernaut. The French inscription across the wall reads: 'I was crushed by grief, but fraternity revived me, and from my wound there sprang a river of freedom.'

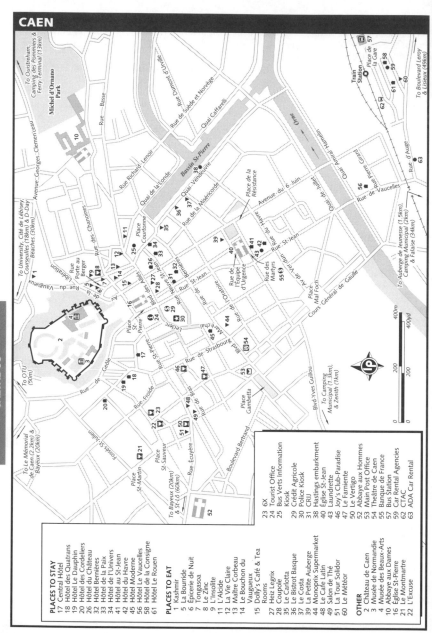

# CAEN

## PLACES TO STAY
17  Central Hôtel
18  Hôtel des Quatrans
19  Hôtel Le Dauphin
20  Hôtel des Cordeliers
26  Hôtel du Château
32  Hôtel Bernières
33  Hôtel de la Paix
34  Hôtel de l'Univers
41  Hôtel au St-Jean
42  Hôtel du Havre
45  Hôtel Moderne
56  Hôtel Le Vaucelles
58  Hôtel de la Consigne
61  Hôtel Le Rouen

## PLACES TO EAT
1  Kashmir
5  La Bouride
6  Épicerie de Nuit
7  Tongasoa
8  Le Zinc
9  L'Insolite
11  L'Alcide
12  La Vie Claire
13  Maître Corbeau
14  Le Bouchon du Vaugueux
15  Dolly's Café & Tea Rooms
27  Heiz Legrix
28  Coupole
35  Le Carlotta
36  Le Bistrot Basque
37  Le Costa
39  La Petite Auberge
44  Monoprix Supermarket
48  Le Cafe Latin
49  Salon de Thé
51  La Tour Solidor
60  Le Météor

## OTHER
2  Château de Caen
3  Musée de Normandie
4  Musée des Beaux-Arts
10  Abbaye aux Dames
16  Église St-Pierre
21  Le Montmartre
22  L'Excuse
23  6X
24  Tourist Office
25  Bus Verts Information Kiosk
29  Crédit Agricole
30  Police Kiosk
31  CRIJ
38  Hastings embarkment
40  Église St-Jean
43  Laundrette
46  Joy's Club-Paradise
47  Le Famiente
50  Le Vertigo
52  Abbaye aux Hommes
53  Main Post Office
54  Theâtre de Caen
55  Banque de France
57  Bus Station
59  Car Rental Agencies
62  CTAC
63  ADA Car Rental

In the middle of the vast entrance hall is a replica of an RAF Hawker Typhoon that looks as though it is poised to strike. Captioned in English, French and German, the exhibition consists of three distinct parts:

• A tunnel spiralling downwards showing Europe's descent into total war. Posters, documents and photos trace the failure of the Versailles agreement that ended WWI, leading to the rise of fascism in Germany and the fear of Bolshevism in France. Vichy France is recalled as well as the Resistance. Photos of German concentration camps and Hitler's voice booming over the loudspeakers convey the sense of urgency facing Allied leaders.
• Three segments of un-narrated film footage (50 minutes in total) are taken from the archives of both the German and Allied sides. Most startling is the split-screen film footage of D-Day from both viewpoints. The documentary material is further enlivened by scenes from the fictional film *The Longest Day*. The second segment deals with the Battle of Normandy and the third with struggles against oppression since WWII. The last film of the day begins at 6 pm (8 pm mid-May to early September).
• An exhibit on Nobel Peace Prize laureates, housed within a former German command post underneath the main building and reached via a futuristic tunnel.

There's a cafeteria in the museum and a park around it, good for a contemplative stroll. The little-used Centre de Documentation above the main hall has an extensive library of books (some in English) covering WWII. There's also a collection of videos in French and English that include documentaries and films about WWII. They can be watched for free.

Le Mémorial de Caen is about 3km northwest of the tourist office on esplanade Dwight Eisenhower. Tickets are sold 9 am to 7 pm daily (to 9 pm in summer and to 6 pm November to mid-February). Admission costs 74FF (students 65FF). WWII veterans get in free. Allow about 2½ hours for a visit.

To reach the museum take bus No 17 from opposite the tourist office at place St-Pierre; the last bus back departs at 8.45 pm (earlier on Sunday). By car head towards Bayeux, following the multitude of signs with the word 'Mémorial'.

## Château de Caen

This enormous fortress was begun by William the Conqueror in 1060 and extended by his son Henry I. It was a royal residence until the reign of Richard the Lion-Heart and then turned into a garrison when Normandy became a part of France in 1204. Eventually it became a town within a town, containing residences, workshops, a church, prison and cemetery. From the Revolution until WWII it served various military functions. Until 1944, a nest of houses pressed up against the fortress but the bombardment had the salutary effect of revealing the entire structure. It opens 6 am to 7.30 pm daily (to 10 pm May to September).

A walk around the **ramparts** is a fine way to appreciate the harmonious layout of reconstructed Caen and its many church steeples. You can visit the 12th-century **Chapelle de St-Georges**, built for the people who were living within the walls of the castle, and the **Échiquier (Exchequer)**, which dates from about AD 1100 and is one of the oldest civic buildings in Normandy. Of special interest is the **Jardin des Simples**, a garden of medicinal and aromatic herbs cultivated during the Middle Ages – some of which are poisonous. A book (in French) on the garden is on sale for 30FF inside the **Musée de Normandie** (☎ 02 31 30 47 50), which contains historical artefacts illustrating life in Normandy. Utensils, tools, coins, jewellery, farm implements and pottery from the Neolithic era to the 20th century are on display. There are explanatory signs in English. The museum opens 9.30 am to 12.30 pm and 2 to 6 pm daily except Tuesday. Admission costs 10FF (students 5FF) but it's free on Wednesday.

The **Musée des Beaux-Arts** (☎ 02 31 30 47 70), in an extravagant modern building nearby, houses an extensive collection of paintings dating from the 15th to 20th centuries including the wonderful *Marriage of the Virgin* painted by Perugino in 1504. The Venetian school is represented by Veronese's *Temptation of St Anthony*. From Flanders, the collection highlights Rubens' *Abraham et Melchisédech* and the French rooms include Poussin's *Venus Mourning Adonis*, Courbet's

*The Sea*, Boudin's *The Beach at Deauville* and *Nymphéas* by Monet. The collection of engravings is particularly noteworthy, including works by Dürer, Rembrandt, Tiepolo and Van de Weyden. For reasons of conservation, not all the engravings are on display at any given time. The museum opens 10 am to 6 pm daily except Tuesday. Admission costs 25FF (students 15FF, free for everyone on Wednesday). A combined ticket allowing admission to the Musée des Beaux-Arts and the Musée de Normandie costs 35FF (students 25FF).

## Abbaye aux Hommes

With its multi-turreted **Église St-Étienne**, Abbaye aux Hommes (☎ 02 31 30 42 81), is a triumphant mixture of Romanesque, Gothic and classical architecture. 'When St-Étienne comes tumbling down, the kingdom of England will perish,' wrote 12th-century Norman poet Robert Wace and it seems nothing short of miraculous that the church and convent buildings remained standing after the fearsome 1944 bombardments. Built by William the Conqueror, it was his chosen resting place but now only his thighbone remains here. His tomb was desecrated during the 16th-century Wars of Religion but his corpse was badly treated even before he was buried. His thieving servants stripped him almost naked and the funeral procession caught fire. Finding him too large for the funeral bier, the pallbearers tried to fold him in half, causing his stomach to burst open. As a final indignity, a peasant launched the ancient cry of 'Haro' at his tomb (see the boxed text 'La Clameur de Haro' later), claiming that he owned the land upon which the grave had been constructed and had not been compensated for its seizure. The peasant was hastily paid off and William was finally laid to rest.

The church was built relatively quickly – from 1066 to 1077 – which explains the unity of its style. The austere, undecorated facade creates an impression of sobriety and grandeur, accentuated by the church's perfect proportions. The 11th-century towers topped by Gothic steeples became a model for churches around the region. The interior

has the same minimalist decorative scheme and the Gothic choir is one of the oldest in Normandy. A modern plaque in front of the altar marks the burial place of William. The church opens 8.15 am to noon and 2 to 7.30 pm. Admission is free.

Alongside the church are the **convent buildings** now housing the majestic town hall. Very little remains of the original abbey after the 18th-century monk-architect Guillaume de la Tremblaye rebuilt it in a classical style. The monks were ejected from the abbey during the French Revolution and Napoleon turned it into a school. The guided visit takes you through the sumptuous interior outfitted in sculpted oak panelling, classical paintings and such wonders as an exquisitely designed staircase that seems to be suspended in mid-air.

Guided tours (in French with an English translation) are at 9.30 am, 11 am, 2.30 pm and 4 pm. Admission costs 10FF.

Also in the convent buildings is the interesting **Musée d'Initiation à la Nature** (☎ 02 31 30 43 27) which has a child-friendly series of exhibits on the fauna and flora of the Normandy countryside. There are dioramas, games, a botanical garden and stuffed animals. It opens 2 to 6 pm Monday to Friday, Easter to All Saints Day (1 November); and Wednesday only the rest of the year. Admission is free.

---

### La Clameur de Haro

Norman tradition allows someone who has been wronged to invoke their rights by raising *la clameur*. In front of two witnesses, the injured party sinks to their knees, recites the Lord's Prayer in French and cries 'Haro! Haro! Á l'aide mon Prince, on me fait tort!' (Haro! Help me my Prince, someone is wronging me). The accused must then stop the offending acts and wait for the legal system to run its course. 'Haro' is thought to derive from the cry of 'Ha' and 'Roi' or 'Rollo', the first duke of Normandy. Although the custom has fallen out of use in Normandy, it survives in parts of the Channel Islands.

---

## Abbaye aux Dames

At the eastern end of rue des Chanoines, Abbaye aux Dames (☎ 02 31 06 98 98) incorporates the **Église de la Trinité**, an even starker church than the Église St-Étienne. The highlights of the church are the stained-glass windows behind the altar and the 11th-century crypt with its finely sculpted capitals. Look for Matilda's tomb behind the main altar. William and Matilda's daughter Cécile was one of the first nuns at the convent, but its most famous boarder was Charlotte Corday. In July 1793, she got a pass from the abbess, headed to Paris and stabbed revolutionary extremist Marat in his bath. She was guillotined within a week. Access to the abbey, which houses regional government offices, is by guided tour at 2.30 pm and 4 pm daily. Admission is free.

The abbey opens onto the 13-acre **Michel d'Ornano Park** which was once part of the abbey grounds. With paths as wide as boulevards, manicured flower beds and a maze, the park is a restful breather from the city. It opens from 8 am daily and admission is free.

## Other Things to See

The most popular old neighbourhood in Caen is **rue du Vaugueux** and its offshoots. The tiny neighbourhood can be overrun with tourists and nightcrawlers but the cobblestone streets and creaky houses convey the charm of working-class Caen. Most of the stone houses date from the 18th century although a couple of half-timbered houses were built in the 16th century. Edith Piaf's grandparents had a bistro here. Less touristy **rue Froide** also escaped bombing and has fine examples of 17th- and 18th-century bourgeois architecture. Behind the elegant facades there are often courtyards with dormer windows and stone staircases. Although these apartments are private residences there's usually not a problem opening the outside door for a look around. Try Nos 10, 22 bis and 49. **Rue Écuyère** is a little more run down but also has some interesting old buildings. Notice the facade of No 9, the string of interior courtyards in No 32 and the 15th-century courtyard in No 42.

## Organised Tours

Boat trips on board the *Hastings* (☎ 02 31 34 00 00) leave from quai Vendeuvre four times daily in July and August, Sunday only the rest of the year. The 1¼-hour cruise travels along the Caen canal to Ouistreham passing by the Pegasus bridge and other sites. It costs 50FF (77FF return).

Le Mémorial de Caen organises guided minibus tours of the D-Day beaches that include Pointe du Hoc, Omaha Beach, the American Military Cemetery, Arromanches and Longues-sur-Mer. The tour leaves at 1 pm daily, April to September (with additional departures at 9 am and 2 pm June to August) and at 1 pm at the weekend and holidays only, the rest of the year. The tour costs 380FF (students and WWII veterans 270FF). The ticket includes a visit to the museum and this can be used on a different day. Reservations are essential.

## Places to Stay

**Camping** On the bank of the River Orne, the *Camping Municipal (*☎ 02 31 73 60 92, route de Louvigny)*, 2.5km south-west of the train station, opens May to September. It charges 20FF per person, 14FF per tent and 11FF per car. Take bus No 13 to the Camping stop (last bus at 8 pm).

Near the coast at Ouistreham, *Camping des Pommiers (*☎ 02 31 97 12 66, fax 02 31 96 87 33, rue de la Haie Breton)* opens year round except from mid-December to mid-February. Prices are 21.20FF per person and the same for a tent site.

**Hostels** The *Auberge de Jeunesse (*☎ 02 31 52 19 96, fax 02 31 84 29 49, 68 rue Eustache Restout)* charges 62FF per person (plus 10FF for breakfast) but opens June to September only. It's 2km south-west of the train station – take bus No 5 or 17 (the last one is at 9 pm) to the Cimetière de Vaucelles stop. In July and August students may stay in the *Cité de Lébisey (*☎ 02 31 46 74 74)* university dormitories for 49/370/741FF per day/fortnight/month for doubles with shower in the hall. Reservations must be made by mail to Cité de Lébisey, 114–116 rue de Lébisey, BP 5153, 14070

CALVADOS

Caen Cedex 5. Its dormitories are just north of the chateau.

**Hotels – Budget** Rooms starting at 115FF (140FF with shower and TV) are available at *Hôtel Le Vaucelles* (☎ 02 31 82 23 14, 13 rue de Vaucelles). Hall showers are free. The hard-to-miss yellow and green *Hôtel de la Consigne* (☎ 02 31 82 23 59, 48–50 place de la Gare) has decent doubles from 140FF. The *Hôtel au St-Jean* (☎ 02 31 86 23 35, fax 02 31 86 74 15, 20 rue des Martyrs) has nicely done singles or doubles for 150FF (with shower) or 190FF (with full bathroom). There's free enclosed parking.

The *Hôtel Le Rouen* (☎ 02 31 34 06 03, fax 02 31 34 05 16, 8 place de la Gare) has decent singles/doubles with washbasin for 130/150FF and ones with shower for 200/220FF. The *Hôtel du Havre* (☎ 02 31 86 19 80, 11 rue du Havre) has average rooms of above-average size from 150FF with washbasin or toilet, and 210/230FF with shower. The hotel has been recently renovated and windows are double glazed. The *Hôtel de la Paix* (☎/fax 02 31 86 18 99, 14 rue Neuve St-Jean) has plain, medium-sized rooms starting at 140/170FF with private WC and shower. Since it's on a busy street, the windows are double glazed to shut out the traffic noise and rooms have telephone and TV.

**Hotels – Mid-Range** The *Central Hôtel* (☎ 02 31 86 18 52, fax 02 31 86 88 11, 23 place J. Letellier) is in a drab building but the interior is cheerfully coloured in yellow and peach. The welcome is as warm as the decor. Rooms with shower only cost 170/190FF and 210/240FF for a private shower and toilet.

*Hôtel de l'Univers* (☎ 02 31 85 46 14, fax 02 31 38 21 33, 12 quai Vendeuvre) overlooks the port. Windows are double glazed to block out noise and each room has a telephone and TV, although the decorative scheme is uninspiring. Rooms with shower cost 170/200FF.

*Hôtel du Château* (☎ 02 31 86 15 37, fax 02 31 86 58 08, 5 avenue du 6 Juin) is a stone's throw from the chateau and has

good-sized rooms with private bath for 220/240FF. Front windows are double glazed and there's an elevator.

*Hôtel des Cordeliers* (☎ 02 31 86 37 15, fax 02 31 39 56 51, 4 rue des Cordeliers) is one of the rare Caen hotels in an 18th-century building. The interior garden is a relaxing haven and some of the rooms open directly onto it. With white walls and plain pine furniture the rooms are easy on the eye and the hotel is located on a quiet old street. Rooms with private bath cost 200/230FF.

In the centre of town, *Hôtel des Quatrans* (☎ 02 31 86 25 57, fax 02 31 86 20 91, 17 rue Gémare) is a sleek, modern establishment with elevator and soundproof rooms equipped with TV and telephone. Rooms with shower/bathtub cost 280/290FF.

*Hôtel Bernières* (☎ 02 31 86 01 26, fax 02 31 86 51 76, 50 rue de Bernières) is a cosy, friendly establishment that offers excellent value for the price. Rooms with showers only cost 160/200FF and 180/220FF with shower and toilet. You can book through its Web site at www.hotelbernieres.com.

**Hotels – Top End** Although *Hôtel Moderne* (☎/fax 02 31 85 37 93, 116 boulevard Maréchal Leclerc) has a plain exterior the modern rooms are large and brightly decorated and the rooftop breakfast room offers a superb view of the city. Rooms start at 340/410FF.

For a touch of class, it's hard to beat *Hôtel Le Dauphin* (☎ 02 31 86 22 26, fax 02 31 86 35 14, 29 rue Gémare). Features such as antiques, polished wood doors and beamed ceilings create an atmosphere of refinement and luxury and the restaurant is one of the best in town. Singles start at 410FF and doubles cost from 510FF to 650FF. Room 310 is particularly romantic.

## Places to Eat
**Restaurants** Caen's restaurants serve a variety of cuisine from local specialities to those from farther afield. There's something to suit all tastes and budgets.

*Around rue du Vaugueux* The pedestrianised quarter around rue du Vaugueux is a

CALVADOS

popular dining area with a wide range of prices and cuisines: North African, Chinese and even Malagasy at **Tongasoa** (☎ *02 31 43 87 15, 7 rue du Vaugueux).* The diverse range of main courses start at 58FF, and *menus* at 79FF (closed Sunday lunch).

Caen's only Indian restaurant is **Kashmir** (☎ *02 31 94 02 19, 78 rue du Vaugueux),* which turns out reasonably authentic dishes at more-than-reasonable prices. The 45FF lunch *menu* (except Sunday) is hearty and gently spiced.

One of the finest restaurants in town is **La Bourride** (☎ *02 31 93 50 76, 15 rue du Vaugueux)* in an ancient house that has been stylishly refitted. The cuisine is sophisticated, top-quality fare and, in a welcome nod to vegetarians, there's a vegetarian *menu* for 220FF. Other *menus* cost 250FF (weekdays only) and 340FF. The restaurant opens daily except Sunday and Monday.

**L'Insolite** (☎ *02 31 43 83 87, rue du Vaugueux)* is another restaurant that prepares vegetarian platters (65FF) and its fish dishes are fresh and copious. *Menus* start at 95FF. It opens daily except Sunday and Monday.

Cheese is the star as an appetiser, main course and dessert at **Maître Corbeau** (☎ *02 31 93 93 00, 8 rue Buquet)* and *menus* start at 90FF. It opens daily except Saturday lunch, Sunday and Monday and has the same management as Au Temps des Cerises in Rouen.

**Le Bouchon du Vaugueux** (☎ *02 31 44 26 26, 12 rue de Graindorge)* fills up with a crowd of regulars who come for the homespun cooking and hearty, imaginative salads. There are *menus* at 69FF and 99FF. The restaurant opens daily except Sunday and Monday.

**La Vie Claire** (☎ *02 31 93 66 72, 3 rue Basse)* is an organic food store that serves delicious lunches noon to 2 pm Tuesday to Saturday. A two-course *menu* costs 45FF and a plate of mixed veggie goodies costs 57FF. Space is limited so it's wise to book ahead. Reservations made before 11 am are awarded free coffee.

A hearty full English breakfast can be a welcome antidote to the French bread and coffee routine. **Dolly's Café & Tea Rooms** (☎ *02 31 94 03 29, 16–18 avenue de la Libération)* serves up bacon, eggs, beans, toast, coffee and juice all day for 56FF. Fish and chips cost 68FF and English-language newspapers and magazines are available next door at The English Shop. The shop and café open 10 am to 7.30 pm Tuesday to Saturday and 9.30 am to 6 pm Sunday.

**City Centre** At **Coupole** (☎ *02 31 86 37 75, 6 boulevard des Alliés)* you'll find a good-value *menu* for 68FF, salads from 38FF and a selection of local dishes including *tripes à la mode de Caen* (a heavily spiced tripe stew). The restaurant opens daily except Sunday.

**La Petite Auberge** (☎ *02 31 86 43 30, 17 rue des Équipes d'Urgence)* is a homely little place with *menus* of home-cooked food from 68FF and *plats du jour* from 55FF. It opens daily except Sunday.

Near the train station is **Le Météor** (☎ *02 31 82 31 35, 55 rue d'Auge)*, a tiny haunt charging only 52FF for a three-course *menu*, including a glass of wine. The restaurant opens daily except Saturday evening and Sunday.

The cheery **Salon de Thé** *(153 rue St Pierre)* has salads from 28FF, quiche from 12FF and sandwiches from 15.50FF. It opens 6 am to 8 pm daily.

Tapas are popular in Caen and **Le Bistrot Basque** (☎ *02 31 38 21 26, 24 quai Vendeuvre)* is the place to sample them. This bright, friendly place offers tapas only Monday to Wednesday (48FF for a healthy assortment) augmented by a selection of other Basque dishes Thursday to Saturday evenings (closed Sunday).

**L'Alcide** (☎ *02 31 44 18 06, 1 place Courtonne)* is an excellent address for sampling Caen cuisine, especially the infamous *tripes à la mode de Caen* served here in a sauce so savoury you can almost forget you're eating intestines. *Menus* cost 85/118/ 139FF and the two higher-priced *menus* include a starter of oysters if you like. It opens daily except Saturday.

**Le Carlotta** (☎ *02 31 86 68 99, 16 quai Vendeuvre)* is decked out in a very Parisian

CALVADOS

*belle epoque* style. The seafood platters also recall a Parisian brasserie except at better prices. The best dishes here are the fish and seafood with *menus* that start at 108FF. The restaurant opens daily except Sunday.

The latest addition to Caen's restaurant scene is the trendy *Le Costa (☎ 02 31 86 28 28, 13 rue Guilbert)*. A revolving door takes you into the sleek, Art Deco interior where you can feast on modern updates of French classics. There's a 100FF lunch *menu* that includes a main course, dessert and glass of wine and also a 150FF evening *menu*. Le Costa opens daily except Saturday lunch, Sunday, and Monday evening.

The restaurant *Le Dauphin* at the hotel of the same name (see Places to Stay earlier) has built a loyal clientele from locals and regular visitors to the hotel. The cuisine is thoroughly Norman, well-executed and reasonably priced considering the quality. *Menus* run from 110FF to 310FF. The restaurant opens daily except Saturday year round, except Sunday lunch in summer and Sunday evening in winter.

**Cafes** Redestrianised rue St-Pierre and rue Écuyère have a number of cafes to take a break from shopping during the day or meet friends at night. *Le Cafe Latin (☎ 02 31 85 26 36, 135 rue St-Pierre)* is a casual student hangout with a small terrace on the street. It opens 11 am to 1 am Monday to Saturday. *La Tour Solidor (☎ 02 31 86 10 35, 24 rue Écuyère)* is larger and warmly decorated in mustard tones. It opens 10 am to 12.45 am Monday to Saturday. Both cafes serve food only between noon and 2 pm.

**Self-Catering** The supermarket downstairs at *Monoprix (45 boulevard Maréchal Leclerc)* opens 8.30 am to 8.30 pm Monday to Saturday. Late-night purchases can be made at *Épicerie de Nuit (23 rue Porte au Berger)*, which opens 8 pm to 2 am Tuesday to Sunday.

Exquisite gateaux and dozens of types of bread are available at *Heiz Legrix (8 boulevard des Alliés)*, open 7 am to 7.30 pm daily except Monday.

For *food markets* head to place St-Sauveur on Friday, boulevard Leroy, behind the train station, on Saturday and place Courtonne on Sunday.

## Entertainment

**Pubs & Bars** Tiny *6X (☎ 02 31 86 36 98, 7 rue St-Sauveur)* is a funky student joint where the drinks are cheap and the crowds spill out onto the street. It opens 5 pm to 1 am Monday to Saturday. *Le Vertigo (☎ 02 31 85 43 12, 14 rue Écuyère)* is a larger bar which is also popular with the university set. It opens noon to 1 am Monday to Saturday.

**Discos & Clubs** One of the coolest student hangouts is *Le Farniente (☎ 02 31 86 30 00, 13 rue Paul Doumer)*, the kind of local place where everyone knows everyone else. Expect lots of Latin sounds. It opens at 2 pm but doesn't heat up until the late evening. It opens to 1 am daily except Sunday. *Le Montmartre (☎ 02 60 21 31 82, 8 rue Pémagnie)* is minuscule but offers house and techno on Saturday, hip-hop on Friday, reggae and ragga on Thursday and a mixture of styles Monday to Wednesday. It opens 7 pm to 1 am but the music doesn't start until around 9 pm.

Hard-core clubbers wind up the evening at *Joy's Club-Paradise (☎ 02 31 85 40 40, 10 rue de Strasbourg)* for dance-till-you-drop sounds in a variety of styles. It opens 11 pm to 5 am. It costs 20FF before 11.30 pm and then 30FF, Sunday to Thursday; 60FF with two drinks Friday and 70FF with two drinks Saturday. Women get in for free weekdays before midnight.

**Gay & Lesbian Venues** Although you'll sometimes find a mixed crowd at *Le Zinc (12 rue du Vaugueux)* it remains the trendiest gay bar in town. The DJ spins house and techno and it can get pretty crowded. It opens 6 pm to 1 am daily (to 2 am Thursday and Friday). Tiny *L'Excuse (☎ 02 31 38 80 89, rue Vauquelin)* is Caen's only lesbian bar although men are also welcome. It opens 10 pm to 4 am from Wednesday to Saturday.

**Classical Music, Opera & Ballet** Located in the centre of town *Théâtre de Caen* (☎ *02 31 30 76 20, 135 boulevard Maréchal Leclerc)* offers a season of opera, dance, jazz and classical concerts that run from October to May. Tickets cost 90FF to 210FF depending on the program and there are reductions for students. Big events with big stars take place at *Zenith* (☎ *08 36 68 17 57, rue Joseph Philippon)* where you might see Mylene Farmer or Enrico Macias. To get there take bus Nos 12 or 16 to the Parc des Expositions stop.

### Getting There & Away
**Air** Caen's airport (☎ 02 31 71 20 10) is 5km west of town in Carpiquet. Bus No 1 runs from Carpiquet to Caen's train station. A taxi costs about 80FF.

**Bus** Bus Verts serves the entire Calvados department, including Bayeux (36FF, 50 minutes), Courseulles-sur-Mer (26.50FF), Deauville-Trouville (53FF), Honfleur (67FF via Cabourg and Deauville, or 86FF by express bus) and the ferry port at Ouistreham (21FF, 25 minutes). It also runs two buses a day to Le Havre (1½ hours). For information on buses to Falaise, Lisieux and Pont l'Évêque see the Getting There & Away sections under those destinations.

Most buses stop both at the bus station and in the centre of town at place Courtonne, where there's a Bus Verts information kiosk. During the summer school holidays (July and August, more or less), the Ligne Côte du Nacre goes to Bayeux (one hour and 20 minutes) twice a day via Ouistreham and the eastern D-Day beaches. Bus No 44 to Bayeux takes in Le Mémorial de Caen, Arromanches, Pointe du Hoc and the American Military Cemetery.

If you arrive in Caen by bus, your ticket is valid on CTAC city buses for one hour. If you purchase your intercity ticket in advance, your ride to the bus station to catch your bus is free.

**Train** Caen is on the Paris–Cherbourg line. There are connections to Paris' Gare St-Lazare (156FF, 2½ hours, 13 daily), Bayeux (31FF, 20 minutes), Cherbourg (99FF, 1½ hours, four daily), Pontorson (122FF, six daily), Rennes (167FF, three hours, two daily), Rouen (116FF, two hours, 10 daily), and Tours (169FF, 3¾ hours, five daily) via Le Mans.

**Car** Rental agencies in Caen include: Hertz (☎ 02 31 84 64 50) 34 place de la Gare; Europcar (☎ 02 31 84 61 61) 36 place de la Gare; Avis (☎ 02 31 84 73 80) 44 place de la Gare; and ADA (☎ 02 31 34 88 89) 26 rue d'Auge.

**Boat** Brittany Ferries (☎ 02 31 36 36 36) sails from Ouistreham, 14km north-east of Caen, to Portsmouth in England. For more information, see under Sea in the Getting There & Away chapter.

### Getting Around
**Bus** CTAC (☎ 02 31 15 55 55) runs city bus No 7 and the more direct No 15 between the train station and the tourist office (stop: St-Pierre). A single ride costs 6.20FF, and a carnet of 10 costs 53FF. Services end between 6 and 8 pm.

Like many French cities, Caen is constructing a tram line that should be in service by 15 September 2002. The line will connect the train station with the University, stopping at quai de Juillet, rue de Bernières, place St-Pierre and the chateau, as well as running out to the suburbs.

**Taxi** To order a taxi, ring ☎ 02 31 26 62 00 or ☎ 02 31 52 17 89.

# Côte Fleuri

The Côte Fleuri between Honfleur and Cabourg is a lovely but highly developed string of beach resorts along a sandy coast. Glamorous Deauville-Trouville attracts the chic set from Paris, Cabourg is more sedate, while Honfleur and Houlgate retain traces of their medieval past amidst the summer hoopla. The landscape is gentle with low cliffs and dunes rising behind wide swathes of sand.

**CALVADOS**

## HONFLEUR
### postcode 14600 • pop 8200

In its strategic coastal position at the mouth of the River Seine some 200km north-west of Paris, Honfleur is a step back in time to an era when fishermen, pirates and explorers set sail from its harbour to seek their fortune. The stone dwellings constructed at the height of Honfleur's glory in the 17th and 18th centuries survive largely intact in a warren of streets around its old harbour. Even though Parisian weekenders sometimes outnumber residents and cruise ships can be more plentiful than fishing boats in the summer, it's still an active maritime centre dispatching shrimp, scallops and mackerel to the interior.

Honfleur may still be gatekeeper to the sea but the sea is farther away now. The Seine has been dumping silt on the seafront for centuries, leaving the houses along boulevard Charles V staring across parkland. Farther west are two wide sandy beaches but the main attraction of Honfleur is the impossibly picturesque old harbour. The changing play of light over slate-fronted buildings proved irresistible to a procession of 19th-century artists. Eugène Boudin was born in Honfleur and was an early mentor of Claude Monet. Painters such as Paul Huet, Corot, Seurat and Dufy came to try their hand at capturing Honfleur's particular charm. The poet Baudelaire spent time in Honfleur and the composer Erik Satie was born and worked in the town. There are still a number of artists' studios in Honfleur, especially along rue du Puits, rue de l'Homme de Bois and rue des Lingots.

### History

Honfleur's seafaring tradition dates back over a millennium. After the Norman invasion of England in 1066, goods bound for the conquered territory were shipped across the Channel from Honfleur. During the Hundred Years' War, Charles V fortified the town but it was conquered by the English and remained in English hands until 1450. With the return of peace, the town rebuilt and re-established its commercial links. Even the creation of Le Havre as a rival port in 1517 only served to spur the town on to developing trade relations with the New World.

In 1608 Samuel de Champlain set sail from here with a crew of local sailors on his way to found Quebec City. More than 4000 Normans migrated to Canada in the 17th century, working as fishermen, merchants and fur traders. In 1681 Cavelier de la Salle started out from Honfleur to explore the New World. He reached the mouth of the Mississippi and named the area Louisiana in honour of King Louis XIV, ruler of France at the time. During the 17th and 18th centuries, Honfleur achieved a certain degree of prosperity through trade with the West Indies, the Azores and the colonies on the western coast of Africa. In order to accommodate the growing maritime traffic, Louis XIV's minister Colbert ordered the construction of a sheltered port, now the Vieux Bassin (old harbour), completed in 1684. It was followed by the construction of the Bassin de l'Est in the 18th century but the age of maritime adventure was passing as England assumed control of the seas. Honfleur's diminishing importance made it unnecessary to undertake any grand renovation projects, leaving the town much as it was when its moment in the spotlight had passed.

### Orientation

Honfleur is centred around the Vieux Bassin. To the east is the heart of the old city, known as the Enclos because it was once enclosed by fortifications. To the north is the Avant Port (outer harbour), where the fishing fleet is based. Quai Ste-Catherine fronts the Vieux Bassin to the west, while rue de la République runs southwards from it. The Plateau de Grâce, with the Chapelle Notre Dame de Grâce on top, is west of town. To reach the beach walk up promenade de la Jetée and head west along the coast.

### Information

**Tourist Office** The tourist office (☎ 02 31 89 23 30, fax 02 31 89 31 82) is in the Enclos at place Arthur Boudin. It opens 9.30 am to 12.30 pm and 2 to 6.30 pm Monday to Saturday, Easter to July and also September;

CALVADOS

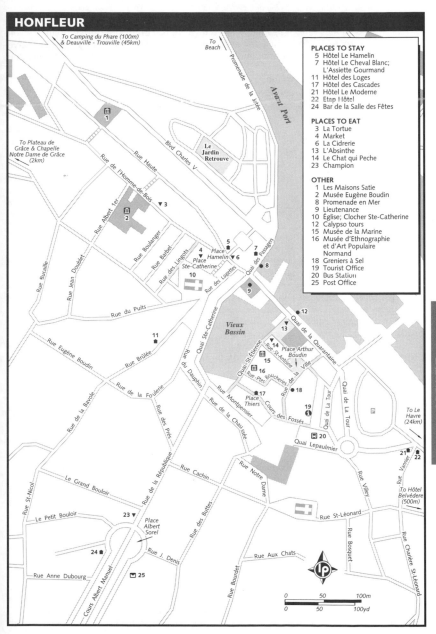

# HONFLEUR

To Camping du Phare (100m) & Deauville - Trouville (45km)

To Beach

Avant Port

Promenade de la Jetée

To Plateau de Grâce & Chapelle Notre Dame de Grâce (2km)

Blvd Charles V

Rue Haute

Le Jardin Retrouve

Rue de l'Homme-de-Bois

▼ 3

Rue Albert 1er

Rue Boulanger

Rue Barbel

Rue des Lingots

Rue Bucaille

Rue Jean Doublet

Place Hamelin

Place Ste-Catherine

Rue des Logettes

5
7
6 ▼

8

10

9

Quai des Passagers

Rue du Puits

Quai Ste-Catherine

Vieux Bassin

▲ 12

13 ▼

Quai de la Quarantaine

11

Rue Eugène Boudin

Rue Brûlée

Rue du Dauphin

14 ▼
15

16

Place Arthur Boudin

Quai St-Étienne

Rue St-Antoine

Rue de la Ville

Rue de la Foulerie

Rue de la Bavole

Rue des Prés

Rue Montpensier

Rue Ptes Boucheries

17

18

Place Thiers

19 ℹ

Cours des Fossés

Quai de la Tour

To Le Havre (24km)

Le Grand Bouloir

Rue St-Nicol

Rue de la République

Rue de la Chaûssée

Rue Cachin

Rue Notre Dame

20

Quai Lepaulmier

21
22

Rue Vanier

Rue Villey

To Hôtel Belvédère (500m)

Le Petit Bouloir

24 ☗

23 ▼

Place Albert Sorel

Rue des Buttes

Rue J. Denis

25

Rue St-Léonard

Rue Bosquet

Rue Anne Dubourg

Cours Albert Manuel

Rue Bourdet

Rue Aux Chats

Rue Charrière St-Léonard

LP

0 — 50 — 100m
0 — 50 — 100yd

CALVADOS

## PLACES TO STAY
- 5 Hôtel Le Hamelin
- 7 Hôtel Le Cheval Blanc; L'Assiette Gourmand
- 11 Hôtel des Loges
- 17 Hôtel des Cascades
- 21 Hôtel Le Moderne
- 22 Etap Hôtel
- 24 Bar de la Salle des Fêtes

## PLACES TO EAT
- 3 La Tortue
- 4 Market
- 6 La Cidrerie
- 13 L'Absinthe
- 14 Le Chat qui Peche
- 23 Champion

## OTHER
- 1 Les Maisons Satie
- 2 Musée Eugène Boudin
- 8 Promenade en Mer
- 9 Lieutenance
- 10 Église; Clocher Ste-Catherine
- 12 Calypso tours
- 15 Musée de la Marine
- 16 Musée d'Ethnographie et d'Art Populaire Normand
- 18 Greniers à Sel
- 19 Tourist Office
- 20 Bus Station
- 25 Post Office

9.30 am to 7 pm daily in July and August; 9.30 am to noon and 2 to 6 pm Monday to Saturday, October to Easter. You can visit the Web site at www.ville-honfleur.fr for more information.

The tourist office runs two-hour guided tours of Honfleur at 3 pm on Wednesday from July to September. The cost is 32FF (students and children 28FF).

**Post & Communications** The main post office is south-west of the centre on rue de la République, just past place Albert Sorel. It has a Cyberposte terminal.

### Église Ste-Catherine

This wooden church, whose stone predecessor was destroyed during the Hundred Years' War, was built by the people of Honfleur during the second half of the 15th and the early 16th centuries. It is thought that they chose wood, which could be worked by local shipwrights, in an effort to save stone in order to strengthen the fortifications of the Enclos. The structure that the town's carpenters created, which was intended to be temporary, has a vaulted roof that looks like an overturned ship's hull. The church is also remarkable for its twin naves. Each nave is topped by vaulted arches supported by oak pillars. Église Ste-Catherine opens 10 am to noon and 2 to 6 pm to visitors, except during services.

### Clocher Ste-Catherine

The church's free-standing wooden bell tower, Clocher Ste-Catherine (☎ 02 31 89 54 00), dates from the second half of the 15th century. It was built apart from the church for both structural reasons (so the church roof would not be subject to the bells' weight and vibrations) and for safety (a high tower was more likely to be hit by lightning). The former bell-ringer's residence at the base of the tower houses a small museum of liturgical objects but the huge rough-hewn beams are of more interest.

The bell tower opens 10 am to noon and 2 to 6 pm daily, except Tuesday, mid-March to September; 2.30 to 5 pm weekdays and 10 am to noon and 2.30 to 5 pm weekends,

the rest of the year. Admission costs 10FF for Clocher Ste-Catherine only and if you pay 30FF (students 25FF) you can have admission to both this and Musée Eugène Boudin.

### Musée Eugène Boudin

Named in honour of the early Impressionist painter born here in 1824, the museum (☎ 02 31 89 54 00), on rue de l'Homme de Bois at place Erik Satie, has a good collection of Impressionist paintings from Normandy, including works by Dubourg, Dufy and Monet. An entire room is devoted to the works of Eugène Boudin whom Baudelaire called the 'king of skies' for his luscious skyscapes. It has the same opening hours as the Clocher Ste-Catherine.

### Harbours

The **Vieux Bassin**, from where ships bound for the New World once set sail, now shelters mainly pleasure boats. The nearby streets, especially **quai Ste-Catherine**, are lined with tall, narrow houses dating from the 16th to 18th centuries. The **Lieutenance**, which was once the residence of the town's royal governor, is at the mouth of the old harbour. It is the sole remaining vestige of the fortifications that once completely circled the town.

The **Avant Port**, on the other side of the Lieutenance, is home to Honfleur's 50 or so fishing vessels. Farther north, dikes line both sides of the entrance to the port.

Either harbour makes a pleasant route for a walk to the seashore.

### Musée de la Marine

Honfleur's small maritime museum (☎ 02 31 89 14 12) is on the eastern side of the Vieux Bassin in the deconsecrated Église St-Étienne, which was begun in 1369 and enlarged during the English occupation of Honfleur (1415–50). Displays include assorted model ships, ships' carpenters' tools and engravings.

It opens 10 am to noon and 2 to 6 pm daily except Monday, April to late September; 2 to 6 pm weekdays and 10 am to noon and 2 to 6 pm at the weekend, late September to mid-November and mid-February to March (closed mid-November to mid-February). Admission to the Musée de la Marine costs 15FF (students 10FF); admission to Musée de la Marine and Musée d'Ethnographie et d'Art Populaire Normand combined costs 25FF (students 15FF).

## Musée d'Ethnographie et d'Art Populaire Normand

Next to the Musée de la Marine on rue de la Prison, the Museum of Ethnography & Norman Folk Art (☎ 02 31 89 14 12) occupies a couple of houses and a former prison dating from the 16th and 17th centuries. It contains 12 furnished rooms of the sort you would have found in the shops and wealthy homes of Honfleur between the 16th and 19th centuries.

It can be visited by guided tour only (in French), which leaves about once an hour. It opens 2 to 5.30 pm Monday to Friday. Admission costs the same as to the Musée de la Marine.

## Les Maisons Satie

This delightful new museum (☎ 02 31 89 11 11) at 67 boulevard Charles V captures the spirit of composer Erik Satie in an unusual way. 'Esoteric' Satie was known for his surrealistic wit ('Like money, piano is only agreeable to those that touch it') as much as for his starkly beautiful compositions. Visitors wander through the museum (located in Satie's birthplace) with a headset playing Satie's music and excerpts from his writings (in French or English). Each room is a surprise. One features a winged pear, another has a light display around a basin. A room called the Laboratory of Emotions has a whimsical contraption that you pedal. The museum opens 10.30 am (10 am June to September) to 7 pm daily, except Tuesday, mid-February to December.

## Greniers à Sel

The two huge salt stores (☎ 02 31 89 02 30) on rue de la Ville, along from the tourist office, were built in the late 17th century to store the salt needed by the fishing fleet to cure its catch of herring and cod. There were originally three warehouses but one burned down in 1892. All three could store up to 10,000 tons of salt. For most of the year the only way to see the Greniers à Sel is to take a guided tour (enquire at the tourist office). During July and August the stores host art exhibitions and concerts.

## Chapelle Notre Dame de Grâce

This chapel, built between 1600 and 1613, is at the top of the Plateau de Grâce, a wooded, 100m-high hill about 1km west of the Vieux Bassin. There's a great view of the town and port.

## Organised Tours

Forty-minute **boat tours** of the Vieux Bassin and port area are available on the *Calypso* for 25FF. Board at the quai de la Quarantaine. There is a 50-minute Promenade en Mer offered by Vedettes Stéphanie, Alphée and Evasion from the quai des Passagers that goes to the Pont de Normandie (40FF; see the boxed text 'The Pont de Normandie' later in the chapter). Tours run from April to mid-October.

## Special Events

Every year on Whit Sunday (the 7th Sunday after Easter) Honfleur's sailors organise a blessing of the sea in front of the old harbour. On Whit Monday (the next day) there's a procession up to Chapelle Notre Dame de Grâce where there's a ceremony. During the two-day festival there's an exposition of model ships at the Greniers á Sel.

## Places to Stay

**Camping** About 500m north-west of the Vieux Bassin, *Camping du Phare (☎ 02 31 89 10 26, boulevard Charles V)*, opens April to September. It costs 28FF per person and 35FF for a tent site and car. To reach it from the centre of town follow rue Haute.

**Hotels** The *Bar de la Salle des Fêtes (☎ 02 31 89 19 69, 8 place Albert Sorel)*, 400m south-west of the Vieux Bassin along rue de la République, charges 160FF (including breakfast) for each of its four double rooms.

## The Pont de Normandie

The Pont de Normandie between Le Havre and Honfleur is a remarkable feat of engineering and a majestic work of architecture. Opened in January 1995, the original idea had been to build the world's longest cable-stayed bridge to connect Upper and Lower Normandy. With a total length of 2141m, the Pont de Normandie was surpassed in 1998 by the Tartara bridge in Hiroshima, Japan, but its elegant structure is unequalled. A delicate web of cables connects the arched span of the bridge with two soaring 215m towers etching a bold silhouette against the sky. At night, the theatrically placed lights create an even more dramatic effect.

The decision to construct a cable-stayed bridge was based in part upon the softness of the river bed which probably would not have supported a suspension bridge. The two towers descend to a depth of 50m to rest upon a sufficiently solid bedrock. Also, one malfunctioning stay doesn't affect the entire bridge. Its aerodynamic design keeps the bridge stable even at tornado-level winds and a battery of computers monitor its stress level.

The bridge is 88km from Caen, 16km from Le Havre and 2km from Honfleur. A visitor centre (☎ 02 35 24 64 90) on the Le Havre side has photos and explanations of the bridge's construction. It opens 8 am to 8 pm daily. There's no charge for walking across the bridge but drivers pay 33FF each way.

The **Hôtel Le Moderne** (☎ 02 31 89 44 11, 20 quai Lepaulmier), has very simple singles/doubles for 125/190FF as well as doubles with shower for 255FF. Across the street **Etap Hôtel** (☎ 02 31 89 71 70) has the charmlessness you would expect from a chain hotel but the rooms have private bath and TV for 180/240FF per room.

**Hôtel Le Hamelin** (☎ 02 31 89 16 25, fax 02 31 89 16 25, 16 place Hamelin) is more central, near Église Ste-Catherine, and has doubles with shower from 180FF. **Hôtel des Cascades** (☎ 02 31 89 05 83, fax 02 31 89 32 13, 17 place Thiers) has sparse but attractive rooms that start at 200FF. There's also a decent restaurant downstairs.

**Hôtel Belvédere** (☎ 02 31 89 08 13, fax 02 31 89 51 40, 36 rue Emile Renouf) is a tranquil retreat less than 1km east of the town centre. The garden and terrace are relaxing and room 11 has a view of the Pont de Normandie. Rooms cost 290/340FF.

**Hôtel des Loges** (☎ 02 31 89 38 26, 18 rue Brûlée) has been renovated and is cheerfully decorated with candles and flowers. The ambience is friendly and rooms cost 335FF. The most luxurious hotel in town is the three-star **Hôtel Le Cheval Blanc** (☎ 02 31 81 65 00, fax 02 31 89 52 80, e lecheval.blanc@wanadoo.fr, 2 quai des Passagers) in a 15th-century mansion beside the port. The rooms are furnished in a traditional style and many have views of the port; they start at 492/514FF.

### Places to Eat
**Restaurants** Places to dine are abundant (especially along quai Ste-Catherine) but the food here doesn't come cheap: *menus* start at about 85FF. The **Hôtel Le Moderne** is one of the less expensive places, with *menus* from 70FF.

**La Cidrerie** (☎ 02 31 89 59 85, 26 place Hamelin) has a *menu* for 59FF that includes a *galette* (a wholemeal or buckwheat pancake) and drink but its main attraction is the wide selection of drinks that are almost exclusively based on apples and pears. Cider (*cidre*), *pommeau* (an aperitif of Calvados and apple juice), *poiré* (pear cider) and Calvados are served in surprising forms and combinations. It opens daily (except Tuesday and Wednesday from October to June).

One highly recommended spot is the cosy **La Tortue** (☎ 02 31 89 04 93, 36 rue de l'Homme de Bois), whose succulent four-course seafood *menus* start at 100FF. It also does a vegetarian *menu* for 77FF and 230FF allows you to choose anything on the *menu*. It opens daily except Tuesday lunch.

**Le Chat qui Peche** (☎ 02 31 89 35 35, 5 place Arthur Boudin) is solid value for correctly executed seafood dishes and the outdoor umbrella-covered terrace is inviting. *Menus* cost 60FF (lunch), 78FF and 150FF.

The best restaurant in Honfleur and one of the finest in Normandy is *L'Assiette Gourmande* (☎ *02 31 89 24 88, 2 quai des Passagers)*, part of Hôtel Le Cheval Blanc. Chef Gérard Bonnefoy comes up with inventive dishes and the portions are large. *Menus* start at 170FF. The restaurant opens daily except Sunday evening, and Monday, October to June.

Located in a ravishing 18th-century mansion, *L'Absinthe* (☎ *02 31 89 39 00, 10 quai de la Quarantaine)* offers sophisticated cuisine, even in its cheapest 175FF *menu*, which might include crispy veg, fish and a crepe with fresh fruit.

**Self-Catering** The Saturday *market* at place Ste-Catherine runs from 9 am to 1 pm. There's a *Champion* supermarket just west of rue de la République, near place Albert Sorel. It opens 8.30 am to 12.30 pm and 2.30 to 7.30 pm Monday to Friday, and 8.30 am to 7.30 pm on Saturday.

## Getting There & Away
**Bus** The bus station (☎ 02 31 89 28 41) is south-east of the Vieux Bassin on rue des Vases. Bus Verts (☎ 02 31 44 77 44 in Caen) No 20 bus runs via Deauville-Trouville (21.20FF, 30 minutes, five a day) to Caen (68.90FF or 86FF by express bus). The same line goes northwards to Le Havre (42.40FF, 30 minutes, five a day) via the Pont de Normandie. Line No 50 goes to Lisieux (one hour). Bus Verts offers a 12% discount for people aged under 26 on Wednesday, Saturday afternoon and Sunday.

## DEAUVILLE-TROUVILLE
Some 15km south-west of Honfleur lie the two seaside resorts of Trouville (population 5600) and Deauville (population 4300) which share many of the same amenities but maintain distinctly different personalities. Chic Deauville couldn't be more impressed with itself. With designer boutiques, an exclusive casino, a racetrack and the yearly American Film Festival, the town is clearly more comfortable with world-class shoppers, gamblers and film stars. Trouville is more down-to-earth. Hotels and restaurants

are less expensive and the town is proud of the 19th-century artists and writers that once flocked to its picturesque port. Both towns boast a wide, sandy beach, marred by lines of bathhouses.

The town of Trouville developed before Deauville. When painter Paul Huet and writer Alexandre Dumas first came in 1826, Trouville was just a small fishing village. Its proximity to Paris (200km) attracted a series of painters and writers at a time when the concept of therapeutic baths began gaining popularity. Flaubert came in 1836 when he was still a teenager and the landscape painter Charles Mozin produced several Trouville paintings. In the 20th century, writer-director Marguerite Duras wrote fondly of her long visits to Trouville and was inspired to make several films in the town. For most of the 20th century, Trouville was overshadowed by Deauville but it has begun to recapture its former glory.

Deauville was the brainchild of the duke of Morny, half-brother of Napoleon III. Enlisting a prestigious doctor and an architect in his scheme, the duke decided to create another spa across the river from Trouville. The developers begun draining the swampy land in 1859, built a racetrack and waited for the new railway to bring visitors. Still Deauville lagged behind Trouville until the construction of the Deauville casino in 1912 followed by the luxury hotels, Normandy and Royal. Designer Coco Chanel opened a boutique in 1913 that was soon patronised by the fashionable set fleeing WWI for their secondary residences. Throughout the 1920s and 1930s Deauville glittered with international royalty, industrialists and such political heavyweights as Winston Churchill. The American Film Festival arrived in 1975 bringing a parade of stars and new glamour to Deauville. The calendar of events revolving around horses, polo and film attracts the highest rungs of Parisian society who sometimes refer to the town as Paris' 21st arrondissement.

## Orientation
The towns are separated by the River Touques, with Trouville on the eastern and Deauville on the western bank, respectively, and

**CALVADOS**

linked by the pont des Belges. The combined train and bus station is just west of the bridge. Beaches line the coast to the north of both towns on either side of the port. Note that there are no beach showers; you must rent a swimming hut (monthly) and they are reserved at least a year in advance for the July/August season.

## Information

**Tourist Office** Deauville's tourist office (☎ 02 31 14 40 00, fax 02 32 88 78 88, **e** info-deauville@deauville.org) is at place de la Mairie and opens 9 am to 12.30 pm

and 2 to 6.30 pm Monday to Saturday, mid-September to April; 9 am to 6.30 pm May to June; 9 am to 7 pm July to September. It opens 10 am to 1 pm and 2 to 5 pm (10 am to 6 pm in July and August) on Sunday. You can pick up a copy of the free, outlandishly glossy magazine *Deauville Passions* for an overview of annual events and you can check out the Web site at www.deauville .org for more information.

The smaller Trouville tourist office (☎ 02 31 14 60 70, fax 02 31 14 60 71, **e** o.t.trou ville@wanadoo.fr) is at 32 boulevard Fernand Moureaux. It opens 9 am to noon and

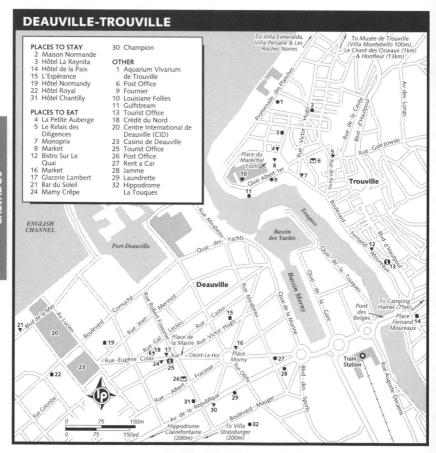

**DEAUVILLE-TROUVILLE**

PLACES TO STAY
2 Maison Normande
3 Hôtel La Reynita
14 Hôtel de la Paix
15 L'Espérance
19 Hôtel Normandy
22 Hôtel Royal
31 Hôtel Chantilly

PLACES TO EAT
4 La Petite Auberge
5 Le Relais des Diligences
7 Monoprix
8 Market
12 Bistro Sur Le Quai
16 Market
17 Glacerie Lambert
21 Bar du Soleil
24 Mamy Crêpe

30 Champion

OTHER
1 Aquarium Vivarium de Trouville
6 Post Office
9 Fournier
10 Louisiane Follies
11 Gulfstream
13 Tourist Office
18 Crédit du Nord
20 Centre International de Deauville (CID)
23 Casino de Deauville
25 Tourist Office
26 Post Office
27 Rent a Car
28 Jamme
29 Laundrette
32 Hippodrome La Touques

CALVADOS

1.30 to 6 pm daily, September to April; and 9 am to 7 pm daily, May to August.

**Money** Banks in Deauville include a Crédit du Nord at 84 rue Eugène Colas. In Trouville there's a Société Générale at 6 rue Victor Hugo. There are also several other banks on boulevard Fernand Moureaux. The post office also exchanges currency.

**Post & Communications** The post office on rue Robert Fossorier in Deauville opens 9 am to 6 pm, Monday to Friday, and Saturday mornings. It has Cyberposte. In Trouville the main post office is at 16 rue Amiral de Maigret but there is no Cyberposte.

**Travel Agencies** Fournier (☎ 02 31 88 16 73), place du Maréchal Foch, Trouville, handles air tickets and represents Avis.

**Laundry** There's a self-service laundrette in Deauville at 41 avenue de la République.

## Things to See & Do

In Deauville, the rich, famous and assorted wannabes strut along the beachside **promenade des Planches**, a 500m-long boardwalk lined with private swimming huts, before losing a wad at the casino.

About 1.5km north-east of Trouville's tourist office stands the **Musée de Trouville** (☎ 02 31 88 16 26) in the magnificent Villa Montebello, 64 rue du Général Leclerc. This former summer residence of Napoleon III was built at the height of Trouville's popularity in 1865 for the marquise de Montebello. The villa has a panoramic view over the beaches, and the museum recounts the history of Trouville in posters, drawings and paintings. Featured artists include Trouville painters Eugène Isabey, Charles Mozin and Eugène Boudin and there are temporary exhibits of local artists. It opens 2 to 6 pm daily except Tuesday, April to September. Admission costs 10FF (those aged over 60, 5FF).

On Trouville beach, La Plage, is the remarkably varied **Aquarium Vivarium de Trouville** (☎ 02 31 88 46 04), which aside from wild and wonderfully colourful fish also houses some fearsome reptiles (snakes, crocodiles and iguanas among them) and weird insects. It opens 10 am to noon and 2 to 7 pm daily, Easter to June and in September and October; 10 am to 7.30 pm July and August; and 2 pm to 6.30 pm November to May. Admission costs 35FF (students 30FF).

Walking up Trouville's beachside promenade, you'll come to several illustrious 19th-century **villas**. Notice the half-timbered Villa Esmeralda, the oriental-style Villa Persane and Les Roches Noires, where Marguerite Duras lived and worked. Following rue Général Le Clerc past the Villa Montebello takes you to La Corniche, a hilly road with spectacular views along the coast.

In Deauville the **Villa Strassburger** on avenue de Strassburger near the Hippodrome was built by the Rothschild family and then given to the town of Deauville. The exterior is an eye-pleasing mixture of towers and gables coalescing in a unique Alsatian–Norman style and the interior is furnished in its original American style. The tourist office conducts visits three times a day Tuesday, Wednesday and Thursday during July and August. Admission costs 15FF.

## Organised Tours

Fournier (see earlier under Travel Agencies) offers a program of excursions to the D-Day beaches, Mont St-Michel and other Normandy highlights for about 280FF a day. On quai Albert 1er the *Gulfstream* boat goes on a half-hour coastal tour (40FF), a two-hour trip to the Pont de Normandie (80FF) and a half-day fishing trip (250FF with equipment included) according to the tides between April and October. Call ☎ 02 31 85 10 11 for further information.

## Special Events

Deauville's answer to Cannes' famous festival is the American Film Festival, which is open to all and attracts a procession of Hollywood stars during the first week of September. Tickets cost 250FF and are available during the festival at the Centre International de Deauville (CID; ☎ 02 31 14 14 14), avenue Lucien Barrière. One ticket

CALVADOS

includes the entire daily program, which may include up to eight films.

Deauville is renowned for its equestrian tradition. The horseracing season, which runs from early July to mid-October, is held at two local racetracks: Hippodrome La Touques (300m south-west of the train station) for gallop races, and Hippodrome Clairfontaine (2km farther west) for galloping, trotting and steeplechase. Admission costs 25FF. Horse lovers will also enjoy the Equi'days which take place for a week in mid-October with seminars, horse shows, jumping and sales. Call ☎ 02 31 84 61 18 or visit the Web site (www.chevalnews.com).

The new Asian Film Festival takes place in March. Tickets are free and available at the tourist office. Trouville hosts a Festival Folkorique, which fills the streets with colourfully clad musicians and dancers the third week of June.

## Places to Stay
*Camping Hamel (☎ 02 31 88 15 56, 55 rue des Soeurs de l'Hopital)*, in a large field near Trouville's local hospital, charges 12FF per adult and 6FF per tent. From the pont des Belges, walk five minutes east through rue Biesta and its continuations. There's another camp site, *Le Chant des Oiseaux (☎ 02 31 88 06 42)*, 1km east of Trouville at 11 route d'Honfleur, with a sweeping view of the coast.

The best-value hotels are all in Trouville and the town participates in the Bon Weekend en Villes two-nights-for-the-price-of-one program from November to March. *Hôtel de la Paix (☎ 02 31 88 35 15, fax 02 31 88 28 44, 4 place Fernand Moureaux)* charges 150FF for cheerful singles/doubles with washbasin and 230FF for doubles with private shower and WC.

About 100m east of Trouville casino, *Hôtel La Reynita (☎ 02 31 88 15 13, fax 02 31 87 86 85, 29 rue Carnot)* has spacious, newly renovated doubles for 195FF (265FF in high season). *La Maison Normande (☎ 02 31 88 12 25, fax 02 31 88 12 25, 4 place de Lattre de Tassigny)* is in an ultra-Norman style with crisscrossing beams outside and an interior that resembles a

local family home. Rooms with private bath start at 345/350FF.

In Deauville, *Hôtel Chantilly (☎ 02 31 88 79 75, fax 02 31 88 41 29, 120 avenue de la République)* is a good moderately priced hotel with renovated, relatively large rooms for 345/405FF. *L'Espérance (☎ 02 31 88 26 88, fax 02 31 88 33 29, 32 rue Victor Hugo)* is a comfortable hotel with a very good restaurant. Half-board is mandatory from July to September and costs 535/681FF. The rest of the year there are rooms with sink only for 220FF and rooms with bathrooms for 330FF.

The most luxurious establishments in Deauville are the *Hôtel Normandy (☎ 02 31 98 66 22, fax 02 31 98 66 23, 38 rue Jean Mermoz)* and the *Hôtel Royal (☎ 02 31 98 66 33, fax 02 31 98 66 34, boulevard Cornuché)* on either side of the casino. Whether or not you're ready to pay 1190FF for a room at the Hôtel Normandy or 1300FF at the Hôtel Royal, the hotels are worth a visit for their fine restaurants, sumptuous lobbies and bars where you might catch sight of a celebrity or two.

## Places to Eat
Among the waterfront eateries in Trouville, the *Bistrot Sur Le Quai (☎ 02 31 81 28 85, 68 boulevard Fernand Moureaux)* has seafood *menus* from 65FF served in its pleasant front terrace. It opens daily except Wednesday.

Just off the pedestrianised rue des Bains, *Le Relais des Diligences (☎ 02 31 81 44 40, 7 rue du Dr Leneveu)* is a cosy place offering filling two-course seafood *menus* for 55FF and 85FF. It opens daily except Tuesday evening and Wednesday. *La Petite Auberge (☎ 02 31 88 11 07, 7 rue Carnot)* is another good bet for Norman specialities; it opens daily except Tuesday and Wednesday.

There's a big *Monoprix* supermarket at the northern end of boulevard Fernand Moureaux which opens daily except for Sunday. A *food market* is held on place du Maréchal Foch on Wednesday and Saturday mornings.

In Deauville *Bar du Soleil (☎ 02 31 88

CALVADOS

*04 74, boulevard de la Mer)* is not especially cheap with mussels at 72FF but its wide terrace on the beach keeps the crowds coming. It opens noon to 4 pm weekends only, November to Easter. *L'Espérance* (see Places to Stay earlier) offers good home cooking and has *menus* for 105FF, 138FF and 168FF. It opens daily (except Wednesday and Thursday, October to June).

The popular *Mamy Crêpe (55 rue Eugène Colas)* is a fine takeaway option for quiche and sandwiches (12FF to 22FF) and crepes (9FF to 21FF). The homemade ice cream at *Glacerie Lambert (76 bis rue Eugène Colas)* is enormously popular in the summer. Look for fine regional products at the *market*, place Morny, every morning in July and August; Tuesday, Friday and Saturday off season. *Champion* supermarket is on avenue de la République and opens daily except Monday.

## Entertainment

Dress at the *Casino de Deauville (☎ 02 31 14 31 14)* is formal but men can borrow a jacket and tie from reception. It opens 11 am to 2 am Monday to Friday, 10 am to 4 am Saturday and 10 am to 3 am Sunday. Admission to some rooms costs 70FF to 100FF. Trouville's casino, *Louisiane Follies (☎ 02 31 87 75 00)* at place du Maréchal Foch on the beachfront, is a more relaxed affair with an adjoining cinema and nightclub. It opens 10 am daily to 2 am Monday to Thursday, 3 am on Friday and 4 am on Saturday; the minimum bet is only 2FF.

## Getting There & Away

**Bus** The bus is generally faster and cheaper than the train. Bus Verts (☎ 08 01 21 42 14) has very frequent services to Caen (53FF, 1¼ hours), Honfleur (21.20FF, 30 minutes) and Le Havre (via Honfleur, 59FF, one hour).

**Train** Most train services from Deauville-Trouville require changes at Lisieux (31FF, 20 minutes, 10 daily). There are trains to Caen (65FF, 1–1½ hours, 13 daily), Rouen (105FF, 3¼ hours, four daily) and Dieppe (via Rouen 138FF, 3–3½ hours, four daily).

## Getting Around

For car rental try Rent a Car (☎ 02 31 88 08 40) 3 bis rue Désiré-Le-Hoc or Avis through the Fournier agency in Trouville. Bike rentals are available at Jamme (☎ 02 31 88 40 22), 11 avenue de la République, for 25/60/80FF per hour/half-day/day.

## AROUND DEAUVILLE-TROUVILLE

Situated 22km south-west of Deauville-Trouville, **Cabourg** is a staid resort whose main claim to fame is as the inspiration for Balbec, a town appearing in Proust's *Du Coté de Chez Swann*. Proust stayed in the *Grand Hôtel (☎ 02 31 91 01 79, fax 02 31 24 03 20, promenade Marcel Proust)*, which is still here, sprawling along a wide beach promenade. It's a magnificent structure, built at the height of Cabourg's turn-of-the-century popularity, and not unreasonably priced considering its history. Rooms start at 400FF for a Sunday night off season and extend to 1300FF for the room occupied by Marcel Proust. The tourist office (☎ 02 31 91 20 00, fax 02 31 24 14 49) in the Jardins du Casino can direct you to cheaper accommodation and provides a useful brochure and town map. It opens 9.30 am to 12.30 pm and 2 to 6 pm Monday to Saturday and 10 am to noon and 2 to 4 pm Sunday, September to June; and 9.30 am to 7 pm daily, the rest of the year.

The quiet family resort of **Houlgate**, 14km south-west of Deauville-Trouville, is also composed of Victorian-era mansions but, unlike Cabourg, there has been little disfiguring new construction. The town's 19th-century elegance has remained intact and prices are more reasonable than other coastal resorts. The tourist office (☎ 02 31 24 34 79, fax 02 31 24 42 27, **e** houlgate@wanadoo.fr), boulevard des Belges, opens 9 am to 12.30 pm and 2 to 6.30 pm daily, off season; and 10 am to 7 pm July and August.

Cabourg shares a train station with Dives-sur-Mer. There are daily trains from Paris to Houlgate and Cabourg in summer changing at Deauville-Trouville (178FF, 2¼ hours) but the service drops to weekends only the rest of the year. There are five

**CALVADOS**

trains daily from Deauville-Trouville to Cabourg (30 minutes) and Houlgate (20 minutes) in summer; weekends only in winter. Bus Verts bus No 20 runs year round from Houlgate and Cabourg to Caen (one hour), Deauville-Trouville (30 minutes) and Honfleur (45 minutes).

# Central Calvados

Falaise lies on the River Ante at the end of the Calvados department, 38km south of Caen. Due west of Falaise, spanning the Calvados and Orne departments, the Suisse Normande in the Orne Valley is a paradise for active travellers.

## FALAISE
### postcode 14700 • pop 8300

The rocky promontory in the western part of town overlooks the Ante Valley giving it a strategic importance that was obvious to the earliest Norman dukes. The 12th-century fortified castle on the hill was the birthplace of William the Conqueror and is now the town's main attraction. Falaise emerged as a prosperous trade and crafts centre in the early Middle Ages, known throughout France for its trade fairs. Although disrupted during the Hundred Years' War, the fairs returned in full force in the 16th century and were the basis for the Falaise economy until the 19th century. Falaise was devastated in WWII. Canadian forces liberated the city on 16 August 1944 and then joined other Allied forces intending to encircle remnants of the German army south of the city in the 'Falaise Pocket'. The Allied failure to close off the German retreat has been one of the more controversial subjects of WWII military history. Eighty-five percent of Falaise was destroyed in the fighting but it has been tidily rebuilt.

## Orientation & Information

The town centre of Falaise is compact and the tourist office (☎ 02 31 90 17 26, fax 02 31 90 98 70, ℮ falaise-tourism@mail.cpod .fr) is at Le Forum, boulevard de la Libération, in the centre of town. It opens 9.30 am to 12.30 pm and 1.30 to 6.30 pm Monday to Saturday and 10 am to 12.30 pm and 3 to 5.30 pm on Sunday, June to September; it closes Sunday and Monday morning the rest of the year. The post office is also in the town centre on rue St-Michel; it has Cyberposte. There's a laundrette at 3 rue Trinité.

## Things to See & Do

With its thick, square walls and circular tower, **Château Guillaume-le-Conquerant** (☎ 02 31 41 61 44) cuts a striking figure. Although the promontory upon which it rests was the site of a 9th-century chateau, it wasn't until the 11th century that Robert, duke of Normandy, built the chateau that served as the birthplace of his son, William, in 1027. Little remains of the 11th-century structure which was probably the oldest chateau in Normandy. In 1123, Henry Beauclerc, the son of William the Conqueror, built a square keep and chapel and, later in the century, Henry II Plantagenet built a small keep on the western side. When Normandy fell to the forces of Philippe-Auguste in 1204, the new king built the round tower, known as the Talbot Tower. After suffering a siege by Henri IV in 1590 during the Wars of Religion the castle fell into disuse and was left to moulder for several centuries.

In 1986 architect Bruno Decaris was hired to restore the castle and completed his work in 1997 to a storm of criticism. Rather than attempting to re-create the original forecourt the architect decided to 'suggest' its military function by erecting unattractive walls of grey concrete. Angry petitions and lawsuits ensued but the walls remain. His other architectural ideas were better received. Replacing the stone floors with translucent glass allows the visitor to gaze down at the remains of the 11th-century castle. The rooms have an austere beauty and plans are afoot to present a 'scenography' with multimedia effects tracing the castle's history within its walls. The top of the tower gives a splendid view of the surrounding landscape. The castle opens 10 am to 6 pm but it will be closed for some time while the presentation is being arranged so it's wise to call ahead to check its open. Admission costs 40FF (those aged 6 to 16, 25FF).

Across the River Ante behind the castle is **La Fontaine d'Arlette**, which commemorates the meeting between Robert and Arlette (William's father and mother). Legend has it that Robert, son of the duke of Normandy, spotted Arlette, daughter of a successful tanner, washing clothes by the river. Struck by her beauty, Robert invited her to spend the night in his chateau. Arlette agreed but, rather than slink in secretly, she entered through the front gate on horseback, dressed magnificently. Nine months later, little William entered the world. A bas-relief tells the story of their encounter next to an old washhouse.

The **Musée Août 1944** (☎ 02 31 90 37 19), chemin des Roches, illustrates the battle of the Falaise pocket with an impressive collection of tanks, jeeps, war memorabilia and figurines, explained by a series of multilingual panels. The museum opens 10 am to noon and 2 to 6 pm daily except Tuesday, April to November (daily, June to August). Admission costs 30FF (those aged 6 to 16, 10FF).

### Places to Stay & Eat

*Camping Municipal (☎ 02 31 90 16 55, route du Val d'Ante)* is in a lovely location at the foot of the chateau near tennis courts and a pool. It charges 17/14FF per person/tent. The cheapest hotel in town is *Hôtel Le Sulky (☎ 02 31 90 14 36, 22 rue du Pavillon)*, over a bar slightly east of the town centre. It has basic rooms for 130FF with toilet and shower in the hall.

*Hôtel de la Place (☎ 02 31 40 19 00, fax 02 31 90 08 90, 1 place St-Gervais)* has simple singles/doubles with private bath for 160/190FF. It's located near the town centre and serves inexpensive meals in the restaurant, which opens daily except Wednesday and Sunday evening. The hotel-restaurant *La Poste (☎ 02 31 90 13 14, fax 02 31 90 01 80, 38 rue Georges Clemenceau)* is a comfortable, friendly establishment that offers well-outfitted rooms for between 200FF and 360FF and good Norman cuisine in the restaurant. The restaurant opens daily except Monday and Sunday evening.

*La Fine Fourchette (☎ 02 31 90 08 59, 52 rue Georges Clemenceau)* is an exquisitely tasteful restaurant in every sense. The cuisine and decor are sophisticated without being pretentious. *Menus* cost from 87FF to 299FF and it opens daily except Tuesday evening. *Le Jardin (☎ 02 31 90 19 00, 7 rue de Paris)* is a more modest alternative that offers a popular 59FF lunch, usually with fish, as well as more expensive *menus*. It opens daily except Monday and Wednesday evening. *Aux Delices du Midi (21 rue St-Gervais)* sells groceries.

### Getting There & Away

Bus 35 links Caen and Falaise (42.40FF, one hour) up to six times a day weekdays, less often on Saturday; there's no service on Sunday.

## LA SUISSE NORMANDE

Lying 25km south of Caen and 14km west of Falaise, the Suisse Normande is defined by jagged cliffs and forested slopes along the path of the River Orne and its tributaries. In summer, kayakers and canoeists paddle up and down the rivers, hang-gliders drift overhead, cyclists pedal the back roads and walkers make their way through the meadows and forests. For further information on what you can do in the area contact the tourist offices in Clécy or Thury-Harcourt or check out the region's Web site www.suisse-normande.com.

Bus No 34 from Caen runs frequently to the main centres of Clécy (50 minutes, four daily) and Thury-Harcourt (40 minutes, nine daily), but your own transport is handy for appreciating the beauty of this unique region.

### Thury-Harcourt
**postcode 14220 • pop 1844**

On the northernmost edge of the Suisse Normande, Thury-Harcourt is built along a hill rising from the Orne. Most shops and services are clustered around place St-Sauveur. A scattering of houses and a hotel lies on the other side of the river. The tourist office at 2 place St-Sauveur (☎ 02 31 79 70 45, fax 02 31 79 15 42, **e** otsi.thury@libertysurf.fr) is

*CALVADOS*

open from 10 am to noon and 2 to 6 pm Monday to Saturday.

The Kayak Club (☎ 02 31 79 40 59), on impasse des Lavandières, rents out canoes (220FF, two people), kayaks (140FF per person) and mountain bikes (100FF half-day).

*Camping du Traspy (☎ 02 31 79 61 80)* is beautifully situated along the riverbanks next to an aquatic centre with a toboggan and waterfalls.

*Hôtel Stop (☎ 02 31 39 23 50, 5 rue St-Sauveur)* is across from the tourist office and has rooms with private facilities for 220FF and 110FF without.

*Hôtel du Val d'Orne (☎ 02 31 79 70 81, fax 02 31 79 16 12, 9 route d'Aunay-sur-Odon)* is a rustic establishment with a facade half-buried under ivy. Rooms with sink only cost 130FF and those with private facilities cost 275FF. *Le Relais de la Poste (☎ 02 31 79 72 12, fax 02 31 39 53 55, avenue du 30 Juin)* is the most expensive with exquisitely decorated rooms for 300FF to 600FF.

## Clécy
**postcode 14570 • pop 1266**

Self-proclaimed 'capital' of the Suisse Normande, Clécy is an engaging town of narrow streets, granite houses and white shutters. The town is on top of a hill which affords marvellous views of the Orne Valley. At the bottom of the hill, the leafy banks of the Orne are lined with *guinguettes* – cafes with riverside terraces. With its natural charms and array of outdoor activities, it's not surprising that Clécy is packed with tourists at sunny weekends and during summer holidays.

The tourist office (☎/fax 02 31 69 79 95, @ otsi.clecy@libertysurf.fr), place Tripot, is on a pretty square behind the town hall and has a list of chambres d'hôtes. They'll also point you in the right direction for walks, hikes and other activities. It opens 10 am to 12.30 pm and 2.30 to 6.30 pm Monday to Saturday and 10 to 12.30 pm Sunday from April to October; 10 am to 5 pm Monday to Friday, and Saturday mornings, the rest of the year.

Canoeing and kayaking are major attractions in Clécy. Rental places are along the river around the Pont de Vey. Try Le Beau Rivage (☎ 02 31 69 79 73), La Potinière (☎ 02 31 69 76 75) or La Guinguette à Tartine (☎ 02 31 69 89 38). A four-hour river trip in canoe costs 180FF for two people; four hours in a kayak costs 110FF per person. Le Relais du Grand Camp (☎ 02 31 69 69 06) rents out mountain bikes as well as canoes and kayaks. The Centre de Pleine Nature Lionel Terray (☎ 02 31 69 72 82), also along the banks of the Orne, will equip you with a canoe (220FF, two people), kayak (140FF per person), mountain bike (100FF per half-day), archery equipment (150FF, two hours) or take you rock climbing (150FF, two hours, four-person minimum).

Four kilometres north-east of Clécy at St-Omer, there's a parachuting centre (☎ 02 31 26 89 13), where hang-gliding costs 150FF.

Across the River Orne the 205m Pain de Sucre (sugarloaf) massif looms over the valley. Several paths lead up to the top.

*Camping Municipal (☎ 02 31 69 70 36)* is along the Orne in Vey, 1km from Clécy just across the river. In the town centre *Au Site Normand (☎ 02 31 69 71 05, fax 02 31 69 48 51, 1 rue des Châtelets)* has a shady, plant-covered terrace and attractive rooms that cost from 280FF to 350FF. The more expensive rooms have a terrace or balcony. *Hostellerie du Moulin du Vey (☎ 02 31 69 71 08, fax 02 31 69 14 14)* is in a converted flour mill on the river at Vey. The setting is enchanting and the romantic rooms have every comfort but you'll pay from 430FF to 600FF for the luxury.

## Pont d'Ouilly
**postcode 14690**

At the confluence of the Rivers Orne and Noireau, Pont d'Ouilly is an inconspicuous little village known for its watersports. The centre is an unremarkable postwar reconstruction but the serene riverbanks overhung with trees and rising to gentle slopes on either side create a lovely setting for a stroll or drive. The tourist office (☎ 02 31 69 29 86 or 02 31 69 39 54) is just over the river on boulevard de la Noë. It opens

10 am to 1 pm and 2.30 to 6.30 pm Wednesday to Sunday in July and August and less frequently in May, June and September. It's closed in winter.

**Things to See & Do** Base de Plein Air (☎ 02 31 69 86 02), on the river, rents out canoes/kayaks for 60/40FF per hour and organises canoe and kayak trips down the River Orne for 180/120FF per half/full day. They also organise competitions in kayak-polo, a unique sport played only in Pont d'Ouilly. You can hire mountain bikes from the service station (☎ 02 31 69 80 35) across from the tourist office for 60/110FF per half-day/day. Fishing enthusiasts can try their luck at Les Sources de la Here pond north of Pont d'Ouilly at St-Christophe. It costs 70/120FF per half-day/day. Call ☎ 02 31 69 26 26 for details.

**Places to Stay** The *Camping Municipal* (☎ 02 31 69 80 20) is along the river.

There are two hotels in town. *Hôtel de la Place* (☎ 02 31 69 40 96) is near the post office and marketplace on a hill overlooking the river. Rooms with sink only cost 140FF and there are a few rooms with private facilities for 170FF. The nearby *Hôtel du Commerce* (☎ 02 31 69 80 16, fax 02 31 69 78 08) has simply furnished but comfortable rooms with private facilities for 200FF to 250FF.

### Around Pont d'Ouilly

**La Roche d'Oëtre**, about 7km south of Pont d'Ouilly, is the most dramatic sight in the Suisse Normande. From this immense cliff rising almost 120m over the gorge of the River Rouvre, waves of forested slopes and steep valleys unfold in a breathtaking panorama. Scattered bald spots on the hills testify to the severity of the storm of December 1999. A number of paths lead down and across the cliff but be careful after rainfall as the rocks can get slippery. Notice the profile of a human face that the wind has carved into the rock face supporting the upper plateau. A cafe is perched near the lookout point but it was badly damaged during the storm and has yet to reopen. The

site is isolated but easily reachable and signposted from the D167 in Pont d'Ouilly.

# Pays d'Auge

Inland from the Côte Fleurie, the Pays d'Auge is a luscious green landscape of hills, pastures and apple trees. The Rivers Risle, Dives and Touques water the lowlands, sprouting streams and brooks that add to the visual allure. Apart from Lisieux, the largest city, Pays d'Auge is composed of the kinds of small towns and villages that make French people sentimental about rural life. The countryside is dotted with half-timbered family farms that usually contain a dairy, an apple barn and a cider press. Parisians have been steadily acquiring the farms as secondary residences, preserving their traditional architecture. Cheese rules the region with three of the finest French cheeses produced here: Camembert, Pont L'Évêque and Livarot, as well as the lesser-known pavé d'Auge. Apple products from the Pays d'Auge are also highly prized; Normandy's best cider and Calvados are made here. Thoroughbred horses from over 200 stables in the region fetch high prices at Deauville's international horse markets.

### LISIEUX
**postcode 14100 • pop 25,600**
Forty-seven kilometres south-east of Caen, Lisieux is the largest city in the Pays d'Auge. After 13 bombardments between 6 June and 31 July 1944, little remains of it's medieval centre. Postwar reconstruction was graceless in Lisieux, replacing sinuous streets with straight wide roads and squat buildings. Yet there is a stunning Gothic cathedral and the city makes a good base to explore the surrounding countryside. Lisieux is of particular interest to devotees of Ste-Thérèse as she grew up here at the end of the 19th century.

The city was inhabited by an ancient Gallic tribe that succumbed to the Romans in the 1st century BC. Traces of the Roman occupation are visible in excavations on the place de la République. Lisieux became the

**CALVADOS**

## The Humble Saint

Born into a devout family in Alençon in 1873, Thérèse Martin lost her mother to breast cancer when she was only four years old. It was a great shock, turning her into a shy introspective child. Her father moved the family to Lisieux and, at the age of 10, Thérèse underwent a second transformation when a statue of the Virgin Mary appeared to smile at her and cured her of a fever. She became even more devout and decided to become a Carmelite nun as her sister had. With a great struggle, she mastered a hypersensitive disposition and, at the age of 14, made a pilgrimage to Rome seeking a special dispensation from the pope to enter the convent. Impressed with her determination and ardour, the Church allowed her to take the veil at the extraordinarily young age of 15.

JANE SMITH

**Thérèse – saint of small deeds**

Joining her two sisters in the Carmelite convent in Lisieux, Thérèse's growing spirituality was severely tested when her father entered a mental hospital after suffering a stroke. 'Jesus isn't doing much to keep the conversation going,' she moaned after a period of unfulfilling prayers. Gradually, the form of her devotion to God emerged. Her 'little way', as she called it, was to approach her life with extreme meekness and humility. She smiled at sisters she didn't like, ate whatever was put in front of her and accepted blame for the misdeeds of others. The point was to find holiness in small sacrifices rather than grand gestures. Her philosophy was that secret acts of goodness are more difficult and thus honour God more than well-publicised great deeds. It is perhaps ironic that the saint Thérèse most admired was the swashbuckling Joan of Arc, who was anything but humble.

Thérèse fell ill with tuberculosis in 1896 and became consumed with the idea of extending her influence past her own rapidly dwindling days. She continued to write and bore her physical suffering with strength and serenity, despite severe and unremitting pain. She died 30 September 1897 at the age of 24.

After her death, her sister sent copies of her book, *Story of a Soul*, to local convents. Thérèse's account of her spiritual journey immediately found an audience. Her tomb attracted the faithful and it wasn't long before miracles were attributed to her intercession. She was beatified in 1923 and canonised two years later. Now considered the greatest modern-day saint, Thérèse was made a doctor of the Church in 1997. There are more than 2000 churches, chapels and religious institutions dedicated to the woman who declared as she lay dying: 'My heaven will be spent on earth.'

seat of a bishopric in the 6th century and controlled most of the Pays d'Auge by the 12th century. Henry II and Eleanor of Aquitaine were married in Lisieux in 1152 (or so it's thought) and the town remained important until the triple troubles of the 14th century – war, famine and plague – reduced its influence. The town's association with St Thérèse, which has been assiduously promoted, has made it one of the more important pilgrimage destinations in Europe, attracting about a million and a half pilgrims each year.

### Orientation & Information

The town centre is dominated by the imposing Cathédrale St-Pierre. The train station is about 1km south of the town centre. The tourist office (☎ 02 31 48 18 10, fax 02 31 48 18 11, ✉ officelx@club-internet.fr) is 400m north of the train station at 11 rue Alençon (follow rue de la Gare). The tourist office opens 8.30 am to 6.30 pm Monday to Saturday, and 10 am to noon and 2 to 5 pm Sunday, June to September; and 8.30 am to noon and 1.30 to 6 pm Monday to Saturday, the rest of the year. There's another temporary tourist office across from Cathédrale St-Pierre open in July and August only. The town's Web site is www.ville-lisieux.fr. The post office is on rue Condorcet across from the cathedral; there's no Cyberposte. You can check email at Web Café (☎ 02 31 62 07 62), 6 place de la République. It opens 8 am to 8 pm Monday to Saturday.

## Things to See & Do

The town's main attraction is the **Cathédrale St-Pierre** on rue Condorcet begun in 1170 and largely completed by the mid-13th century. The interior is marked by an elegant sobriety, characteristic of early Gothic architecture. A statue of St Thérèse stands in the choir where she came to pray and the main altar was a gift from her father. The chapel was built to the order of Pierre Cauchon who became bishop of Lisieux after presiding over the trial and sentence of Joan of Arc. His tomb is to the left of the altar. The stained-glass windows date from the 13th century and the side chapels contain fine examples of painting and sculpture from the 14th to 18th centuries. Behind the church, the **Jardin de l'Evêché** was designed by Le Nôtre who also designed the gardens of Versailles. The church opens 9 am to noon and 2 to 7 pm June to September and 9.30 am to noon and 2 to 6 pm the rest of the year.

The **Basilique Ste-Thérèse** behind the train station is hard to miss. Grand and grandiose, it combines Romanesque and Byzantine styles in one of the largest churches built this century. This stone and concrete behemoth was begun in 1924 and consecrated in 1954. The interior, which can accommodate 4000 people, is covered with mosaics and it's possible to climb to the top of the 100m dome. Take a look, especially, at the multicoloured mosaics that cover the crypt. It opens 8.30 am to 8 pm June to September and 9 am to 6 pm the rest of the year.

The Saturday morning **market** on place de la République is replete with local food products and there's a Wednesday market from 4 pm in July and August that offers more elaborate gastronomic adventures accompanied by music.

## Places to Stay & Eat

*Camping Municipal de la Vallée (☎ 02 31 62 00 40)* is on route de la Vallée, 2km east of the town centre. Take bus No 1.

The cheapest hotel in town is *Les Capucines (☎ 02 31 62 28 34, 6 place Fournet)*, about 200m north of the train station on the way into town. Singles/doubles cost 130/200FF without private bath and 230FF with private bath. Closer to the town centre, *Hôtel de Lourdes (☎ 02 31 31 19 48, fax 02 31 31 08 67, 4 rue au Char)* has simple, bright rooms for 185/350FF with private bath. The town's best hotel is *Azur Hôtel (☎ 02 31 62 09 14, 15 rue au Char)*, a colourful and fully renovated three-star establishment near the cathedral. Well-appointed rooms cost 380/480FF.

Rue Henry Chéron along the side of the cathedral is awash in cheap eateries but for a special meal try *Le France (☎ 02 31 62 03 37, 4 rue au Char)*, a favourite haunt of actors from the nearby theatre. Many of the dishes use such local products as cider, pommeau and Livarot cheese. *Menus* cost 89FF and 128FF and it opens daily except Monday. Self-caterers can pick up supplies at the *Champion* supermarket in the Nouvelle Galleries shopping centre on place de la République. See Things to See & Do earlier for details of markets.

## Getting There & Away

There are no buses from Caen but trains run at least hourly from there to Lisieux (45FF, 30 minutes) and there are five direct trains from Rouen daily (88FF, 1½ hours). There are also up to 10 trains daily from Deauville-Trouville (31FF, 45 minutes).

One bus connects Lisieux and Le Havre daily (79.50FF, 1½ hours); there's one bus daily Monday to Friday from Deauville (37.10FF, one or two hours) and up to seven from Honfleur (42.40FF, one hour).

## PONT L'ÉVÊQUE
**postcode 14130 • pop 4130**

Located 18km north of Lisieux, Pont l'Évêque is an unpretentious little town that has been known for its cheese since the 13th century. Pont l'Évêque is a strongly flavoured

CALVADOS

soft cheese with a rind that, as an *appellation controllée*, must be produced in the region. Although 65% of the town was destroyed in the 1944 bombings, a careful reconstruction has preserved much of the town's layout. The rivers meandering through the town centre give a sense of connection to the surrounding countryside and the banks contain pleasant footpaths.

## Orientation & Information

The church, tourist office, bank and post office are grouped together on rue St-Michel in the town centre, about 200m north of the train station. The tourist office (☎ 02 31 64 12 77, fax 02 31 64 76 96, **e** pontleveque-tourisme@wanadoo.fr), 16 bis rue St-Michel, opens 9.30 am to 7 pm Monday to Saturday and 10 am to 1 pm Sunday, July and August; 10 am to 12.30 pm and 2 to 6 pm Monday to Saturday, September, October and March to June (to 5.30 pm November to February). It makes hotel reservations for a 5FF fee.

## Things to See & Do

The **Église St-Michel** in the centre of town was built between 1483 and 1519 although the stained-glass windows date from 1963. **La place du Tribunal** has a number of 16th-century residences and the nearby **Couvent des Dames Dominicaines** is marked by a Renaissance building with a lovely balustrade and stone stairway. The most intact part of the town is along **rue de Vaucelles**, the western extension of rue St-Michel. Notice the old houses leaning into the River l'Yvie just after avenue de la Libération.

The tourist office has information about several chateaux to visit in the region, most notably the **Château du Breuil** (☎ 02 31 65 60 00), open 9 am to noon and 2 to 6 pm. They can also direct you to cheese-making farms that offer visits and tastings. The lake south-west of the train station has a leisure centre (☎ 02 31 65 29 21) that offers sailing, jet-skiing, canoeing and horse-riding.

Two **Calvados distilleries** outside town offer visits. The closest is Père Magloire (☎ 02 31 64 30 31) about 1km north-east of the town centre on the road to Deauville. Visits cost 15FF and include a tasting and

tour of the small museum. Tours are given at 10.30 am, 11.30 am, 2.30 pm, 3.30 pm, 4.30 pm and 5.30 pm from May to September; 11 am, 2.30 pm, 3.30 pm and 4.30 pm in April and October.

Cheese-lovers won't want to miss the Fête du Fromage **cheese festival** held on place Foch the second weekend in May where there are prizes for the best cheese and displays of regional products. If you miss the cheese festival try for the Marché Campagnard à l'Ancienne, regularly held on Sundays 10 am to 1 pm on place des Dominicaines, where you can enjoy folk dances, craft demonstrations and local costumes while downing your fill of cider and cheese.

## Places to Stay & Eat

There's an excellent camp site, *La Cour de France* (☎ 02 31 64 17 38), near the leisure centre on the lake, which charges 32/32FF per person/tent, and another, *La Stade* (☎ 02 31 64 15 03), 1km north-west of the town centre on the route to Beaumont. It charges 62FF for two people with a tent or car. In the town centre, *Hôtel de France* (☎ 02 31 64 30 44, fax 02 31 64 98 90, 1 rue de Geôle) has recently been restored and offers cheerfully decorated rooms without/with private bath for 165/260FF. Next to the train station, you'll find simple rooms with sink only at *La Station* (☎ 02 31 64 11 13) for 150FF.

*Restaurant Le Rollon* (☎ 02 31 64 28 13, 44 rue Hamelin) is a favourite for local dishes at reasonable prices. It opens daily in July and August and daily except Wednesday and Sunday evening the rest of the year. *Auberge de l'Aigle d'Or* (☎ 02 31 65 05 25, 68 rue de Vaucelles) is expensive but worth it for the atmosphere alone. It's located in a 16th-century building that served as a post office. It also opens daily in July and August and daily except Wednesday and Sunday during the rest of the year.

## Getting There & Away

Pont l'Évêque is on the train line that runs from the coast to Lisieux. There are up to 15 trains a day between Deauville-Trouville and Pont l'Évêque (10 minutes) and an

**CALVADOS**

equal number to Lisieux (20FF, 12 minutes). Less practical are the late-afternoon buses from Deauville (37FF, one hour) or the early morning bus from Lisieux (21FF, 35 minutes). There are also three daily buses from Caen (53FF, one hour).

## ST-PIERRE-SUR-DIVES
postcode 14170 • pop 4500

Midway between Falaise and Lisieux, St-Pierre-sur-Dives is a marketplace for regional produce and is also Normandy's box-maker. The town doesn't produce cheese but manufactures the light wooden boxes that protect Norman cheeses. There's also a substantial tannery trade. The town formed around a powerful 11th-century Benedictine abbey that endured until the French Revolution. The abbey is the official highlight of St-Pierre-sur-Dives but the Monday markets afford an indelible glimpse of small-town Norman life.

### Orientation & Information

The tourist office (☎ 02 31 20 97 90, fax 02 31 20 36 02), rue St-Benoit, is in the town centre, west of rue de Lisieux (the main road running through town). It opens 9.30 am to 12.30 pm and 1.30 to 6 pm Monday to Friday year round; to 5.30 pm on Saturday, April to November; and 10 am to noon and 2 to 5 pm on Saturday, December to March. The post office is on the other side of rue de Lisieux next to place du Marché.

### Things to See & Do

Established in the 11th century, reconstructed in the 12th and 13th centuries and modified in the 16th and 17th centuries, the **abbey** is the most extensive monastical structure in Normandy. The church towers have the tapered elegance that characterises Norman Gothic architecture and the bright, harmonious interior has carved Renaissance choir stalls and a gold-leaf altar that dates from the 17th century. The chapter room has recently been restored to its former glory and now displays works by the painter André Lemaître.

One of the convent buildings houses the **Musée des Techniques Fromagèrs** and the tourist office. The new museum is well-conceived and covers every aspect of cheese-making from the production of milk to the latest techniques. The visit also includes a tasting. Guided visits take place every 30 minutes while the tourist office is open. The church and chapter room open 8 am to noon and 2 to 7 pm and admission is free. The museum opens 9.30 am to 12.30 pm and 1.30 to 5.30 pm Monday to Saturday. Admission costs 15FF.

The market building in the town centre, **Les Halles**, is nearly as impressive as the abbey. Although burned in 1944, the 13th-century building was faithfully reconstituted using the original 290,000 handmade wooden pegs. The regular **markets** in Les Halles are local events. The weekly market is on Monday morning and offers local produce and regional dishes as well as pigs, calves, sheep and goats to local breeders. The first Sunday of the month is given over to the **Marché aux Antiquaires** where everything from crafted furniture to postcards are for sale. It opens 8 am to 6 pm. Not enough markets? Try the Monday **cattle auction** in the Zone Industrial Sud (from 10 am) and pick up a Normandy heifer.

### Places to Stay & Eat

The *Camping Municipal (☎ 02 31 20 73 28)* is 1km south of town on the D102 and is next to a sports complex. It costs 15/12FF per adult/tent. *Les Agriculteurs (☎ 02 31 20 72 78, 118 rue de Falaise)* has a rustic flavour in the centre of town and serves inexpensive meals. Rooms without/with private bath cost 170/200FF.

### Getting There & Away

Getting to St-Pierre-sur-Dives on public transport is highly problematic since it is only connected by school bus with Falaise and Lisieux, which means that there's no bus service during school holidays. There's a midday bus on Wednesday, and two late-afternoon buses from Lisieux and Falaise (50 minutes) as well as early buses in either direction Monday to Friday, so it's possible to stop in St-Pierre-sur-Dives overnight on your way to either Lisieux or Falaise.

CALVADOS

## AROUND ST-PIERRE-SUR-DIVES

The **Château de Vendeuvre** (☎ 02 31 40 93 83), 6km south of St-Pierre-sur-Dives on the road to Falaise, is an 18th-century manor that testifies to the enviably luxurious life of pre-Revolutionary aristocrats. The manor presides over a vast estate that includes several manicured gardens enlivened by a marvellous water park with a shellfish grotto. The interior re-creates the 18th-century lifestyle with period furniture and *objets d'art*.

The chateau's main feature is the unique **Musée des Meubles Miniatures** that presents a hundred or so miniature pieces of furniture created from the 16th to the 19th centuries. Made with the same material as standard furniture, these exquisite pieces served as models for larger items and sometimes were created simply as a hobby by furniture artisans. Among other wonders, notice the bed made for the cat of Louis XV's daughter.

The museum opens 10 am to 6 pm daily, May to September; 2 to 6 pm Sunday and holidays only March, April, October and until November 11. Admission costs 49FF (those aged 7 to 18 and students, 40FF) for the gardens, chateau and museum; 33FF (reduced price 25FF) for the gardens alone. You'll need your own transport to get here.

# Bayeux & the D-Day Beaches

The D-Day landings, code-named Operation Overlord, were part of the largest military operation in history. Early on the morning of 6 June 1944, swarms of landing craft – part of a flotilla of almost 7000 boats – hit the beaches, and tens of thousands of soldiers from the USA, UK, Canada and elsewhere began pouring onto French soil.

Most of the 135,000 Allied troops stormed ashore along 80km of beach north of Bayeux code-named (from west to east) Utah and Omaha (in the US sector) and Gold, Juno and Sword (in the British and Canadian ones). The landings on D-Day –

called Jour J in French – were followed by the Battle of Normandy, which would lead to the liberation of Europe from Nazi occupation. In the 76 days of fighting, the Allies suffered 210,000 casualties, including 37,000 deaths. German casualties are believed to be around 200,000, and another 200,000 German soldiers were taken prisoner. Le Mémorial de Caen provides the best introduction to the history of what took place here and also attempts to explain the rationale behind each event. Once on the coast, travellers can take a well-marked circuit that links the battle sites, close to where holiday-makers sunbathe.

Fat Norman cows with udders the size of beach balls use the bombed-out bunkers to shield themselves from the wind. Many of the villages near the D-Day beaches have small museums with war memorabilia on display collected by local people after the fighting.

Maps of the D-Day beaches are available at *tabacs* (tobacconists), newsagents and bookshops in Bayeux and elsewhere. The best one is called *D-Day 6.6.44 Jour J* and costs 29FF. The area is also known as the Côte du Nacre (Mother-of-Pearl Coast).

## BAYEUX
### postcode 14700 • pop 15,000

Stately Bayeux is the proud possessor of the only pictorial record of William the Conqueror's trans-Channel invasion in 1066 – the Bayeux Tapestry. This invaluable stretch of embroidered cloth is the magnet for several million tourists each year and, with a majestic cathedral, the British War Cemetery and museums of art, lace and WWII, a visitor can easily pass an absorbing day or two here. The River Aure cuts through the town centre composed of austere stone buildings, some dating as far back as the 16th century. Bayeux was the first town liberated after the D-Day landings and is one of the few in Calvados to have survived WWII unscathed.

### Orientation

Cathédrale Notre Dame, the major landmark in the centre of Bayeux and visible

# BAYEUX

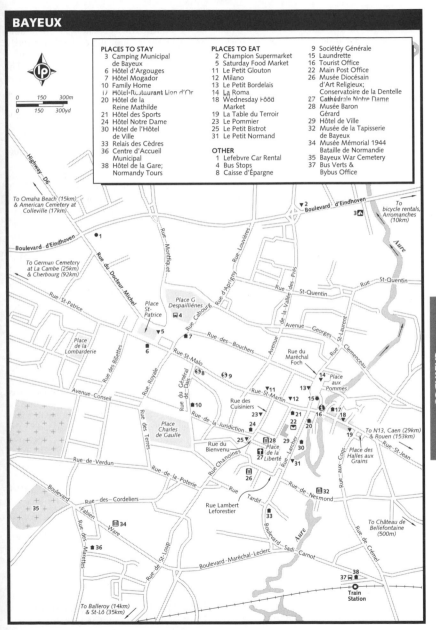

**PLACES TO STAY**
3 Camping Municipal
  de Bayeux
6 Hôtel d'Argouges
7 Hôtel Mogador
10 Family Home
17 Hôtel-Restaurant Lion d'Or
20 Hôtel de la
   Reine Mathilde
21 Hôtel des Sports
24 Hôtel Notre Dame
30 Hôtel de l'Hôtel
   de Ville
33 Relais des Cèdres
36 Centre d'Accueil
   Municipal
38 Hôtel de la Gare;
   Normandy Tours

**PLACES TO EAT**
2 Champion Supermarket
5 Saturday Food Market
11 Le Petit Glouton
12 Milano
13 Le Petit Bordelais
14 La Roma
18 Wednesday Food
   Market
19 La Table du Terroir
23 Le Pommier
25 Le Petit Bistrot
31 Le Petit Normand

**OTHER**
1 Lefebvre Car Rental
4 Bus Stops
8 Caisse d'Épargne

9 Sociétéy Générale
15 Laundrette
16 Tourist Office
22 Main Post Office
26 Musée Diocésain
   d'Art Religieux;
   Conservatoire de la Dentelle
27 Cathédrale Notre Dame
28 Musée Baron
   Gérard
29 Hôtel de Ville
32 Musée de la Tapisserie
   de Bayeux
34 Musée Mémorial 1944
   Bataille de Normandie
35 Bayeux War Cemetery
37 Bus Verts &
   Bybus Office

**CALVADOS**

throughout the town, is 1km north-west of the train station. The River Aure, with several attractive little mills along its banks, flows northwards on the eastern side of the centre.

## Information

**Tourist Office** The tourist office (☎ 02 31 51 28 28, fax 02 31 51 28 29, @ bayeux-tourisme@mail.cpod.fr) is at pont St-Jean, just off the northern end of rue Larcher. It opens 9 am to noon and 2 to 6 pm Monday to Saturday year round; and 9.30 am to noon and 2.30 to 6 pm Sunday, July and August. Staff book accommodation for a 10FF fee.

A multipass ticket *(billet jumelé)* valid for four of the museums listed in this section (Musée de la Tapisserie de Bayeux, Musée Diocésain d'Art Religieux, Musée Baron Gérard and Conservatoire de la Dentelle) is available at each costs 41FF (16FF students).

**Money** There's a Société Générale at 26 rue St-Malo, and a Caisse d'Épargne at No 59 on the same street. The tourist office will change money when the banks are closed (Monday and public holidays). The post office also exchanges currency.

**Post & Communications** The main post office, near the town hall at 14 rue Larcher, opens 8 am to 6.30 pm Monday to Friday and to noon on Saturday. It has Cyberposte. You can use the Internet at the tourist office (25FF per 15 minutes, with a Cyberis card bought from the counter).

**Laundry** The laundrette at 13 rue du Maréchal Foch opens 7 am to 10 pm daily.

## Bayeux Tapestry

The world-famous Bayeux Tapestry – actually a 70m-long strip of coarse embroidered linen – was commissioned by Bishop Odo of Bayeux, half-brother of William the Conqueror, sometime between the Norman invasion of England in 1066 and 1082. The tapestry, which was probably made in England, recounts the dramatic story of the Norman invasion and the events that led up

to it – from the Norman perspective. The story is told in 58 panels, with action-packed scenes following each other in quick succession. The events are accompanied by written commentary in dog Latin. The scenes are filled with depictions of 11th-century Norman and Saxon dress, food, tools, cooking utensils and weapons. The Saxons are depicted with moustaches and the backs of the Norman soldiers' heads are shaved. Halley's Comet, which passed through our part of the solar system in 1066, also makes an appearance.

The tapestry is housed in the **Musée de la Tapisserie de Bayeux** (☎ 02 31 51 25 50) on rue de Nesmond. It opens 9 or 9.30 am to 12.30 pm and 2 to 6 pm, mid-September to April; to 7 pm without a midday break the rest of the year. Admission with the multipass ticket costs 41FF (students 16FF). The excellent taped commentary (5FF) makes viewing the upstairs exhibits a bit unnecessary. A 14-minute film on the 2nd floor is screened eight to 13 times a day in English (last showing 5.15 pm, or 5.45 pm May to mid-September).

## Cathédrale Notre Dame

Most of Bayeux's spectacular cathedral, a fine example of Norman Gothic architecture, dates from the 13th century, though the crypt, the arches of the nave and the lower portions of the towers on either side of the main entrance are 11th-century Romanesque. The central tower was added in the 15th century; the copper dome dates from the 1860s. The cathedral opens 8.30 am to 6 pm daily (8 am to 7 pm July and August).

## Musée Diocésain d'Art Religieux

The Diocesan Museum of Religious Art (☎ 02 31 92 14 21), an Aladdin's cave of vestments and liturgical objects, is just south of the cathedral at 6 rue Lambert Leforestier. It opens 10 am to 12.30 pm and 2 to 6 pm daily (9 am to 7 pm July to September). Admission costs the same as for the Musée de la Tapisserie de Bayeux.

## Conservatoire de la Dentelle

The fascinating Lace Conservatory (☎ 02

# THE BAYEUX TAPESTRY

Nine and a half centuries ago, William the Bastard sailed across the English Channel with 6000 men and defeated Harold at the Battle of Hastings to become William the Conqueror, King of England. It was the epic that defined the 11th century in much the same way as the D-Day landings defined the 20th century in Europe. The Norman Conquest changed the course of history and the Normans had no doubt that they were right to vanquish the duplicitous Harold.

Bayeux's Bishop Odo, along with an unknown artist and a team of highly skilled embroiderers, set out to tell this tale of ambition, betrayal, war and conquest. The result was the splendid Bayeux Tapestry. From Harold's journey to Normandy, to his broken oath of loyalty to William and defeat at the Battle of Hastings, the tapestry is a vivid pictorial record of the Norman Conquest of England and a window upon 11th-century life.

The tapestry is really a 70m-long piece of embroidered linen, once called 'Queen Matilda's tapestry' in the erroneous belief that William the Conqueror's wife was responsible for it. It is unlikely that the busy Queen could have executed the work herself however and, if she had, the tapestry would have ended up in Caen, where she and William lived, rather than Bayeux. Because the earliest reference to the tapestry indicates that it hung in Bayeux's cathedral, scholars believe that Bishop Odo of Bayeux, William's half-brother, commissioned it for the opening of the cathedral in 1077. The Bishop was energetic and ambitious, and appears no less than four times in the tapestry.

Bishop Odo was also the earl of Kent and probably assigned the job to the renowned school for decorative embroidery in Canterbury. The distinctively English spelling of the Latin inscriptions on the tapestry argue in favour of English involvement in the tapestry's production. Women may have embroidered the tapestry, but the realism and detail of the battle scenes indicate that a man must have designed it.

**Top:** Harold takes one in the eye! (By special permission of the City of Bayeux)

**Right:** Harold of Wessex gives his oath to William that the Crown of England will pass to Normandy. (The Bayeux Tapestry – 11th Century)

## The Bayeux Tapestry

Bishop Odo knew that he had an important story to tell future generations and made sure that his tapestry would be around to tell it. The two-ply wool on coarse linen has weathered well, especially given the tapestry's turbulent history. In 1792, the tapestry was narrowly saved from use as a wagon cover, and in 1794 it was almost cut up into decorative little pieces. Napoleon displayed it in Paris for a few years to drum up support for an invasion of England, but the tapestry was eventually returned to Bayeux where the priceless work underwent a careful restoration. In 1939 it was placed in an air-raid shelter, then in 1944 it was sent to Paris and hidden in a cellar of the Louvre.

The tapestry tells the story of the Norman Conquest cartoon style with 58 scenes, briefly captioned in Latin, and a cast of hundreds. The main narrative fills up the centre of the canvas while the daily life of Norman France unfolds in the top and bottom edges. In addition to the lead roles, William (the Good) and Harold (the Bad), and supporting players King Edward and Bishop Odo, there are 619 extras, from knights and nobles to peasants ploughing the fields. Like modern blockbusters, it's a man's story – there are only five female figures – with men's labours, animals, weapons, feasts and battles rendered in startling detail.

From the tapestry we have learned that 11th-century Saxons wore moustaches and had long hair, while the Normans were clean-shaven. Military outfits are scrupulously rendered. We see that weapons decorated with dragon motifs were popular on both sides, that the Saxons preferred to fight with battle axes and that they had few archers during the Battle of Hastings. We see men hunting birds with a sling, felling trees and sharpening axes. Animals were an important part of 11th-century life – there are over 200 horses galloping and prancing across the tapestry; 55 dogs hunting, playing or dashing into battle; and hundreds of birds including eagles, falcons and peacocks.

One scene is entirely devoted to a Norman feast; birds are roasting on a spit while a baker takes loaves of bread from an oven and a servant announces the meal with a horn.

Norman spiritual life included myths, fables, superstitions and

**Left:** Norman servants cook up a pre-battle feast.
(The Bayeux Tapestry – 11th Century)

astrology, all of which are alluded to in the tapestry. The Normans considered Halley's Comet to be an important omen and its appearance in 1066 is depicted in the tapestry along with a cluster of clearly astonished onlookers. Mythical creatures decorate the upper and lower borders of the tapestry. There are griffins with the head and wings of an eagle but the body of a lion; fish that represent the Pisces constellation; dragons; and half-man, half-beast figures. Aesop's fable of an ape asking a lion to become king of the animals is depicted in the tapestry, with the implication that Harold is the ape and William is the lion.

There are a few mysterious panels in the tapestry that seem to refer to events that were a matter of local 11th-century gossip, further evidence that the tapestry was made soon after the Norman Conquest. A woman stands under the caption 'where a certain clerk and Aelfgyva'. A man in a clerical outfit appears to be chastising her. Who is Aelfgyva? Was she involved in a scandal? Is that the significance of the

**Top:** Halley's Comet, which appeared in 1066, was widely regarded as an important omen.

**Right:** William's army marches on past Mont St-Michel. (The Bayeux Tapestry – 11th Century)

# The Bayeux Tapestry

BY SPECIAL PERMISSION OF THE CITY OF BAYEUX

naked man squatting beneath her? The reference remains obscure.

The epic moves to a thrilling climax at the Battle of Hastings. A woman flees a burning house; cavaliers hurl javelins; archers unleash their arrows and men tumble to the ground, their bodies broken and their heads severed. The artist's conception of battle seems curiously modern; there is more death than glory on this battlefield. Finally Harold falls, either by an arrow in the eye or under the hooves of a Norman horse. Some scholars identify Harold as the man under the final inscription while others place him in the middle of the picture. With the death of Harold the battle is over and the tapestry ends with the fleeing English soldiers.

The farthest border of the tapestry is unfinished, indicating that there may have been another scene. Having vanquished the faithless Harold, William became the king of England – an image that might have furnished the tapestry's final scene.

BY SPECIAL PERMISSION OF THE CITY OF BAYEUX

**Top:** The sands of Mont St-Michel bay were as troublesome in 1066 as they can be today!

**Left:** The Battle of Hastings draws to a close when King Harold is finally killed. (The Bayeux Tapestry – 11th Century)

31 92 73 80) is dedicated to the preservation of traditional Norman lace-making. It is claimed that this is the only place where you can watch some of France's most celebrated lace-makers, who are creating the intricate designs using dozens of bobbins and hundreds of pins.

The Conservatory also gives lace-making classes and sells materials (pins, bobbins, thread and so on). Small lace objects, the product of something like 50 hours work, are on sale for around 750FF. The museum opens 10 am to 12.30 pm and 2 to 6 pm daily, October to June; 9 am to 7 pm the rest of the year. Admission costs the same as for the Musée de la Tapisserie de Bayeux.

### Musée Baron Gérard

This pleasant museum (☎ 02 31 92 14 21), near the cathedral at place de la Liberté, specialises in local porcelain, lace and 15th- to 19th-century paintings (Italian, Flemish, Impressionist). In front of the museum is a huge plane tree known as the Arbre de la Liberté, which, like many such 'Freedom Trees', was planted in the years after the Revolution. It is one of only nine left in France. The museum opens 10 am to 12.30 pm and 2 to 6 pm daily, mid-September to May; 9 am to 7 pm the rest of the year. Admission costs the same as for the Musée de la Tapisserie de Bayeux.

### Musée Mémorial 1944 Bataille de Normandie

Bayeux's huge war museum (☎ 02 31 92 93 41), boulevard Fabien Ware, rather haphazardly displays thousands of photos, uniforms, weapons, newspaper clippings and lifelike scenes associated with D-Day and the Battle of Normandy. It opens 10 am to 12.30 pm and 2 to 6 pm daily, mid-September to April and 9.30 am to 6.30 pm daily May to mid-September. Admission costs 33FF (students 16FF). A 30-minute film in English is screened two to five times a day (always at 10.45 am and 5 pm).

### Bayeux War Cemetery

This peaceful cemetery, on boulevard Fabien Ware a few hundred metres west of the war museum, is the largest of the 18 Commonwealth military cemeteries in Normandy. It contains 4868 graves of soldiers from the UK and 10 other countries. Many of the 466 Germans buried here were never identified, and the headstones are simply marked 'Ein Deutscher Soldat' (A German Soldier). There is an explanatory plaque in the small chapel to the right as you enter the grounds. The large structure across boulevard Fabien Ware commemorates the 1807 Commonwealth soldiers missing in action.

### Special Events

The Fêtes Médiévales de Bayeux takes place the first weekend in July to commemorate the anniversary of the Battle of Formigny which put an end to the Hundred Years' War. Expect medieval songs, dances, parades and street theatre. In July and August the city sponsors a series of concerts around town for the Eté Musical (Musical Summer). The tourist office has the schedule.

### Places to Stay

**Camping** About 2km north of the town centre, just south of boulevard d'Eindhoven, is *Camping Municipal de Bayeux* (☎ 02 31 92 08 43). It opens mid-March to mid-November and you can check in from 8 to 9 am and 5 to 7 pm (7 am to 9 pm in July and August). A tent site costs 9.20FF, adults 17.10FF and children aged over seven 9.20FF. Bus No 3 stops three times daily at Les Cerisiers, near the camp site.

A few tents can be pitched in the back garden of *Family Home* hostel (see Hostels) for about 30FF per person including breakfast.

**Hostels** An excellent old hostel and a great place to meet other travellers is *Family Home* (☎ 02 31 92 15 22, fax 02 31 92 55 72, 39 rue du Général de Dais). A bed in a dorm room costs 105FF (95FF if you've got a Hostelling International card) including breakfast. Singles cost 160FF. The hostel opens all day, but curfew is (theoretically) at 11 pm; just ask for a key to the main door. Multicourse French dinners including wine cost 65FF. Vegetarian dishes are available on request or you can cook for yourself.

CALVADOS

The **Centre d'Accueil Municipal** (☎ 02 31 92 08 19, 21 rue des Marettes) is in a large, modern building 1km south-west of the cathedral. Antiseptic but comfy singles (all that's available) are a great deal at 90FF including breakfast. Telephone reservations are usually accepted.

**Chambres d'Hôtes** The tourist office has a list of chambres d'hôtes in the Bayeux area. The cheapest cost about 150FF for two people with breakfast.

**Hotels** The old but well-maintained **Hôtel de la Gare** (☎ 02 31 92 10 70, fax 02 31 51 95 99, 26 place de la Gare) has singles/doubles from 85/100FF. Two-bed triples/quads are 160FF and showers are free. There are no late trains so it's usually pretty quiet at night.

**Hôtel de l'Hôtel de Ville** (☎ 02 31 92 30 08, 31 ter rue Larcher) has large, quiet rooms for 140/160FF including free showers. An extra bed costs 50FF. Telephone reservations aren't accepted.

**Hôtel des Sports** (☎ 02 31 92 28 53, 19 rue St-Martin) is a cut above, with tastefully appointed rooms (most with shower or free use of those in the hall) starting at 160/200FF.

**Relais des Cèdres** (☎ 02 31 21 98 07, 1 boulevard Sadi Carnot) is an old mansion done up in 'French country' style. Doubles cost 150FF with washbasin and toilet, 200FF with shower, and 250FF with shower or bath and toilet. Showers are free.

**Hôtel Notre Dame** (☎ 02 31 92 87 24, fax 02 31 92 67 11, 44 rue des Cuisiniers) is a family-run hotel-restaurant with an impressive view of the western facade of the cathedral. Doubles cost 250FF to 270FF with shower or bath, but they have cheaper rooms without a shower for 160FF. Hall showers cost 20FF.

For a few more francs, there's the **Hôtel Mogador** (☎ 02 31 92 24 58, fax 02 31 92 24 85, 20 rue Alain Chartier), a two-star establishment with calm, comfortable rooms, some of which face a pleasant interior courtyard. Beamed ceilings and the old-fashioned decor add a touch of warmth. The single/double rooms here cost from 260/290FF.

**Hôtel de la Reine Mathilde** (☎ 02 31 92 08 13, fax 02 31 92 09 93, 23 rue Larcher) is another pleasant option; the rooms are named after Anglo-Saxon kings and queens, who probably would have been happy with the en-suite bathrooms. Rooms cost 285FF.

**Hôtel d'Argouges** (☎ 02 31 92 88 86, fax 02 31 92 09 93, @ dargouges@aol.com, 21 rue St-Patrice) is an 18th-century mansion with a peaceful inner garden and elegant rooms. It's within walking distance of the town centre and there are parking facilities. Rooms cost from 210FF to 550FF.

**Hôtel-Restaurant Lion d'Or** (☎ 02 31 92 06 90, fax 02 31 22 15 64, 71 rue St-Jean), is a sprawling three-star hotel in an old coaching inn, part of which dates from the 17th century. The cheerful rooms are quiet because they face a courtyard. Prices run from 370FF to 505FF depending on room size and view.

You can live like the duke of Normandy in **Château de Bellefontaine** (☎ 02 31 22 00 10, fax 02 31 22 19 09, 49 rue de Bellefontaine), about 500m east of the train station in a groomed five-acre park. A canal runs through the property and the hotel is in a luxuriously renovated 18th-century building. The best rooms are Nos 4, 5 and 6, which have chimneys and views over the park. Rooms cost from 450FF to 700FF.

## Places to Eat

**Restaurants** Serving traditional Norman food prepared with apple cider, **Le Petit Normand** (☎ 02 31 22 88 66, 35 rue Larcher) is popular with English tourists. Simple fixed-price *menus* start at 58FF; more expensive *menus* cost 78/98/128FF. The restaurant opens daily July and August; daily except Wednesday and Sunday evening in summer (closed Thursday also in winter).

**Milano** (☎ 02 31 92 15 10, 18 rue St-Martin) serves very good pizza. It opens 11.30 am to 10 pm Monday to Saturday and also opens Sunday in June and August.

The food at the **Hôtel Notre Dame** (see Places to Stay earlier) provides good value for money; count on 60FF for a lunch *menu* and 95FF per person minimum at dinner for traditional Norman cuisine. It opens daily (except Sunday lunch and Monday, November to March). *Le Petit Bistrot (☎ 02 31 51 85 40, 2 rue du Bienvenu)* is a charming little eatery with excellent fish and duck *menus* from 98FF. It opens daily except Sunday and Monday.

*Le Pommier (☎ 02 31 21 52 10, 40 rue des Cuisiniers)* turns out impeccably executed Norman dishes such as *filet mignon* (a small fillet steak) in Camembert sauce and a compote of rabbit in cider. *Menus* cost 76FF (lunch) and 145FF (dinner).

For a change of pace try *La Roma (☎ 02 31 51 94 14, 1–3 place aux Pommes)*, which serves authentic Italian pastas, fish and meat dishes. The *plat du jour* costs 59FF and there's an 82FF two-course *menu*. The restaurant opens daily except Monday evening and Sunday.

For lunch pop into *Le Petit Bordelais (☎ 02 31 92 06 44, 15 rue du Maréchal Foch)*, a tiny wine bar that is an extension of a wine cellar. The vintages are inexpensive and good to wash down the 47FF *plat du jour* or an assortment of cheeses (35FF). The wine bar opens noon to 7 pm from Tuesday to Saturday but meals are served only between noon and 2.30 pm.

Meat is king at *La Table du Terroir (☎ 02 31 92 05 53, 42 rue St-Jean)*, with excellent Norman-style *menus* costing from 60FF during the week. The restaurant is an extension of a butcher shop so the cuts are of high quality. The big wooden tables here attract plenty of tourists but locals come as well. It opens daily except Sunday evening and Monday.

**Self-Catering** There are lots of takeaway shops along or near rue St-Martin and rue St-Jean including *Le Petit Glouton (42 rue St-Martin)*.

Rue St-Jean has an open-air *food market* on Wednesday morning, as does place St-Patrice on Saturday morning. Don't miss *tergoule*, a sweet, cinnamon-flavoured rice pudding typical of the Bayeux region.

The *Champion* supermarket across the road from the Camping Municipal opens 9 am to 8 pm Monday to Saturday.

## Entertainment

Bayeux is not known for its hot nightlife but there are frequent concerts and theatrical events staged in venues around town. The free booklet *Sorties Plurielles* highlights the various concerts, exhibitions and festivals in Bayeux and is available at the tourist office.

## Getting There & Away

**Bus** Bus Verts (☎ 02 31 92 02 92, or ☎ 02 31 44 77 44 in Caen) offers rather infrequent services from the train station and place St-Patrice to Caen, the D-Day beaches (see Getting There & Away under D-Day Beaches later), Vire and elsewhere in the Calvados department. The schedules are arranged for the convenience of school children coming into Bayeux for school in the morning and going home in the afternoon. The Bus Verts office, across the car park from the train station, opens 10 am to noon and 3 to 6 pm Monday to Friday, year round except most of July.

**Train** Services from Bayeux include Paris' Gare St-Lazare (171FF) via Caen (31FF, 20 minutes, 15 a day) as well as Cherbourg (81FF, one hour, 10 a day). There's a service to Quimper (266FF, 5¾ hours, three a day) via Rennes.

## Getting Around

**Bus** The local bus line, Bybus (☎ 02 31 92 02 92), which shares an office with Bus Verts, has two routes traversing Bayeux, all of which end up at place St-Patrice. From the train station, take bus No 3 (direction J Cocteau). The bus service is geared to students and is thus infrequent. There's no bus service on Sunday.

**Bicycle** Family Home (see Places to Stay earlier in the chapter) rents out 10-speed bicycles for 60FF per day plus 100FF deposit. Tandem (☎ 02 31 92 03 50) and Roué (☎ 02 31 92 27 75), both on boulevard Winston Churchill, also rent out bikes.

**Taxi** You can order a taxi 24 hours a day on ☎ 02 31 92 92 40 or ☎ 02 31 92 04 10.

CALVADOS

## AROUND BAYEUX
### Balleroy

Fourteen kilometres south-west of Bayeux, Balleroy is a humble village with a grand avenue leading to a grandiose **chateau** (☎ 02 31 21 60 61). In 1631, one of Louis XIII's top advisors commissioned François Mansart, the most prestigious architect of the day, to construct a magnificent residence. For centuries the counts of Balleroy presided over the grounds, but in 1970 leather-clad press prince Malcolm Forbes bought the property and restored it. He also created a museum devoted to ballooning, a hobby he pursued avidly in his time away from running *Forbes* magazine. Balloon history and examples of elephant, sphinx, Beethoven and minaret balloons are amusing even if you're not allowed to forget Forbes, his exploits, his friends or his magazine for an instant. Every two years in the third week of June there's a balloon festival (the next one is in June 2003) on the grounds of the chateau. In case you're not a balloon buff, there's always the sumptuously outfitted residential area to explore. Staid royal portraits, oak panelling and floors alternate with more whimsical features such as a ceiling painted with, you've guessed it, balloons. The chateau and museum open 9 am to noon and 2 to 6 pm daily except Tuesday, mid-March to mid-October; and 10 am to 6 pm daily in July and August. Admission costs 45FF (students 35FF). There's no public transport to the chateau.

## ARROMANCHES
postcode 14117 • pop 552

To make it possible to unload the quantities of cargo necessary, the Allies established two prefabricated ports code-named Mulberry Harbours. The harbour established at Omaha Beach was completely destroyed by a ferocious gale just two weeks after D-Day, but one of them, Port Winston, can still be viewed at Arromanches, a seaside town 10km north-east of Bayeux.

The harbour consists of 146 massive cement caissons towed from England and sunk to form a semicircular breakwater in which floating bridge spans were moored. In the three months after D-Day, 2.5 million men, four million tonnes of equipment and 500,000 vehicles were unloaded there. At low tide you can walk out to many of the caissons. The best view of Port Winston is from the hill, east of town, topped with a statue of the Virgin Mary.

In addition to its historical interest, Arromanches is a low-key resort with a wide, sandy beach. The tourist office (☎ 02 31 22 36 45, fax 02 31 22 95 06, e off-tour@mail.cpod.fr), 2 rue Maréchal Joffre, is one block in from the sea. It opens 10 am to 12.30 pm and 1.30 to 5 pm except in July and August when it opens 9 am to 7 pm. You can change money there and there's a list of chambres d'hôtes. Check out the Web site at www.arromanches.com for more information.

### Things to See & Do

The well-regarded **Musée du Débarquement** (Invasion Museum; ☎ 02 31 22 34 31), on place de 6 Juin right in the centre of Arromanches, explains the logistics and importance of Port Winston and makes a good first stop before visiting the beaches. The museum opens 9 am to 6 pm daily except Monday, April; 9 am to 7 pm May to September; and 9.30 am to 5 pm October to December and February to March. It closes throughout January. Admission costs 35FF (20FF students). The last guided tour (in French, with text in English) leaves 45 minutes before closing time. An unimpressive seven-minute slide show in English is held throughout the day.

### Places to Stay & Eat

The *Camping Municipal* (☎ 02 31 22 36 78, avenue de Verdun) is a block away from the tourist office. *Hôtel de la Marine* (☎ 02 31 22 34 19, fax 02 31 22 98 80, 2 quai du Canada) is right on the sea and has renovated rooms that run from 300FF to 390FF depending on whether there's a view. *Hôtel d'Arromanches* (☎ 02 31 22 36 26, fax 02 31 22 23 29, 2 rue du Colonel René Michel) is a block inland and has comfortable rooms for 320FF. Both hotels have good restaurants. Friendly brasserie *Le 6 Juin* (☎ 02 31 22 34 84, 27 rue du Maréchal Joffre) has daily specials beginning at 35FF.

## LONGUES-SUR-MER

The massive 152mm German guns on the coast near Longues-sur-Mer, 6km west of Arromanches, were designed to hit targets some 20km away, which in June 1944 included both Gold Beach (to the east) and Omaha Beach (to the west). Half a century later, the mammoth artillery pieces are still sitting in their colossal concrete emplacements. (In wartime they were covered with camouflage nets and tufts of grass.)

Parts of an American film about D-Day, *The Longest Day* (1962), were filmed both here and at Pointe du Hoc. On clear days, Bayeux's cathedral, 8km away, is visible to the south.

## OMAHA & JUNO BEACHES

The most brutal fighting on D-Day took place 15km north-west of Bayeux along 7km of coastline known as Omaha Beach, which had to be abandoned in storms two weeks later. As you stand on the gently sloping sand, try to imagine how the US soldiers must have felt running inland towards the German positions on the nearby ridge. A memorial marks the site of the first US military cemetery on French soil, where soldiers killed on the beach were buried. Their remains were later reinterred at the American Military Cemetery at Colleville-sur-Mer or in the USA.

These days, Omaha Beach is lined with holiday cottages and is popular with swimmers and sunbathers. Little evidence of the war remains apart from a single concrete boat used to carry tanks ashore and, 1km farther west, the bunkers and munitions sites of a German fortified point (look for the tall obelisk on the hill).

Dune-lined Juno Beach, 12km east of Arromanches, was stormed by Canadian troops on D-Day. A Cross of Lorraine marks the spot where General Charles de Gaulle came ashore shortly after the landings.

## AMERICAN MILITARY CEMETERY

The American Military Cemetery (☎ 02 31 51 62 00), Colleville-sur-Mer, 17km northwest of Bayeux contains the graves of 9386

American soldiers. The remains of an additional 14,000 soldiers were repatriated to the USA.

The huge, immaculately tended expanse of lawn, with white crosses and Stars of David, set on a hill overlooking Omaha Beach, testifies to the extent of the killings that took place in this area in 1944. At the overlook is an orientation table marked with the landing sites of all the invasion forces, making it easy to visualise the D-Day actions. Steps and a path to the beach lead down from the orientation table.

There's a large colonnaded memorial with a map carved into the north loggia showing the progress of the invasion forces across Europe. Behind the memorial is a wall inscribed with the names of 1557 soldiers missing in action whose remains were never found. Opposite the visitor centre and embedded in the lawn is a time capsule containing news reports of the invasion. It is dedicated to the journalists who covered the war and is due to be opened 6 June 2044. A reflecting pond and a chapel encourage silent meditation.

Veterans are invited to sign a special register at the visitor centre. The visitor centre will also help you locate a specific tomb. The cemetery opens 8 am to 5 pm (9 am to 6 pm from mid-April to mid-October). It can be reached from Bayeux by Bus Verts' bus No 70, but the service is infrequent. Bus No 44 from Caen also stops here.

## POINTE DU HOC RANGER MEMORIAL

At 7.10 am on 6 June 1944, 225 US Army Rangers scaled the 30m cliffs at Pointe du Hoc, where the Germans had emplaced a battery of huge artillery guns. The guns, as it turned out, had been transferred elsewhere, but the Americans captured the gun emplacements (the two huge circular cement structures) and the German command post (next to the two flagpoles) and then fought off German counterattacks for two days. By the time they were relieved on 8 June, 81 of the rangers had been killed and 58 more had been wounded.

Today the site, which France turned over

in perpetuity to the US government in 1979, looks much as it did half a century ago. The ground is still pockmarked with 3m bomb craters. Visitors can walk among and inside the German fortifications, but they are warned not to dig; there may still be mines and explosive materials below the surface. In the German command post, you can see where the wooden ceilings were charred by American flame-throwers. As you face the sea, Utah Beach, which runs roughly perpendicular to the cliffs here, is 14km to the left. Pointe du Hoc, which is 12km west of the American Military Cemetery, is always open. The command post is open the same hours as the cemetery.

## ORGANISED TOURS

A bus tour is an excellent way to see the D-Day beaches. Normandy Tours (☎ 02 31 92 10 70), based at the Hôtel de la Gare in Bayeux, has four-hour tours stopping at Longues-sur-Mer, Arromanches, Omaha Beach, the American Military Cemetery and Pointe du Hoc for 200FF (students/children 150FF). Times and itineraries are flexible.

Bus Fly (☎ 02 31 22 00 08) is best booked through the Family Home hostel (see Places to Stay under Bayeux earlier in the chapter). An afternoon tour to major D-Day sites costs 200FF (students 180FF), including museum admission fees. They'll collect you from your hotel or the tourist office in Bayeux. See Organised Tours under Caen for details of tours of the beaches from Caen.

## GETTING THERE & AWAY
### Bus

Bus No 70 run by Bus Verts (☎ 02 31 92 02 92 in Bayeux, ☎ 02 31 44 77 44 in Caen) goes westwards to the American Military Cemetery at Colleville-sur-Mer and Omaha Beach, and onto Pointe du Hoc and the town of Grandcamp-Maisy. Bus No 74 (No 75 during summer) serves Arromanches, Gold and Juno beaches, and Courseulles. During July and August only, the Côte du Nacre line goes to Caen via Arromanches, Gold, Juno and Sword beaches, and Ouistreham; and Circuit 44 links Bayeux and Caen via Pointe du Hoc, the American Military Cemetery, Arromanches and Le Mémorial de Caen.

### Car

For three or more people, renting a car can be cheaper than a tour. Lefebvre Car Rental (☎ 02 31 92 05 96), on boulevard d'Eindhoven (at the Esso petrol station) in Bayeux, charges 350FF per day with 200km free (more than enough for a circuit to the beaches along coastal route D514) and 699FF for two days with 400km free. The office opens 8 am to 8 pm daily.

*euro currency converter  10FF = €1.52*

# Manche

The department of Manche, surrounded on three sides by the English Channel (La Manche), includes the entire Cotentin Peninsula. Its 320km-coastline stretches from Utah Beach north-westwards to the port city of Cherbourg and then south to the magnificent Mont St-Michel. The fertile inland areas, criss-crossed with hedgerows, produce an abundance of cattle, dairy products and apples.

Sadly, over the past 20 years, part of the Manche region has become known as 'Europe's nuclear dump'. On the peninsula's western tip at Cap de la Hague is France's first nuclear waste treatment plant, which is well hidden until you reach its heavily fortified perimeter. Farther south at Flamanville is a sprawling nuclear power plant, and at the Cherbourg shipyards the latest nuclear submarines are built.

Trains run to and from Cherbourg, but local buses are few and far between in the Manche region.

## Cotentin Peninsula

The Cotentin Peninsula's north-western corner is especially lovely, with unspoiled stretches of rocky coastline sheltering tranquil bays and villages. Due west lie the Channel Islands of Jersey (25km from the coast) and Guernsey (45km), accessible by ferry from St-Malo in Brittany and, in season, from the Norman towns of Carteret, Granville and Dielette.

### CHERBOURG
**postcode 50100 • pop 25,000**
At the tip of the Cotentin Peninsula sits Cherbourg, one of the largest artificial ports in the world. Transatlantic cargo ships, passenger ferries from Britain, yachts, warships and nearly everything else that floats on water pass in and out of Cherbourg's monumental port. It was Napoleon's idea to build a port here in preparation for the Eng-

### Highlights

- Watching the high tide roll in at Mont St-Michel
- Hiking the coast between the Nez de Jobourg and the Baie d'Ecalgrain
- Partying at the Granville carnival
- Experiencing the splendour of Coutances' cathedral
- Examining the illuminated manuscripts at Avranches
- Shopping for copper pots in Villedieu-les-Poêles

lish invasion he never got around to launching. Napoleon III completed the project around the same time that the Paris to Cherbourg railroad line opened in 1831. The port welcomed transatlantic passenger ships at the turn of the century and took on an enormous strategic importance during the D-Day landings. As the region's only deep water port, Cherbourg was indispensable in resupplying the invasion forces.

Cherbourg has a small old town huddled behind the sprawl of maritime installations, but the city is not nearly as romantic as that portrayed in Jacques Demy's 1964 classic film *Les Parapluies de Cherbourg* (The

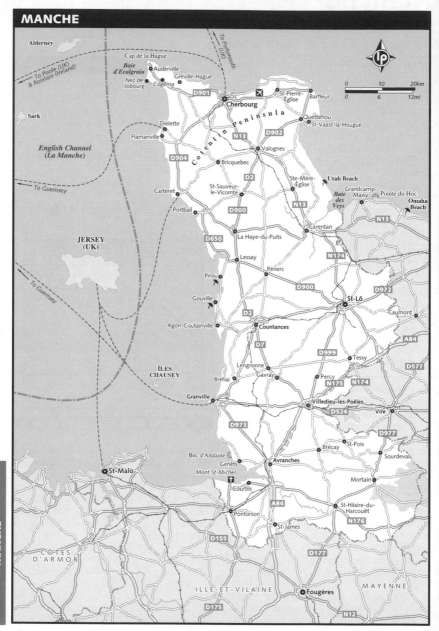

## MANCHE

**Alderney**

To Portsmouth (UK)

To Poole (UK) & Rosslare (Ireland)

Cap de la Hague
*Baie d'Eculgrain*
Auderville
*Nez de Jobourg*
Cogéma
Gréville-Hague

**D901**

**Cherbourg**

St-Pierre-Eglise
Barfleur

**Sark**

Quettehou
St-Vaast-la-Hougue

Dielette

**N13**

**D902**

Flamanville

Valognes

**English Channel (La Manche)**

**D904**

Bricquebec

To Guernsey

**D2**

Ste-Mère-Eglise

**Utah Beach**

**Baie des Veys**

Grandcamp-Maisy
Pointe du Hoc

**Omaha Beach**

Carteret

St-Sauveur-le-Vicomte

Portbail

**N13**

**N13**

**JERSEY (UK)**

**D900**

Garentan

**N174**

La Haye-du-Puits

**D650**

Lessay

**D900**

St-Lô

**D972**

Pirou

Périers

Caumont

Gouville

**D2**

**A84**

Agon-Coutainville

Countances

**D577**

To Guernsey

**D7**

**D999**

Tessy

Lengronne

Percy

**ÎLES CHAUSEY**

Gavray

**N175**

**N174**

Bréhal

**Granville**

Villedieu-les-Poêles

**D524**

**Vire**

**D973**

**D977**

Brécay
St-Pois

Bec d'Andaine
Genêts

**Avranches**

Sourdeval

**St-Malo**

*Mont St-Michel*

Courtils

Mortain

**A84**

St-Hilaire-du-Harcouët

**MANCHE**

Pontorson

**N176**

St-James

**D155**

**CÔTES D'ARMOR**

**D177**

**ILLE-ET-VILAINE**

**MAYENNE**

**Fougères**

**D175**

**N12**

0  10  20km
0  6  12mi

Forget beer – cider is the preferred tipple here!

There's a *crêperie* round every corner in Calvados.

Fiery Calvados takes the sting out of a rainy day.

Cider, cider everywhere and not a drop to drink!

You'll be spoilt for choice with the local cheese.

MARTIN MOOS

Caen's triumphant Abbaye aux Hommes

HANNAH LEVY

Joan of Arc – heretic or French heroine?

HANNAH LEVY

The huge dome of Lisieux's Basilique St-Thérèse

MARTIN MOOS

Spectacular Cathédrale Notre Dame, Bayeux

Umbrellas of Cherbourg). There is an umbrella factory, although the city is no rainier than any other in Normandy. Residents even recall that the downpours and drizzles in the film were artificially produced. There are enough shops and cafes, as well as a couple of museums and a boat trip, to keep you occupied if you must spend time in Cherbourg, but there is little reason to go out of your way to visit it, particularly since it is not well connected to other sights on the Cotentin peninsula.

## Orientation

The Bassin du Commerce, a wide central waterway, separates the 'living' half of Cherbourg to the west from the deserted streets to the east. The attractive Avant Port (outer harbour) lies to the north.

## Information

**Tourist Offices** The tourist office (☎ 02 33 93 52 02, fax 02 33 53 66 97, e ville .cherbourg@wanadoo.fr), 2 quai Alexandre III, opens 9 am to noon and 2 to 6 pm weekdays and on Saturday morning (9 am to 6.30 pm Monday to Saturday, July and August). The annexe (☎ 02 33 44 39 92) at the ferry terminal opens 7 to 9 am and 2 to 3 pm daily. The tourist office makes hotel reservations for 10FF. Its Web site is at www.ville-cherbourg.fr.

**Money** The Banque de France, 22 quai Alexandre III, exchanges money from 9 am to noon. Crédit Lyonnais is at 16 rue Maréchal Foch. The post office also exchanges currency.

**Post & Communications** The main post office, 1 rue de l'Ancien Quai, opens weekdays from 8 am to 7 pm and on Saturday until noon. It has Cyberposte.

The cybercafe in the upper floor of the Forum Espace Culture bookshop (☎ 02 33 78 19 30), place Centrale, charges 15FF per half-hour. It opens 2 to 7 pm on Monday and 10 am to 7 pm Tuesday to Saturday.

**Laundry** The laundrette at 62 rue au Blé opens 7 am to 8 pm daily.

## Musée Thomas Henry

This museum (☎ 02 33 23 02 23), upstairs in the cultural centre on rue Vastel, has 200 works by French, Flemish, Italian and other artists. Highlights include *Atalante et Maleagre* by Van Dyck, *Conversion de St-Augustin* by Fra Angelico and 30 paintings by Jean-François Millet, born in nearby Gréville-Hague, which alone make it worth the visit. The museum opens 9 am (10 am on Sunday) to noon and 2 to 6 pm daily; it is closed on Monday. Admission costs 15FF (students 7FF).

## Musée de la Liberation

Devoted to the role played by Cherbourg's port in the Battle of Normandy, this interesting museum (☎ 02 33 20 14 12) is housed in the strategically located Fort du Roule. Built under Napoleon III, the fort was intended to defend against an English attack. After falling into disuse, it was again occupied by French soldiers in the 1930s. On 19 June 1940 it finally fell to Field Marshal Rommel. The German troops stationed there put up a fierce resistance to Allied liberators In 1944, but the fort fell on 26 June. Photos, posters, and audiovisual aids document the period of the occupation and the fall of Cherbourg. The museum opens 6.30 am to noon and 2 to 5.30 pm Tuesday to Sunday, October to April; and 10 am to 6 pm daily, May to September.

## Organised Tours

From June to September *La Vega* (☎ 02 33 93 75 27) cruises Cherbourg harbour three times an afternoon (and once in the morning in July and August) for 1½ hours. It costs 46FF and the boat leaves from Port de Plaisance Chantereyne (pontoon J).

## Walking

The tourist office organises walks of 12km or more in the surrounding countryside some Saturdays from April to October, and every Saturday in July and August.

## Sailing

Cherbourg is a major sailing centre and an excellent place to learn the basics or polish

MANCHE

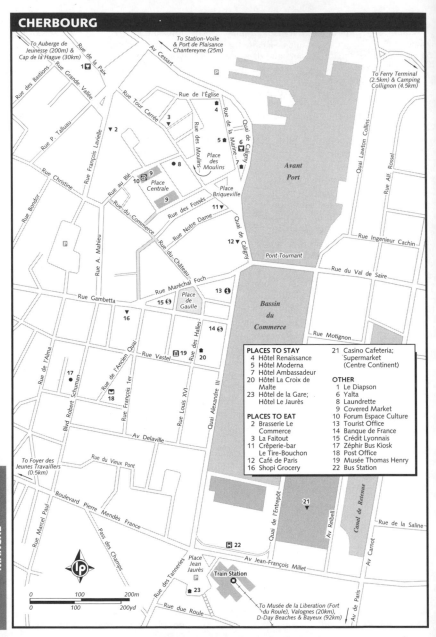

# CHERBOURG

To Auberge de
Jeunesse (200m) &
Cap de la Hague (30km)

To Station-Voile
& Port de Plaisance
Chantereyne (25m)

To Ferry Terminal
(2.5km) & Camping
Collignon (4.5km)

Rue de la Paix
Rue Grande Vallée
Av Cessart
Rue des Bastions
Rue P. Talluau
Rue François Lavieille
Rue Tour Carrée
Rue de l'Église
Rue Christine
Rue au blé
Rue du Commerce
Rue Bondor
Rue des Moulins
Rue de la Marne
Quai de Caligny
Place
des
Moulins
Place
Centrale
Place
Briqueville
Rue des Fossés
Rue Notre Dame
Rue du Château
Rue A. Mahieu
Quai de Caligny
Avant
Port
Quai Lawton Collins
Rue Alf Rossel
Rue Ingenieur Cachin
Pont Tournant
Rue du Val de Saire
Rue Maréchal Foch
Place
de
Gaulle
Rue Gambetta
Bassin
du
Commerce
Rue Motignon
Rue de l'Alma
Rue de l'Ancien Quai
Rue Vastel
Rue des Halles
Blvd Robert Schuman
Rue de François 1er
Rue Louis XVI
Quai Alexandre III
Av Delaville
To Foyer des
Jeunes Travailleurs
(0.5km)
Rue du Vieux Pont
Boulevard Pierre Mendès France
Rue Marcel Paul
Pass des Champs
Quai de l'Entrepôt
Av Reibell
Canal de Retenue
Rue de la Saline
Av Carnot
Av de Paris
Rue des Tarnettes
Place
Jean
Jaurès
Av Jean-François Millet
Train Station
Rue due Roule
To Musée de la Liberation (Fort
du Roule), Valognes (20km),
D-Day Beaches & Bayeux (92km)

0   100   200m
0   100   200yd

**MANCHE**

| PLACES TO STAY | 21 Casino Cafeteria; |
| --- | --- |
| 4 Hôtel Renaissance | Supermarket |
| 5 Hôtel Moderna | (Centre Continent) |
| 7 Hôtel Ambassadeur | |
| 20 Hôtel La Croix de | OTHER |
| Malte | 1 Le Diapson |
| 23 Hôtel de la Gare; | 6 Yalta |
| Hôtel Le Jaurès | 8 Laundrette |
| | 9 Covered Market |
| PLACES TO EAT | 10 Forum Espace Culture |
| 2 Brasserie Le | 13 Tourist Office |
| Commerce | 14 Banque de France |
| 3 La Faitout | 15 Crédit Lyonnais |
| 11 Crêperie-bar | 17 Zéphir Bus Kiosk |
| Le Tire-Bouchon | 18 Post Office |
| 12 Café de Paris | 19 Musée Thomas Henry |
| 16 Shopi Grocery | 22 Bus Station |

your skills. Station-Voile Cherbourg-Hague (☎ 02 33 78 19 29), at the entrance to the Port de Plaisance Chantereyne, offers sailing courses for 1200FF a week and a range of other watery activities such as kayaking, rowing and paragliding.

## Places to Stay

**Camping** The nearest camp site is *Camping Collignon* (☎ 02 33 20 16 88) in Tourlaville, on the coast about 5km northeast of town. It opens June to September. Adults pay 20FF each and 29FF for a tent site. Bus No 5 makes two runs a day Monday to Saturday from the train station and there are frequent shuttles *(navettes)* in summer. There's a large indoor swimming pool nearby.

**Hostels** The comfortable, ultra-modern *Auberge de Jeunesse* (☎ 02 33 78 15 15, fax 02 33 78 15 16, 55 rue de l'Abbaye) charges 70FF per night, including breakfast. Take bus No 3 or 5 to the Hôtel de Ville stop.

*Foyer des Jeunes Travaillers* (☎ 02 33 78 19 78, fax 02 33 53 51 76, 33 rue Maréchal Leclerc) is 1km from the centre of town but offers clean, efficient rooms for 80FF per person with shared bath, including breakfast. Rooms are doubles, triples, quads and quins. Take bus No 8 to the cemetery.

**Hotels** Quai de Caligny has plenty of mid-range options. There are cheaper places in the backstreets north of the tourist office. *Hôtel Moderna* (☎ 02 33 43 05 30, fax 02 33 43 97 37, 28 rue de la Marine), one block back from the harbour, has decent, basic rooms from 140FF (190FF with a shower).

*Hôtel Renaissance* (☎ 02 33 43 23 90, fax 02 33 43 96 10, 4 rue de l'Église) provides excellent value. The comfortable, well-equipped rooms (ask for a port view) are decorated in soft pastels. Singles/doubles without a shower start at 140/160FF or with a shower for 160/180FF. *Hôtel La Croix de Malte* (☎ 02 33 43 19 16, fax 02 33 43 65 66, 5 rue des Halles) near the sumptuous Théâtre de Cherbourg (built in

1882), has well equipped doubles costing from 160FF.

*Hôtel de la Gare* (☎ 02 33 43 06 81, fax 02 33 43 12 20, 10 place Jean Jaurès) has decent rooms with shower from 160/180FF. A couple of doors along, *Hôtel Le Jaurès* (☎ 02 33 43 06 35, 4 place Jean Jaurès) has basic rooms for 120/130FF and ones with shower for 150/170FF. The hotel is closed on Sunday. The brasserie below can get pretty lively.

*Hôtel Ambassadeur* (☎ 02 33 43 10 00, fax 02 33 43 10 01, 22 quai de Caligny) is in the centre of the action, overlooking the Avant Port, but the comfortable rooms have double glazed windows to ensure quiet. Rooms have a private bath and TV and cost 180/310FF; hair dryers are available.

## Places to Eat

**Restaurants** One fine seafood restaurant, with *menus* from around 110FF, is the *Café de Paris* (☎ 02 33 43 12 36, 40 quai de Caligny). It's not the place for a romantic tête-à-tête with the constant crowds and bustle, but the seafood is the freshest in town. It opens daily except Sunday dinner and Monday in the low season.

Rue Tour Carrée, rue de la Paix and around place Centrale offer a wide choice of both cuisine and price. *La Faitout* (☎ 02 33 04 25 04, 25 rue Tour Carrée) is an atmospheric place with wonderful lunch dishes (55FF to 60FF) and a show-stopping *menu* for 115FF. It opens daily except Sunday and Monday lunch. It's best to book at the weekend.

*Brasserie Le Commerce* (☎ 02 33 53 18 20, 42 rue François Lavieille) is a bustling brasserie that serves food from 11 am to midnight. There are no culinary surprises here but a copious, tasty *plat du jour* (dish of the day) costs only 54FF and there are *menus* from 82FF. It opens daily except Sunday.

*Crêperie-bar Le Tire-Bouchon* (☎ 02 33 53 54 69, 17 rue Notre Dame) is a cool bar-creperie where the motherly Charlette watches over a brood of hungry and thirsty students. It opens daily except Monday night and Sunday.

MANCHE

If you can forgo the atmosphere, the *Casino Cafeteria*, on the 1st floor of the Centre Continent at quai de l'Entrepôt has two-course *menus* from just 29FF and lots of other cheap eats.

**Self-Catering** There is a *market* on Tuesday and Thursday until about 5 pm at place de Gaulle and place Centrale. The latter, which is covered, also operates on Saturday morning. The Centre Continent at quai de l'Entrepôt has a huge *supermarket* open all day, seven days a week.

The little *Shopi grocery store (57 rue Gambetta)* opens 8.30 am to 12.30 pm and 2.30 to 7.30 pm Monday to Saturday.

## Entertainment

The sizzling centre of Cherbourg nightlife, attracting sailors, students and sophisticates alike, is *Yalta (☎ 02 33 43 02 81, 46 quai de Caligny)*. There are usually two or three jazz, rock or blues concerts a month and occasionally French singers. The pub opens 4.30 pm to 3 am.

*Le Diapson (☎ 02 33 01 21 43, 21 rue de la Paix)* has a little bit of everything – a philosophy night, art exhibits, an occasional concert. There's a good selection of beer to wash down a varied musical program. It opens 5 pm to 1 am daily except Sunday.

## Getting There & Away

**Air** Cherbourg's airport is 9km east of town at Maupertus-sur-Mer.

**Bus** The main regional bus line (which stops at the station on avenue Jean-François Millet) is STN (☎ 02 33 88 51 00 in Tourlaville), which has services to the camp site in Tourlaville (12.80FF). There are also buses to Valognes (30 minutes, six daily) and Barfleur (40 minutes, two daily).

**Train** The train station (☎ 02 33 57 50 50) opens 6 am to 10 pm. Destinations served include Paris' Gare St-Lazare (218FF, 3½ hours, seven daily) via Caen (99FF, 1½ hours, eight daily). Most destinations involve a change at either Caen or Lisons. There are connections to:

| destination | cost (FF) | duration (hours) | trains daily |
| --- | --- | --- | --- |
| Avranches | 139 | 2¼ | 4 |
| Bayeux | 101 | 1 | 8 |
| Bernay | 161 | 2–3½ | 11 |
| Évreux | 179 | 2½–3½ | 11 |
| Lisieux | 125 | 2–3 | 9 |
| Pontorson | 131 | 2½ | 2 |
| Rennes | 175 | 3½ | 2 |
| St-Lô | 175 | 1½ | 10 |

**Boat** The three companies with services to either England or Ireland have bureaus in the ferry terminal *(gare maritime)*. Their desks are open two hours before departure and for 30 minutes after the arrival of each ferry.

Brittany Ferries (☎ 02 33 88 44 44) covers the route to Poole in England; Irish Ferries (☎ 02 33 23 44 44) sails to Rosslare, Ireland; and P&O (☎ 02 33 88 65 70) handles the link to Portsmouth. For further details and schedules see the Sea section in the Getting There & Away chapter. Local buses run between the ferry terminal and the tourist office between three and 10 times daily, depending on the season. The fare is 6.20FF.

## Getting Around

**To/From the Airport** There's no public transportation into town and a taxi will cost about 120FF.

**Bus** City buses are run by Zéphir (☎ 02 33 22 40 58). The information kiosk at 40 boulevard Robert Schuman opens from 9 to 11.45 am and 1.30 to 6.30 pm weekdays, and 9.30 to 11.45 am on Saturday. Buses leave from either outside the kiosk or at various points around place Jean Jaurès, in front of the train station. Single tickets cost 6FF and a carnet of 10 costs 51FF.

**Taxi** Taxis can be called on ☎ 02 33 53 36 38. The trip between the train station and ferry terminal costs about 40FF.

**Bicycle** Station-Voile (see sailing earlier in the chapter) rents out mountain bikes for 50FF a half-day.

## BARFLEUR
**postcode 50760 • pop 630**
Little more than a cluster of granite houses on a finger of land, Barfleur is the smallest village in the Manche. The sea has been creeping up on the town for centuries turning the most important commercial harbour on the Cotentin peninsula into a scenic but relatively minor fishing port. At one time Barfleur had a population of 9000 installed on much more than the sliver of land that now constitutes the town centre. Dikes have been erected on the northern shore but the town still seems on the verge of disappearing under the waves, which lends it a fragile beauty. There's a small beach but Barfleur is mainly attractive for its laid-back village-on-the-sea ambience.

In its heyday under the Norman dukes, Barfleur was involved in two pivotal events. It was a local, Étienne, that built and piloted the ship – the *Mora* – that carried William the Conqueror to England in 1066. A stele across from the tourist office commemorates the fact. Less happily, it was from Barfleur that the infamous *Blanche Nef* was launched in 1120. William the Conqueror's son, Henry I of England, was returning home to England and entrusted a local seaman with the boat carrying his son and heir to the throne, William, William's wife and 300 courtiers. King Henry's vessel set out and began to outpace the *Blanche Nef*. Considerably intoxicated, the sailors of the *Blanche Nef* tried to outmanoeuvre the king's boat but were swept away by currents and crashed onto the offshore rocks. All the nobles were drowned, ending the line of William the Conqueror and giving rise to the Plantagenet dynasty. The site is marked by a lighthouse, visible from the town centre.

### Orientation & Information
The two main streets of Barfleur are quai Henri Chardon, which runs along the western side of the port, and the intersecting rue St-Thomas à Becket, which contains most hotels and restaurants. The main square is place Général de Gaulle near the post office. The post office also changes money.

The tourist office (☎ 02 33 54 02 48, fax 02 33 23 43 09) on quai Henri Chardon is at the tip of the port near the church and the monument to William the Conqueror. It opens 10.30 am to noon and 2.30 to 6.30 pm April to October (10.30 am to noon on Tuesday and Friday during the rest of the year). Visit its Web site at www.ville-barfleur.fr.

### Things to See & Do
Barfleur is museum-free but there is a simple 17th-century church, **Église St-Nicolas**, clearly built to withstand maritime gusts.

Admiring the granite houses that line the straight, narrow streets, strolling along the coast and waiting for the fishing boats to return are typical Barfleur activities. For livelier pursuits, there's the sailing school (☎/fax 02 33 54 79 08) at the camp site.

### Places to Stay & Eat
*Camping de la Blanche Nef* (☎ 02 33 23 15 40) is next to the seaside promenade. It costs 70FF for up to two people with a tent or car.

Two-star *Hôtel Le Conquérant* (☎ 02 33 54 00 82, fax 02 33 54 65 25, 16 rue St-Thomas à Becket) is in a handsome 17th-century house with a flourishing rear garden. Rooms with a sink only cost 200FF; those with a private bath cost from 340FF to 400FF.

Nearby is the simple *Hôtel du Phare* (☎ 02 33 54 10 33, fax 02 33 54 63 90, rue St-Thomas à Becket), which has rooms with a sink only for 180FF and with a full bathroom for 250FF.

### Getting There & Away
There are two buses from Cherbourg daily (40 minutes).

## VALOGNES
**postcode 50700 • pop 7200**
The architectural unity of Valognes creates a startling effect. From the banks of the narrow river to mansions, townhouses and bridges, everything is constructed from the same beige-grey granite. At first glance the town centre seems to be all angles, corners and walls, but closer examination reveals elaborate decoration on the sober facades.

MANCHE

In the late 17th and early 18th centuries many noble families with chateaux in the countryside constructed opulent winter quarters in Valognes. With its new burst of money and prestige, Valognes became known as the 'little Versailles of Normandy'. Its moment of glory ended abruptly with the Revolution of 1789 but the town continued to prosper, turning out porcelain for a while, then butter and now material for the nearby nuclear industry. Proud of its heritage, Valognes was rebuilt with style after WWII, recovering a large part of its aristocratic allure.

## Orientation & Information

The centre of town is place du Château and the main street is boulevard Division-Leclerc, which becomes boulevard Félix Buhot in the north-west and boulevard de Verdun in the south-east. The tourist office (☎ 02 33 40 11 55, fax 02 33 40 00 14, **e** mairie.office-tourisme.valognes@wanadoo.fr) is on place du Château and distributes a helpful leaflet of

walking tours of the city. It opens 10 am to noon and 3 to 6 pm Monday to Friday (2 to 6.30 pm in July and August). The post office is also on place du Château across from the tourist office and it has Cyberposte terminal. You can change money at Crédit Mutuel, 25 boulevard Division-Leclerc.

## Things to See & Do

The 18th-century **Hôtel de Beaumont** (☎ 02 33 40 12 30) is an elegant mansion featuring a fine columned facade and wrought iron balcony. It is still inhabited but in the part open to visitors you'll find a monumental stairway leading to rooms furnished in 17th-, 18th- and 19th-century style. The visit is completed by a stroll of the manicured gardens. The mansion is at the corner of the rue Barbey d'Aurevilly and rue Petit Versailles south-east of the tourist office. It opens 2.30 to 6.30 pm daily and 10.30 am to 12.30 pm and 2.30 to 6.30 pm Tuesday in July and August. Admission costs 28FF.

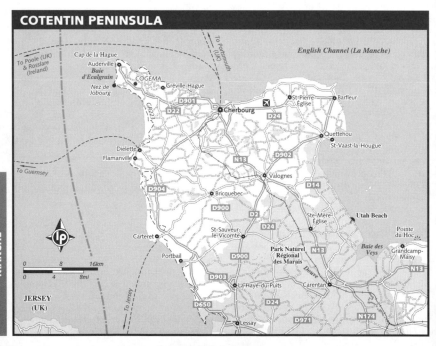

COTENTIN PENINSULA

Off boulevard de Verdun the **Abbaye de Valognes** (☎ 02 33 21 62 82), 8 rue des Capucins, makes an interesting visit. The abbey was built for Bénédictine monks in the 17th century and was reconstructed after damage caused during WWII. It now houses a community of nuns. Seventeenth-century sculptures and windows in the church contrast with more recent acquisitions. Admission is free but expect heavy sales pressure to buy the sweets that are made in the abbey.

A two-part museum is devoted to Normandy's most famous thirst-quenchers – cider and Calvados. **Le Musée Regional du Cidre** (☎ 02 33 40 22 73) on rue du Petit Versailles has three floors of cider tools and equipment plus a video explaining the process in one building. Up the street on rue Pelouze **Le Musée du Calvados et des Vieux Métiers** (☎ 02 33 40 26 25) is in a 17th-century mansion that functioned as a lace factory, barracks and firehouse before it became a museum displaying the barrels, pipes and casks used to make Calvados. The stone, iron and leather trades are also explained. The museums open 10 am to noon and 2 to 6 pm Monday and Wednesday to Saturday, except in July and August when they open Monday to Saturday. Admission costs 20FF including both museums.

### Places to Stay & Eat
The three hotels in Valognes are reasonably priced. The cheapest is ***Hôtel St-Malo*** *(☎ 02 33 40 03 24, fax 02 33 40 15 08, 7 rue St-Malo)*, which has basic rooms for 120FF and rooms with private facilities for 230FF. Both ***Hôtel du Louvre*** *(☎ 02 33 40 00 07, fax 02 33 40 13 73, 28 rue des Religieuses)* and ***Hôtel de l'Agriculture*** *(☎ 02 33 95 02 02, fax 02 33 95 29 33)* provide excellent value, offering large, comfortable rooms that cost from 140FF to 280FF.

Hôtel du Louvre has a more romantic atmosphere, while the ivy-covered Hôtel de l'Agriculture is in a rustic style.

### Getting There & Away
For transportation options from Cherbourg see Getting There & Away in that section.

## STE-MÈRE-ÉGLISE
**postcode 50480 • pop 1500**
In perhaps the most celebrated image of D-Day, the American parachutist, John Steele, drifted down from the skies on the night of 6 June 1944 and entangled himself on the church clock in Ste-Mère-Église. The episode was featured in the film *The Longest Day*, and Mr Steele became something of a local celebrity, returning every so often to re-enact the drama. Since his death, a mannequin has taken his place on the church roof. Ste-Mère-Église was the first village to be invaded on D-Day. It is now point zero for *La Voie de la Liberté* (Liberty Way) the route marked out by white milestones that follows the 1944 march of General Patton's Third Army across Normandy.

The 12th-century **church** is probably the only one in existence that has a stained-glass window depicting the Virgin and Child surrounded by parachutists. Another recent window shows St Michel, the patron saint of parachutists.

The only other interesting site in Ste-Mère-Église is the **Musée des Troupes Aéroportées** (☎ 02 33 41 41 35) which tells the story of the landings through films, documents and photos. Jeeps, tanks and even a C47 transport plane help convey the intensity of the experience. The museum opens 9 am to 6.45 pm from May to September but closes between noon and 2 pm during the rest of the year, except in December and January when it's closed. Admission costs 30FF.

### Getting There & Away
STN bus No 5 travels between Cherbourg and Ste-Mère-Église on weekdays (about 50 minutes, five times daily).

## THE HAGUE PENINSULA
The wild landscape on the north-western tip of Normandy has often been compared to Ireland.

Pastures roll up to the edge of cliffs while underneath an ice-blue sea pounds the lonely coves. The sound of wind and waves is unbroken by any whirring motors since the area has few residents and only a smattering of

MANCHE

## COGEMA vs Greenpeace

The struggle between Greenpeace and COGEMA has been extraordinarily acrimonious. Created in 1976, government-controlled COGEMA handles every stage of the nuclear industry from uranium mining to reprocessing spent fuel. Its plant in Cap la Hague receives nuclear waste from around the world, processes it and dumps it into the Channel to the tune of 230 million litres a year. The environmental organisation, Greenpeace has labelled COGEMA's plant as 'the single largest source of radioactive contamination in the EU'.

In 1997 Greenpeace discovered that an exposed waste pipe at the nearby beach of Les Moulinets had left radioactive contamination 3000-times higher than normal and sued to stop further discharges. In response, COGEMA undertook an operation to clean up the residue in the pipe despite Greenpeace's allegations that such an operation could diffuse the radioactive mess.

After Greenpeace monitoring equipment found that the ocean bed was so contaminated that it qualified as a nuclear waste dump, the organisation revealed that it's sampling devices had been stolen and demanded that COGEMA be charged with the theft. COGEMA continued the residue removal process. The following year a government study found that the radioactive material had indeed dispersed onto the sea floor and that the radiation level around the pipe was higher than it was before the clean-up operation began.

Greenpeace continued staging protests against COGEMA throughout 1998 and 1999 but achieved its most dramatic success at the conference of the Oslo–Paris Commission (OSPAR) in June 2000. The commission was set up to protect marine life in the north-eastern Atlantic Ocean. In April, a Greenpeace water sample showed that COGEMA was illegally discharging radioactive particles larger than the authorised 25 microns (about the size of a grain of salt), which means that the insoluble particles will remain radioactive for centuries.

During OSPAR's June conference, Greenpeace attached a webcam to an underwater discharge pipe and relayed the images directly to the conference in Copenhagen. A few days later the cable link to the camera was 'accidentally' cut by divers; Greenpeace promptly repaired it. COGEMA responded by filing a lawsuit alleging that Greenpeace had damaged its property in the course of filming, but so far Greenpeace has had the last word. At the end of the conference, OSPAR delegates adopted a decision condemning the dumping of radioactive waste into the sea. The decision will have no immediate effect since France and the UK (the only EU countries with waste treatment plants) abstained from the vote and are not legally bound to follow it. Greenpeace hopes that public pressure will force the French government to limit the discharges in the near future and eventually ban them.

visitors. It feels like the end of the world – or at least the end of Europe – although it is clearly neither.

Perhaps it was the remoteness of the site that inspired the French government to turn a hunk of the territory over to the nuclear power industry. The eerie constellation of white tanks, tubes, towers and offices at the sprawling **COGEMA plant** (☎ 02 33 02 61 04) at La Hague are devoted to the reprocessing and disposal of spent nuclear fuel. Because of the controversy surrounding the site, the COGEMA people are happy to offer free guided tours of the plant in which they will explain that the disposal of radio-

active material is as sanitary as their lustrous facilities suggest. By the time they're done, you'll be ready to take a bath in the stuff. The facility opens 10 am to 6 pm daily from April to September; there are several visits per week for which you must reserve one week in advance. Visits are available at the weekend only the rest of the year. The minimum age is 13.

For further enlightenment on the wonders of nuclear power you can tour the **Flamanville nuclear power plant** (☎ 02 33 04 12 99). Each tour lasts about three hours, and you must present your passport or national ID card. It opens 9 am till noon and

MANCHE

2 to 6.30 pm, Monday to Saturday There is one afternoon visit per day in July and August for which you must book no later than the morning of the visit. Visits are scarcer the rest of the year and reservations must be made one month in advance.

At 126m, the cliff at **Nez de Jobourg** is the highest in continental Europe. The GR223 trail *(Sentier des Douaniers)* winds along the steep cliffs offering breathtaking sea views. You can follow it north to the **Baie d'Ecalgrain**, a majestic coastal curve that qualifies as the most romantic spot in Normandy. Windswept skies, tossing waves and low cliffs capped with meadows create an unforgettable sight.

From Ecalgrain, the trail takes you to **Auderville**, 22km north-west of Cherbourg, with the only places to stay in the area. The tiny village is an artful arrangement of stone houses built to withstand the gusty winds that rip over the peninsula.

*Hôtel de la Hague (☎/fax 02 33 52 71 00,* e *regishamelin@wanadoo.fr)* is a sturdy stone house in town that has rooms running from 120FF to 250FF. Some rooms have views of the sea. A little further down is *Hôtel du Cap (☎ 02 33 52 71 00, fax 02 33 01 56 30)* that has a garden, sea view and private baths in all rooms. It costs 230FF to 270FF per room. Eat at the *Auberge d'Auderville (☎ 02 33 52 77 44)* and enjoy home-smoked fish among other local treats in a rustic, beamed dining room behind the bar. It opens daily except Tuesday.

### Getting There & Away

There's no public transport out here so you'll need your own wheels.

# Central Manche

WWII veterans remember with a shudder the 'bocage' country that stretches from the bottom of the Cotentin peninsula south-east to Vire and the Suisse Normande. The zigzagging hedgerows that lend the region its distinctive character were used to devastating effect by the defending Germans, who were able to launch surprise attacks

## Normandy Cows

There are cows and there are cows and then there are Normandy cows. Easily recognisable by the distinctive spectacle markings around their eyes, Normandy cows are a breed unto themselves. They're relatively new, dating only from the 19th century when the need to feed a growing population forced farmers to look for ways to increase the quality and output of their cows. For the best milk and meat, breeders mixed three regional cows: the large, heavy Cotentine; the Augeronne, which was smaller but produced good meat; and the Cauchoise of Flemish stock. The breed was officially recognised in 1883.

*La race normande* is a cow with qualities. It's hardy, not fussy about its climate or cuisine. It produces more milk than other breeds and the milk is of a higher quality, with more curds, making it more expensive. The meat is highly prized by chefs around France for its tenderness and flavour.

Since 1976 the *Unités Nationales de Sélection et de Promotion des Races Bovines* (UPRA) in Normandy has worked hard to promote the breed, advertise its qualities and advise breeders. The recent BSE scare has undone years of hard work, however, threatening Normandy cows with the same uncertain fate as the rest of French cattle. Fortunately, the breed is doing well around the world. French consumers could well end up savouring Normandy beef imported from Brazil.

JANE SMITH

**Keep an eye out for hardy Norman cattle**

from their leafy hideouts. From low bushes to higher trees, the bocage was designed to delineate small or irregular parcels of land and has existed for centuries. Its green patchwork carpets the low hills and gentle valleys formed by the Soulles and Sienne rivers. Small towns and hamlets dot this region, which is predominantly agricultural, producing milk by the tanker.

## COUTANCES
**postcode 50200 • pop 9700**
The medieval hilltop town of Coutances, 77km south of Cherbourg, is the administrative and commercial centre of bocage country but its remarkable old cathedral recalls the days when it was an influential episcopal centre. The contours of the cathedral are visible from afar and its lofty towers and steeples dwarf the modest structures surrounding them. Religious life in Coutances reached its apogee in the 16th century, attracting wealthy and powerful people to set up residences in the town. For a while, it was the capital of the Manche department but since it lost that role in 1796, Coutances has resigned itself to serving as a market for local agricultural products. In addition to the cathedral, Coutances boasts splendid botanical gardens.

### Orientation & Information
The town centre is compact and confined by boulevard Alsace-Lorraine in the northwest and boulevard Jeanne Paynel to the east. At the centre of town is the cathedral and town hall.

The tourist office (☎ 02 33 19 08 10, fax 02 33 19 08 19, ⓔ tourisme-coutances@ wanadoo.fr) is at place Georges Leclerc behind the town hall. It opens 10 am to 12.30 pm and 2 to 6 pm Monday to Friday, and to 5 pm on Saturday, September to June; 10 am to 12.30 pm and 1.30 to 7 pm Monday to Saturday, and 3 to 7 pm Sunday, July and August.

The train and bus stations are about 1km south-east of the town centre.

There's a Société Générale opposite the tourist office at 8 rue Daniel. The post office at 10 rue St-Dominique opens 8 am to

6.30 pm on weekdays and also Saturday morning; it exchanges money and has a Cyberposte terminal.

### Things to See & Do
The soaring 13th-century Gothic **Cathédrale de Coutances** is one of France's finest, prompting Victor Hugo to call it the prettiest he'd seen after the one at Chartres. Constructed in creamy limestone, the cathedral combines Gothic and Romanesque styles to stunning effect. Initially erected in the 11th century, the cathedral was transformed by the wave of Gothic architecture that accompanied Philippe-Auguste's takeover of Normandy in the 13th century. A new layer of stone created soaring Gothic towers from the original Romanesque structures.

A rare octagonal lantern tower is the focal point of the light, bright interior and a series of parallel arches makes the cathedral look higher than it is. The dizzying sense of verticality was meant to create the impression that the church was rising to the floors of heaven. Look for the 13th-century stained-glass window in the north transept which shows scenes from the lives of Thomas à Becket, St George and St Blaise. In the Chapel of St-Lô is one of the cathedral's oldest windows, dating from the early 13th century. In the south transept, notice the 14th-century window showing a frightening Last Judgement. Tours in English are held at 3.30 pm on weekdays in summer, and afford sweeping views from the galleries in the lantern tower. It costs 30FF (those aged 12 to 18, 20FF).

Opposite place Georges Leclerc lies the splendid **Jardin des Plantes**, a grand 19th-century landscape garden. Conceived by a civil engineer and painter, the garden tastefully blends symmetrical French lines with Italianesque terraces, English-style copses, a maze and fountains. Its varied stock of ornamental trees includes giant redwood, cedar of Lebanon, New Zealand beech and Canadian nut. Look out for the hedges trimmed into the shape of human figures and flower beds arranged to suggest a boat. Kids will like the labyrinth in the south-western corner. Like the cathedral, the gardens are illuminated on summer nights. It opens 9 am to 8 pm daily

MANCHE

(5 pm from October to March, 11.30 pm from July to mid-September). Admission is free.

The **beaches** of Agon-Coutainville, Gouville and Pirou lie a short distance from the town. The beach at Agon-Coutainville is the oldest and also the most popular; Pirou has the longest beach and a remarkable **chateau** 2km inland surrounded by an artificial lake.

## Special Events
The jazz festival during Ascension week in May, *Jazz Sous les Pommiers*, is the most important annual music event in Normandy. In cafes, churches and on the streets, local and international musicians strut their stuff to an appreciative public. For further information call ☎ 02 33 76 78 50 or visit the Web site at www.jazzsouslespommiers.com.

## Places to Stay & Eat
Situated about 1.2km north-west of town on the D44, *Camping Municipal Les Vignettes (☎ 02 33 45 43 13, route de Coutainville)* charges 16FF for each adult, tent site and car.

*Hôtel de Normandie (☎ 02 33 45 01 40, fax 02 33 46 74 54, 2 place Général du Gaulle)* is an old-fashioned place with a homely atmosphere. It charges 120/160FF for roomy singles/doubles with TV and hall shower, some with a cathedral view. The restaurant does great fish *menus* for 53FF (except Sundays) and bouillabaisse (90FF).

The *Hôtel des Trois Piliers (☎ 02 33 45 01 31, 11 rue des Halles)* has smallish but well-equipped rooms with washbasin for 125FF (135FF with private shower). The bar downstairs draws a young, noisy crowd.

The most comfortable digs are at *Hôtel le Parvis (☎ 02 33 45 13 55, fax 02 33 45 68 00, place de la Cathédrale)*, which has rooms for 210/260FF with private bath, TV and telephone.

*Restaurant le Vieux Coutances (☎ 02 33 47 94 78, 55 rue Geoffroy de Montbray)* is a small, intimate Norman eatery with excellent fish or meat *menus* for 70FF or 85FF. It opens daily except Sunday. For a meal on Sunday, try *Restaurant Notre Dame (☎ 02 33 45 00 67, 4 rue d'Harcourt)* which has all the usual suspects such as *magret de canard* (fillet of duck) as well as

excellent crepes and *galettes* (wholemeal or buckwheat pancake) and even organic wine. *Menus* cost 50FF, 65FF and 95FF.

The **market** is Thursday morning. Look for the delicious local Coutances cheese with its creamy interior.

## Getting There & Away
STN (☎ 02 33 50 77 89) runs buses to Granville (41FF, 30 minutes, up to five daily). In July and August there are buses to the beaches (20 minutes, three daily). Regular train services include Cherbourg (94FF, 2 hours, six daily), Caen (83FF, 1½ hours, six daily) and Paris Gare du Nord (210FF to 243FF, four hours, twice daily).

## GRANVILLE
**postcode 50400 • pop 15,000**
At the foot of the Cotentin peninsula, the coastal port of Granville likes to call itself the 'Monaco of the North'. Like the tiny principality to the south, Granville has an old town crowded onto a rocky promontory overlooking the sea and a lower town built on land reclaimed from the sea. The straight rows of granite houses and white shutters in the walled upper town however, have a uniquely Norman austerity. Despite the no-nonsense buildings, Granville is a popular destination for pleasure-seekers. In summer, the narrow beach is crowded with visitors and the coastal views from the upper town are extraordinary.

Much of the upper town dates from the 18th century when shipbuilders and privateers built residences. The 19th-century vogue for sea bathing brought the first beach lovers to Granville, speeded by a new railroad line. Liberated on 31 July 1944, the town was surprised to find itself under assault by German commandos everyone had forgotten were still garrisoned at Jersey. The Germans left 20 dead before making off with a cargo of coal and GI prisoners.

## Orientation
Granville is divided into two parts – a modern lower town that contains most shops and services, and a walled upper town overlooking the sea. The beach runs north-east

MANCHE

of the casino and the southern part of town is given over to several ports. There are promenades along the beach, around the upper town and along rue du Port. The train station is on avenue de la Gare, 1km east of the town centre.

## Information

### Tourist Offices
The tourist office (☎ 02 33 91 30 03, fax 02 33 91 30 19, e office .tourisme@ville-granville.fr), 4 cours Jonville, opens 9 am to noon (to 1 pm in July and August) and 2 to 6.30 pm (7.30 pm in July and August) Monday to Saturday, and 11 am to 12.30 pm Sunday. Its Web site is at www.ville-granville.fr. The STN office (☎ 02 33 50 77 89), across the street, is a good source of information for local and regional buses.

### Money
You can change money at Caisse d'Epargne, 18 cours Jonville. It is closed on Sunday and Monday.

### Post & Communications
The post office is also on cours Jonville, a block east of the tourist office, and there's Cyberposte.

### Travel Agencies
Émeraude Vacances (☎ 02 33 90 62 24), 1 rue Lecampion, sells train, air and sea tickets.

### Laundry
There's a self-service laundrette at 10 rue St-Sauveur.

## Things to See & Do
All of Granville's sights are in the walled upper city. The **Musée du Vieux Granville** (☎ 02 33 50 44 10), 2 rue Le Carpentier, concentrates on the maritime history of the town, displaying painted and ceramic seascapes, model boats, posters, postcards and photographs. There are also rooms of local furniture, traditional Norman costumes and head-dresses. The museum opens 10 am to noon and 2 to 6 pm Wednesday to Monday in summer, Wednesday to Sunday April to

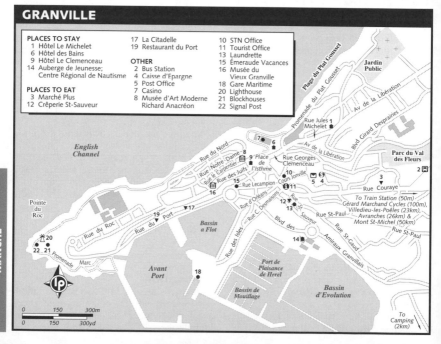

**GRANVILLE**

| PLACES TO STAY | 17 La Citadelle | 10 STN Office |
|---|---|---|
| 1 Hôtel Le Michelet | 19 Restaurant du Port | 11 Tourist Office |
| 6 Hôtel des Bains | | 13 Laundrette |
| 9 Hôtel Le Clemenceau | **OTHER** | 15 Émeraude Vacances |
| 14 Auberge de Jeunesse; | 2 Bus Station | 16 Musée du |
| Centre Régional de Nautisme | 4 Caisse d'Epargne | Vieux Granville |
| | 5 Post Office | 18 Gare Maritime |
| PLACES TO EAT | 7 Casino | 20 Lighthouse |
| 3 Marché Plus | 8 Musée d'Art Moderne | 21 Blockhouses |
| 12 Crêperie St-Sauveur | Richard Anacréon | 22 Signal Post |

June, and Wednesday, Saturday and Sunday afternoons October to March. Admission costs 20FF.

**Le Musée d'Art Moderne Richard Anacréon** (☎ 02 33 51 02 94), place de l'Isthme, houses an eclectic collection of modern art that includes such well-known names as Picasso, Derain, Vlaminck, Utrillo, Laurencin and Signac. The collection was a donation from Granville resident Richard Anacréon who owned a bookshop for many years in Paris' Latin Quarter. The shop window of his bookshop has been re-created and the museum contains mementos from Colette, Cocteau, Apollinaire, Genet and other Parisian literary figures. The museum opens the same hours as the Musée du Vieux Granville, admission costs 15FF.

La Pointe du Roc at the south-western tip of the upper town has a **lighthouse** built in 1869, a **signal post** and several **blockhouses** built by the Germans between 1942 and 1944.

### Organised Tours

Boat trips aboard the ferry *Jolie France II* or the catamaran *Jeune France* take in the rugged Chausey islands, 17km offshore. Departures are at 9 to 10.30 am daily (depending on the tides) from March to September, weekends only October to December. Boats leave from the Gare Maritime and the cost is 92FF return for the day. Reservations are required. Call ☎ 02 33 50 31 81. Alizes Émeraude (☎ 02 33 50 16 36) offers the same service plus day trips to St-Malo (115FF return) and Jersey (200FF return).

### Places to Stay

Two kilometres south of the town centre and 200m from the beach, *Camping La Vague* (☎ 02 33 50 29 97) costs 27FF per person and 30FF per tent.

The *Auberge de Jeunesse* (☎ 02 33 91 22 62, fax 02 33 50 51 99) is well-situated in the Regional Nautical Centre at Port de Plaisance de Herel. A bed in a two- to four-bed room costs 72FF with private facilities.

*Hôtel Le Michelet* (☎ 02 33 50 06 55, fax 02 33 50 12 25, 5 rue Jules Michelet) is a small family-run hotel in the upper town.

## Granville's Carnival

Granville's annual Mardi Gras celebration is the biggest event in the region. For four days floats, bands and majorettes file down the narrow streets, while kids head to the Ferris wheel and grown-ups head to the bars. The festivities culminate on the final day of 'intrigue' when all the townspeople put on masks or disguises and try to surprise their friends and acquaintances. Finally the 'carnival man' mascot is burned on the beach and the party's over.

The origins of the festival stretch back several centuries when most of the town's male population was employed on fishing boats that brought cod back from Newfoundland. Before leaving on their eight months of hard labour, the fishermen partied hard for three or four days, spending money like, well, drunken sailors. Often they borrowed money from the shipowner against their wages and dressed up in disguises. The children made it into a game, pulling off their masks and taunting them: *'Il a mangé ses 400 francs; il s'en ira le cul tout nu au Banc'.* (He ate up his 400 francs; he'll go bare-assed to the fishing banks.)

Rooms are different sizes but most are bright and furnished with a flourish of style. Rooms with a sink only cost 140FF, 185FF with a toilet and 220FF to 300FF with private facilities.

*Hôtel Le Clemenceau* (☎ 02 33 50 19 87, 1 rue Georges Clemenceau) is centrally located and has small, simple rooms that start at 150FF for a sink only and run to 220FF for private facilities.

*Hôtel des Bains* (☎ 02 33 50 17 31, ☎ 02 33 50 89 22, 19 rue Georges Clemenceau) is a three-star modern establishment across from the casino and near the beach. Cheerful, bright rooms cost from 220FF to 790FF. The more expensive rooms have sea views; its restaurant is excellent.

### Places to Eat

There are a number of inexpensive creperies in the upper town especially on rue

Cambernon and rue Notre Dame. In the lower town, *Crêperie St-Sauveur (☎ 02 33 90 20 77, 4 rue St-Sauveur)* is on a colourful street and turns out tasty crepes and galettes in a friendly atmosphere. It opens daily except Tuesday dinner and Wednesday.

*Restaurant du Port (☎ 02 33 50 00 55, 19 rue du Port)* is a delightful spot on the port with a cosy dining room and an outdoor terrace. Locals come for the delicious seafood paella at 65FF or the 69FF daily *menu*. It is closed Sunday dinner and Monday. *La Citadelle (☎ 02 33 50 34 10, fax 02 33 50 15 36, 34 rue du Port)* has a talented young chef who concocts such treats as crabcake with a cream sauce and a special grilled lobster. *Menus* cost 85FF or 190FF. It opens daily July and August and daily except Tuesday and Wednesday, the rest of the year.

The supermarket *Marché Plus* is at 107 rue Couraye. It opens 7 am to 9 pm daily.

### Getting There & Away
**Bus** There is a daily evening bus to Coutances, Valognes and Cherbourg, four weekday buses to Coutances (35.20FF, one hour and 10 minutes), and seven weekday buses to Avranches (34.50FF, one hour).

**Train** There are regular services to Paris (218FF, three hours, six daily), Coutances (41FF, 30 minutes, four daily) and Villedieu-les-Poêles (31FF, 20 minutes, four daily).

### Getting Around
STN runs local buses in Granville. There are infrequent services between the train station and the post office. Tickets cost 7FF.

You can hire a bicycle at Gérard Marchand Cycles (☎ 02 33 61 53 62), 35 avenue Maréchal Leclerc; it costs 40/70FF per half/full day.

## AROUND GRANVILLE
Twenty-three kilometres east of Granville is a 'city of God' (villedieu) and 'pans' (poêles). **Villedieu-les-Poêles** was founded in 1130 by the Hospitallers of St John of Jerusalem, who eventually became the Knights of Malta. This ancient stone town is known for its copper pans. The origins of

the copper industry remain obscure but it seems that the religious character of the town in the 12th century gave rise to various tax breaks that favoured artisans. Workshops began to produce church ornaments and eventually developed an expertise in kitchen implements, church bells and in pewter.

After a decline in the 19th century, the industry has once again flowered to feed a demand for luxury kitchenware. A number of workshops in town are open for visits, from which you can also buy copper pans. Atelier du Cuivre (☎ 02 33 51 31 85), 54 rue Général Huard, presents a short film and a tour of the facilities (25FF). It opens 9 am to noon and 1.30 to 6 pm daily in July and August; daily except Sunday the rest of the year.

The tourist office (☎ 02 33 61 05 69), place des Costils, has information on other workshop tours, accommodation and excursions. It opens 10 am to 12.30 pm and 2 to 6.30 pm Tuesday to Saturday.

Villedieu-les-Poêles is linked by train to Granville (see the Getting There & Away section for Granville for details) and Paris (184FF, three hours, four daily).

## AVRANCHES
**postcode 50300 • pop 10,400**
Avranches is inextricably intertwined with Mont St-Michel, which is 19km to the south-west and visible across the bay. It was Bishop Aubert of Avranches that commanded the first oratory on Mont St-Michel and it was the abbot of Mont St-Michel, Robert de Torigni, that called a council in Avranches to decide the fate of Henry II. Embroiled in a power struggle with his popular archbishop, Thomas à Becket, Henry had cried out in exasperation: 'Will no one rid me of this turbulent priest?' His courtiers interpreted it as an order and murdered Becket in Canterbury Cathedral 29 December 1170. In the cathedral of Avranches, Henry was most contrite in front of the bishops and submitted himself to public flagellation outside the cathedral as his penance. The cathedral has long since crumbled but a plaque marks the spot.

Avranches was also the site of Patton's 'Avranches breakthrough' of 31 July 1944. Avranches was the last barrier to the Allied advance into Brittany and southern Normandy. Since the Germans had abandoned their positions, the Allies were able to enter the city unopposed and proceed to the critical junction of Pontaubault. Nearly three-quarters of the city was destroyed by post- D-Day bombardments, but after its liberation the city proceeded speedily with the reconstruction process.

Avranches is perched on a high granite spur overlooking Mont St-Michel bay and offers some stirring views and the opportunity to visit several unique museums.

## Orientation & Information

The compact town centre of Avranches is at the end of rue de la Constitution, which is the main street for shops and services. The tourist office (☎ 02 33 58 00 22, fax 02 33 68 13 29, ✉ avranches-tourisme@wanadoo.fr) is in the centre of town on rue du Général de Gaulle. It opens 9 am to noon and 2 to 5 pm Monday to Saturday as well as Sunday in July and August. You can visit its Web site at www.ville-avranches.fr. The post office is on rue St-Gervais a block east of rue de la Constitution, and there's Cyberposte. There are numerous banks along rue de la Constitution. The train station is 1km north-west of the town centre; there are four buses a day between the train station and the town centre.

## Things to See & Do

Across from the tourist office, **Le Musée Municipal d'Avranches** (☎ 02 33 58 25 15), place du Tribunal, is an essential prelude to a tour of the Mont St-Michel illuminated manuscripts (see below). A reconstruction of a monastic studio explains the techniques involved in creating the medieval manuscripts although there's only one example on display. The rest of the museum displays furniture, clothes and *objets d'art* from the 19th century, and vestiges of the former cathedral. It opens 9.30 am to noon and 2 to 5 pm daily Easter to September; daily except Tuesday, April and May.

**Les Manuscrits du Mont St-Michel** (☎ 02 33 58 25 15) is in the town hall library and contains a priceless collection of illuminated manuscripts from Mont St-Michel Abbey. Considered the most important collection of its kind in France, the manuscripts date from the 8th to the 15th century and have been kept in Avranches since the French Revolution. The exquisitely illustrated documents concern both religious and temporal subjects. Of the 203 manuscripts in the museum's possession only 30 are displayed at any given time. The library has the same opening hours as the museum except that it opens June to September only.

No visit to Avranches is complete without a stop at the **Trésor** (treasury) of **Église St-Gervais**, which contains the skull of Bishop Aubert, marked by the penetrating finger of St Michael. Also on display is a precious collection of liturgical objects and robes. The Trésor opens the same hours as the town hall library. A ticket good for the museum, town hall library and Trésor costs 30FF.

The site of the old cathedral where Henry II did penance is marked by a **platform** surrounded by a chain. To find it, head west on rue d'Office, which is one block north of the tourist office.

General George S Patton's 'Avranches breakthrough' is commemorated by a monument on **place Patton**. It's a slice of American territory; the earth and the trees were brought over from the USA.

For a view of Mont St-Michel bay, head to **Le Jardin des Plantes**, 200m south-west of the tourist office, which also hosts a wide variety of rare plants and trees.

## Places to Stay & Eat

The centrally located *Hôtel La Renaissance* (☎ 02 33 58 03 71, 17 rue des Fossés) is a sweet little place with French windows and white curtains. Simple doubles/triples/quads cost 145/180/210FF (sink only). The restaurant downstairs offers sandwiches, crepes and basic dishes. *Hôtel Le Jardin des Plantes* (☎ 02 33 58 03 68, fax 02 33 60 01 72, 10 place Carnot) is a

MANCHE

large country house near the Jardin des Plantes. Rooms vary in size but are cheerfully decorated in bright fabrics. Prices run from 170FF (sink only) to 490FF for a spacious room with private facilities. The elegant restaurant is well-regarded and has *menus* from 75FF to 185FF. It is closed at the weekend from September to Easter.

### Getting There & Away
**Bus** STN (☎ 02 33 58 03 07) bus No 12 connects Avranches with Granville (34FF, 1¼ hours, five daily) and Mont St-Michel in summer only (27FF, one daily). Effia (☎ 02 35 98 13 38) has a daily bus to Pontorson (13FF, 30 minutes).

**Train** Avranches is on the Caen–Rennes line. There are services to/from Coutances (40 minutes, two daily), Pontorson (15 minutes, two daily), Cherbourg (139FF, 2½ hours, six daily), Bayeux (92FF, 1½ hours, two daily), Granville (34FF, 40 minutes, three daily) and Caen (110FF, two hours, six daily).

## LE MONT ST-MICHEL
**postcode 51016 • pop 42**
It's difficult not to be impressed with your first sighting of Mont St-Michel. Covering the summit is the massive abbey, a soaring ensemble of buildings in a hotchpotch of architectural styles. The abbey (80m above the sea) is topped by a slender spire with a gilded copper statue of the Archangel Michael slaying a dragon. Around the base are the ancient ramparts and a jumble of buildings that house the handful of true residents. At night the whole structure is brilliantly illuminated.

Mont St-Michel's fame derives equally from the bay's extraordinary tides. The Mont either looks out onto bare sand stretching many kilometres into the distance or, at high tide, the same expanse under water.

The word 'unforgettable' can be bandied about too often in guidebooks (not in this one, of course) but there's no other word to describe the sight of the island abbey at high tide. Watching the water creep up from the horizon and advance upon the island

abbey until it is nearly surrounded by waves is worth flying across oceans to see (though the Mont and its causeway are completely surrounded by the sea only at the highest of tides – for more information see the boxed text 'Turning Tides').

A visit to Mont St-Michel can be one of the most awesome experiences of your travelling life or one of the most acutely disappointing. The 'merchants of the Mont' have honed the art of tourist-gouging to the fine edge of perfection. Nowhere in France is commercialism as crass. Scarves and biscuits, trinkets and toys, crepes and dishes are sold with unbelievable mark-ups. As a general rule, anything that isn't cemented to the ground can be found elsewhere in Normandy at least 50% cheaper.

Avoiding the rip-offs is easier than avoiding the tourist hordes. The tiny island has only one slim street leading up to the abbey and it's shoulder-to-shoulder with people from June to September. To soak up the wonder of Mont St-Michel, try to be there when tourists aren't. Even at the height of the season, you'll have enough breathing room early morning before the tour buses arrive and in the early evening.

### History
According to Celtic mythology, Mont St-Michel was one of the sea tombs to which the souls of the dead were sent. In AD 708 the St Michel appeared to Bishop Aubert of Avranches and told him to build a devotional chapel at the top of the summit. According to legend, the bishop paid no attention until, in exasperation, the saint appeared to him in a dream. To drive his point home, he drove his finger into the bishop's head, penetrating his skull. (Aubert's head with the hole can be seen in the St-Gervais church in Avranches). The oratory was built. In 710 King Childebert deposited his crown at the foot of the oratory and a few years later, the Pope donated some relics, turning the chapel into a pilgrimage destination.

During the next few centuries, the region was beset by Norman invasions, but as soon as the dukes of Normandy consolidated their power, Mont St-Michel emerged from

Escape the island's crowds with a visit by night.

Watch out for Mont St-Michel's dramatic tides.

Slippery seaweed in Mont St-Michel bay.

Mont St-Michel's busy single street leads you past tacky souvenir shops to the majestic abbey.

The monumental abbey looms large over the homes of Mont St-Michel's handful of true residents.

Try the island's famous fluffy omelettes.

The enchanting forests of the Perche, Orne

## Turning Tides

Mont St-Michel has the most dramatic tides in Europe with a difference of 15m between the lowest and highest. Some 61,000 acres of sand is regularly exposed, covered with water and exposed again as the tides advance and recede. Although it used to be said that the tide advances with the speed of a galloping horse, it would be more accurate to say that it advances at the speed of a brisk walk, or at about 10km an hour. It can take as little as 4½ hours for the bay to fill up. To take full advantage of the experience, get there two hours before the tide reaches its peak.

Although there's a high and low tide in the bay each day, the water must reach a level of at least 12m to be perceptible in Mont St-Michel, which only occurs 15 or 16 days a month. The gravitational pull of the sun and moon cause the tides. When the sun, moon and earth are aligned, the tides are at their highest; when they are at right angles, tides are lowest. The tides reach their peak twice a month during the full-moon and new-moon periods, but the most impressive 15m tides only occur twice a year: around the full-moon period of the vernal equinox (around 21 March) and the new-moon period of the autumnal equinox (around 23 September).

For the first six months of the year the highest tides are around the full-moon period. They increase with each full moon until they reach a peak during the full-moon period around the vernal equinox. Thereafter the full-moon tides decrease and the new-moon tides increase until the summer solstice (21 June) when the highest tide is at the new-moon period. For the last six months of the year high tides increase around the new moon until they peak near the autumnal equinox. Then the new-moon tides decrease and the full-moon tides increase until the winter solstice (21 December) when you have the highest tides at the full moon.

For a traveller, the best plan is to come during the full-moon period of the vernal equinox or the new-moon period of the autumnal equinox. The next best plan is to come during the full-moon period during the first six months of the year or the new-moon period the rest of the year. Otherwise, come during the full- or new-moon period any time of the year. To be even more precise, the days you're targeting are 36 to 48 hours after the full or new moons.

---

the shadows. It was Richard I, duke of Normandy, who invited the first Benedictine monks to populate the rock in 966. These first monks built a small church but their sanctuary proved to be too small as the Benedictine order blossomed. The monks supported William the Conqueror's 1066 invasion and, in return, he awarded them with enough money to begin building the first abbey. The first three-storey Romanesque church and abbey buildings were soon completed.

King Philippe-Auguste's conquest of Normandy in 1204 brought stability to a region buffeted by rivalries between the king of France and the duke of Normandy. In the new atmosphere of peace and with a generous donation from Philippe-Auguste, the first stones were laid for the construction of the Gothic abbey known as 'La Merveille'. Much of the design and construction was effected by monks from the abbey at St-Wandrille who brought stones from the offshore Chausey islands, cut them and hoisted them into place.

The abbey was fortified at the end of the 14th century as the country descended into the Hundred Years' War. The English blockaded and besieged Mont St-Michel three times in the early 15th century but the fortified abbey withstood these assaults; it was the only place in western and northern France not to fall into English hands. During the Hundred Years' War, the English authorities allowed safe conduct to pilgrims, which allowed the religious – and commercial – life of Mont St-Michel to continue. In fact, the crack tourism industry of the Mont can be traced back to these medieval merchants selling fake relics to the faithful.

Mont St-Michel was again assaulted during the 16th-century Religious Wars;

monastic life fell into decline and the last monks were chased out during the Revolution. The revolutionaries baptised it Mont Libre and turned it into a prison, which it remained until 1863. Restoration of the abbey was begun under Napoleon III and in 1966 the abbey was symbolically returned to the Benedictines as part of the celebrations marking its millennium. The monks maintain a small, symbolic presence in the abbey.

## Orientation

There is only one opening in the ramparts, Porte de l'Avancée, immediately to the left as you walk down the causeway. The Mont's single street – Grande Rue – is lined with restaurants, a few hotels, souvenir shops and entrances to some rather tacky exhibits in the crypts below. There are several large car parks (15FF) near the Mont.

Pontorson (see that section later in the chapter), the nearest town to Mont St-Michel, is 9km south and the base for most travellers. Route D976 from Mont St-Michel runs right into Pontorson's main thoroughfare, rue du Couësnon.

## Information

**Tourist Offices** The tourist office (☎ 02 33 60 14 30, fax 02 33 60 06 75, ⓔ ot.mont .saint.michel@wanadoo.fr) is up the stairs to the left as you enter Porte de l'Avancée. It opens 9 am to 7 pm daily, July and August; 9.30 am to noon and 1 to 6.30 pm daily, Easter to September; and 9 am to noon and 2 to 5.45 pm Monday to Saturday, the rest of the year. Visit its Web site at www.le-mont-saint-michel.org for further information.

If you're interested in what the tides will be doing, look for the *horaire des marées* posted outside. You will also find a schedule of the tides at www.mont-saintmichel .com. In July and August – when up to 9000 people a day visit – children under eight can be left with a *gardien* (baby-sitter) near the abbey church. A detailed map of the Mont is available at the tourist office for 20FF.

**Money** There's a Société Générale ATM just inside the Porte de l'Avancée.

**Post & Communications** The post office on Grand rue opens from 8.30 am to noon and 2 to 5.30 pm weekdays, and also on Saturday morning.

**Books** *The Mont St-Michel*, written by Lucien Bély and published by Éditions Ouest-France, is a surprisingly readable history of the abbey and its inhabitants. Souvenir shops along Grande Rue sell it for 50FF; it is one of the rare things worth buying in the Mont.

## Walking Tour

When the tide is out, you can walk all the way around Mont St-Michel, a distance of about 1km, but it is essential to check with the tourist office for the schedule of tides. Every year dozens of people need to be rescued from the bay after getting trapped in a rising tide. There are also shifting patches of quicksand in the bay from which Norman soldiers are depicted being rescued in one scene of the Bayeux Tapestry. Watch out for mists that roll in quickly, making it easy to become disoriented.

## Abbaye du Mont St-Michel

The Mont's major attraction is the renowned abbey (☎ 02 33 89 80 00), open 9.30 am to 5.30 pm daily (to 5 pm from October to April). To reach it, walk to the top of Grande Rue and then climb the stairway. From mid-May to September (except Sunday) there are self-paced night-time illuminated visits of Mont St-Michel, complete with music, starting at 9.30 or 10 pm and lasting for three hours. They cost 60FF (those aged under 25, 35FF).

Most rooms can be visited without a guide, but it's worthwhile taking the guided tour included in the ticket price of 40FF (those aged 18 to 25 and students 22FF, children free). One-hour tours in English depart three to eight times daily (the last one leaves about half an hour before closing).

The **Église Abbatiale** (abbey church) was built at the rocky tip of the mountain cone. The transept rests on solid rock while the nave, choir and transept arms are supported by the massive rooms below. The church is famous for its mixture of architectural styles: the nave and south transept (11th and 12th centuries) are Norman Romanesque, while the choir (late 15th century) is Flamboyant Gothic. Mass is said here at 12.15 pm daily year-round.

The buildings on the northern side of the Mont are known as **La Merveille** (literally, 'the marvel'). The famous cloître (cloister) is an ambulatory surrounded by a double row of delicately carved arches resting on granite pillars. The early-13th-century **réfectoire** (dining hall) is illuminated by a wall of recessed windows – remarkable, given that the sheer drop precluded the use of flying buttresses – which diffuse the light beautifully. The Gothic **Salle des Hôtes** (guest hall), which dates from 1213, has two giant fireplaces. Watch out for the **promenoire** (ambulatory), with one of the oldest ribbed vaulted ceilings in Europe, and **La Chapelle de Notre de Dame sous Terre** (Underground Chapel of Our Lady), one of the earliest rooms built in the abbey and rediscovered in 1903.

The masonry used to build the abbey was brought to the Mont by boat and then pulled up the hillside using ropes. What looks like a treadmill for gargantuan gerbils was in fact powered in the 19th century by half a dozen prisoners who, by turning the wheel, hoisted the supply sledge up the side of the abbey.

## Museums
At times Grande Rue resembles a fair, with touts trying to rope you into visiting the 20-minute **Archéoscope** (☎ 02 33 48 09 37) multimedia show or the **Musée Grévin** (☎ 02 33 60 14 09), a wax museum with a mishmash of pseudo-historical exhibits. The **Musée Maritime** (☎ 02 33 60 14 09) is a bit more serious with explanations about the bay. A combined ticket for the three venues costs 75FF (students 60FF, children 45FF); individually they're 45FF (concessions 30FF). The museums open from 9 am to 6 pm daily.

## Organised Tours
In order to fully explore the Mont St-Michel bay you need to leave Mont St-Michel. Découverte de la Baie du Mont St-Michel (☎ 02 33 70 83 49, fax 02 33 48 25 67), La Maison du Guide, 1 rue Montoise, is in Genêts (32km north of the Mont by road) and offers an extensive program of walking tours. Guided walking tours leave from Bec d'Andaine (the point across the bay directly opposite Mont St-Michel) almost daily in July and August, less often the rest of the year, and cost from 30FF for a 14km 4½-hour tour.

Also in Genêts is La Maison de la Baie (☎ 02 33 89 64 00, fax 02 33 89 64 09), which offers walking and wildlife tours leaving from Bec d'Andaine that cost 33FF.

For wildlife tours of the bay contact Maison de la Baie (☎ 02 33 89 66 00, fax 02 33 89 66 09, ⓔ smet.courtils@wanadoo.fr) in Courtils, 9km east of the Mont, which also has a museum devoted to the bird, animal and fish life of the bay. Experienced riders can explore the bay on horseback. Contact Cheval Plaisir (☎/fax 02 33 60 52 67, ⓔ cheval-plaisir@wanadoo.fr), Le Champ du Genêts, 50300 St-Senier-sous-Avranches. A two-day exploration of the bay will cost around 1350FF including accommodation and breakfast.

## Places to Stay
**Camping** At the end of the causeway, only 2km from the Mont, is *Camping du Mont St-Michel* (☎ *02 33 60 09 33, fax 02 33 68 22 09*). This grassy camp site opens early February to October, and charges 22FF per person and 20FF for a tent and car. It also has bungalows with shower and toilet for two people costing 220FF.

There are several other camping grounds – one called *Camping sous les Pommiers* (☎ *02 33 60 11 36, fax 02 33 60 25 81*) – a couple of kilometres farther south towards Pontorson. It opens April to mid-October and charges 13FF per person and 23FF for car and tent.

**Hotels** Mont St-Michel has plenty of hotels. None of them are cheap but you're paying for the ability to experience Mont St-Michel in off-hours. You have the choice of either staying on the Mont or 2km away

MANCHE

## Mont St-Michel – New and Improved

Mont St-Michel has hardly changed at all in centuries. Now everything's about to change. Over the past several decades it's become clear that the mainland has been moving ever closer to Mont St-Michel as the bay silted up. Until the late 19th century, the natural movement of the tides and the River Couësnon regularly flushed out the bay. With the canalisation of the river as well as the creation of polders, an underwater dike and the causeway, sediment began to build up.

Although the underwater dike was removed in 1983, the problem has persisted. The very real danger that Mont St-Michel would one day be in the midst of a field rather than water prompted the authorities to consider a more dramatic solution. After the usual interminable studies, the causeway and the canalised Couësnon were fingered as the major culprits blocking the natural movement of the waters.

A far-reaching 780 million-franc project is being implemented to solve the problem. The floodgates at the mouth of the river will be enlarged, allowing a greater volume of water into the bay. In addition, the river will be divided into two parts, flowing on either side of the Mont. Together the tides and the powerful new river are expected to wash away the sand deposits.

Of keener interest to Mont St-Michel's millions of prospective visitors is the projected destruction of the causeway. A low bridge will replace the current embankment that is choking the bay. A tram will shuttle visitors between car parks on the mainland, 2km away, and the entrance to the Mont. There will also be pedestrian walkways on either side of the tram lines, allowing access by foot. The current car parks outside the Mont will be destroyed and the entrance to the Mont redesigned to accommodate the new approach, which will be slightly to the east of the current embankment.

The project is scheduled to begin in 2001 and the tram is scheduled to make its first voyage in the summer of 2006, but the Mont will remain open for the duration. Although the construction work may spoil photo opportunities for a while, the ultimate result should be more aesthetically pleasing since it should make the views at high tide even more dramatic. Plans are also afoot to expand opportunities for walking, cycling and horse riding in and around the bay in the hopes that some of the abbey's visitors will stay and explore the region.

at the end of the causeway. If you stay on the Mont, meals will be expensive but if you stay at the end of the causeway you can self-cater, plus you get dramatic views of Mont St-Michel silhouetted against the sky. Many people opt to stay in nearby Pontorson, but it's not advisable if you're planning to catch a high tide and are relying on public transport. The buses are on a 9 am to 6 pm schedule but the tides are not.

**Mont St-Michel** The cheapest place to stay on the Mont is the small, two-star *Hôtel du Guesclin* (☎ 02 33 60 14 10, fax 02 33 60 45 81) which has doubles from 200FF. It closes from November to March. *Hôtel Le St-Michel* (☎/fax 02 33 60 14 37) is also reasonable with simple doubles costing from 250FF. *Hôtel de la Mère Poulard*

(☎ 02 33 60 14 01, fax 02 33 48 52 31, e hotel.mere.poulard@wanadoo.fr, Grand rue), is a pretty museum-piece hotel on your left as you enter town, offering doubles with shower from 300FF. The three-star *Hôtel de la Croix Blanche* (☎ 02 33 60 14 04, fax 02 33 48 59 82) is a good luxury alternative with a decent restaurant. Rooms cost from 505FF to 720FF.

**Entrance to the Causeway** You'll find modern but bland doubles/triples/quads/quins at *Hôtel Formule Verte* (☎ 02 33 60 14 13, fax 02 33 60 14 44) for 200/270/340/410FF. *Hôtel Motel Vert* (☎ 02 33 60 09 33, fax 02 33 68 22 09) also has reasonably priced doubles starting at 200FF. Three-star *Hôtel de la Digue* (☎ 02 33 60 14 02, fax 02 33 60 37 59) is a comfortable,

MANCHE

family-run establishment that has doubles costing from 350FF to 460FF.

## Places to Eat
The tourist restaurants around the base of the Mont have lovely views, but they aren't bargains; *menus* start at about 80FF, and the quality can be mediocre. Mention must be made about Mont St-Michel's most celebrated restaurant though, *La Mère Poulard* (☎ 02 33 60 14 01, Grande Rue), which turns out omelettes at stratospheric prices. Movie stars, politicians, and tycoons have made this restaurant an institution, leaving behind autographed photos to adorn the walls. The delicious egg concoctions more closely resemble soufflés than omelettes, but the cheapest *menu* is 180FF.

A number of establishments offer their own cheaper versions of the Poulard omelette as well as the other culinary speciality of Mont St-Michel, lamb *pre-salé*. The sheep grazing on the salty marshes around the island abbey produce a distinctive, delicately salted meat. Restaurants connected with the better hotels offer decent meals at what passes for reasonable prices here. *Crêperie La Sirène* (☎ 02 33 60 08 60) over a souvenir shop turns out good crepes for about 50FF in a cosy dining room. The restaurant opens daily except Friday.

The nearest *supermarket* is next to Camping du Mont St-Michel on the D976. It opens 8 am to 8 pm (to 10 pm in July and August) daily except Sunday, from mid-February to October.

## Getting There & Away
Bus No 15 run by STN (☎ 02 33 58 03 07 in Avranches) goes from Pontorson train station to Mont St-Michel (14.10/22.60FF for a single/return). There are nine buses daily in July and August (six at the weekend) and three or four during the rest of the year. Most buses connect with trains to/from Paris, Rennes and Caen.

Courriers Bretons (☎ 02 99 19 70 70) has regular services from Pontorson (48.50FF, one hour) and Mont St-Michel (55FF, 1¼ hours) to St-Malo in Brittany. The daily bus

from St-Malo to Mont St-Michel leaves at 9.50 am and returns around 4.30 pm.

## PONTORSON
**postcode 50170 • pop 4100**
Pontorson, 9km south of Mont St-Michel, frequently serves as a base for travellers visiting the Mont. There's a wide variety of accommodation options here and its small-village atmosphere is appealing.

## Orientation & Information
Route D976 from Mont St-Michel runs right into Pontorson's main thoroughfare, rue du Couësnon. The friendly staff at Pontorson's tourist office (☎ 02 33 60 20 65, fax 02 33 60 85 67, e mont.st.michel.pontorson@wanadoo.fr), in place de l'Église just west of the town hall, are on duty from 9.30 am to 6 pm Tuesday to Friday (7 pm daily mid-June to mid-September), 10 am to noon and 2 to 5 pm on Saturday (to 6 pm in summer) and 10 am to noon on Sunday in summer.

To change money, try CIN bank, 98 rue du Couësnon, in Pontorson. It is closed Sunday and Monday. There are more banks on rue du Couësnon and place de l'Hôtel de Ville.

The post office (☎ 02 33 60 01 66) on the eastern side of place de l'Hôtel de Ville opens 8.30 am to noon and 2 to 5.30 pm on weekdays, and on Saturday morning.

## Things to See & Do
**Église Notre Dame de Pontorson** is no match for its dramatic sister to the north, but this 12th-century church is a good example of Norman Romanesque architecture. To the left of the main altar is a 15th-century relief of Christ's Passion, which was mutilated during the Religious Wars and again during the Revolution.

## Places to Stay
About 1km west of the train station, *Centre Duguesclin* (☎/fax 02 33 60 18 65, e aj@ville-pontorson.fr, boulevard du Général Patton) is situated in an old three-storey stone building opposite No 26. This modern, newly renovated hostel opens Easter to mid-September and charges 48FF per night

MANCHE

in a four- to six-bed room. There are kitchen facilities. The hostel closes between 10 am and 6 pm, but there's no curfew.

Across place de la Gare from the train station are a couple of cheap hotels. *Hôtel de l'Arrivée (☎ 02 33 60 01 57, 14 rue du Docteur Tizon)* has doubles for 95FF with washbasin, 120FF with washbasin and toilet, and 165FF with shower. Triples/quads with washbasin or toilet cost 170/190FF and from 220FF with shower. Hall showers cost 15FF.

*Hôtel Le Rénové (☎ 02 33 60 00 21, 4 rue de Rennes)*, has simple doubles for 160FF with washbasin, and 180FF with WC and shower. Triples/quads cost 230/250FF. Hall showers are free. *Hôtel La Tour de Brette (☎ 02 33 60 10 69, fax 02 33 48 59 66, 8 rue du Couësnon)* is an excellent deal. Its cheerful rooms – all with shower and TV – cost 169FF (220FF in summer).

At the top end, *Hôtel Montgomery (☎ 02 33 60 00 09, fax 02 33 60 37 66, e hotel .montgomery@wanadoo.fr, 13 rue du Couësnon)*, in a lovely 16th-century townhouse, has rooms with a private WC and shower from 250FF.

## Places to Eat

You can get decent pizza from 36FF, salads from 16FF and pasta for lunch and dinner at *La Squadra (☎ 02 33 68 31 17, 102 rue Couësnon)* It opens daily except Monday and Tuesday. For crepes and savoury galettes (10FF to 30FF), try *La Crêperie du Couësnon (☎ 02 33 60 16 67, 21 rue du Couësnon)*.

The splendid restaurant at the *Hôtel La Tour de Brette* (see Places to Stay) has *menus* for 60FF, 80FF and 95FF. For something a little more formal, try the dining room of the *Hôtel de Bretagne (☎ 02 33 60 10 55, 59 rue du Couësnon)* with excellent food and service. *Menus* cost from 80FF.

The *8 à 8 (5 rue du Couësnon)* supermarket opens 8.30 am to 12.45 pm and 2.30 to 7.30 pm Monday to Saturday, and 9 am to 12.30 pm on Sunday.

## Getting There & Away

**Bus** The Pontorson office of the Courriers Bretons bus company (☎ 02 33 60 11 43) is 50m west of the train station at 2 rue du Docteur Bailleul. Courriers Bretons buses on their way to Mont St-Michel from St-Malo do *not* pick up passengers in Pontorson, but do so in the opposite direction.

**Train** Services to/from Pontorson include Caen (125FF, 2¼ hours, two daily) via Folligny, Rennes (69FF, 50 minutes, two daily) via Dol, Coutances (59FF, 55 minutes, three daily) and Cherbourg (131FF, 2½ hours, two daily). From Paris, take the train to Caen (from Gare St-Lazare), or Rennes (from Gare Montparnasse), or travel directly to Pontorson via Folligny (from Gare Montparnasse, 210FF). The train station has a left-luggage service for 30FF.

## Getting Around

**Taxi** Call a taxi on ☎ 02 33 60 33 23 or ☎ 02 33 60 26 89.

**Bicycle** Bikes can be rented at the train station (55FF per day plus 1000FF deposit) and from E Videloup (☎ 02 33 60 11 40) at 1 bis rue du Couësnon, which charges 50FF per day for city bicycles and 80FF for mountain bikes. E Videloup opens 8.30 am to 12.30 pm and 2 to 7 pm Monday to Saturday. It is closed on Monday morning.

# Orne

Two major autoroutes circle around the Orne department, forming a kind of shell that has protected it from urbanisation. Normandy's most rural department has been left to its forests, hillsides, horses and rivers. Cities are few and far between. To appreciate the Orne, take the backroads – there's hardly anything but backroads anyway – and stop off in the rural villages and hamlets that have sprouted up along the region's many rivers. The River Orne in the north-west stretches into the Suisse Normande while the Sarthe Valley in the south offers ravishing vistas. Take a walk or bike ride through the Forêt d'Écouves north of Alençon or the Perche forests – Forêt de Bellême, Forêt de Saussay and the Parc Regional Normandie-Maine. If you want to unwind, there's always the curative waters in Bagnoles de l'Orne. The Orne is not a good department to explore by public transport – buses throughout the region are either rare or non-existent.

## ALENÇON
### postcode 61000 • pop 34,000
In the far south of Normandy, on the edge of the Normandie Maine nature reserve, lies vibrant Alençon. The elegant buildings that make up the town centre recall the days when Alençon was the lace-making hub of Europe. From the 17th to 19th centuries Alençon supplied fashionable women everywhere with astonishingly intricate lace and grew prosperous in the process. The lace industry has withered away but, thanks to the opening of Moulinex appliance factories, Alençon is still thriving. With the Rivers Sarthe and Briante meandering through a town centre largely composed of pedestrianised shopping streets, Alençon makes a perfect base from which to explore the Orne.

## Orientation & Information
The old town and its sights are about 1.5km south-west of the train station, via avenue

### Highlights

- Strolling through Alençon's town centre
- Taking the waters at Bagnoles de l'Orne
- Walking along the River Sarthe from St-Céneri-le-Gérei to St-Léonard-des-Bois
- Attending the annual *boudin* (blood sausage) fair in Mortagne-au-Perche

du Président Wilson and rue St-Blaise. The bus station is 400m south-west of the train station on square des Déportés.

**Tourist Offices** The tourist office (☎ 02 33 80 60 33, fax 02 33 80 60 32, [e] alençon .tourisme@wanadoo.fr) is in the turreted Maison d'Ozé on place La Magdelaine. It opens 9.30 am to noon and 2 to 6.30 pm Monday to Saturday year round; and 10 am to 12.30 pm and 2.30 to 5.30 pm Sunday in July and August. It books accommodation for free and has a free English-language brochure, *Alençon on Foot*, showing a walking tour of the town. You can visit its Web site at www.ville-alencon.fr. The Bureau Information Jeunesse (☎ 02 33 80 48 90), 4–6 place Poulet Malassis, opens 9.30 am to 12.30 pm and 1.30 to 5.30 pm Monday to Saturday. It provides information

## ORNE

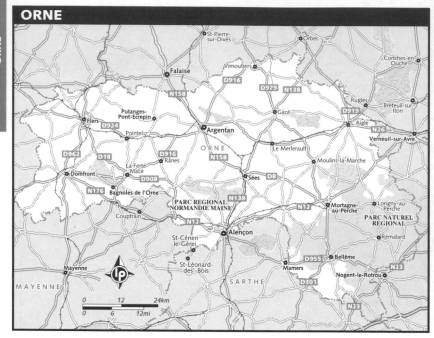

about local transport and accommodation options. Its Web site is at www.bijbus.com.

**Money** The Banque de France on rue Docteur du Becquembois exchanges money from 8.40 am to noon Monday to Friday. There's a Crédit Mutuel at 89 bis rue aux Sieurs. The post office has a currency window.

**Post & Communications** The post office at 16 rue du Jeudi opens 8.15 am to 7 pm Monday to Friday and Saturday mornings. It has Cyberposte. There's a free Internet connection at Espace Internet (☎ 02 33 32 40 33), 6–8 rue des Filles Notre Dame, which opens 8.30 am to 7 pm Monday to Saturday.

**Laundry** There's a self-service laundrette at 5 rue du Collège, open 7 am to 9 pm daily.

### Things to See & Do
The old town, especially along **Grand Rue**, is full of atmospheric Second-Empire houses

with forged iron balconies dating from the 18th century. To the south-east looms the crowned turret of the **Château des Ducs**, which was used by the Nazis as a prison during WWII. It is closed to the public.

The **Musée des Beaux-Arts et de la Dentelle** (☎ 02 33 32 40 07) occupies a restored Jesuit school building at 12 rue Charles Aveline. It houses a so-so collection of Flemish, Dutch and French artworks from the 17th to 19th centuries as well as an exhaustive exhibit on the history of lacemaking and its techniques. The intricacy of the work on display is astonishing. There's also an unexpected section of Cambodian artefacts – including Buddhas, spears and tiger skulls – donated by a former (French) governor of Cambodia. It opens 10 am to noon and 2 to 6 pm daily except Monday; admission costs 18FF (students 15FF).

Serious lace-lovers can try the **Musée de la Dentelle 'Au Point d'Alençon'** (☎ 02 33 26 27 26), 33 rue du Pont Neuf, which offers

## Alençon Lace

During the mid-17th century, Louis XIV's finance minister Jean-Baptiste Colbert had a problem. Too much French money was being spent on fashionable Venetian lace. Venetian artisans were expert in a particular technique that resulted in extraordinarily fine, durable lace.

JANE SMITH

**Intricate Alençon lace**

Colbert decided that it would make more sense to bring 20 or so lace-makers to Alençon, where there was already a tradition of lace-making, to instruct the local needlewomen.

In 1665, he set up the Royal Lace Manufacture in Alençon with the instructions for the Alençon women to develop a new and unique style. His will was done. The new technique was time-consuming but allowed for a more precise design and a wider variety of motifs.

Not only did the Alençon needlewomen create a new technique but, under the supervision of a Madame La Perrière, they created a new production process allowing better lace to be produced more efficiently. Rather than the one-woman-one-product method, Madame La Perrière set up an assembly line in which each woman contributed her own speciality to the production of a magnificent piece of lace. It wasn't long before Alençon lace had outstripped that from Venice.

Alençon lace became world renowned and was designated the 'Queen of Lace' at the 1851 World Fair in London. The demand for such a fine and expensive product dropped in the 20th century and, in 1976, the Alençon Point National Workshop was created to keep the technique alive. Although only about a dozen women are currently producing lace (mostly for Parisian couture houses) their fingers are flying. It takes 25 hours of work to produce a piece of lace the size of a postage stamp and years to produce a tablecloth.

guided visits that include a short film on lace-making and about 60 pieces of lace. There's also a shop where you can buy it. The museum and shop open 10 am to noon and 2 to 6 pm from Monday to Saturday. Admission costs 20FF.

**Église Notre Dame** on Grande Rue has a stunning Flamboyant Gothic portal from the 16th century, and some superb stained glass in the chapel where St Theresa was baptised. It opens from 8.30 am to noon and 2 to 5.30 pm daily.

**St-Theresa's birthplace** is remarkable for its extreme simplicity. The entrance is through an adjacent chapel dedicated to the saint. It opens 9 am to noon and 2 to 6 pm Wednesday to Monday; admission is free.

The **Musée Leclerc** (☎ 02 33 26 27 26), 33 rue du Pont Neuf, details the history of Alençon during WWII and has some fascinating wartime photos. The town was liberated in August 1944 by General Leclerc,

whose statue stands proudly out front. It opens 10 am to noon and 2 to 6 pm Monday to Saturday. Admission costs 15FF (those aged 12 to 18, 8FF).

### Places to Stay & Eat

South-west of town on the Sarthe, *Camping Municipal* (☎ 02 33 26 34 95, 69 rue de Guéramé) charges 12FF per adult and 13FF per tent site. It opens year round.

There are a number of small hotels around the train station. *Hôtel de Paris* (☎ 02 33 29 01 64, fax 02 33 29 44 87, 26 rue Denis Papin), just east of the train station, has basic singles/doubles with washbasin for 130/140FF. Rooms with private shower and WC cost 180/200FF.

Closer to the town centre is *Hôtel de L'Industrie* (☎ 02 33 27 19 30, fax 02 33 28 49 56, 20 place du Général de Gaulle), a friendly place with 1950s-style rooms and a good restaurant, which opens daily except

ORNE

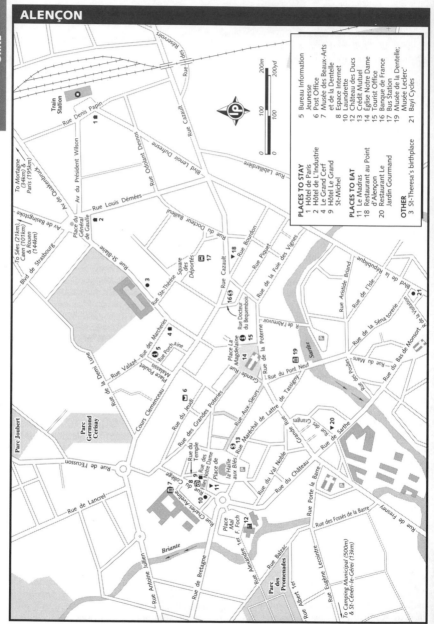

# ALENÇON

PLACES TO STAY
1  Hôtel de Paris
2  Hôtel de L'Industrie
4  Le Grand Cerf
9  Hôtel Le Grand
   St-Michel

PLACES TO EAT
11  Le Madras
18  Restaurant au Point
    d'Alençon
20  Restaurant Le
    Jardin Gourmand

OTHER
3  St-Theresa's birthplace

5  Bureau Information
   Jeunesse
6  Post Office
7  Musée des Beaux-Arts
   et de la Dentelle
8  Espace Internet
10 Laundrette
12 Château des Ducs
13 Crédit Mutuel
14 Église Notre Dame
15 Tourist Office
16 Banque de France
17 Bus Station
19 Musée de la Dentelle;
   Musée Leclerc'
21 Bayi Cycles

*euro currency converter  10FF = €1.52*

Saturday. Simple singles cost from 180FF to 280FF; doubles with a private bathroom cost 350FF.

In the centre of old Alençon on a quiet street, *Hôtel Le Grand St-Michel* (☎ 02 33 26 04 77, fax 02 33 26 71 82, 7 rue du Temple) has the air of a traditional country house. The renovated rooms are comfortable in a casual, thrown-together way. Rooms with sink only cost 180FF, and 280FF to 350FF with private facilities.

Two-star *Le Grand Cerf* (☎ 02 33 26 00 51, fax 02 33 26 63 07, 21 rue St-Blaise), on the edge of the old town, offers more luxury, with plush rooms for 250/290FF. The decor is delightfully traditional but the welcome could be friendlier. It has a good French restaurant with three-course *menus* for 80FF. For just a few francs more you could eat at the far superior *Restaurant Le Jardin Gourmand* (☎ 02 33 32 22 56, 49 rue des Granges). The chef takes simple fresh ingredients and magically transforms them into mouth-watering dishes. *Menus* cost 115FF and 190FF. It opens daily except Tuesday dinner and Wednesday.

*Le Madras* (☎ 02 33 26 19 30, 7 rue des Filles Notre Dame) does Caribbean specialities such as *boudin à l'antilliase* (Caribbean-style blood sausage) with filling *menus* for 49FF and 59FF. It opens daily except Monday dinner and Sunday.

*Restaurant au Point d'Alençon* (☎ 02 33 26 01 68, 116 rue Cazault) is a family-style restaurant that attracts crowds of students who come for its cheap, tasty 58FF *menu*. It opens daily except Sunday dinner and Monday.

## Getting There & Away
**Bus** TIS (☎ 02 43 39 97 30) runs buses between Alençon and Le Mans (55FF, 1¾ hours, three to four daily). STAO (☎ 02 33 29 11 11) connects Alençon with Sées (20 minutes, once daily) and Mortagne-au-Perche (one hour, four daily).

**Train** Alençon has frequent services to Gare Montparnasse in Paris (213FF to 278FF, 1¾ hours), Caen (86FF, 1¾ hours), Granville (142FF, three hours), Pontorson

(136FF, two hours) and Le Mans (50FF, 45 minutes), among other destinations.

## Getting Around
**Bus** Altobus (☎ 08 00 50 02 29) has three lines that serve the city including one, Line A, that runs from the train station to the town centre.

**Bicycle** Bikes can be rented at Bayi Cycles (☎ 02 33 29 65 13) on 104 boulevard de la République.

## AROUND ALENÇON
### Sarthe Valley
Following the Sarthe south-west of Alençon takes you through an enchanting landscape of steep forested hills and fairy-tale villages. The most delightful is **St-Céneri-le-Gérei**, 13km to the south-west. Classified as one of the France's most beautiful villages, its allure has the government seal of approval. The stone village is on a tiny peninsula in the midst of the Sarthe and gives the impression of just holding its own against the encroaching greenery. A map posted at the entrance to the village is a helpful aid in finding the main highlight – the Romanesque church built in the 11th century.

Campers can stay at the idyllic *Camping de St-Céneri* (☎ 02 33 26 60 00) only 100m from the village along the river, but there's nowhere else to stay in town.

**St-Léonard-des-Bois**, 6km south of St-Céneri, is a sleepy town along the Sarthe at the foot of high cliffs. There's a tourist office at the *Camping Municipal* (☎ 02 43 33 81 79) to provide you with a list of *chambres d'hôtes* (B&Bs) and an inexpensive hotel, *L'Hôtel de France* (☎ 02 43 97 92 29), which has simple rooms from 150FF.

There's no public transport to either town but the back roads make a pretty bike ride and there's a path from St-Céneri that takes you along the river to St-Léonard.

### Sées
It's no surprise that French director Luc Besson chose Sées, 17km north of Alençon, as the setting for several scenes in his movie *Jeanne d'Arc*. The town centre is crammed

**ORNE**

with medieval buildings, mostly religious structures dating from the days when Sées was the seat of the archbishop. Of the churches, chapels, basilicas, convents and abbeys, the most outstanding building is the **cathedral**. Built from the 13th to 14th centuries but badly damaged in the Hundred Years' War, the 70m towers dwarf the town centre. Passing through the elaborate central doorway, you're faced with a cavernous interior marked by splendid 13th-century rose windows in the northern and southern transepts.

The tourist office (☎ 02 33 28 74 79) is on place Charles de Gaulle, a few metres north of the cathedral. It opens 10 am to noon and 2 to 6.30 pm Monday to Saturday.

There's only one impracticably timed bus from Alençon each day, so it's best to have your own transport.

## BAGNOLES DE L'ORNE
**postcode 61140 • pop 783**

Hugging the banks of the River Vée and its lake, Bagnoles is the most attractive spa town in Normandy. The vast Forêt des Andaines presses around the town, leaving the air fresh and fragrant. The town is also architecturally interesting. Avenues of opulent buildings date from the turn of the century when the rich and titled found various ailments to send them down to Bagnoles for a relaxing 'cure'. It may no longer be royalty's spa of choice, but Bagnoles has no trouble attracting clients to its luxurious thermal baths. The median age of its visitors stretches into the higher double-digits but there's plenty to do apart from relaxing in warm baths or getting pummelled by water jets. Paths lead along the river and around the lake; there's tennis, golf, horse-riding, rock-climbing, a casino, buggy rides and a packed schedule of concerts and shows in the summer.

### Orientation & Information

The lake provides an orientation point in the town. The casino is on its north-western shore and the commercial centre of town stretches down from the south-eastern shore. The thermal baths are in the midst of the *Parc Thermal*, a spacious wooded park, along the southern course of the Vée.

The tourist office (☎ 02 33 37 85 66, fax 02 33 30 06 75) on place du Marché has ample documentation on the sporting and cultural activities in and around Bagnoles as well as accommodation. It opens 10 am to noon and 2 to 6 pm daily from April to October, but closes Saturday afternoon and Sunday the rest of the year.

The post office is situated on rue de l'Hippodrome, next to the southern shore of the lake.

### Things to See & Do

**L'Établissement Thermal** (☎ 02 33 30 38 00) is worth a visit if only for its eye-catching *belle epoque* architecture. According to local legend, the underground spring that furnishes its famous water was discovered by a local landholder who noticed that his tired old horse gained new vitality after daily baths in the fountain. The elderly gentleman began bathing in the spring and found himself blessed with a youthful new vigour. The water comes from a granite pocket about 5m deep and is lightly radioactive. Doctors prescribe it for circulatory troubles, skin disorders and, naturally enough, stress. Although the French healthcare system pays for extended, prescribed treatments, it's possible to enjoy a two-hour curative bath with water-jet massages for 165FF. The establishment opens April to October and there are free visits on Tuesday and Friday at 5 pm.

The **old town** is an exuberant mixture of over-the-top architectural flourishes on villas built during Bagnoles' golden age. The tourist office publishes a small free brochure containing a map and explanations.

### Places to Stay & Eat

It's gratifying that a town as well-heeled as Bagnoles still provides plenty of affordable accommodation, but book well in advance. Bagnoles has a long season that runs from April to October. During those months it's crammed, and outside them it's deserted.

Two kilometres south of town along avenue Président Coty, *Camping de la Vée*

(☎ 02 33 37 87 45) costs 50FF for two people with a tent or car.

All of the hotels below have good restaurants, making it worthwhile to consider taking half-board.

One of the most agreeable of the budget hotels, **Hôtel Les Capucines** (☎ 02 33 37 82 59, fax 02 33 38 91 38, 36 boulevard Lemeunier-de-la-Raillère), is in the old town. The high-ceilinged rooms are well maintained and some have balconies. Basic rooms cost 100FF; those with private facilities cost 220FF. Also in the old town for about the same price is **Le Grillon** (☎ 02 33 30 70 95, 42 boulevard Paul Chalvet), a stately old villa separated from the street by a small yard.

Close to the lake, you can't miss **La Potinière du Lac** (☎ 02 33 30 65 00, fax 02 33 38 49 04, rue des Casinos). Look for the conical tower and the cross-hatched half-timbered facade that scream 'Normandy'! Rooms here cost from 110FF to 260FF with the higher-priced rooms having private facilities.

Modern **Le Cetlos** (☎ 02 33 38 44 44, fax 02 33 38 46 23, rue des Casinos), overlooking the lake, offers amazing luxury for the price. Rooms are large and comfortable and there's an indoor swimming pool, sauna, steam room and gym. Rooms cost from 305FF to 355FF.

### Getting There & Away
There are three buses daily from Alençon during the week, scheduled to make a day trip possible (one hour and 10 minutes).

### Getting Around
You can rent mountain bikes from Librairie du Lac (☎ 02 33 30 80 27), on 4 rue des Casinos, for 70FF per day.

## MORTAGNE-AU-PERCHE
**postcode 61400 • pop 5200**
Located about 34km north-east of Alençon, Mortagne-au-Perche sits on a hill overlooking the Perche region, an underpopulated land marked by a massive regional park in its southern reaches. The park was created in 1998 and covers nearly half a million acres. Known for its particular breed of horse, the Percheron, much of the region is given over to fields and forests. There are no cities, no autoroutes and just a few large towns. In addition to exporting its popular horses, the Perche exported many of its people to Canada centuries ago, furnishing much of the population for French Canada.

Mortagne-au-Perche makes an excellent base for exploring the Perche region. Its 18th-century buildings have been immaculately restored, recalling the days when the town was the capital of the Perche region. Although Mortagne-au-Perche is no longer the important commercial centre it once was, the town remains a vital marketplace for the agricultural products of the region. If blood sausage (boudin) is to your taste, this is the place to sample it. The annual Lent boudin fair draws many locals and even more Parisians, many of whom have second homes in and around town.

### Orientation & Information
The centre of the town is busy place du Général de Gaulle, dominated by the 19th-century Halle aux Grains (grain market). The tourist office (☎ 02 33 85 11 18, fax 02 33 83 76 76) is in the Halle aux Grains and has a wealth of information about walks and cycle routes in the region. It opens 9.30 am to 12.30 pm and 2.30 to 6 pm Monday to Saturday from mid-May to mid-September. The Caisse d'Épargne bank is at 10 place du Général de Gaulle and changes money. The post office is at 16 rue des 15 Fusillés, the main street leading from place du Général de Gaulle.

### Things to See & Do
The tourist office publishes a helpful pamphlet mapping out the aristocratic residences that were constructed during the town's heyday. Along the route is the **Porte St-Denis** on rue du Portail St-Denis, which is the last remaining remnant of the walls that once surrounded the town.

Also noteworthy is **Église Notre Dame**, reconstructed at the end of the 16th century in Flamboyant Gothic style. Notice the 18th-century wood panelling around the choir.

**ORNE**

## Places to Stay & Eat

In the centre of town is the ***Hôtel de la Poste*** *(☎ 02 33 25 08 01, 15 place de la République)*, which has simple rooms costing 135FF; rooms with private facilities cost 230FF. The restaurant below is a popular lunch favourite serving up tasty 58FF *menus*. It opens daily except Friday.

***Hôtel du Tribunal*** *(☎ 02 33 25 04 77, fax 02 33 83 60 83, 4 place du Palais)* is in a beautifully renovated 16th-century building. The old features have been preserved while modern comforts have been added. Rooms cost from 260FF to 320FF and the restaurant is excellent.

## Getting There & Away

STAO buses in Alençon (☎ 02 33 29 11 11) runs four buses daily between Mortagne-au-Perche and Alençon (one hour).

## Getting Around

Bikes can be rented from Roue Libre (☎ 02 33 25 36 20), 14 rue des 15 Fusillés.

# Language

## FRENCH

While the French rightly or wrongly have a reputation for assuming that all human beings should speak French – until WWI it was the international language of culture and diplomacy – you'll find that any attempt to communicate in French will be much appreciated. Probably your best bet is to approach people politely in French, even if the only sentence you know is: *Pardon, madame/monsieur/mademoiselle, parlez-vous anglais?* (Excuse me, madam/sir/miss, do you speak English?)

Basic French words and phrases are listed below. For a more comprehensive guide to the French language get hold of Lonely Planet's *French phrasebook*.

## Grammar

An important distinction is made in French between *tu* and *vous*, which both mean 'you'. *Tu* is only used when addressing people you know well, children or animals. When addressing an adult who is not a personal friend, *vous* should be used unless the person invites you to use *tu*. In general, younger people insist less on this distinction, and you may find that they use *tu* from the beginning of an acquaintance.

All nouns in French are either masculine or feminine and adjectives reflect the gender of the noun they modify. The feminine form of many nouns and adjectives is indicated by a silent 'e' added to the masculine form, as in *étudiant* and *étudiante*, the masculine and feminine for 'student'. In the following phrases we have indicated both masculine and feminine forms where necessary; the masculine form comes first, separated from the feminine by a slash. The gender of a noun is also often indicated by a preceding article: *le/un/du* (m), *la/une/de la* (f) (the/a/some); or a possessive adjective, *mon/ton/son* (m), *ma/ta/sa* (f) (my/your/his/her). With French, unlike English, the possessive adjective agrees in number and gender with the thing possessed: *sa mère* (his/her mother).

## Pronunciation

Most letters in French are pronounced more or less the same as their English equivalents. A few which may cause confusion are:

j   as the 's' in 'leisure', eg, *jour* (day)
c   before **e** and **i**, as the 's' in 'sit'; before **a**, **o** and **u** it's pronounced as English 'k'. When undescored with a cedilla (ç) it's always pronounced as the 's' in 'sit'.

French has a number of sounds that are difficult for Anglophones to produce. These include:

- The distinction between the 'u' sound (as in *tu*) and 'oo' sound (as in *tout*). For both sounds, the lips are rounded and projected forward, but for the 'u' the tongue is towards the front of the mouth, its tip against the lower front teeth, whereas for the 'oo' the tongue is towards the back of the mouth, its tip behind the gums of the lower front teeth.

- The nasal vowels. With nasal vowels the breath escapes partly through the nose and partly through the mouth. There are no nasal vowels in English; in French there are three, as in *bon vin blanc* (good white wine). These sounds occur where a syllable ends in a single **n** or **m**; the **n** or **m** is silent but indicates the nasalisation of the preceding vowel.

- The **r**. The standard **r** of Parisian French is produced by moving the bulk of the tongue backwards to constrict the air flow in the pharynx while the tip of the tongue rests behind the lower front teeth. It's similar to the noise made by some people before spitting, but with much less friction.

## Greetings & Civilities

| | |
|---|---|
| Hello/Good morning. | *Bonjour.* |
| Hello. (informal) | *Salut.* |

| | |
|---|---|
| Good evening. | *Bonsoir.* |
| Good night. | *Bonne nuit.* |
| Goodbye. | *Au revoir.* |
| Yes. | *Oui.* |
| No. | *Non.* |
| Please. | *S'il vous plaît.* |
| Thank you. | *Merci.* |
| You're welcome. | *Je vous en prie.* |
| Excuse me. | *Excusez-moi.* |
| Sorry/Forgive me. | *Pardon.* |
| How are you? | *Comment allez-vous?* (polite) |
| | *Comment vas-tu?/ Comment ça va?* (informal) |
| Fine, thanks. | *Bien, merci.* |
| What's your name? | *Comment vous appelez-vous?* |
| My name is ... | *Je m'appelle ...* |
| I'm pleased to meet you. | *Enchanté* (m)/ *Enchantée* (f). |
| How old are you? | *Quel âge avez-vous?* |
| I'm ... years old. | *J'ai ... ans.* |
| Do you like ...? | *Aimez-vous ...?* |
| Where are you from? | *De quel pays êtes-vous?* |
| I'm from ... | *Je viens ...* |
| Australia | *d'Australie* |
| Canada | *du Canada* |
| England | *d'Angleterre* |
| Germany | *d'Allemagne* |
| Ireland | *d'Irlande* |
| New Zealand | *de Nouvelle Zélande* |
| Scotland | *d'Écosse* |
| Wales | *du Pays de Galle* |
| the USA | *des États-Unis* |

## Language Difficulties

| | |
|---|---|
| I understand. | *Je comprends.* |
| I don't understand. | *Je ne comprends pas.* |
| Do you speak English? | *Parlez-vous anglais?* |
| Could you please write it down? | *Est-ce que vous pouvez l'écrire?* |

## Getting Around

| | |
|---|---|
| I want to go to ... | *Je voudrais aller à ...* |
| I'd like to book a seat to ... | *Je voudrais réserver une place pour ...* |

| | |
|---|---|
| What time does ... leave/arrive? | *À quelle heure part/arrive ...?* |
| the aeroplane | *l'avion* |
| the bus (city) | *l'autobus* |
| the bus (intercity) | *l'autocar* |
| the ferry | *le ferry(-boat)* |
| the train | *le train* |
| Where is ...? | *Où est ...?* |
| the bus stop | *l'arrêt d'autobus* |
| the train station | *la gare* |
| the ticket office | *le guichet* |
| I'd like a ... ticket. | *Je voudrais un billet ...* |
| one-way | *aller-simple* |
| return | *aller-retour* |
| 1st class | *de première classe* |
| 2nd class | *de deuxième classe* |
| How long does the trip take? | *Combien de temps dure le trajet?* |
| The train is ... | *Le train est ...* |
| delayed | *en retard* |
| on time | *à l'heure* |
| early | *en avance* |
| Do I need to ...? | *Est-ce que je dois ...?* |
| change trains | *changer de train* |
| change platform | *changer de quai* |
| left-luggage locker | *consigne automatique* |
| platform | *quai* |
| timetable | *horaire* |
| I'd like to hire ... | *Je voudrais louer ...* |
| a bicycle | *un vélo* |
| a car | *une voiture* |
| a guide | *un guide* |

## Around Town

| | |
|---|---|
| I'm looking for ... | *Je cherche ...* |
| a bank | *une banque* |
| the city centre | *le centre-ville* |
| the ... embassy | *l'ambassade de ...* |
| an exchange office | *un bureau de change* |
| the hospital | *l'hôpital* |
| my hotel | *mon hôtel* |
| the market | *le marché* |
| the police | *la police* |

## Signs

| Entrée | Entrance |
|--------|----------|
| **Sortie** | Exit |
| **Ouvert** | Open |
| **Fermé** | Closed |
| **Chambres Libres** | Rooms Available |
| **Complet** | No Vacancies |
| **Renseignements** | Information |
| **Interdit** | Prohibited |
| **(Commissariat de) Police** | Police Station |
| **Toilettes, WC** | Toilets |
|   *Hommes* | Men |
|   *Femmes* | Women |

| | |
|---|---|
| the post office | *le bureau de poste/ la poste* |
| a public phone | *une cabine téléphonique* |
| a public toilet | *les toilettes* |
| the tourist office | *l'office de tourisme/ le syndicat d'initiative* |

| | |
|---|---|
| Where is ...? | *Où est ...?* |
| the beach | *la plage* |
| the bridge | *le pont* |
| the castle | *le château* |
| the cathedral | *la cathédrale* |
| the church | *l'église* |
| the island | *l'île* |
| the lake | *le lac* |
| the main square | *la place centrale* |
| the mosque | *la mosquée* |
| the old city | *la vieille ville* |
| the palace | *le palais* |
| the quay/bank | *le quai/la rive* |
| the sea | *la mer* |
| the square | *la place* |
| the tower | *la tour* |

| | |
|---|---|
| What time does it open/close? | *Quelle est l'heure d'ouverture/ de fermeture?* |
| I'd like to make a telephone call. | *Je voudrais téléphoner.* |
| I'd like to change ... | *Je voudrais changer ...* |
| some money | *de l'argent* |
| travellers cheques | *chèques de voyage* |

## Directions

| | |
|---|---|
| How do I get to ...? | *Comment dois-je faire pour arriver à ...?* |
| Is it near/far? | *Est-ce près/loin?* |
| Can you show me on the map/ city map? | *Est-ce que vous pouvez me le montrer sur la carte/le plan?* |
| Go straight ahead. | *Continuez tout droit.* |
| Turn left. | *Tournez à gauche.* |
| Turn right. | *Tournez à droite.* |

| | |
|---|---|
| at the traffic lights | *aux feux* |
| at the next corner | *au prochain coin* |
| behind | *derrière* |
| in front of | *devant* |
| opposite | *en face de* |
| north | *nord* |
| south | *sud* |
| east | *est* |
| west | *ouest* |

## Accommodation

| | |
|---|---|
| I'm looking for ... | *Je cherche ...* |
| the youth hostel | *l'auberge de jeunesse* |
| the camping ground | *le camping* |
| a hotel | *un hôtel* |

| | |
|---|---|
| Where can I find a cheap hotel? | *Où est-ce que je peux trouver un hôtel bon marché?* |
| What's the address? | *Quelle est l'adresse?* |
| Could you write it down, please? | *Est-ce vous pourriez l'écrire, s'il vous plaît?* |
| Do you have any rooms available? | *Est-ce que vous avez des chambres libres?* |

| | |
|---|---|
| I'd like (to book) ... | *Je voudrais (réserver) ...* |
| a bed | *un lit* |
| a single room | *une chambre pour une personne* |
| a double room | *une chambre double* |
| a room with a shower and toilet | *une chambre avec douche et WC* |

I'd like to stay in a dormitory. — *Je voudrais coucher dans un dortoir.*

How much is it ...? — *Quel est le prix ...?*
per night — *par nuit*
per person — *par personne*

Is breakfast included? — *Est-ce que le petit déjeuner est compris?*
May I see the room? — *Est-ce que je peux voir la chambre?*

Where is ...? — *Où est ...?*
the bathroom — *la salle de bains*
the shower — *la douche*

Where is the toilet? — *Où sont les toilettes?*

I'm going to stay ... — *Je resterai ...*
one day — *un jour*
a week — *une semaine*

## Health

I'm sick. — *Je suis malade.*
I need a doctor. — *Il me faut un médecin.*
Where is the hospital? — *Où est l'hôpital?*
I have diarrhoea. — *J'ai la diarrhée.*
I'm pregnant. — *Je suis enceinte.*

I'm ... — *Je suis ...*
diabetic — *diabétique*
epileptic — *épileptique*
asthmatic — *asthmatique*
anaemic — *anémique*

I'm allergic ... — *Je suis allergique ...*
to antibiotics — *aux antibiotiques*
to penicillin — *à la pénicilline*

antiseptic — *l'antiseptique*
aspirin — *l'aspirine*
condoms — *les préservatifs*
contraceptive — *un contraceptif*
medicine — *le médicament*
nausea — *la nausée*
painkillers — *des analgésiques*
sunblock cream — *la crème solaire haute protection*
tampons — *les tampons hygiéniques*

## Time & Dates

What time is it? — *Quelle heure est-il?*
It's (two) o'clock. — *Il est (deux) heures.*
When? — *Quand?*
today — *aujourd'hui*
tonight — *ce soir*
tomorrow — *demain*
day after tomorrow — *après-demain*
yesterday — *hier*
all day — *toute la journée*
in the morning — *du matin*
in the afternoon — *de l'après-midi*
in the evening — *du soir*

Monday — *lundi*
Tuesday — *mardi*
Wednesday — *mercredi*
Thursday — *jeudi*
Friday — *vendredi*
Saturday — *samedi*
Sunday — *dimanche*

January — *janvier*
February — *février*
March — *mars*
April — *avril*
May — *mai*
June — *juin*
July — *juillet*
August — *août*
September — *septembre*
October — *octobre*
November — *novembre*
December — *décembre*

## Numbers

| 1 | *un* |
| 2 | *deux* |
| 3 | *trois* |
| 4 | *quatre* |
| 5 | *cinq* |
| 6 | *six* |
| 7 | *sept* |
| 8 | *huit* |
| 9 | *neuf* |
| 10 | *dix* |
| 11 | *onze* |
| 12 | *douze* |
| 13 | *treize* |

## Emergencies

| Help! | *Au secours!* |
|---|---|
| Call a doctor! | *Appelez un médecin!* |
| Call the police! | *Appelez la police!* |
| Leave me alone! | *Fichez-moi la paix!* |
| I've been robbed. | *On m'a volé.* |
| I've been raped. | *On m'a violée.* |
| I'm lost. | *Je me suis égaré/ égarée.* (m/f) |

| 14 | *quatorze* |
|---|---|
| 15 | *quinze* |
| 16 | *seize* |
| 17 | *dix-sept* |
| 18 | *dix-huit* |
| 19 | *dix-neuf* |
| 20 | *vingt* |
| 21 | *vingt-et-un* |
| 22 | *vingt-deux* |
| 23 | *vingt-trois* |
| 30 | *trente* |
| 40 | *quarante* |
| 50 | *cinquante* |
| 60 | *soixante* |
| 70 | *soixante-dix* |
| 80 | *quatre-vingts* |
| 90 | *quatre-vingts-dix* |
| 100 | *cent* |
| 1000 | *mille* |
| 2000 | *deux mille* |

| one million | *un million* |
|---|---|

## FOOD
### Basics

| breakfast | *le petit déjeuner* |
|---|---|
| lunch | *le déjeuner* |
| dinner | *le dîner* |
| vegetable | *légume* |
| fish | *poisson* |
| meat | *viande* |
| poultry | *volaille* |
| game | *gibier* |
| dessert | *dessert* |
| grocery store | *l'épicerie* |
| chip shop | *friture* |

I'd like the set menu.
*Je prends le menu.*
I'm a vegetarian.
*Je suis végétarien/végétarienne.* (m/f)
I'm a vegan.
*Je suis végétalien/végétalienne.* (m/f)
I'm allergic to nuts.
*Je suis allergique aux noix.*

| I don't eat ... | *Je ne mange pas de ...* |
|---|---|
| meat | *viande* |
| chicken | *poulet* |
| fish | *poisson* |
| seafood | *fruits de mer* |

## Menu Decoder
### Starters, Soups & Snacks

| *croque monsieur* | grilled ham and cheese sandwich |
|---|---|
| *entrées chaudes* | warm starter |
| *entrées froides* | cold starter |
| *frites* | chips or french fries |
| *potage* | soup |
| *sandwich garni* | filled sandwich |
| *tartine* | slice of bread |

### Meat

| *agneau* | lamb |
|---|---|
| *bœuf* | beef |
| *boudin noir* | black pudding |
| *brochette* | kebab |
| *canard* | duck |
| *cerf* | venison |
| *cervelle* | brains |
| *charcuterie* | cooked/prepared meats |
| *cheval* | horse |
| *dinde* | turkey |
| *entrecôte* | rib steak |
| *escargot* | snail |
| *faisan* | pheasant |
| *foie* | liver |
| *jambon* | ham |
| *jambonneau* | ham on the bone |
| *langue* | tongue |
| *lapin* | rabbit |
| *marcassin* | boar |
| *mouton* | mutton |
| *pintade* | guinea fowl |
| *porc* | pork |
| *poulet* | chicken |
| *saucisson* | large sausage |
| *veau* | veal |

### Fish & Seafood

| | |
|---|---|
| *anchois* | anchovy |
| *anguille* | eel |
| *brème* | bream |
| *calmar* | squid |
| *coquille St-Jacques* | scallop |
| *crabe* | crab |
| *crevette* | shrimp |
| *daurade* | sea bream |
| *hareng* | herring |
| *homard* | lobster |
| *huître* | oyster |
| *langouste* | crayfish |
| *lotte* | monkfish |
| *maquereau* | mackerel |
| *morue* | cod |
| *moule* | mussel |
| *palourde* | clam |
| *raie* | ray |
| *rouget* | red mullet |
| *saumon* | salmon |
| *scampi* | prawn |
| *sole* | sole |
| *thon* | tuna |
| *truite* | trout |

### Vegetables

| | |
|---|---|
| *ail* | garlic |
| *artichaut* | artichoke |
| *asperge* | asparagus |
| *aubergine* | eggplant |
| *avocat* | avocado |
| *carotte* | carrot |
| *celeri* | celery |
| *champignon* | mushroom |
| *chicon* | chicory |
| *chou* | cabbage |
| *citrouille* | pumpkin |
| *concombre* | cucumber |
| *courgette* | zucchini |
| *échalote* | shallot |
| *épinards* | spinach |
| *haricot* | bean |
| *maïs* | sweet corn |
| *oignon* | onion |
| *olive* | olive |
| *persil* | parsley |
| *petit pois* | peas |
| *poireau* | leek |
| *poivron rouge/ vert* | red/green pepper (capsicum) |
| *pomme de terre* | potato |
| *truffe* | truffle |

### Desserts

| | |
|---|---|
| *bourdelot* | apple cooked in pastry |
| *douillon* | pear cooked in pastry |
| *crêpe* | pancake |
| *gâteau* | cake |
| *gaufre* | waffle |
| *glace* | ice cream |
| *sucre de pomme* | sweet apple dessert |
| *tarte* | tart (pie) |
| *tarte normande* | apple tart |
| *teurgoule* | sweet, cinnamon-flavoured rice pudding |

### Miscellaneous

| | |
|---|---|
| *beurre* | butter |
| *confiture* | jam |
| *fromage* | cheese |
| *fromage de chèvre* | goat's cheese |
| *galette* | wholemeal or buck-wheat pancake |
| *œuf* | egg |
| *pain* | bread |
| *poivre* | pepper |
| *riz* | rice |
| *sel* | salt |
| *sucre* | sugar |
| *vinaigre* | vinegar |

### Cooking Methods

| | |
|---|---|
| *à la broche* | spit-roasted |
| *à la normande* | with a cream or butter sauce |
| *à la vapeur* | steamed |
| *au feu de bois* | cooked over a wood stove |
| *au four* | baked |
| *farci* | stuffed |
| *fumé* | smoked |
| *gratiné* | browned on top with cheese |
| *grillé* | grilled |
| *pané* | coated in breadcrumbs |
| *rôti* | roasted |
| *sauté* | sautéed |

## Regional Specialities

*bonhomme normande*  duck in a cider and cream sauce

*canard flambé au Calvados*  duck with Calvados

*marmite Dieppoise*  fish soup from Dieppe

*poulet vallée d'Auge*  chicken in cream and cider

*salade Fécampoise*  salad of potatoes, smoked herring and eggs

*sole à la normande*  sole with mussels, shrimps and mushrooms

*tripes à la mode de Caen*  a heavily spiced tripe stew

## Drinks

*eau*  water

*lait*  milk

*citron pressé*  iced water with lemon and sugar

*sirop*  squash, fruit syrup

*tisane/infusion*  herbal tea

*un café/espresso*  espresso

*café au lait*  hot milk with a little coffee

*café crème*  espresso with milk or cream

*noisette*  espresso with just a dash of milk

*un déca*  decaffeinated coffee

*chocolat chaud*  hot chocolate

*bière*  beer

*cidre*  cider

*Calvados*  apple brandy

*pommeau*  aperitif of Calvados and apple juice

*vin*  wine

# Glossary

(m) indicates masculine gender, (f) feminine gender and (pl) plural

**accueil** (m) – reception
**achat** (m) – buy rate (when changing money)
**alimentation** (f) – grocery store
**alpinisme** (m) – mountaineering
**annuaire** (m) – directory
**arrêt** (m) – stop
**auberge de jeunesse** (f) – (youth) hostel
**autorisation de travail** (f) – work permit

**baie** (f) – bay
**billet** (m) – ticket
**billet jumelé** (m) – combination ticket, good for more than one site, museum etc
**billeterie** (f) – ticket office or counter
**biologique** (f) – organic
**bois** (m) – wood
**boisson** (f) – drink
**boisson comprise** (f) – drink included
**boîte** (f) – nightclub
**bon bère** (m) – another name for cider
**boucherie** (f) – butcher
**boucherie chevaline** (f) – butcher selling horse meat
**boulangerie** (f) – bakery, bread shop
**brasserie** (f) – restaurant usually serving food all day (original meaning: brewery)
**brocante** (f) – second-hand goods
**brut** (m) – dry
**bureau de change** (m) – exchange bureau
**bureau de poste** (m) or *poste* (f) – post office

**Calvados** (m) – apple-flavoured brandy
**Camembert** (m) – a soft creamy cheese
**camping sauvage** (m) – freelance camping
**canard** (m) – duck
**capitainerie** (f) – harbour master's office
**carnet** (m) – a book of five or 10 bus, tram or metro tickets sold at a reduced rate
**carrefour** (m) – crossroad
**carte** (f) – card; menu; map
**carte de séjour** (f) – residence permit
**caserne** (f) – military barracks

**cathédrale** (f) – cathedral
**cave** (f) – wine cellar
**chambre** (f) – room
**chambre de bonne** (f) – maids' quarters
**chambre d'hôte** (f) – B&B
**charcuterie** (f) – pork butcher's shop and delicatessen
**chars à voile** (m pl) – sand yachts
**cidre** (m) – cider
**cimetière** (m) – cemetery
**coffre** (m) – hotel safe
**colombier** (m) – pigeon house, or dovecote
**commissariat** (m) – police station
**confiserie** (f) – chocolate/sweet shop
**consigne** (f) – left-luggage office
**consigne automatique** (f) – left-luggage locker
**consigne manuelle** (f) – left-luggage office
**cordonnier** (m) – shoe-repair shop
**correspondance** (f) – linking tunnel or walkway; rail or bus connection
**couchette** (f) – sleeping berth on a train or ferry
**cour** (f) – courtyard
**crémerie** (f) – dairy, cheese shop
**crêpe** (f) – pancake, especially a sweet one
**cyclisme** (m) – cycling

**dégustation** (f) – tasting
**deltaplane** (m) – hang-gliding
**demi** (m) – 330mL glass of beer
**demi-pension** (f) – half-board (B&B with either lunch or dinner)
**demi-tarif** (m) – half-price
**dentelle** (f) – lace
**département** (m) – administrative division of France
**digestif** (m) – a drink taken to aid the digestion, especially before or after a meal
**douane** (f) – customs
**doux/douce** (m/f) – soft

**eau** (f) – water
**église** (f) – church
**embarcadère** (m) – pier, jetty

**épicerie** (f) – small grocery store
**équitation** (f) – horse riding
**escalade** (f) – rock climbing
**escargot** (m) – snail

**faïence** (f) – ceramics
**fauteuil** (m) – seat on trains, ferries or at the theatre
**fauteuil roulant** (m) – wheelchair
**fête** (f) – festival
**foire** (f) – fair
**forêt** (f) – forest
**formule** (f) or *formule rapide* – similar to a *menu* but allows choice of whichever two of three courses you want (eg starter and main course or main course and dessert)
**foyer** (m) – workers or students hostel
**fromagerie** (f) – cheese shop
**funiculaire** (m) – funicular railway

**galerie** (f) – covered shopping centre or arcade
**galette** (f) – wholemeal or buckwheat pancake
**gare** (f) – railway station
**gare maritime** (f) – ferry terminal
**gare routière** (f) – bus station
**gaufre** (f) – waffle with various toppings, usually eaten as a snack
**gazeuse** (f) – fizzy, carbonated
**gendarmerie** (f) – police station; police force
**gîte d'étape** (m) – hikers accommodation, usually in a village
**gîte rural** (m) – country cottage
**grande école** (f) – prestigious educational institution offering training in such fields as business management, engineering and the applied sciences

**halles** (f pl) – covered market, central food market
**halte routière** (f) – bus stop
**horaire** (m) – timetable or schedule
**hôtes payants** (m pl) or *hébergement chez l'habitant* (m) – homestays
**hôtel de ville** (m) – city or town hall
**huile d'olive** (f) – olive oil
**hydroglisseur** (m) – hydrofoil or hydroplane
**hypermarché** (m) – hypermarket

**jambon** (m) – ham
**jardin** (m) – garden
**jardin botanique** (m) – botanical garden
**jours fériés** (m pl) – public holidays

**laverie** (f) or *lavomatique* (m) – laundrette
**légume** (m) – vegetable

**mairie** (f) – city or town hall
**maison de la presse** (f) – newsagent
**maison du parc** (f) – a national park's headquarters and/or visitor centre
**mandat postal** (m) – postal money order
**marché** (m) – market
**marché aux puces** (m) – flea market
**marché couvert** (m) – covered market
**menu** (m) – fixed-price meal with two or more courses
**météo** (f) – weather forecast
**Mobylette** (f) – moped
**musée** (m) – museum

**navette** (f) – shuttle bus, train or boat
**nettoyage à sec** (m) – dry cleaning

**ordonnance** (f) – prescription

**pain** (m) – bread
**palais de justice** (m) – law courts
**parapente** (m) – paragliding
**parc** (m) – park
**parlement** (m) – parliament
**pâtisserie** (f) – cake and pastry shop
**pensions de famille** (f pl) – similar to B&Bs
**pharmacie** (f) – pharmacy
**pichet** (m) – jug
**piste cyclable** (f) – bicycle path
**place** (f) – square, plaza
**plage** (f) – beach
**plan** (m) – city map
**plan du quartier** (m) – map of nearby streets
**plat du jour** (m) – daily special in a restaurant
**poissonnier** (m) – fishmonger
**pont** (m) – bridge
**port** (m) – harbour, port
**port de plaisance** (m) – marina or pleasure-boat harbour
**porte** (f) – gate in a city wall

**poste** (f) or *bureau de poste* (m) – post office
**poste** (m) – telephone extension
**pourboire** (m) – tip
**préfecture** (f) – prefecture (capital of a *département*)
**préservatif** (m) – condom
**presqu'île** (f) – peninsula
**pression** (f) – draught beer

**quai** (m) – quay, railway platform
**quart** (m) – quarter of a litre (25cL)
**quartier** (m) – quarter, district

**refuge** (m) – mountain hut, basic shelter for hikers
**rez-de-chausée** (m) – ground floor
**rive** (f) – bank of a river
**riverain** (m) – local resident
**rond point** (m) – roundabout
**routier** (m) – trucker or truckers' restaurant

**salon de thé** (m) – tearoom
**sentier** (m) – trail
**service des urgences** (f) – casualty ward
**sortie** (f) – exit
**spectacle** (m) – performance, play, theatrical show
**square** (m) – public garden
**supermarché** (m) – supermarket
**supplément** (m) – supplement, additional cost
**syndicat d'initiative** (m) – tourist office

**tabac** (m) – tobacconist (also selling bus tickets and phonecards)
**table d'orientation** (f) – viewpoint indicator
**taxe de séjour** (f) – municipal tourist tax
**télécarte** (f) – phonecard
**thalassothérapie** (f) – sea-water therapy
**thermalisme** (m) – water cures
**toilettes** (f pl) – public toilets
**tour** (f) – tower
**tour d'horloge** (f) – clock tower
**tranche** (f) – slice

**v.f.** (f) – *version française*; a film dubbed in French

**v.o.** (f) – *version originale*; a nondubbed film with French subtitles
**vallée** (f) – valley
**vieille ville** (f) – old town or old city
**ville neuve** (f) – new town or new city
**vin** (m) – wine
**voie** (f) – train platform
**vol** (m) – theft

## ACRONYMS

The French love acronyms as much as the British and Americans do. Many transport companies are known by acronyms whose derivations are entirely unknown by the average passenger.

**BP** – *boîte postale* (post office box)
**CRIJ** – Centre Régional d'Information Jeunesse (regional youth association)
**FFRP** – Fédération Française de la Randonnée Pédestre (French ramblers' association)
**FIYTO** – Federation of International Youth Travel Organisations
**FN** – Front National (far right-wing political party)
**FUAJ** – Fédération Unie des Auberges de Jeunesse (united federation of youth hostels)
**GR** – *grande randonnée* (long-distance hiking trail)
**LFAJ** – Ligue Française pour les Auberges de la Jeunesse (French league of youth hostels)
**RPR** – Rassemblement pour la République (centre-right political party)
**SAMU** – Service d'Aide Médicale d'Urgence (emergency medical aid service)
**SMIC** – *salaire minimum interprofessionel de croissance* (minimum wage)
**SNCF** – Société Nationale des Chemins de Fer (state-owned railway company)
**TEOR** – Transport Est Ouest Rouennais
**TGV** – *train à grande vitesse* (high-speed train, bullet train)
**TTC** – *toutes taxes comprises* (all taxes included)
**TVA** – value-added tax
**UDF** – Union pour la Démocratie Française (centre-right political party)
**VTT** – *vélo tout terrain* (mountain bike)

# LONELY PLANET

You already know that Lonely Planet produces more than this one guidebook, but you might not be aware of the other products we have on this region. Here is a selection of titles that you may want to check out as well:

**Cycling France**
ISBN 1 86450 036 0
US$19.99 • UK£12.99

**Europe on a shoestring**
ISBN 1 86450 150 2
US$24.99 • UK£14.99

**France**
ISBN 0 86450 151 0
US$24.99 • UK£14.99

**French phrasebook**
ISBN 1 86450 136 7
US$5.95 • UK£3.99

**Mediterranean Europe**
ISBN 1 86450 154 5
US$27.99 • UK£15.99

**Paris**
ISBN 1 86450 125 1
US$15.99 • UK£9.99

**Provence & the Côte d'Azur**
ISBN 1 86450 196 0
US$17.99 • UK£11.99

**Read This First: Europe**
ISBN 1 86450 136 7
US$14.99 • UK£8.99

**Walking in France**
ISBN 0 86442 601 1
US$19.99 • UK£12.99

**Western Europe**
ISBN 1 86450 163 4
US$27.99 • UK£15.99

**World Food France**
ISBN 1 86450 021 2
US$12.99 • UK£7.99

**Available wherever books are sold**

# LONELY PLANET

## Guides by Region

Lonely Planet is known worldwide for publishing practical, reliable and no-nonsense travel information in our guides and on our Web site. The Lonely Planet list covers just about every accessible part of the world. Currently there are 16 series: Travel guides, Shoestring guides, Condensed guides, Phrasebooks, Read This First, Healthy Travel, Walking guides, Cycling guides, Watching Wildlife guides, Pisces Diving & Snorkeling guides, City Maps, Road Atlases, Out to Eat, World Food, Journeys travel literature and Pictorials.

**AFRICA** Africa on a shoestring • Cairo • Cairo City Map • Cape Town • Cape Town City Map • East Africa • Egypt • Egyptian Arabic phrasebook • Ethiopia, Eritrea & Djibouti • Ethiopian Amharic phrasebook • The Gambia & Senegal • Healthy Travel Africa • Kenya • Malawi • Morocco • Moroccan Arabic phrasebook • Mozambique • Read This First: Africa • South Africa, Lesotho & Swaziland • Southern Africa • Southern Africa Road Atlas • Swahili phrasebook • Tanzania, Zanzibar & Pemba • Trekking in East Africa • Tunisia • Watching Wildlife East Africa • Watching Wildlife Southern Africa • West Africa • World Food Morocco • Zimbabwe, Botswana & Namibia
**Travel Literature:** Mali Blues: Traveling to an African Beat • The Rainbird: A Central African Journey • Songs to an African Sunset: A Zimbabwean Story

**AUSTRALIA & THE PACIFIC** Auckland • Australia • Australian phrasebook • Australia Road Atlas • Cycling Australia • Cycling New Zealand • Fiji • Fijian phrasebook • Healthy Travel Australia, NZ & the Pacific • Islands of Australia's Great Barrier Reef • Melbourne • Melbourne City Map • Micronesia • New Caledonia • New South Wales • New Zealand • Northern Territory • Outback Australia • Out to Eat – Melbourne • Out to Eat – Sydney • Papua New Guinea • Pidgin phrasebook • Queensland • Rarotonga & the Cook Islands • Samoa • Solomon Islands • South Australia • South Pacific • South Pacific phrasebook • Sydney • Sydney City Map • Sydney Condensed • Tahiti & French Polynesia • Tasmania • Tonga • Tramping in New Zealand • Vanuatu • Victoria • Walking in Australia • Watching Wildlife Australia • Western Australia
**Travel Literature:** Islands in the Clouds: Travels in the Highlands of New Guinea • Kiwi Tracks: A New Zealand Journey • Sean & David's Long Drive

**CENTRAL AMERICA & THE CARIBBEAN** Bahamas, Turks & Caicos • Baja California • Belize, Guatemala & Yucatán • Bermuda • Central America on a shoestring • Costa Rica • Costa Rica Spanish phrasebook • Cuba • Dominican Republic & Haiti • Eastern Caribbean • Guatemala • Havana • Healthy Travel Central & South America • Jamaica • Mexico • Mexico City • Panama • Puerto Rico • Read This First: Central & South America • World Food Mexico • Yucatán
**Travel Literature:** Green Dreams: Travels in Central America

**EUROPE** Amsterdam • Amsterdam City Map • Amsterdam Condensed • Andalucía • Austria • Baltic States phrasebook • Barcelona • Barcelona City Map • Belgium & Luxembourg • Berlin • Berlin City Map • Britain • British phrasebook • Brussels, Bruges & Antwerp • Brussels City Map • Budapest • Budapest City Map • Canary Islands • Central Europe • Central Europe phrasebook • Copenhagen • Corfu & the Ionians • Corsica • Crete • Crete Condensed • Croatia • Cycling Britain • Cycling France • Cyprus • Czech & Slovak Republics • Denmark • Dublin • Dublin City Map • Eastern Europe • Eastern Europe phrasebook • Edinburgh • England • Estonia, Latvia & Lithuania • Europe on a shoestring • Europe phrasebook • Finland • Florence • France • Frankfurt Condensed • French phrasebook • Georgia, Armenia & Azerbaijan • Germany • German phrasebook • Greece • Greek Islands • Greek phrasebook • Hungary • Iceland, Greenland & the Faroe Islands • Ireland • Italian phrasebook • Italy • Krakow • Lisbon • The Loire • London • London City Map • London Condensed • Madrid • Malta • Mediterranean Europe • Mediterranean Europe phrasebook • Moscow • Munich • Netherlands • Normandy • Norway • Out to Eat – London • Out to Eat – Paris • Paris • Paris City Map • Paris Condensed • Poland • Polish phrasebook • Portugal • Portuguese phrasebook • Prague • Prague City Map • Provence & the Côte d'Azur • Read This First: Europe • Rhodes & the Dodecanese • Romania & Moldova • Rome • Rome City Map • Russia, Ukraine & Belarus • Russian phrasebook • Scandinavia & Baltic Europe • Scandinavian phrasebook • Scotland • Sicily • Slovenia • South-West France • Spain • Spanish phrasebook • St Petersburg • St Petersburg City Map • Sweden • Switzerland • Tuscany • Ukrainian phrasebook • Venice • Vienna • Walking in Britain • Walking in France • Walking in Ireland • Walking in Italy • Walking in Spain • Walking in Switzerland • Western Europe • World Food France • World Food Ireland • World Food Italy • World Food Spain
**Travel Literature:** After Yugoslavia • Love and War in the Apennines • The Olive Grove: Travels in Greece • On the Shores of the Mediterranean • Round Ireland in Low Gear • A Small Place in Italy

# LONELY PLANET

## Mail Order

Lonely Planet products are distributed worldwide. They are also available by mail order from Lonely Planet, so if you have difficulty finding a title please write to us. North and South American residents should write to 150 Linden St, Oakland, CA 94607, USA; European and African residents should write to 10a Spring Place, London NW5 3BH, UK; and residents of other countries to Locked Bag 1, Footscray, Victoria 3011, Australia.

**INDIAN SUBCONTINENT & THE INDIAN OCEAN** Bangladesh • Bengali phrasebook • Bhutan • Delhi • Goa • Healthy Travel Asia & India • Hindi & Urdu phrasebook • India • Indian Himalaya • Karakoram Highway • Kerala • Madagascar • Maldives • Mauritius, Réunion & Seychelles • Mumbai (Bombay) • Nepal • Nepali phrasebook • Pakistan • Rajasthan • Read This First: Asia & India • South India • Sri Lanka • Sri Lanka phrasebook • Tibet • Tibetan phrasebook • Trekking in the Indian Himalaya • Trekking in the Karakoram & Hindukush • Trekking in the Nepal Himalaya
**Travel Literature:** The Age of Kali: Indian Travels and Encounters • Hello Goodnight: A Life of Goa • In Rajasthan • Maverick in Madagascar • A Season in Heaven: True Tales from the Road to Kathmandu • Shopping for Buddhas • A Short Walk in the Hindu Kush • Slowly Down the Ganges

**MIDDLE EAST & CENTRAL ASIA** Bahrain, Kuwait & Qatar • Central Asia • Central Asia phrasebook • Dubai • Farsi (Persian) phrasebook • Hebrew phrasebook • Iran • Israel & the Palestinian Territories • Istanbul • Istanbul City Map • Istanbul to Cairo • Istanbul to Kathmandu • Jerusalem • Jerusalem City Map • Jordan • Lebanon • Middle East • Oman & the United Arab Emirates • Syria • Turkey • Turkish phrasebook • World Food Turkey • Yemen
**Travel Literature:** Black on Black: Iran Revisited • The Gates of Damascus • Kingdom of the Film Stars: Journey into Jordan

**NORTH AMERICA** Alaska • Boston • Boston City Map • Boston Condensed • British Columbia • California & Nevada • California Condensed • Canada • Chicago • Chicago City Map • Florida • Great Lakes • Hawaii • Hiking in Alaska • Hiking in the USA • Las Vegas • Los Angeles • Los Angeles City Map • Louisiana & the Deep South • Miami • Miami City Map • Montreal • New England • New Orleans • New York City • New York City City Map • New York City Condensed • New York, New Jersey & Pennsylvania • Oahu • Out to Eat – San Francisco • Pacific Northwest • Rocky Mountains • San Francisco • San Francisco City Map • Seattle • Southwest • Texas • Toronto • USA • USA phrasebook • Vancouver • Virginia & the Capital Region • Washington, DC • Washington, DC City Map • World Food New Orleans
**Travel Literature:** Caught Inside: A Surfer's Year on the California Coast • Drive Thru America

**NORTH-EAST ASIA** Beijing • Beijing City Map • Cantonese phrasebook • China • Hiking in Japan • Hong Kong • Hong Kong City Map • Hong Kong Condensed • Hong Kong, Macau & Guangzhou • Japan • Japanese phrasebook • Korea • Korean phrasebook • Kyoto • Mandarin phrasebook • Mongolia • Mongolian phrasebook • Seoul • Shanghai • South-West China • Taiwan • Tokyo • World Food Hong Kong
**Travel Literature:** In Xanadu: A Quest • Lost Japan

**SOUTH AMERICA** Argentina, Uruguay & Paraguay • Bolivia • Brazil • Brazilian phrasebook • Buenos Aires • Chile & Easter Island • Colombia • Ecuador & the Galapagos Islands • Healthy Travel Central & South America • Latin American Spanish phrasebook • Peru • Quechua phrasebook • Read This First: Central & South America • Rio de Janeiro • Rio de Janeiro City Map • Santiago de Chile • South America on a shoestring • Trekking in the Patagonian Andes • Venezuela
**Travel Literature:** Full Circle: A South American Journey

**SOUTH-EAST ASIA** Bali & Lombok • Bangkok • Bangkok City Map • Burmese phrasebook • Cambodia • Hanoi • Healthy Travel Asia & India • Hill Tribes phrasebook • Ho Chi Minh City • Indonesia • Indonesian phrasebook • Indonesia's Eastern Islands • Java • Lao phrasebook • Laos • Malay phrasebook • Malaysia, Singapore & Brunei • Myanmar (Burma) • Philippines • Pilipino (Tagalog) phrasebook • Read This First: Asia & India • Singapore • Singapore City Map • South-East Asia on a shoestring • South-East Asia phrasebook • Thailand • Thailand's Islands & Beaches • Thailand, Vietnam, Laos & Cambodia Road Atlas • Thai phrasebook • Vietnam • Vietnamese phrasebook • World Food Thailand • World Food Vietnam

**ALSO AVAILABLE:** Antarctica • The Arctic • The Blue Man: Tales of Travel, Love and Coffee • Brief Encounters: Stories of Love, Sex & Travel • Chasing Rickshaws • The Last Grain Race • Lonely Planet ... On the Edge: Adventurous Escapades from Around the World • Lonely Planet Unpacked • Not the Only Planet: Science Fiction Travel Stories • Sacred India • Travel Photography: A Guide to Taking Better Pictures • Travel with Children

# LONELY PLANET

## ON THE ROAD

**Travel Guides** explore cities, regions and countries, and supply information on transport, restaurants and accommodation, covering all budgets. They come with reliable, easy-to-use maps, practical advice, cultural and historical facts and a rundown on attractions both on and off the beaten track. There are over 200 titles in this classic series, covering nearly every country in the world.

 **Lonely Planet Upgrades** extend the shelf life of existing travel guides by detailing any changes that may affect travel in a region since a book has been published. Upgrades can be downloaded for free from **www.lonelyplanet.com/upgrades**

For travellers with more time than money, **Shoestring** guides offer dependable, first-hand information with hundreds of detailed maps, plus insider tips for stretching money as far as possible. Covering entire continents in most cases, the six-volume shoestring guides are known around the world as 'backpackers bibles'.

For the discerning short-term visitor, **Condensed** guides highlight the best a destination has to offer in a full-colour, pocket-sized format designed for quick access. They include everything from top sights and walking tours to opinionated reviews of where to eat, stay, shop and have fun.

**CitySync** lets travellers use their Palm™ or Visor™ hand-held computers to guide them through a city with handy tips on transport, history, cultural life, major sights, and shopping and entertainment options. It can also quickly search and sort hundreds of reviews of hotels, restaurants and attractions, and pinpoint their location on scrollable street maps. CitySync can be downloaded from **www.citysync.com**

## MAPS & ATLASES

Lonely Planet's **City Maps** feature downtown and metropolitan maps, as well as transit routes and walking tours. The maps come complete with an index of streets, a listing of sights and a plastic coat for extra durability.

**Road Atlases** are an essential navigation tool for serious travellers. Cross-referenced with the guidebooks, they also feature distance and climate charts and a complete site index.

# LONELY PLANET

## ESSENTIALS

**Read This First** books help new travellers to hit the road with confidence. These invaluable predeparture guides give step-by-step advice on preparing for a trip, budgeting, arranging a visa, planning an itinerary and staying safe while still getting off the beaten track.

**Healthy Travel** pocket guides offer a regional rundown on disease hot spots and practical advice on predeparture health measures, staying well on the road and what to do in emergencies. The guides come with a user-friendly design and helpful diagrams and tables.

Lonely Planet's **Phrasebooks** cover the essential words and phrases travellers need when they're strangers in a strange land. They come in a pocket-sized format with colour tabs for quick reference, extensive vocabulary lists, easy-to-follow pronunciation keys and two-way dictionaries.

Miffed by blurry photos of the Taj Mahal? Tired of the classic 'top of the head cut off' shot? **Travel Photography: A Guide to Taking Better Pictures** will help you turn ordinary holiday snaps into striking images and give you the know-how to capture every scene, from frenetic festivals to peaceful beach sunrises.

Lonely Planet's **Travel Journal** is a lightweight but sturdy travel diary for jotting down all those on-the-road observations and significant travel moments. It comes with a handy time-zone wheel, a world map and useful travel information.

**Lonely Planet's eKno** is an all-in-one communication service developed especially for travellers. It offers low-cost international calls and free email and voicemail so that you can keep in touch while on the road. Check it out on **www.ekno.lonelyplanet.com**

## FOOD & RESTAURANT GUIDES

Lonely Planet's **Out to Eat** guides recommend the brightest and best places to eat and drink in top international cities. These gourmet companions are arranged by neighbourhood, packed with dependable maps, garnished with scene-setting photos and served with quirky features.

For people who live to eat, drink and travel, **World Food** guides explore the culinary culture of each country. Entertaining and adventurous, each guide is packed with detail on staples and specialities, regional cuisine and local markets, as well as sumptuous recipes, comprehensive culinary dictionaries and lavish photos good enough to eat.

## OUTDOOR GUIDES

For those who believe the best way to see the world is on foot, Lonely Planet's **Walking Guides** detail everything from family strolls to difficult treks, with 'when to go and how to do it' advice supplemented by reliable maps and essential travel information.

**Cycling Guides** map a destination's best bike tours, long and short, in day-by-day detail. They contain all the information a cyclist needs, including advice on bike maintenance, places to eat and stay, innovative maps with detailed cues to the rides, and elevation charts.

The **Watching Wildlife** series is perfect for travellers who want authoritative information but don't want to tote a heavy field guide. Packed with advice on where, when and how to view a region's wildlife, each title features photos of over 300 species and contains engaging comments on the local flora and fauna.

With underwater colour photos throughout, **Pisces Books** explore the world's best diving and snorkelling areas. Each book contains listings of diving services and dive resorts, detailed information on depth, visibility and difficulty of dives, and a roundup of the marine life you're likely to see through your mask.

## OFF THE ROAD

**Journeys**, the travel literature series written by renowned travel authors, capture the spirit of a place or illuminate a culture with a journalist's attention to detail and a novelist's flair for words. These are tales to soak up while you're actually on the road or dip into as an at-home armchair indulgence.

The range of lavishly illustrated **Pictorial** books is just the ticket for both travellers and dreamers. Off-beat tales and vivid photographs bring the adventure of travel to your doorstep long before the journey begins and long after it is over.

Lonely Planet **Videos** encourage the same independent, tough-minded approach as the guidebooks. Currently airing throughout the world, this award-winning series features innovative footage and an original soundtrack.

Yes, we know, work is tough, so do a little bit of deskside dreaming with the spiral-bound Lonely Planet **Diary** or a Lonely Planet **Wall Calendar**, filled with great photos from around the world.

Chasing Rickshaws

## TRAVELLERS NETWORK

**Lonely Planet Online**. Lonely Planet's award-winning Web site has insider information on hundreds of destinations, from Amsterdam to Zimbabwe, complete with interactive maps and relevant links. The site also offers the latest travel news, recent reports from travellers on the road, guidebook upgrades, a travel links site, an online book-buying option and a lively traveller's bulletin board. It can be viewed at **www.lonelyplanet.com** or AOL keyword: lp.

**Planet Talk** is a quarterly print newsletter, full of gossip, advice, anecdotes and author articles. It provides an antidote to the being-at-home blues and lets you plan and dream for the next trip. Contact the nearest Lonely Planet office for your free copy.

**Comet**, the free Lonely Planet newsletter, comes via email once a month. It's loaded with travel news, advice, dispatches from authors, travel competitions and letters from readers. To subscribe, click on the Comet subscription link on the front page of the Web site.

# Index

## Text

**Bold** indicates maps.

Bold indicates maps.

## Boxed Text & Special Sections

**Bold** indicates maps.

# MAP LEGEND

## BOUNDARIES

▪▪▪▪▪▪▪ .............. International
▪▪▪▪▪▪▪ .................. Regional

## HYDROGRAPHY

................... Coastline
................ River, Creek
......................... Lake
.................... Swamp

+ × × ......... Cemetery
.......................... Forest

## ROUTES & TRANSPORT

................................. Freeway
................................. Highway
............................ Major Road
............................. Minor Road
═══════ ........... Unsealed Road
............................ City Freeway
............................ City Highway
................................. City Road

...................... City Street, Lane
........................ Pedestrian Mall
─)─ ─── ─── ── .................... Tunnel
╟──╂───●──╢ ... Train Route & Station
╟──╂───▣──╢ .................. Cable Car
─ ─ ─ ─ ─ ─ .............. Walking Track
· · · · · · · · · · · · · · .......... Walking Tour
─ ─ ─ ─ ─ ─ ─ ─ .................. Ferry Route

## AREA FEATURES

........................ Building
................... Park, Gardens

.......................... Market
.................. Beach, Desert

## MAP SYMBOLS

| | | |
|---|---|---|
| ◉ **Rouen** .......... Provincial Capital | ↗ ........................... Beach | ☀ .................... Lighthouse |
| ◉ Évreux .......................... Town | ⊟ ⊟ ........ Bus Stop, Station | ☼ ¦ ................... Lookout |
| ● Damville .......................... Village | ⬚ ......... Castle or Chateau | ⚑ ................... Monument |
| | ⬛ ▮ ....Cathedral or Church | ⬜ ................... Museum |
| ⬛ ................... Place to Stay | ⊟ ...................... Cinema | ← .......... One Way Street |
| ⬛ ......... Camping Ground | ⌒⌒ ...... Cliff or Escarpment | ⊡ ..................... Parking |
| ⬛ ................ Caravan Park | ◉ ... D-Day Parachute Site | ⬛ ............ Police Station |
| | ⬛ ... Embassy or Consulate | ▱ ................. Post Office |
| ▼ ................. Place to Eat | ⬚ ...Ferry or Boat Terminal | ⬛ ......... Shopping Centre |
| ⬛ ................ Pub or Bar | ⚓ ...................Fountain | ⬛ Stately Home or Palace |
| | ⊚ ............... Golf Course | ⬛ ........... Swimming Pool |
| ⊠ ...................... Airport | ⊕ .................. Hospital | ⬚ ................... Telephone |
| ....Ancient or City Wall | ⬚ ............... Internet Cafe | ⬚ ................... Theatre |
| ⬛ ........ Archaeological Site | | ⬤ ...... Tourist Information |
| ⊝ ........................ Bank | *Note: not all symbols displayed above appear in this book* | ⬚ ........................ Zoo |

---

# LONELY PLANET OFFICES

## Australia
Locked Bag 1, Footscray, Victoria 3011
☎ 03 8379 8000  fax 03 8379 8111
email: talk2us@lonelyplanet.com.au

## USA
150 Linden St, Oakland, CA 94607
☎ 510 893 8555  TOLL FREE: 800 275 8555
fax 510 893 8572
email: info@lonelyplanet.com

## UK
10a Spring Place, London NW5 3BH
☎ 020 7428 4800  fax 020 7428 4828
email: go@lonelyplanet.co.uk

## France
1 rue du Dahomey, 75011 Paris
☎ 01 55 25 33 00  fax 01 55 25 33 01
email: bip@lonelyplanet.fr
www.lonelyplanet.fr

**World Wide Web: www.lonelyplanet.com or AOL keyword: lp
Lonely Planet Images: lpi@lonelyplanet.com.au**